From Love Zero to Love 360

God's Unconditional Love for Us,
and Our Love for Him, Ourselves, and One Another

Robert George

From Love Zero to Love 360

Copyright © 2021 by Robert George

Tri-Pillar Publishing
Anaheim Hills, California

International Standard Book Number: 978-1-942654-08-7

Library of Congress Control Number: 2020951588

First edition, January, 2021
Printed in the United States of America

Back cover photographs:
    Upper: The author with his mother, Edith in 1963
    Lower: The author with his sister, Polly in 1965

Cover design: Peter Dibble, Wilsonville, Oregon

To my representative person,

I'm sorry, and I forgive you.

R.G.

Table of Contents

Prologue – Why Me?

I found an interesting and consistent reaction when people who know me discovered that I was writing a book about love. This reaction lies somewhere between disbelief and amusement – I will call it bewilderment. Yes, from one perspective I am the last person they would expect to write about love. You see, I am fairly quiet and reserved; I am generally not expressive with my emotions; I have never been accused of public displays of affection; and I have yet to be called a social butterfly. Those things may not seem too terrible, but add the following: I am famous for being able to detect *(and point out!)* the smallest of flaws; I can be incredibly patient until I suddenly am not; I have been known to get mopey from time to time; I have it from good sources that I am at times downright annoying; I can have impetuous outbursts of acerbic yet impressively fluent acrimony; I – well, I think you get the idea.

I admit that these attributes don't make me seem particularly lovable or capable of giving much love. But you see, so far I have been focusing on the negative. I can turn the table and list my strengths – *(Actually, I do this at some length in Chapter 4)* – but do those things make me lovable? Perhaps a few people would feel a twinge of what some call love, but that's not what this book is about. I cannot say much about worldly, superficial love, based only on outward surface perceptions.

No, I have not written about beefing up positive attributes to attract more love. And I have not written about how to eliminate weaknesses to achieve chick- or hunk-magnet status. I'm sorry if this leaves you disappointed, but such approaches lead to exactly that – disappointment. Whenever we change something about ourselves in an attempt to feel loved, we are actually scurrying away from true love. True love – what I and others refer to as unconditional love – by its very definition (Chapter 1) means that we are loved exactly as we are at any given moment. For example, (I don't understand how she can do it, but) my wife loves me immensely whether I'm exhibiting a strength or I'm being a pain in the a$$. She doesn't love me more or less – she loves me the same, and the reason is… *(wait for it…)* just because. Does this mean that I should be a pain in the a$$ all the time? (It's easier for me, after all…) Of course it doesn't mean that! If my attitude was that I could be, then that would mean I don't love her!

A main theme of this book is that we don't need to change anything about ourselves to be loved. Does an infant need to change anything to be loved by her mother? Of course not! Unfortunately, such unconditional love between parent and child can wear off over time; I've done a little research and have become aware of something called the Terrible Twos – perhaps you've heard of it. At such times, the love between parent and child can become less than perfect... I did just enough research on this to decide that I'm not going to write about parenting skills!

~

OK, I've delayed long enough. You now know several things that I have *not* written about. So, what *have* I written about? And why am I qualified to write about it?

Some of what I've written about is a feeling that is the polar opposite of being loved unconditionally. Love is difficult to define – *(Although, I try in Chapter 1!)* – and sometimes a definition is best understood by antonyms (opposites). I'll get to antonyms shortly, but before I go there let me remind you that a difficult definition is also better grasped with illustrations. Yes, sometimes we're fortunate to get glimpses of what love looks like: Maybe we see it as a child when being cared for by our mother. Maybe we see it when opening up to a friend about something that has been troubling us, and they offer a sympathetic ear. Maybe we see it when becoming engaged to be married, and then starting life together as husband and wife. Maybe we see it at the birth of our child. Maybe we see it when facing a challenge and receiving support from family and friends. Maybe we see it when messing up badly and experiencing forgiveness. Maybe we see it when being cared for by a friend or family member during an illness or old age. These experiences are to be cherished!

For many of us, however, such times are too few, they can fade from our memories, and we crave more love in our life. Instead of nurtured, we feel neglected. Instead of desired, we feel self-conscious and ugly. Instead of appreciated, we feel taken for granted. Instead of connected to others, we feel lonely. Instead of supported, we feel let down and even betrayed. Instead of forgiven and accepted, we feel judged and rejected. If it gets bad enough, such feelings can leave us wondering if anyone really loves us. I have written about this feeling, even as it hits rock bottom where it seems that there is no one – no friend, no family member, not anyone, not even God Himself – who loves us and will ever love us. I call this feeling Love Zero. It's the feeling of having no value, with no chance of a reevaluation – of being unlovable in perpetuity. If you've never experienced this blackness, you're in the majority, and – *Never fear!* – this book is for you too. On this journey, we don't spend much time in utter darkness, but to appreciate whatever shade of gray we're in, it's helpful to consider both white and black. To this end, let me turn the lights off, just for a moment: If you've never felt Love Zero, the best I can do to describe it for you is mild to moderate physical pain (pressure) in the chest / abdomen, and intense to almost unbearable emotional pain that boils down to a bitter brew of despair and hopelessness. If you do occasionally feel this way, and especially if this includes recently, I refer you to p. 331 ("What if you hit rock bottom?"), and before you go there won't you do one of the following right now?

- If you believe that Jesus is your Savior, then I would like you to pray the following: *Heavenly Father, whenever I feel this pain, it seems that I hardly know You. But You know me through and through, and somehow You love me anyway. I don't really understand such love – I have never received it from anyone else, and sometimes that even makes me doubt that You love me. I'm begging You to alleviate such doubts. Please help me to experience Your love. And please help me understand that since You love me right now, even with everything You know about me, You also want me to love myself right now, even with everything I know about myself. It's not easy for most people to understand this feeling that I get sometimes, but it helps to know that You understand. Please help me not feel this way! In Jesus' name, Amen.*

- If you're not sure whether you believe that Jesus is your Savior, but you haven't thoroughly and persistently rejected Him – *(And if you're reading this Prologue with any compassion and interest, then I don't see how you could have thoroughly and persistently rejected Jesus)* – then I would like you to think about the following: *I am disheartened by this pain, and I want it to go away. I'm searching for some way for this to happen. So far, I haven't found consistent relief in any of my personal relationships. I feel an emptiness that isn't being filled by the people I know. Because I've made it this far into this book, including looking at the back cover, the Table of Contents, and the Index, it seems that I have some curiosity about God and the Christian faith.*

I want to remain curious. It seems the author has experienced this feeling of being unlovable, and I'm encouraged that I'm not alone in having had such feelings.

But this feeling is not all that I have written about. Have you noticed that I've been calling Love Zero a feeling? I've done this on purpose. More accurately, Love Zero is a cognitive distortion (a.k.a., thought distortion), but I've been calling it a feeling to emphasize that – like a vivid dream – it sure does feel real when you're experiencing it. While the thought distortion feels real, it doesn't come close to representing reality. I have also written about this reality – this clarity for the heart and soul.

~

I apologize to most – perhaps all – of you, but before we proceed I need to address something. What I've written after this paragraph describes the richness of God's mercy and grace, and you, dear reader, are prepared to take this to heart, with one exception. And this one exception is entirely up to you – you cannot blame God. The one exception is that you are thoroughly and persistently reject- ing Jesus as your Savior, and doing this in such a flagrant fashion that you are causing tangible spiritual damage to a person in your life. (Friendly reminder: You are a person in your life, whether you like it or not!) If this is the situation that you find yourself in, then I'm prescribing a detour to one of the distant out- posts of this book. There is no generic for this prescription. Specifically, I'd like you to proceed immediately to Appendix A – "What if you are thoroughly and persistently rejecting Jesus as your Savior?" – and take all the time you need to take that message to heart. There is a certain kind of openness that comes from acknowledging your absolute dependence on God for *all* things – most impor- tantly your need for a Savior. This is the kind of openness that I'd like all readers to have, at least by the time you finish Chapter 10. In the meantime, I'm quite satisfied with a glimmer of hope. I will close this paragraph with comforting words for any of you who are concerned that this one exception could possibly apply to you. If you're concerned, then it does *not* apply to you! Your concern is a symptom of your desire or at least curiosity – maybe just a small, hardly percep- tible, desire or curiosity at this point – to have or at least explore a relationship with God, and this means that there is much more than a glimmer of hope. If my last several sentences are not even remotely comforting but instead make you extremely irate – really ready to fly off the handle in fury because of my Christ-centered attitude – then I'm compelled to say that the one exception probably *does* apply to you… (I am finally done with this paragraph, and elsewhere in this book I refer to it as the "unfortunate but necessary paragraph.")

~

Now we're ready to proceed. And by "we," I'm including you even if you've arrived at this launching pad via a successful detour through Appendix A; I'm also including you even if you're currently on a dusky odyssey that I refer to as a convoy of doubts. Maybe you have doubts about the Triune God – Father, Son (Jesus), and Holy Spirit – Christianity, heaven, hell, Satan, the world, society, your friends, your extended family, your spouse, yourself. There is plenty of room on this journey for your doubts. You just have to promise that you'll keep an open mind and be receptive to change in your life.

OK, where were we? Oh, yes, I was telling you that I've written not only about the thought distortion of Love Zero but also about reality. This reality is as far away as we can get from Love Zero – "as far as the east is from the west" (Psalm 103:12). And it really is this far away even in the unlikely and extreme case that you literally don't know one person who loves you (rare, but it can happen). Even in such seemingly dire circumstances, the reality is that there is someone who loves you. Even if you're not aware of it yet, there is someone who already loves you more than any definition can describe, or antonym oppose. Even though we cannot understand it, there is someone who loves us just the way we are… and, yes, they *do* know the way we are... every bit… Even though we cannot come close to reciprocating such love, there is someone who keeps pouring it on… and has no plan to stop… Even though we cannot come close to meeting their high standards, there is someone who keeps forgiving again and again… and has no plan to stop…

How can they do this? Why do they do this? You'll have to wait until Chapter 10 for me to thoroughly address the second question, although I do drop a few hints along the way. In the meantime, let's focus on *how* they can do this.

- Yes, how can they love us just the way we are?
  - They can love us – no, they *do* love us – just the way we are because they understand what it's like to be us; they have "been tempted in every way, just as we are" (Hebrews 4:15 NIV). They perfectly empathize with us.
- And how can they keep pouring it on, with no plan to stop, when we cannot come close to reciprocating?
  - They can keep pouring it on – no, they *do* keep pouring it on – because it's their nature "not to be served but to serve" (Matthew 20:28). They are perfectly selfless.
- And how can they keep forgiving again and again, with no plan to stop, when we cannot come close to meeting their high standards?
  - They can keep forgiving again and again – no, they *do* keep forgiving again and again – because they "delight to show mercy" (Micah 7:18 NIV). They are perfectly merciful.

Who am I talking about? … If you have eyes to see, you've seen Him before. You see Him every time you look at nature (John 1:3; John 1:10; Colossians 1:16); "The sky above proclaims his handiwork" (Psalm 19:1). … And you've probably heard about Him before. If you have ears to hear, you hear about Him every Christmas season, unless you are wearing earplugs in every store: "Holy Infant, so tender and mild."[1] And you may even have heard that this baby grew up to die on a cross. … You may already know who I'm talking about.

Why did this baby – why did Jesus – why did God the Son (John 1:14; Matthew 3:17; Matthew 17:5; Matthew 27:54) – why did True God (Colossians 2:9) – grow up to die on a cross? Was this a tragedy? No, this is the polar opposite of a tragedy. This is the culmination of Jesus' earthly ministry. God the Son came to this earth to live the perfect life that we cannot, and this enabled Him to die on the cross as a perfect sacrifice, validated on Easter morning, to fully quench God the Father's wrath – His wrath that was stoked by our failure to meet His high standards (Exodus 20:3-17; Matthew 5:48). Yes, Jesus died on the cross because He is perfectly empathetic, perfectly selfless, and perfectly merciful – perfectly loving. True God died on the cross because He loves us.

In my vernacular, the apex of love is an intimate thing, and from this perspective it involves two, and only two. When I speak of intimate love such as this (Chapter 1), it's clear that we don't love groups of people with the degree of intimacy with which we love individuals within these groups. Likewise, God loves the world (John 3:16) in the sense that He intimately loves individuals of the world. Indeed, God truly loves every one of us, not as a faceless mass of humanity, but each one of us as an individual. Presuming anything less would be placing a limit on God's love, and in light of Ephesians 3:18-19 I wouldn't recommend making such an allegation. He knows us "by name" (John 10:3). And, yes, God loves us right now, before any change that He wants for us in our life. He does not withhold His love, waiting for us to change. He loves us with our doubts. He loves us with our baggage. He loves us with our weaknesses. And not only does God love us now, He has since the beginning of time (Psalm 139:1-18)! How can I be so confident? I don't know what you've done. I don't know what you've said. I don't know your innermost thoughts. That's true, I don't. But it doesn't matter! No matter how heinous it might be, nothing we have done, or said, or thought will cause God to love us any more or any less. He loves us because He created us (Genesis 1:26-27; Genesis 5:1-2; Psalm 139:13-14). He loves us because He promises to love us (Psalm 100:5; Isaiah 54:10; Jeremiah 31:3; Lamentations 3:22-23; Romans 8:38-39), and He never breaks His promises (Numbers 23:19; Psalm 18:30; Psalm 145:13; 2 Timothy 2:13; Hebrews 10:23). He loves us just because. Does this mean that we should continue to do, and say, and think heinous things? (It's easier for us, after all…) Of course it doesn't mean that (Romans 6:1-2)! If our attitude was that we could keep on doing such things, then that would mean we don't love God! And I don't recommend facing the time of God's judgment (generally the end of our life – see Appendix B) with that attitude.

Here, finally, is a summary of what I *have* written about:

- Despite any negative feelings we struggle with or hardships we've experienced, not only are we lovable, we are already loved
- This does not require us to change anything about ourselves
- Even if no one else loves us this way, God does
- When we bask in God's unconditional love, it's natural that we love ourselves, even with our flaws and quirks, and it follows that it's natural that we love others God has placed in our life, even with their flaws and quirks
  - o We cannot do this perfectly, but this does not deter us from expressing our love for God, for ourselves, and for others in our life; we do this with the help of the Holy Spirit

- When we live according to the Spirit, while we love despite our flaws we do not continue in willful sin as that is unloving

~

I still have not addressed why I am qualified to write about such things.

Foremost, I have felt Love Zero once, as I will describe shortly. Based on that experience – specifically, being rescued from that thought distortion – I learned that, until the time of God's judgment, **God loves us no matter what**.

Secondly, despite this experience, I subsequently had a similar feeling, but this time it was unconditional love from fallible human beings that I wanted to be assured of. I also elaborate on this below. In a nutshell, after praying fervently to see unconditional love from people, I had several experiences within one week that I deemed qualified as such. Even during my exhilaration, it didn't take long for me to realize that these were simple examples that just about any week in my life could produce. Don't you see? I learned that when I looked for it, it was already all around me. I had been too inwardly focused to see it clearly before. Based on that experience, I learned that **our awareness of being loved and our ability to give love are stifled by egoism (which is when our values are based on self-interest)**.

~

Let me now back up and give some background related to my eventually feeling Love Zero.

I will start with memories about my mom. Shall I lie down on a couch before I get started?

- My earliest memory is playing with a toy airplane on the floor of the hair-dresser's while she was having her hair done
- I remember nightly prayers with her before I would go to bed; this always included:

> *Ah, dearest Jesus, holy Child, / Prepare a bed, soft, undefiled,*
> *A quiet chamber set apart / For You to dwell within my heart.*[2]

- One of her favorite expressions was "In due time." I usually hated it when she said that because it meant she wanted me to be patient about something.
- I remember lying on the floor whining about breakfast, complaining that she was on the phone a long time. You're right! She *did* say "In due time"!
- One time when I was about four, she said that our family was going to move. I had no idea what that meant, but it did sound kind of fun. Then I found that we suddenly changed our house from one in the city to one about forty miles away in the suburbs. That's when I learned what "move" meant, and it wasn't as fun as I was anticipating…
- A couple blocks away from our house in the suburbs is a small hill, about a couple hundred feet high. There is a dirt path that curves its way along the side of the hill before it finally winds its way to the top. My mom and I would walk up that hill about once a month. One time, she started to have some kind of a pain (I think in her leg), and she had a bit of a hard time getting back to the house.
- Around that time, she started spending more time in bed
- Our dad put Christmas tree lights on a tree in the backyard. It was a tree that could easily be seen through our dad and mom's bedroom window. I thought it was a little weird that the lights stayed up long after Christmas, but the lights were pretty at night.
- I remember a lot of visitors to the house
- She enjoyed car trips to the desert
- One of her favorite hymns was "Take My Life and Let It Be"[3]
- I noticed that her hair looked different from before
- My favorite memory occurred on one of our walks up the hill near our house. (I don't remember if it was before or after the time she felt the pain I mentioned above. I don't think it was the same trip.) This time, instead of following the path all the way up to the top like usual, for some reason somewhere along the way the two of us got off the winding path and headed straight up the hill. Not far into this, I stopped at a big boulder (or at least it seemed big to me) and said something like, "I can't make it any further," and as far as I was concerned there was no way I was going to make it to the top of the hill. But my mom said something like, "You're closer than you think. Come on just a little bit more." And sure enough, just beyond that boulder was the top!

- I remember being happy when she came home from spending some time at the hospital
- I remember her being very calm – not easily angered or agitated
- I saw oxygen tanks being delivered to the house
- I remember her being optimistic and content – never bitter or negative

Those are all my meaningful memories of my mom. One morning, when I was six, I woke up to be told that she had died the night before. I didn't really know what that meant, other than the person who had shown me love most clearly was gone and wasn't coming back.

This came as a shock to me because I had not been given any warning. I knew she was sick, but I didn't know where that was leading. My parents had plenty of time to prepare me – she had breast cancer for a few years. They made a mistake by not talking to me about it. (By the way, if you find yourself in such a situation, I urge you to tell children what is forthcoming. Even if it's hard and even if they don't completely understand, it's worth having that conversation. In Chapter 9, I provide an example of what a mother who knows she is going to die within a few months could tell her young son.) Do I sound angry that my parents didn't do more to prepare me for my mother's impending death? I may have been a little bitter about this a few times, but I have moved past that. I have forgiven my parents for making an innocent mistake. Part of what has made me who I am today is my processing of my mother's death after it was presented to me in the way it was. It is neither logical nor healthy to hold grudges about experiences that have shaped us, even if they caused some difficulties.

Maybe the biggest burden I've carried because I wasn't given any warning is that I had no opportunity to say anything meaningful to her before she left. My memories that far back are pretty hazy, and I was obviously rather immature, so, as far as I know, it didn't occur to me to say "I love you" or even "I love you too." My recollection is that such sentiments were *never* (not only not toward the end) expressed by me to her. I cannot help but regret that. (Logically, I understand that under the circumstances I shouldn't feel bad about such things, but not all our feelings are logical!)

I also don't remember anything specific that she said to me (other than our nightly prayer, her catch phrase, "In due time," and, very few times, the gist of what she said, for example during my favorite memory). While she probably told me many times that she loved me, I don't remember a single time. Having no memory of verbal affirmation exacerbated some doubts that I'll get to shortly.

No, I didn't drop all the way down to Love Zero when my mom died. I was extremely sad, acutely lonely, and a little confused, but I generally felt adequately supported by my three siblings and our dad. However, there were some nagging feelings that may not seem logical, although to a six year old they made some sense. It boiled down to feeling abandoned. In my mind, abandonment was a viable explanation because maybe my mom didn't have much incentive to fight her disease: maybe I was too much trouble to take care of – maybe I really was a mistake (Appendix E). As a preadolescent, such feelings seemed natural, and I didn't think much of it then. As I got older, while logically I deduced that my mom had not downright abandoned me, those nagging feelings didn't completely go away. What if there was a grain of truth to it? What if she had even just a twinge of weariness that resulted in losing some of her motivation to fight? What if I had something to do with that weariness? What if it made a difference in the outcome? What if … ?

Sometimes we overthink things, build a house of cards, and reach illogical conclusions. On this line of thinking, it went even further. In light of such doubts, how could I be so sure that she had loved me as much as I thought she did? Likewise, how could I be so sure that others in my life loved me, or that they would not decide to leave me or hurt me in some other way? And with no warning! Maybe there was something I should do differently, so they wouldn't do that. Maybe there was some way to convince them that I'm not a mistake. Maybe there was something I could do to make them love me. … I would oscillate between not feeling these doubts at all, and being convinced that they must represent reality. I needed a lot of verbal affirmation from others to keep from swinging back to the negative side of this…

One night, I remember it very well, the doubts got so dark and pervasive that I thoroughly convinced myself that I have no value, and that not one person, alive or dead, had ever loved me and ever would, and what's worse I included God in this. I was convinced that even God Himself did not love me and could never – never, ever – love me. This is Love Zero, and I'm sorry if you've ever felt this way.

~

I cannot adequately put into words how I came out of that (which took a few days – days of hopelessness followed by a sharp transition to its antonym), but here are the basics. My feeling that God didn't love me was based on my knowledge of my sinfulness and that I cannot change from this nature. In my despair, I considered this to be sufficient reason for God not to love me – for God to abandon me as worthless. As I was contemplating this, I felt that it's unfortunate that God doesn't talk to us directly and in such a way tell us what He thinks of us. At the same time *(My mind was busy!)*, I felt that because people don't tell me very often that they love me, then the simplest conclusion is that they really don't. Somehow – I guess the Holy Spirit rescued me from my overthinking – it dawned on me that some people don't talk about love very often but you know they love based on their actions and, more impactful for me at that particular juncture, based on being loyal to a promise that they had made. Minds like mine can – unfortunately, and especially when depressed – find a way to misconstrue people's actions as having been done for selfish motives, and find a way to ignore evidence of God's actions in my life; so, considering that love is sometimes made evident by actions wasn't what launched me out of my dark place. Fortunately, even minds like mine can never misconstrue loyalty to a promise. Yes, those were the words that rescued me – *loyalty* and *promise*. I very abruptly (it truly was quite a rush) realized that of course God loves me! Why did I suddenly know? Because I remembered that He promised, and that He does not break His promises! This was truly euphoria (I felt the influence of oxytocin and/or similar hormone(s) for almost a week) – a bolus epiphany of 200-proof true love – and I now know with certainty that God loves me. (For more on God's promise to love us, please see Chapter 2.)

~

In hindsight, I can see that my doubting God's love for me is related to a common misconception that people have, namely that we need to have saving faith in Jesus as our redeemer (i.e., be assured of our salvation) in order for God to love us. In other words, the misconstruction is that God's love is conditional, marching in lockstep with our faith. But this is most certainly not the case during earthly life – before the time of God's judgment. (When we are judged, we do need to be saved by faith alone in order to abide [remain] in God's love for all eternity.) Until the time of God's judgment, God loves us no matter what – it's not conditional upon anything. God's love is *not* in lockstep with our belief: "For God so loved the world … that whoever believes in him [God the Son – Jesus] should not perish but have eternal life" (John 3:16). Some may ask: *Does it really matter that God presently loves me no matter what, if He's going to damn me to hell if I reject Jesus as my Savior at the time of God's judgment?* My answer to this is: *Yes, it matters immensely, and here's why: Since it is God's nature to love (1 John 4:8, 16), come what may, we're assured that God is approachable; throughout this life, we never have anything to fear about entering into a relationship with Him, regardless of what our past looks like. To Him, we are precious – no matter what – and He greatly desires an intimate relationship with each of us. He very much wants to save us from the awful consequences of our sins, even if they are indescribably heinous and innumerable.* When I felt Love Zero, I was wrong about God's regard for me. But my feeling of unworthiness is correct from the perspective of salvation. To be sure, I was – and still am – utterly undeserving of spending eternity in the presence of God (the result of salvation). The only thing that saves me is the redeeming work of Jesus and my not rejecting the Holy Spirit's gift of faith in Jesus as my Savior. Knowing that God loves me – no matter what – was the key I needed to realize that God really does want to have an intimate relationship with me. At Love Zero, I thought I was undeserving (lacking merit) *and* unlovable (lacking value), and that is a hopeless feeling. Now that the Holy Spirit has rescued me from Love Zero, I realize that I'm simply undeserving, and that fills me with blessed hope, for I know with certainty: "Christ died for the ungodly … God shows his love for us in that while we were still sinners, Christ died for us" (Romans 5:6, 8). That's not lockstep by any stretch. (I'm a little sad that this important paragraph is drawing to a close, and elsewhere in this book I fondly refer to it as the "fortunate and necessary paragraph.")

*Oh I can see You now / Oh I can see the love in Your eyes
Laying Yourself down / Raising up the broken to life*[4]

~

As I mentioned, after that experience, I now know with certainty that God loves me – that God considers me inherently valuable.

Since that time, have I doubted that *others* love me? ... *Sort of...* What I mean is that I've doubted whether people love me unconditionally (defined in Chapter 1). If you can't tell by now, let me inform you that I'm a recovering perfectionist. I want – oh, excuse me, I mean I used to want... – everything to be just so, and I get upset – oh, I mean I used to get upset... – by anything less than ideal. In those days, I never saw a glass half full, but I could see it 1% empty. Now, *that's* a perfectionist! Anyway, one day my mind got to wandering and I started to consider how awesome unconditional love is; but then I went down the rabbit hole of realizing that I cannot perfectly love others unconditionally, and (other than God Himself) neither can anyone else. I slid down pretty far (but not all the way down to Love Zero). I was upset for two reasons. First, I was disappointed in myself because it's clear that I'm incapable of loving the people in my life the way that I want to love them – with irreproachable, incessant, and unfettered unconditional love. And second (selfishly – proving my inability to perfectly love unconditionally), I felt resentment that no one seemed to come close to loving me that way either; specifically, some of my friends (not including my wife), on separate recent occasions, had strongly implied that there were things about me that they would rather I change. This flew in the face of my enlightened way of thinking – that God loves me just the way I am. And while I hadn't forgotten that God loves me unconditionally, I was bitter that I wasn't feeling this from people too. What did I do? I prayed about it. I told God that I'm sorry for my inability to love others the way that He wants me to, asked for His help to do better, and, yes, against my nature I went ahead and asked to see evidence that people love me unconditionally. A couple days went by and I didn't see any tangible evidence, and I started to fret about that. Actually, as it turns out, this anxiety did lead to the first of several occurrences of my experiencing unconditional love – see the list below. These all occurred within a week of my prayer. One lesson I learned is that this deluge of love started with me reaching out to a friend (my wife); in other words, if we want more love in our life, it helps to stop focusing on ourselves. Yes, love is all around us, and we see it better when we stop gazing at our navel.

- A couple days after my prayer, I finally told my wife that something was bothering me. Someone I considered a friend had told me that they generally cannot tolerate people with certain characteristics – characteristics that I clearly have. My wife listened attentively, did not accuse me of overreacting, sympathized with me, and did not try to fix the problem, other than to encourage me to talk to my friend and tell them how I felt about what they said.
  - This is an example of loving empathetically
- The next day, I met with my friend, and told them how I felt. They apologized and clarified that they care about me and really do accept me the way I am.
  - From this, I was reminded that true friends love us despite our quirks
- A couple days later, I really blew up at my wife about something pretty stupid (sentence structure in a draft email, of all things!). She was remarkably unfazed, and her love for me was obviously unmoved. Yes, I did eventually apologize for flying off the handle, but her forgiveness was not really dependent on that.
  - This is an example of loving despite occasional falterings
- One week after my prayer, a quiet friend who doesn't often initiate conversations initiated a conversation with me, and this was simply to touch base – not to request something from me
  - From this, I was reminded that sometimes we need to be patient and not jump to conclusions (for example, that an apparent lack of communication means that we are not cared for)
  - It is meaningful to me that this occurred a full week ("in due time") after my prayer
- This final example is an observation that I made in the middle of the week after my prayer. At a track meet, I was at the finish line and saw a fifth-grade boy just barely get passed at the last moment, causing him to finish second in the race. He was quite upset – even crying a bit. His mother took him aside and held him and comforted him for several minutes, appropriately oblivious to others who were asking what was going on. She was completely focused on her son.
  - While I wasn't directly involved, this made an impression on me – it was a clear expression of unconditional love

One thing you'll notice about this list is that these are in some ways small things. But I nevertheless experienced love – true love. Yes, a week of true love is not always a honeymoon vacation. More often, a week of true love is appreciating the little things that we experience in our life, and being thankful for each of the relationships that we have.

And I learned that it's not limited to a week. Within two weeks of the above list, it was Mother's Day, and my wife and I were on the phone with my stepmother. As we were getting toward the end of the conversation, my stepmom said much more than a simple, off-the-cuff "Love you." She reminded us that she keeps my wife and I and our kids in her prayers, and that she loves us. She has become increasingly good about emphasizing this over the years, but for whatever reasons I had not noticed it as much before.

Yes, it should not be just a week, or two or three weeks, of love surrounded by months and even years of barren landscape. We should open our eyes to a new way of viewing the world around us: not just the world in a general sense, but more importantly the individual people in our lives – the individual people whom God wants us to love. It is living in this love that the rest of this book describes. I invite you to stop your navel-gazing, experience God's perfect unconditional (true) love for you, and learn how to better reflect love back to Him, yourself, and everyone God has placed in your life.

~   ~   ~

After-hours

At the end of each chapter, as well as here in the Prologue, I provide a few life-application prompts that I hope you find thought-provoking. Some prompts are geared for parents and other intimate couples; however, I'm sure they won't mind if everyone takes a peek at those.

Each time, I start these "After-hours" prompts with a cooldown period that I refer to as "Bob unplugged." This is always followed by "Step up to the microphone" – several prompts that are generally shorter and designed as mini-launching pads from which you can choose whatever flight path that suits your fancy.

Bob unplugged

Do you feel guilty when you have doubts about God? I think many of us do, but we don't need to. Doubts mean that we're giving the subject some thought, and that's better than apathy. Doubts can even strengthen our faith, if we keep thinking with an open mind, and keep praying with an open heart. In the Prologue, I've made it clear that there was a time when I doubted that God loves me. My doubts about this became so severe that for several days I came to the conclusion that – no doubt about it – He doesn't. It made sense to me, so I accepted it. But I kept processing it, and in due time the Holy Spirit blessed me by turning me upside down and shaking such doubts, and my erroneous conclusion, out. I now know with certainty that God always has, does, and always will love me, and I feel this is a good example of how doubts can lead to a stronger faith.

Now, I'd like you to consider your doubts about God, and choose the most significant question that you have. I know it can be difficult to pray about something we have doubts about, but I want you to do it. Be transparent with God and tell Him (as if He doesn't already know…) that you're having doubts about a certain matter. Ask Him to bless you with closure on this. Ask Him to guide you to trustworthy, God-fearing mentors whom you can talk to openly about your doubts. Ask Him to turn you upside down and shake. After thinking, discussing, and praying in this way every day for a month, look around to see what now lies scattered on your cutting-room floor. Is there anything that seemed to make sense to you, but God is saying instead, "Be still, and know that I am God" (Psalm 46:10)?

Remember that, as humans, it's natural for us to have doubts; and, for believers, an effective counterbalance to our spiritual doubts is faith, which is a gift from God. While saving faith does not infer the absence of all doubt about spiritual matters, scattering doubts to our cutting-room floor is an effective way to strengthen our faith and our relationship with God.

Step up to the microphone

"Anything that savors of dejection spiritually is always wrong."[5] (Allow me to paraphrase this Oswald Chambers quote: *Until the time of God's judgment, any interpretation of God's nature that causes us to feel hopeless is incorrect.*)
• Do you agree or disagree, with either the quote or my paraphrase?

On p. 12, I provide several general examples of "glimpses of what love looks like." Think back to at least one specific time in your life when you got a glimpse of love. Close your eyes and try to remember as many specifics about these experience(s) as you can. Please say a prayer of thanksgiving, and include in this how you felt at the time of your glimpse(s), and how it feels now as you're remembering.

If one or more people related to the glimpse(s) of love you just remembered are still alive, why not tell them about your fond memories?

Thinking is overrated. On p. 21, I describe anxiously thinking about what others were thinking about me, and I ended up building a house of cards in my mind.
• Do you ever worry about what someone else is thinking, and then proceed to build a teetering skyscraper?
• What are better approaches than fancying ourselves a mind-reading architect?

For parents: At least once in the coming month, I'd like you to tell each of your children that you love them. If you have more than one child, please don't tell them all at once as a group – rather, tell each one individually. And maximum effect is achieved if you use their name in close proximity to the L-word. If they no longer live with you, don't expect a pass from me on this. Why not call them on the phone, have a videoconference, or send them a written message?

For intimate couples: Both of you, in turn, tell your partner *two* fond memories: your favorite memory that does *not* involve them, and your favorite memory that *does* involve them.

From Love Zero to Love 360

Chapter 1 – Short Definitions of Love
(If Indeed This Is Possible!)

Let us start with definitions! Usually, that's an easy task, but not so when we're talking about love. It's made especially difficult in English because the single word "love" is used to encompass so many concepts. The ancient Greeks had the right idea by having several words to represent different aspects of love. Four *(There are more!)* of the most commonly referenced ancient Greek words related to love are: *agape* (ἀγάπη) (essentially what we refer to as unconditional love), *storge* (στοργή) (essentially familial love), *philia* (φιλία) (essentially friendship), and *eros* (ἔρως) (most definitely sexual desire and intimacy). But breaking love down into bins such as this is not entirely satisfying. Each loving relationship is unique, and the vast majority of them should include contents from more than one of these bins. For example, a healthy sexual relationship should include, in addition to a hefty dose of *eros*, some measure of *philia* and *agape*. So, in a sense, we're right back where we started from – juggling words to try to describe the diversity of loving relationships.

The ancient Greeks had specific words to describe love; we have specific phrases, such as unconditional love and conditional love. I will soon juggle *many* words to give you my definitions of such phrases.

But before I get to that, the time has come for me to greet the new students.

Orientation Day

All those days anxiously checking the mailbox are behind you now. *Will the acceptance letter ever come?* you thought. Remember the rollercoaster ride? You were just about to give up hope, but then you finally realized that Bob U doesn't mail any acceptance letters. (It's not in our budget…) All acceptance is communicated in a World Wide, ebb and flow, fashion.

Over the years, we've found that the two most frequently asked questions on Orientation Day are: Are the dorms coed? And what is Bob U's acceptance rate? For the first, you'll find out soon enough. For the second, we don't like to brag, but the records show that our standards are very extreme. We have taken stringency to a whole new level – to a place that "no eye has seen, no ear has heard, and no mind has imagined" (1 Corinthians 2:9 GW). That's right, it's a little-known fact that we have a 100% acceptance rate.

And we are delighted that you have not rejected our offer. Thank you for matriculating.

As I look around, I see some nervous faces, I see some confused faces, and I see that apparently a few of you were enjoying your newfound freedom all the way until the wee hours of this morning, or at least that's how I'm going to interpret your drooping eyelids.

OK, let's sweep away the cobwebs and get to know one another better. My favorite way to break the ice is to do a little brainstorming. And what better way to do that than to put our heads together and take a peek into the four bins I mentioned on the previous page. That's right – I want you to help me list some descriptions of love that others have already given us. … Yes, just shout them out, and I'll try to keep up with you as I jot their descriptions down on the whiteboard. I'll do my best to write them in chronological order.

> *"Love is as overpowering as death. Devotion is as unyielding as the grave. / Love's flames are flames of fire, flames that come from the LORD. / Raging water cannot extinguish love, and rivers will never wash it away."* – Author unknown (Song of Solomon 8:6-7 GW)

> *"When nobody in the world loves any other, naturally the strong will overpower the weak, the many will oppress the few, the wealthy will mock the poor, the honoured will disdain the humble, the cunning will deceive the simple"* – Mozi[1]

> *"The madness of love is the greatest of heaven's blessings"* – Plato[2]

> *"Love is composed of a single soul inhabiting two bodies"* – Aristotle[3]

> *"Love is patient and kind; love does not envy or boast; it is not arrogant or rude. It does not insist on its own way; it is not irritable or resentful; it does not rejoice at wrongdoing, but rejoices with the truth. Love bears all things, believes all things, hopes all things, endures all things. Love never ends."* – St. Paul (1 Corinthians 13:4-8)

"Love is from God" – St. John (1 John 4:7)

"God is love" – St. John (1 John 4:8, 16)

"Love is itself the beauty of the soul" – St. Augustine[4]

"Love is the astrolabe [inclinometer for making astronomical measurements] of God's mysteries" – Rumi[5]

"To love is to will the good of another" – Thomas Aquinas[6]

"Love is a smoke raised with the fume of sighs" – Shakespeare[7]

"Love sought is good, but given unsought better" – Shakespeare[8]

"Love in our hearts makes us one" – Goethe[9]

"The more a man judges the less he loves" – Honoré de Balzac[10]

"Love is a celestial respiration of the air of paradise" – Victor Hugo[11]

"If the light were not in your eyes, dear Mr. Brooks, you would understand better how happy your little Helen was when her teacher [Anne Sullivan] explained to her that the best and most beautiful things in the world cannot be seen nor even touched, but just felt in the heart" – Helen Keller[12]

"With truth for sword, he needs neither steel nor gunpowder. He conquers the enemy by the force of the soul, which is Love." – Gandhi[13]

"We are never so defenceless against suffering [vulnerable] as when we love" – Sigmund Freud[14]

"Of all forms of caution, caution in love is perhaps most fatal to true happiness" – Bertrand Russell[15]

"What is love but acceptance of the other, whatever he is" – Anaïs Nin[16]

"Love is not affectionate feeling, but a steady wish for the loved person's ultimate good as far as it can be obtained" – C.S. Lewis[17]

"Love is not a thing of the mind. It is only when the mind is really quiet, when it is no longer expecting, asking, demanding, seeking, possessing, being jealous, fearful, anxious – when the mind is really silent, only then is there a possibility of love." – Jiddu Krishnamurti[18]

"Love is the only force capable of transforming an enemy into a friend. ... Love transforms with redemptive power." – Martin Luther King, Jr.[19]

"A purpose of human life ... is to love whoever is around to be loved" – Kurt Vonnegut[20]

"'Love' is that condition in which the happiness of another person is essential to your own" – Robert Heinlein[21]

"Love is all you need" – John Lennon and Paul McCartney[22]

"The smile is the beginning of love" – Mother Teresa[23]

"LOVE has nothing to do with what you are expecting to get – only with what you are expecting to give – which is everything" – Katharine Hepburn[24]

"Anyone who falls in love is searching for the missing pieces of themselves. So anyone who's in love gets sad when they think of their lover. It's like stepping back inside a room you have fond memories of, one you haven't seen in a long time." – Haruki Murakami[25]

So, what do you think of our list? I always enjoy doing this. Every time I have a brainstorming session on the topic of love, I learn something new. But here's something I've known for a long time. Everyone quoted in a list like this is smarter than me in at least one way: They gave short descriptions of love. As you'll soon discover, all but two of my descriptions – no, I'm going to be so bold as to call them attempts at *definitions* – of love are not at all short.

The first exception is my current answer to a homework assignment that I gave myself some time ago. Here's what I assigned myself: *Define love in 58 words or less*. … Why 58? … Because that's the number of words in the longest description in our brainstorming list. I haven't finished my homework, but I'll share with you what I have so far. And note that I've narrowed my attempt down to a description – no, a definition – of love between people. (Please wait patiently for my attempts related to other aspects of love.)

> *To love is to remain tenaciously true to our authentic self, allowing our intrinsic unique attributes to shine through unfettered as they guide and shape our prayers, thoughts, words, and actions – our special gifts handpicked for another specific individual, keeping in mind their pref-erences, with our gifts given for no reason other than our counterpart's physical, emotional, psychological, and spiritual benefit – blessing our counterpart by showing them their inherent value in a new way.*
>
> *To be loved is when another does this for us.*
>
> *To be in love (an apt phrase for* any *loving relationship) is when two do this for one another.*

103 words… *Not even close! This is tough!* But it is also rewarding to try to express what love means to us. I invite you to try, and I'll make it easier for you by allowing you to use many more than 58 words – let's say, oh, 103 words. *How generous of me!* While you're working on that, if you will indulge me, I will soon cast off the shackles of draconian limitations to the number of words that we can use. As you know by now – *(You didn't forget to read the Prologue, did you?)* – I typically ignore any such limitations…

Autumn snow day

But before I try to give any more definitions of love, let me say a little more about why love is so difficult to describe or define. As I alluded to above, there are so many facets to love, and each loving relationship has its own blend of these facets. Allow me to make a comparison: Our love for ourselves, and each of our loving relationships, including the one we have with God – each is a snowflake.

Is it a good description of a snowflake to say that it's a beautiful meadow covered with freshly fallen snow? Is it a good description of a snowflake to say that it's an exhilarating ski run? Is it a good description of a snowflake to say that it's a very slippery sidewalk, and we can get hurt if we're not careful? While these are accurate descriptions of what snowflakes sometimes give rise to, they are terrible descriptions of a snowflake. What I'm attempting to do in this book is to describe a snowflake… and another… and another… By the end, you'll know what several different snowflakes look like and how each is beautiful in its own way, and that some snowflakes are even exquisite. I'm not going to try to describe a blizzard, a whiteout, an avalanche, or other manifestations of billions upon billions of snowflakes.

No, let us appreciate individual snowflakes.

Intimate love

Careful readers have already noticed something about my view of love. … What have you noticed? … For starters, you've already lost count of how many times I've used the word "relationship." That's not very surprising, but you've also gotten the sense that my use of this word is typically in the context of an interaction between two individuals – *only two* individuals. I can't tell you how happy I am that you've picked up on that. While I agree that it's often reasonable to consider a special connection that we have with a group of people to be love, my view is that settling for this type of love is too limiting – not scaling the heights that can be achieved. What do I mean? … Allow me to draw a two-part analogy.

- In the first part, my special connection *with a group of people* is analogous to us (the said group and me) being an unmarried couple walking along the beach, holding hands, occasionally stopping to embrace and share a pro-longed, moonlit kiss, and then going back to the parking lot to get into our separate cars and drive off in different directions. … During such an evening, are we expressing our love for one another? Of course we are! Likewise, of course it's possible for me to have a special, loving connection with a group of people; I refer to such connections as "living in love with" a group of people.

- In the second part of my analogy, my loving relationship *with an individual (ANY individual)* is analogous to us (my companion and me) being a married couple walking along the beach, holding hands, occasionally stopping to embrace and share a prolonged, moonlit kiss, and then going back to our hotel room to express our love for one another in other ways. ... *These are the analogies, people!*

In this book, we're not driving off in different directions; no, we're going back to our hotel room and disturbing our neighbors. ... I enjoy a stroll on the beach as much as the next person, but I crave the satisfaction of supplementing this with something more intimate.

Setting analogies aside for a moment – (and if you're more than a little flushed right now, I advise reading Appendix X) – I'm now going to rephrase my last sentence in literal terms: *I am positively impacted by living in love with groups of people, but overall I am* more *positively impacted by the love I share with specific individuals who make up these groups.*

I think you get the idea, but to be sure I haven't left you standing aghast outside of my hotel room door, let me take a moment to be clear about what I mean by intimate love. For one thing, I usually am not talking about a sexual relationship. I am in intimate love with scores of people, but of course (Chapter 7 – "Dr. Bob's sex advice" section) only one of these people is my sexual partner. By intimate love, I mean that it's an emotionally close relationship that involves only two individuals (or one, when referring to our love for ourselves).

Why am I so focused on loving individuals? ... We can all agree that love is a broad topic – an expansive mountain range, to be sure. We may disagree on details of the topography, but from my vantage point the highest peaks of love are inherently intimate – inherently one-on-one relationships.

Look back at my 103-word definition of love between people. Read it again, and you'll agree that a more accurate characterization of what I've tried to define is *intimate* love between people, and naturally the highest level – *(Why settle for anything lower?)* – of intimacy means it involves two, and only two.

Many times in life, we need to zoom out to see the bigger picture in order to understand a difficult concept. However, to better appreciate the concept of love,

I ask you to zoom in. In various ways throughout this book, I try to convince you that we are most positively impacted by intimate love. And when it comes to surveying intimate love, we need to get very close to get even a glimpse of the ecstatic heights that are achievable. So, I implore you to set your telescope aside, stop gazing at the stars, and dust off your microscope – we will be focusing in on what I like to call the wee beasties[26] (Antonie van Leeuwenhoek and I will accept "animalcules"[27] for partial credit) of intimate love.

Semantics 101, Fall Semester

For starters, to help you get your feet wet with the wee beasties, when you write your short definitions – *(Yes, now you can see that you may want to try to write more than one!)* – of love, with at least one I'd like you to focus on trying to define intimate love between people. When doing this, by now you know that I don't want you to fall into the trap of trying to describe intimate love for humanity. Whether or not any one of us – besides God Himself – can honestly say that we love humanity to this depth is a topic for another book, and it won't be a book that I write. To whatever extent I can say that I have intimate love for humanity is only accurate from the perspectives that I have intimate love for individuals who are part of humanity, and I do go so far as to say that I have intimate love for what I refer to as my "representative person" (Chapter 6 – "Loving our representative person" section, and Chapter 8 – "Love is … kind" section). In a nutshell, all the individuals I know and love, taken together, create my representative person, and my love for people I don't know is made possible by my love for my representative person – who is very flexible indeed, and constantly evolving to mesh with my environment at any given moment.

Oh, I see a hand up. Do you have a question? … Why does my representative person need to be so flexible? … Good question. If they weren't, the implication would be that I love each of my counterparts in the same way. Those who think it's reasonable to love in such a generic manner are way, way... *way...* too zoomed out! They might as well just go ahead and say that every snowflake is the same! *Preposterous!* I am but one person, to be sure, but my love for each of my counterparts is unique. Why? Because each of my counterparts is unique. To give our love to more than one person in exactly the same way is disrespectful to our counterparts. If we were actually able to intimately love all humanity, I would certainly intimately love each person in a different manner, and I hope you would too. God is the only One who I'm confident actually *does* intimately love all humanity, and He absolutely loves each of us in a different manner. If you disagree, I'd like you to ask yourself why you're placing such limitations on God; I'd also like you to consider this: God invites you to have an intimate relationship with Him, and He would never be so discourteous as to have a relationship with you that is the same as He has with anyone else.

The apex of love – ecstatic love – is intimate, which means two, and only two. (*Zoom in…*)

~

OK, we can now check that wee beastie off the list. Let's wade a little deeper into the pool and check off another similar point. When writing your short definition of intimate love between people, also don't become ensnared in an attempt to describe intimate love for specific groups of people. This is even worse than the trap of describing intimate love for all humanity. Why is it even worse? Besides the limiting nature of the monotonic style of love that I described earlier this semester, saying that we intimately love specific groups of people infers that we are biased – including specific groups at the exclusion of others. For example, I'm a Christian, but the concept that I should love Christians at the exclusion of unbelievers is abhorrent to me. Another example is that I'm a U.S. citizen, but the notion that I should love other members of my country at the exclusion of others is detestable to me. Let us not be biased in these or other ways.

Love is inclusive.

What's that? … Am I saying that we should interact with all groups in the same way? … *Uh, have you been dozing off in class?* … I'd like you to apply the same approach you learned earlier this semester to how we are to live in love with groups. Have I lost you? I hope this example will help get us back on the same page: I think we can all agree that we are to live in love with our family in a special way – different from how we live in love with any other group. So, there you have it: Just as we should love each individual in a different manner, we should live in love with each group in a different manner.

Semantics 101, Spring Semester

How are you doing so far? Are you feeling pretty comfortable? Well, today's class presents a simple concept for me – *(I like to dive right into the pool!)* – but if you're slowly wading in, we've reached an uncomfortable point for many. In case I'm not being clear, we have waded in deep enough that the next step is submerging our … *How do I put this?* … submerging our "nether region." Yes, we've reached the juncture where I remind you that we sometimes use the word "love" to describe feelings that certainly are not love. This is an unfortunate fallout of English having one word that is often used to cover so many different feelings that we have. (My conclusion for why we use this one word in so many ways is it provides a mechanism for us to distance ourselves from the intimacy of ecstatic love – to dilute what is too strong [uncomfortable] for some.)

- My first example of how we misuse the word love is that we do not love things (food, clothes, homes, cars, music, movies, TV shows, etc.)
  - No, these are inanimate objects or creations that provide us with satisfaction or enjoyment
- My second example is that we do not love places or events
  - No, these are delightful locales, uplifting experiences, and the like, where we go to relax, have fun, be inspired
- My third example is that we do not love hobbies and similar activities
  - No, these are pleasant things we do to brighten our days
- My fourth example is that we do not love characteristics about people, for example aspects of their personality ("I love how positive and upbeat you are, even in light of this challenge"), their physical appearance ("I love your hair!"), and the like
  - No, these are attributes we appreciate, admire, or desire about people we love
- It looks like we're starting to approach some gray areas here. Do you agree? Many times in life, topics are best not presented in black-and-white, heavy-handed ways. To this end, I'll present one of my favorite gray-area topics – bonds between people and animals – in a very gray, light-handed way. What do I mean?

As you already know, this book is zoomed in on intimate love. I've already provided a definition of intimate love between people, and – as you may have gathered by now – the rest of this book elaborates on this topic as well as our intimate love of ourselves and, most importantly, the intimate relationship that God wants to have with each of us. Suffice it to say that while I appreciate that people can form tangible, deeply meaningful bonds with animals – yes, to love animals *(There, I said it)* – this happens to be outside of the field of view that I've asked you to zoom in on.

I will end this class session with a warning. In all five of my examples, it's possible for us to go too far and allow such things and majestic creatures to inhibit our interactions with others. Whether it be our motorcycle with sidecar, our ice-fishing shack, our collection of empty soup cans, our boyfriend's chartreuse toenails, or our pet iguana (even if he is the most cuddly iguana imaginable), let us not become so enamored by our lov… – I'm going to say fondness – of such things and affectionate creatures that we are distracted, to the detriment of our most important relationships. While we often supplement our dissemination of love to ourselves and others in ways such as the following example – enjoying a day at the park, highlighted by listening to an outdoor concert featuring our favorite musician, as we braid our daughter's hair between handfuls of trail mix, with our faithful tricolor rough collie lying on the cool grass next to us – let's use such activities and circumstances to enhance, not detract from, the intimate (emotionally close, one-on-one) loving relationships that we should be developing with God and the people in our lives.

I enjoy sharing a chocolate malt at the soda shop as much as the next person, but I crave… Oh, you already know where this is leading… Let's try another one: The foothills are charming, but let me take you up where the air is thinner.

Spring snow day

I'm perceiving an icy breeze from a few of you. Yes, it can be a little chilly and even uncomfortable when first wading into the wee beastie pool, but you'll get used to it. At this point, you might as well just get all the way in. Don't worry – the water's fine.

When I get chilly, I look for snowflakes. Speaking of which, it has been said that no two snowflakes are alike. It has also been said by certain egghead scientists that this is not necessarily true. If there ever have been two natural snowflakes alike, then the analogy of loving relationships being like snowflakes has completely collapsed! Why has the analogy collapsed? Because surely – without any doubt – no loving relationship is like any other. No scientist, regardless of the shape of their head, is ever going to disprove this, no matter how hard she or he may try! I've often thought to myself: *Has there ever been – in all of history – another loving relationship like the one I have with my counterpart?* Every time I ask myself this question, considering every counterpart I've ever had, the answer is always: *No! There never has been, and there never will be again!* That's how special each of our loving relationships is. For each of your counterparts, ask yourself the same question, and I'll be very surprised – and very skeptical… – if your answer is, "Yes, there has been another loving relationship just like one of mine."

Love is inimitable.

Definitions of love

OK, I've rested long enough since my 103-word definition above. I'm now reenergized and ready to attempt more definitions of specific types of love. As promised, I'm surely springing free from the confines of word limitations!

I've amply explained that love is difficult to describe, and I'm sure some would argue impossible to define. Nevertheless, I do give it a shot, if nothing else so you and I are on the same page – in the same hotel room – as you read this book, within which I do refer to these concepts many times.

Undoubtedly, you'll notice that my definitions related to our giving love (to ourselves and to others) are from an idealistic viewpoint, such that it's clear that consistently achieving these heights is not attainable. Yes, this is indeed the case, but if we – with the Holy Spirit's guidance – don't aspire for such pinnacles then we're certainly not giving our best loving. Our best loving is given in the striving, even though we all understand that none of us will reach perfection on this side of eternity.

Without further ado, below I elaborate on what I mean by the following six types of love. I generally avoid using the word "love" in these definitions, except when quoting Scripture and in the bulleted footnotes. Note that many of the referenced (but not quoted) Scripture passages use the word "love" as well. Check them out!

God's perfect unconditional (true) love for all people

Despite our rebellion against Him that started in the Garden of Eden (Genesis 3) and continues to this day (Romans 3:9-23; Romans 8:7; Galatians 1:4), God considers all people to be inherently valuable (Matthew 13:44-46; Luke 15), and He wants all of us to be saved (1 Timothy 2:3-4; Titus 2:11 NIV; 2 Peter 3:8-9) from the consequence of our sins (Ezekiel 18:4; Romans 6:23) and to live for eternity with Him (Romans 6:23; John 6:40). God is continuously mindful of our greatest need – a Savior – and is equipped to satisfy this need, freely providing the gift of faith in the blessed truth that it's only the redeeming work of His only Son (Jesus) that saves us (Ephesians 2:8; John 14:6). At all times until the time of God's judgment (Appendix B), God patiently (2 Peter 3:8-9) longs (Luke 13:34) for all people (John 3:16) to live in His compassion (Micah 7:18-20), forgiveness (Nehemiah 9:17), mercy (not punishing us, even though we deserve it – Psalm 145:9; Jeremiah 3:12; Joel 2:13), and grace (blessing us, even though we don't deserve it – Romans 5:20-21; Joel 2:13). He has promised that this is the case under all circumstances: even when we sin against Him (Romans 5:8; Ephesians 2:1-5), even when we don't reciprocate (Luke 13:34), even when we deny Him (Luke 22:54-62, John 21:15-19), even when we're unfaithful to Him (Hosea 3), even when we feel no one could be worse than us (1 Timothy 1:13-16), even when we're severely depressed and feel worthless (Psalm 40:1-3), and even no matter what* (Psalm 100:5; Isaiah 54:10; Jeremiah 31:3; Lamentations 3:22-23; Romans 8:38-39). And God always keeps His promises – they are everlasting (Numbers 23:19; Psalm 18:30; Psalm 145:13; 2 Timothy 2:13; Hebrews 10:23).

> This definition has so many references that it does read a bit choppy. Do you agree? … Yes? OK, let me rewrite it, but this time leaving out all the references.
>
> Despite our rebellion against Him that started in the Garden of Eden and continues to this day, God considers all people to be inherently valuable, and He wants all of us to be saved from the consequence of our sins and to live for eternity with Him. God is continuously mindful of our greatest need – a Savior – and is equipped to satisfy this need, freely providing the gift of faith in the blessed truth that it's only the redeeming work of His only Son (Jesus) that saves us. At all times until the time of

God's judgment, God patiently longs for all people to live in His compassion, forgiveness, mercy, and grace. He has promised that this is the case under all circumstances: even when we sin against Him, even when we don't reciprocate, even when we deny Him, even when we're unfaithful to Him, even when we feel no one could be worse than us, even when we're severely depressed and feel worthless, and even no matter what*. And God always keeps His promises – they are everlasting.

- The only way to escape God's love is if, at the time of God's judgment, you reject Jesus as your Savior
  - In this way, God's unconditional love does not equate to universal salvation (Appendices H-4 and J)
- If someone tries to convince you that God's love is conditional before God's judgment of you, they are wrong and please see Appendices H to H-4 where I handily refute every one of their flimsy arguments
- God's unconditional love does not mean that He doesn't want us to change anything about ourselves. Times when God wants us to change include: if we are injuring someone (including ourselves) – physically, emotionally, psychologically, or spiritually; if we are disrespecting someone (including ourselves) – even without imparting tangible injury; if we are not doing something that God wants us to do; if we are ensnared in a persistent, habitual sin (1 John 3:4-10); and last but most, if you (I cannot include myself in this statement) do not yet believe that Jesus is your Savior. But wherever we are in this journey, God cannot love us any more or any less than He has since the beginning of time. God's love is unwavering and everlasting (Psalm 100:5; Isaiah 54:10; Jeremiah 31:3; Lamentations 3:22-23; Romans 8:38-39)!
- While God's unconditional love for us is perfect, we cannot reciprocate perfectly because of our selfish, sinful, human nature. We will experience perfect love (what I call perfectly requited love) only in heaven, and that will last into eternity.

   *Note: If "no matter what" caused you to raise your eyebrows, I suggest you read Appendix H-3, as there I provide my commentary on whom God "hates" and when He does so.

God's perfect unconditional (true) love for each of us as individuals

Everything in the previous definition applies, and don't go down the rabbit hole of thinking that with countless googolplexes of meteoroids, asteroids, comets, moons, dwarf planets, planets, stars, galaxies, and black holes for God to juggle, and more importantly billions of people for God to keep track of, that He doesn't care for you as an individual. No, look at the personal pronouns Paul uses in Galatians 2:20. "I have been crucified with Christ. It is no longer I who live, but Christ who lives in me. And the life I now live in the flesh I live by faith in the Son of God, who loved *me* and gave himself for *me*" (emphasis mine). And look at the personal and possessive pronouns referring to Job in this comforting passage. "For I know that *my* Redeemer lives, and at the last he will stand upon the earth. / And after my skin has been thus destroyed, yet in my flesh I shall see God, / whom I shall see for myself" (Job 19:25-27, emphasis mine). "Does he not leave the ninety-nine on the mountains and go in search of the one" (Matthew 18:12)? And when He finds what He's looking for, the two of us rejoice – "My beloved is mine, and I am his" (Song of Solomon 2:16). God calls us "by name" (John 10:3), and has an intimate knowledge of everything about us (Psalm 139:1-16; Matthew 10:30). Furthermore, Jesus' earthly ministry made it very clear that He came to serve (Matthew 20:25-28) not only the whole world but individuals (John 13:3-9); for example, Jesus' care for individuals is demonstrated in His miracles, many of which are the healing of one person. In this and other ways, God demonstrates that He cherishes us as inherently valuable individuals. As St. Augustine wrote, "O Thou Good omnipotent, who so carest for every one of us, as if Thou caredst for him only; and so for all, as if they were but one!"[28]

Our unconditional (true) love for ourselves

Our total acceptance of ourselves as an inherently valuable human being, just the way we are, despite our limitations and flaws, and despite how others feel about us, knowing that God created us as a unique individual for a reason and cares about us. This is true at every moment, even when we learn that we need to change, for example because we are disrespecting or injuring ourselves or others in our life. We have a high regard for ourselves, always taking good care of our physical and emotional needs, and never putting up with harmful behavior from others.

- We cannot love this way perfectly because of our selfish, sinful, human nature. We will experience perfect love (what I call perfectly requited love) only in heaven, and that will last into eternity.
- Unconditional love for ourselves is not selfishness when we rightly prioritize, as follows
  - We are to love God more than we love ourselves (Matthew 22:36-38; Exodus 20:3)
  - While we are equal with all other people with respect to how inherently lovable we are, we are to serve others (Matthew 20:25-28; Galatians 5:13; 1 Peter 4:10) and as a demonstration of our love for them, in humility, prioritize their needs above our own (Philippians 2:3-4; John 15:13; Matthew 5:38-42; Romans 12:10), provided that they're not injuring* us, and provided that we do not slip into codependency (i.e., the dysfunctional behavior of sacrificing our own needs as we try to meet the needs of others in a chronically unbalanced fashion). A healthy way to deprioritize our needs in a balanced way involves trusting God's provision, as described in Matthew 6:25-33.

    *Note: For my commentary on Jesus' command that we turn the other cheek (Matthew 5:39), see Appendix C, henceforth to be referred to as Appendix Ɔ.

- Pop quiz! *Define intimate love for ourselves in 58 words or less! …* Give me a minute here… … OK, I'm done with my quiz, and I'll show it to you: *To love ourselves is to remain tenaciously true to our authentic self, allowing our intrinsic unique attributes to shine through unfettered, as we express our thankfulness to God, serve others in meaningful ways that are edifying to them, all the while attending to our own needs and never discounting our inherent value, no matter what.* 55 words… *I could go on! You know I could!*

Our unconditional (true) love for others

Our total acceptance of others as inherently valuable human beings, just the way they are, despite their limitations and flaws, and despite how others feel about them, knowing that God created them as unique individuals for a reason and cares about each of them. This is true at every moment, even when they don't realize that they should change, for example because they are disrespecting or injuring themselves or others in their life. Under such circumstances, we should pray for them, aspire to forgive them – even if they don't show any remorse (Chapter 9), offer to help them if they know us or if it's otherwise appropriate, and distance ourselves from them if necessary for our physical and emotional wellbeing. We are to treat others this way even when it's not appreciated or reciprocated – ourselves not becoming mired in feelings of bitterness and resentment. Under all circumstances, if someone makes themselves vulnerable to us (i.e., opens up to us), we are to treat them with respect and not judge them (Matthew 7:1-5). We always want the best for them, and encourage or otherwise help them to take good care of their physical and emotional needs, and never to tolerate harmful behavior from others.

So the people in our lives will experience the above blessings, we don't hoard our thoughts but rather communicate (demonstrate and verbally express) effectively and frequently. We do this in a respectful way that does not cause them to feel uncomfortable or burdened. We treat them in the way that we would want to be treated (Luke 6:31; Luke 10:25-37) if we were them (i.e., keeping in mind that their preferences may be different from ours), such that in all aspects of their life – sorrows, joys, defeats, achievements, relapses, positive developments – they experience empathy and know that they're supported, no matter what.

- We cannot love this way perfectly because of our selfish, sinful, human nature. We will experience perfect love (what I call perfectly requited love) only in heaven, and that will last into eternity.
- As you can see from this definition, it's possible for unconditional love to be completely one-sided. But even in such circumstances – which in many cases are difficult circumstances – it's true love nevertheless.
- A classic example of unconditional love is mother and infant. By the way, I consider this to be mutual (not completely one-sided) unconditional love, even from the beginning. (For example, look at the first picture on the back cover. Isn't it saturated with love? Look at all that love spilling over the edges! Oh, and so far I've only addressed the love coming from the baby.)

Conditional love

A mutual attraction – physical and/or emotional – resulting in a bond between two people (counterparts), with each looking to please the other, while not neglecting their own needs. While not "keeping score" and not necessarily like for like, reasonably balanced reciprocation is necessary for a healthy relationship.

Each time either counterpart pleases the other, *both* feel joy.

Each time either counterpart becomes aware of the other experiencing joy based on something outside of the relationship, the first empathizes and feels some measure of joy.

Each time either counterpart becomes aware of the other experiencing sadness, anxiety, fear, illness, or other emotional or physical hardship, the first empathizes and feels some measure of pain, while the receiver of this empathy experiences some measure of comfort.

Both are comfortable being vulnerable to one another, provided that their counterpart is consistent in their respect and support, and of course is not hurtful.

Both are forgiving of the other, which means: always offering forgiveness, and truly forgiving if their counterpart shows some measure of remorse for what they did wrong and an openness to change (Chapter 9).

Both care about the emotional, psychological, and spiritual development of their counterpart, and about building a stronger relationship, and will therefore identify things they feel should change, communicate their thoughts to their counterpart, and if a mutual understanding is reached both will work together to reach a common goal. If in such a circumstance a mutual understanding is *not* reached or a common goal is *not* agreed upon, either counterpart can decide that it's best for them to distance themselves from the other, at least temporarily (have a "timeout"), and this should absolutely be done if there is the potential for any type of abuse (emotional, physical, etc.) (Appendix Ɔ). The desired outcome of a timeout is a cooling-off period followed by reconciliation.

Mutual trust, transparency, open communication, and frequent affirmation of positive feelings for the other – demonstrated and verbally expressed – are necessary for a healthy relationship.

All conditional love relationships should include some measure of mutual unconditional love.

- Friendships are in this category
- Sexual relationships are also in this category, with the addition of physical intimacy
- There's no such thing as one-sided conditional love. It takes two! For example, a one-sided infatuation with someone, who doesn't share our desire to

form a bond, is not love, at least not in the conditional love category. In such circumstances, it's possible for love to be experienced via unconditional love.

- Based on my definition, there's no such thing as a conditional love relationship involving more than two people. In my view, the love experienced within families of three or more, and similar camaraderie in other groups, is better described as a series of one-on-one, intimate relationships, involving both conditional and unconditional love. In my vernacular, you may love everyone in the group, but you don't love the group per se, at least not in an intimate way. As I said before, ecstatic love is an intimate thing – thus, my view is that conditional love is best described as involving two, and only two.
  - o And a corollary, based on ecstatic love being an intimate thing, is that of the two definitions I wrote related to God's love for us, the second is more accurate
- Conditional love is inherently imperfect (because it's based on conditions) but can nevertheless be a very beautiful and heartwarming thing
- Conditional love is obsolete (see Chapter 10 for why) after our earthly life. *But don't worry!* We will experience perfect love (what I call perfectly requited love) in heaven, and that will last into eternity.

Perfectly requited love

In heaven, the relationships that all who are saved (i.e., all who have not rejected Jesus as their Savior at the time of God's judgment) have with God and with one another. Unlike the prior five definitions, I'm incapable of even trying to describe this, other than to say that each believer will experience a consummated relationship with God, and restored relationships with fellow believers. I very much look forward to the time when I'll be able to describe this fully!

"As it is written, 'What no eye has seen, nor ear heard, nor the heart of man imagined, / what God has prepared for those who love him'" (1 Corinthians 2:9).

"What we will be has not yet appeared; but we know that when he appears we shall be like him, because we shall see him as he is" (1 John 3:2).

"For now we see in a mirror dimly, but then face to face. Now I know in part; then I shall know fully, even as I have been fully known" (1 Corinthians 13:12).

"Let him lead me to the banquet hall, and let his banner over me be love" (Song of Solomon 2:4 NIV).

- It's not unconditional love as I've defined it because unconditional love involves loving despite flaws, but there will be no flaws in heaven
- It's not conditional love as I've defined it because conditional love involves two people maintaining a loving relationship with one another provided that certain conditions are met. As discussed in Chapter 7, each of these conditions lies somewhere within the spectrum established by the two extremes of a dichotomy. Here are examples of such dichotomies: kindness – insensitivity; respect – disrespect; selflessness – selfishness; support – neglect; amenability – stubbornness; reliability – irresponsible, capricious behavior; gentleness – harshness; forgiving attitude – mercilessness. There are no such dichotomies in heaven.

Antonyms of love

That's a lot of words! Way over 103! I'm not sure how successful I was at defining these aspects of love; the saying "words cannot express" certainly does seem to fit. As I mentioned in the Prologue, sometimes a definition is better understood by antonyms (opposites or antitheses). Certain things are seen more clearly with the opposite as the backdrop. For example, how can we understand light without considering darkness? How can we appreciate good without being disgusted by evil? How can we "fear, love, and trust in God above all things"[29] without rejecting Satan and his ways?

One thing that makes love hard to see clearly is its brilliance. Like the sun, it's too much for us to stare straight into it. But – wait – there *are* circumstances where we can look directly at the sun with our own, unprotected eyes. And it is beautiful, isn't it? Why are we able to look at the sun during a sunrise or a sunset? It's because the intensity of the sun's light is reduced by the atmosphere, and there's more atmosphere for its light to penetrate when the sun is low on the horizon. And the more polluted the atmosphere is, the more the sun's intensity is attenuated. Likewise, with our world's filthy atmosphere of antonyms such as neglect, indifference, selfishness, revulsion, manipulation, abuse, cruelty, malevolence, vindictiveness, and hate, there are times when we can look straight at love and see its splendor, even if just for a brief moment. Let us travel far to discover the best vantage points, welcoming all we encounter as we are "going down that road" (Luke 10:31), and together wait patiently (Psalm 37:7a) for the right times, and surely we will be blessed to catch a glimpse of an exquisite spectacle.

As we prepare for such a journey, let's learn more about the world's atmosphere, so we better understand its filthiness.

Neglect

When we neglect a family member or friend, we are shirking our duty to help and support them.

Neglect says: *Deep down, I know that one of my accountabilities is to care for you one way or another – maybe I'm your parent, maybe I called you friend – but can't you handle this on your own?* Love says: *I'm right here beside you; I'll never leave you behind.*

Love does not race ahead and abandon; love slows down and nurtures.

Indifference

When we are indifferent toward someone, we are disrespecting their inherent value.

Indifference says: *I know that you're suffering, and I really don't care.* Love says: *I know that you're suffering, and, if it's OK, I'd like to learn more about what you're going through. I'll pray for you and do what I can to help you in tangible ways.*

Love is not indifferent; love is empathetic and compassionate.

Selfishness

When we are selfish, we devalue others – prioritizing our interests over theirs.

Selfishness says: *Stop whatever you're doing, and serve me.* Love says: *If it's OK, I'd like to learn more about what you're doing. And can we do it together?*

Love is not selfish; love is symbiotic.

Revulsion

When we are repulsed or disgusted by someone, either physically or emotionally, we are fixated on their flaws, forgetting that they are "fearfully and wonderfully made" (Psalm 139:14) by God, in His image and likeness (Genesis 1:26-27; Genesis 5:1-2; James 3:9).

Revulsion says: *Back away, so I can whip your self-image to shreds.* Love says: *Come closer, so I can soothe you.*

Love is not repulsed or disgusted; love embraces any imperfection.

Manipulation

When we manipulate someone, we are trampling on their autonomy.

Manipulation says: *I'm going to play mind games with you to try to get what I want; you can't trust what I say – for example, when I say "I love you," it really means that I want something from you.* Love says: *I'm going to be transparent and trustworthy – for example, when I say "I love you," it really means just that.*

Love is not manipulative or phony; love is authentic, genuine, and trustworthy.

Abuse

When we abuse someone, we are taking terrible advantage of their vulnerability.

Abuse says: *I know you well enough that I feel comfortable hurting you; I have trapped you, and am in control of you.* Love says: *I respect you and set you free.*

Love is not abusive; love is kind, fair, and liberating.

Cruelty

When we are cruel to someone, we are demeaning them – treating them in an inhumane way – because we want to feel powerful.

Cruelty says: *I will do whatever it takes to make you submit to me.* Love says: *Tell me how you'd like me to serve you.*

Love is not cruel; love is caring and submissive.

Malevolence

When we are malevolent toward someone, we have ill will for them, often because we are trying to feel better about ourselves.

Malevolence says: *I want you to fail; I want you to be mired in problems; I want you to be miserable.* Love says: *I want you to succeed; I want you to be blessed, even through your challenges; I want you to have a joy-filled life.*

Love is not malevolent; love always wants the best for others.

Vindictiveness

When we are vindictive toward someone, we want to get back at them for something they did to hurt us. "An eye for an eye and a tooth for a tooth" (Matthew 5:38), and that's just for starters.

Vindictiveness says: *Not only do I not forgive you for what you did to me or my loved one, but also I am going to make you pay; I will get my revenge.* Love says: *I forgive you, I encourage you to turn to Jesus (to repent), and if you don't: "Vengeance is mine, I will repay, says the Lord" (Romans 12:19).*

Love is not vindictive; love is forgiving and merciful.

Hate

When we hate someone, we have completely given up on them, and we want nothing but the worst for them. This may be because of something they have done to us or a loved one. Or this may be because of our biased / prejudiced attitude: Even though we don't know them personally, we have already made up our mind that we hate them, no matter what they do; I call this unconditional hate.

Hate says: *Because of what you did to me or my loved one, I will never forgive you and want only the worst for you.* Love says: *Despite what you did to me or my loved one, I forgive you and want only the best for you.*

Unconditional hate says: *Based on my biased / prejudiced attitude, I'm afraid of what you might do to me or my loved one, and there's nothing you can do to change my mind.* Love says: *I will not assume the worst about you.*

Love is not hateful; love is tolerant, nonjudgmental, and hopeful.

I told you that our world's atmosphere is filthy. The antitheses of love are surely putrid and vile! Minimally, I'd like you to be able to say the following after reading this book: *I'm still not really sure that I understand what love is, but I certainly understand what it is not! And in the midst of this gritty smog, thick with the choking stench of the fumes from Satan's cesspit, I will fix my eyes on Jesus (cf. Hebrews 12:2 NIV), whose brilliance can penetrate even this.* Yes, Satan's schemes are surely thwarted when he throws everything he has at us, yet it only helps us see more clearly Jesus, who is "the light of the world … the light of life" (John 8:12). Satan is strong and can cause much trouble, but God is stronger: "For he who is in you is greater than he who is in the world" (1 John 4:4).

~

I've written a plethora of words, many about love and fewer about opposites. You now know plenty about what I mean when I use specific words and short phrases, as well as what I certainly do *not* mean… This has gone on long enough; even I can agree: *Enough with the semantics!*

Oh, for heaven's sake, look at the time! Have we been cooped up in this classroom that long? … I wonder if it's here yet. Let me look out the window. … Oh, good, it's just pulling up now. … OK everybody, I'm prescribing a change of scenery. The bus is here, and we're going on a field trip!

On this trip, I'll be driving the bus, and from time to time I'll be pointing out more elaborate descriptions of individual snowflakes. Remember the four ancient Greek bins of love I mentioned at the beginning of this chapter? We'll be scooping out contents from each of those bins – a ladle-full here, a dollop there, a dash for flavor – and sometimes we'll see what happens when grime from Satan's cesspit interferes with the formation of our snowflakes. But even such snowflakes, as imperfect as they may be, can be made beautiful – yes, even exquisite – if we allow their ever-evolving form to be shaped by the Holy Spirit's hand.

~ ~ ~

After-hours

Bob unplugged

Our unconditional (true) love for others includes, according to my definition, that we "help them to take good care of their physical and emotional needs." When thinking about *why* (Chapter 10) we love other people in our life, to me one of the most compelling reasons is becoming aware that my counterpart has a specific need.

- Has this been your experience as well? Think of the people closest to you in your life. Was your closeness facilitated by one or both of you having a need that the other was equipped to mitigate or satisfy?
- Are there any people who have no needs whatsoever?

Step up to the microphone

Look again at the brainstorming list of descriptions of love. When considering those descriptions that are not quotes from the Bible, which are your favorites? … Why?

In the "Antonyms of love" section, I briefly introduce the concept of unconditional hate. Please consider this viewpoint for a few moments and, ideally, discuss it with a few others, all the while comparing and contrasting unconditional hate with unconditional love.

- How does such thinking help you better understand the concept of unconditional love?
- Which is easier for our selfish, sinful, human nature to understand: unconditional hate or unconditional love?
- Which is more commonly actualized in our world?

Read the parable of The Good Samaritan (Luke 10:25-37). Which antonym(s) of love do you think best describe the attitude(s) of the priest and Levite?

Read Genesis 2:18-20, which provides a description of Adam's vastly numerous interactions with animals.

- Was "a helper fit for him" (vv. 18 and 20) found within these verses?
- Who was Adam's suitable companion?
- Who are your suitable companions?

For parents: Tell each of your children that you've been giving this topic some thought, and you're interested in hearing them describe to you any one of the following types of love: God's love for us, our love for God, the love of a parent, love between any two people.

For intimate couples: In my definition of conditional love, I include the two points listed below. Read these again, and I'd like both of you, in turn, to empathize with your partner after they tell you a recent example in both categories. It's fine if the two of you have already discussed these examples, provided that this time you get into more depth than before.

- Each time either counterpart becomes aware of the other experiencing joy based on something outside of the relationship, the first empathizes and feels some measure of joy
- Each time either counterpart becomes aware of the other experiencing sadness, anxiety, fear, illness, or other emotional or physical hardship, the first empathizes and feels some measure of pain, while the receiver of this empathy experiences some measure of comfort

Chapter 2 – God's Perfect Unconditional (True) Love for Each of Us

I apologize to all but one of you, but I need to pull this bus to the side of the road. I'm looking in the rearview mirror, and I'm seeing something that cannot be tolerated. … *I already warned you, didn't I?!* … It's a narrow shoulder, but I have no choice but to pull over immediately. … OK, here will have to be good enough. It won't take me long to take care of this. … All but one of you look a little fearful as I walk down the aisle, my face like stone and my eyes on fire. All but one of you look a little fearful, and that's good – for all but one of you. We shouldn't get too comfortable on this journey. A healthy amount of fear is appropriate (Proverbs 22:4; Psalm 128:1; Psalm 33:18-19; Psalm 147:11; Psalm 103:11; Malachi 4:2). One of you should be especially fearful. You should be saturated with terror (Hebrews 10:26-31)! To him I say – *(Note: The rest of you are welcome to listen from a distance)* – you boarded this bus with wide eyes and a spring to your step, but you have regressed to stubbornness and an unrepentant heart (Romans 2:5). Did you think I wouldn't see or hear you because you sat in the back row? I didn't mind the smoking, the sips from the small flask you're hiding in that paper bag, the gawking at the worn magazine you keep holding up sideways, the spit wads aimed toward the front, and even the churlish jokes about me, but you went too far when you started hurting your seatmate. Don't roll your eyes… *I saw you!* Nothing gets by me, and I saw you hurt a fellow bus rider – the one and only thing that may get you thrown off this bus. I also heard your seatmate try to talk to you about it, but you wouldn't listen to them. I also heard the entire back row try to talk to you about it, but you wouldn't listen to any of them. So, now I'm here to join the conversation. I'm very interested to hear more about your viewpoint on your sinfulness – your need for a Savior. I heard you say that your sins aren't that bad. I heard you say that you can name many people worse than you. I heard you say that you can look at the headlines on any day, and there are more people to add to the list of those who are worse than you. You don't get it, do you? *God demands perfection (Matthew 5:48)!* Can you give Him that? … Was that a smirk? … OK, that's it! … This is always difficult for me, but sometimes it comes to this. The best thing for everyone – yes, including you – is for you to get off this bus, for as long as it takes. There is another journey that will be of great benefit to you, if you open your heart to God's guidance. You've got a lot of thinking to do, and what better place to do it than in the desert that's right next to us here. You'll have plenty of time as you make progress toward that valley in the distance. Looks like it might take oh, say, 40 days to reach your destination. There is only one path across this wilderness. If you get off that path, you will wander forever, with the closest thing to water being mirages that are always just a little bit farther on... But I assure you that there is one way through to the other side. This path – this Way (John 14:6) – has Bread and Water, more than enough to sustain you (John 6:35). I am familiar with this detour, and I promise that every evening I will drive the dune buggy that we're dragging behind this bus to check on your progress and to help you find your way back to the one path, if you are willing. Friend, I pray that after your 40 days in the wilderness, you are convicted of your sinfulness – especially your sin of hurting a fellow bus rider – and convicted of your need for a Savior in order to stand before God. Then, you will be ready; there will be another bus for you to get on, and then you will be allowed to stay on the bus for the duration of the journey. I am but one bus driver among many. Yes, there are many bus drivers like me, and for this journey we all follow the same route.

...

OK, now that that's settled, are the rest of you ready to get going again? ... Oh... wait... I see that we can't go quite yet. One of you is crying... Here, let me come kneel next to you. ... What's wrong? ... Did I upset you? ... Was it when I yelled that God demands perfection? ... Oh, come here. Let me hold you – there, there. ... I know that you're not perfect, and guess what? I'm going to let you in on a little secret. It's not much of a secret, actually. I'm not perfect either – far from it (Romans 7:18). Not one person is perfect, except God's Son, Jesus. God demands perfection, yes, but His high standards are met through the perfection of the One who is both True Man and True God – Jesus (Matthew 5:17). If we put our trust in Jesus, His righteousness becomes ours (Romans 1:17; 1 Corinthians 1:30; 2 Corinthians 5:21; Philippians 3:9). So, in that way, God actually does see us as perfect – but only through the lens of Jesus. All you have to do is trust in Jesus (Romans 8:1-11). Do you know that Jesus said, "Whoever comes to me I will never cast out" (John 6:37)? That is a promise from Jesus.

Thinking about this promise helps me when something I've done, said, or thought makes me remorseful because I know that it's not in line with God's will. Can you remember this promise too, as we continue on our journey? … Good. … Here, let me wipe your eyes – there now. … Are you ready to go? … Oh, not quite yet. You have a question? Yes, I want to hear it. … … You're right. My tone was quite different with the man I threw off the bus. That's because he was hurting one of his fellow bus riders, and he doesn't feel remorse – doesn't feel sorry – for his sins. He doesn't understand yet that he needs a Savior. The man I cast off the bus needs to understand this. … What's that? How do I know that you understand? Because you were crying. … And how do I know that the rest of the folks on the bus understand? Because they looked fearful when I came down the aisle. Does that make sense? … Are you ready to go? … Oh, not quite yet. You have another question? Yes, I want to hear it. … … No, I don't hate him, but I can see how you might think that. No, I love him. If I didn't love him, I wouldn't have thrown him off the bus. … Before we go, would you like to pray with me for our friend whom I sent on a detour? … Does that sound good? … OK, let's join hands. … *Heavenly Father, we ask that the Holy Spirit work in the heart of our friend whom I sent into the wilderness, and in the hearts of all unrepentant sinners who are causing spiritual damage to or are otherwise hurting one of Your dear children. We plead with You! Please convict them to repent, to turn to Jesus – to trust Jesus, not themselves – so they too will stand alongside us before God. We pray this in Jesus' name. … I also want to pray for my new friend here. I ask that the Holy Spirit comfort her and make her confident that every one of her sins is forgiven because of Jesus. Help her to fix her eyes on Jesus (cf. Hebrews 12:2 NIV), the One who alleviates all our fears. Please build her trust in You, so she may live a life full of peace and joy. I pray this in Jesus' name. Amen.*

A preemptive strike

Does it surprise you that I love both the woman and the man in the preamble to this chapter? Does it surprise you that I call them both friends? … It surprises me. I'm always surprised whenever the Holy Spirit amps up my sanctification such that I actually do something Christlike. I'm surprised because it goes against every fiber of my selfish, sinful, human nature. I generally don't like surprises, but a sanctification-surprise is an exception. I'm delighted every time that I'm surprised in this way.

How can I call the man I threw off the bus my friend? If you're a careful reader, then you're surely thinking: *It doesn't make sense! A friend is a type of conditional love relationship. But the man cast into the wilderness is not feeling love for the bus driver. Where's the bond?* … First of all, I'd like to thank you for making it through Chapter 1 – *All the way through!* – and reading it so carefully. Second of all, you're right! A friendship *is* a form of conditional love. While a part of me is tempted not to, I'm going to jump straight to the punchline, and here it is: Sometimes in life, we need to pursue what I like to call a preemptive-strike friendship. I allude to this in the "What if your love for someone is not reciprocated?" section (Chapter 9). There, I explain that when we feel that our love is not reciprocated – (And remember that reciprocation is a conditional love concept) – we should respond with unconditional love, and in such a way drop our fishing line into the lake, drop our net into the sea. Who knows? Maybe in time our counterpart will come to appreciate our unconditional love, and maybe we'll even find ourselves on our way toward a new friendship. In the preamble to this chapter, I've taken this concept one step further. I've recognized that especially my first counterpart is in dire need of spiritually mature friends. What is my response? I call him friend, even though forming a friendship with me is the furthest thing from his mind at the moment. I want him to know that despite his perilously erroneous self-perception and his appalling attitude about this, I am willing – no, I want – to be his friend. As I am yelling at him, I am surely loving him unconditionally – yes, with tender affection (Chapter 6 – "The myth of 'tough love' … " subsection) – but he may have a hard time appreciating that at this particular time. So, I want to be bold and give him something to hang his hat on. I want him to hear me call him the F-word. … *Oh, come on people! I mean "friend"!* … Perhaps he'll remember this when the dust has settled and if we happen to see each other in the valley – his destination on the other side of the desert. I very much want to see him complete his journey across the wilderness. I am praying for this. I'm also praying that if we meet in the valley, we hardly recognize each other: He calmed and refreshed by the cool water of forgiveness for his acknowledged sins, and me with a warm and smiling countenance, with tears forming in my eyes. Will he call me friend? Will he make my tears fall? I am praying for this.

~

What does this have to do with God's love for us? Since I now know that you've read Chapter 1 carefully, I feel comfortable proceeding to expand on this immediately. You already know that God loves us unconditionally, not conditionally. One of the primary ways that God shows His unconditional love for us is to kick us in the keister when we do not acknowledge our sinfulness and need for a Savior. "Those whom I love, I reprove and discipline, so be zealous and repent" (Revelation 3:19). This is surely loving most gently.

Do you think of God as angry or loving? … Your answer should be: "Yes – that is, if you change that 'or' to an 'and'!" To be clear, the answer is, "All of the above." … What is God angry about? … He is angry about sin (disobedience to God's commands); He is angry about unrepentance (not acknowledging our sin – not feeling sorrow for it – not wanting to change – not turning to Jesus, our Savior, for forgiveness and guidance toward obedience); and He is angry about unbelief (not believing that forgiveness and everlasting life with God are found only in Jesus). … How does this apply to us? There are only two answers to this. Which answer applies to you?

- When we are a believer, God has smoldering anger about our willful sins but sees us as sinless. … *How is this possible?!* … Jesus has already taken *all* our sins (willful and unwillful) upon Himself and bore them on the cross, Himself taking the full brunt of God the Father's anger toward our sin (Isaiah 53:5; 1 Peter 2:24). In the circumstance of repentance and belief, God's smoldering anger withers to ashes based on Jesus' sacrifice, and He sees us as sinless.

- When you are an unbeliever, God is angry about your willful sins, especially your willful sins of unrepentance and unbelief, but is patient with you. "With the Lord one day is as a thousand years, and a thousand years as one day. The Lord is not slow to fulfill his promise as some count slowness, but is patient toward you, not wishing that any should perish, but that all should reach repentance" (2 Peter 3:8-9). What is God waiting for? He is waiting for you to submit to the Holy Spirit such that you repent and believe. If you stop rejecting Jesus by the time of God's judgment of you, then He still has smoldering anger about your willful sins but sees you as sinless. … *How is this possible?!* … Jesus has already taken *all* your sins (willful and unwillful) upon Himself and bore them on the cross, Himself taking the full brunt of God the Father's anger toward your sin (Isaiah 53:5; 1 Peter 2:24). In the circumstance of repentance and belief, God's smoldering anger withers to ashes based on Jesus' sacrifice, and He sees you as sinless.

As I've amply expounded upon above, God is angry – *very angry!* He has a *lot* to be angry about! And this is the case when considering only my willful sins, let alone anyone else's willful sins, especially their willful sins of unrepentance and unbelief.

If God is so angry, can He still love us? ... I'd like you to answer this question for me. Whom shall I call on? ... Let me see here. As I look around, I can tell which of you are parents, from the smiles on your faces. Go ahead – give us the answer. ... *Yes, you're right!* Righteous anger and love can mix – actually, they do mix very nicely. Just as we discipline our children when we have righteous anger about their misbehavior, and just as I cast the man off the bus in my righteous anger about his unrepentant attitude, God disciplines those He loves (Proverbs 3:11-12; Hebrews 12:5-11; Revelation 3:19). This is gentle love. *But wait – there's more.* Because justice must be served, God the Father has no choice but to mete out severe punishment for sin, unrepentance, and unbelief. ... How does this apply to us? How do we respond? There are only two responses to consider. Which response applies to you?

- If we are a believer, we say, *"Thank You, Jesus! Thank You for suffering on the cross to pay the penalty for my sins – every one of them. Thank You for Your gentle love."*
- If, at the time of God's judgment, you reject Jesus as your Savior, then you will be saying something else. I'm not sure what that is, exactly, but it will have something to do with your eternal regret for finally realizing that you were wrong about who Jesus is. It will also have something to do with you having to take upon yourself – *Remember, you rejected Jesus...* – the full brunt of God the Father's wrath because of your unrepentance and your unbelief in Jesus' redeeming work. It will also have something to do with you embarking on an eternal odyssey that explores the antipode (direct opposite) of love in all its blackness. If, at the time of God's judgment, you reject Jesus as your Savior, then none of what you experience will be love, gentle or otherwise.

God's gift & the one condition

Just as words cannot describe the depth of God's love for us, words cannot describe the anguish that will be experienced by all who reject Jesus as their Savior at the time of God's judgment.

Does God want anyone to experience this misery? No, "As surely as I live, declares the Sovereign LORD, I take no pleasure in the death of the wicked, but rather that they turn from their ways and live" (Ezekiel 33:11 NIV). "God our Savior … desires all people to be saved and to come to the knowledge of the truth" (1 Timothy 2:3-4). Just as I want the man I cast off the bus to call me friend, God wants each of us to call Him friend as well. … I know what you're thinking: *But a friendship implies conditions, right? I thought God's love is unconditional...* Yes, until the time of God's judgment, God's love for us is unconditional; He loves us no matter what. But for us to *continue* in God's love *at and after* His judgment of us – there is a condition that must be met. … *Anyone want to take a shot at this?* … Do you need a hint? … OK, here you go. There's only one condition: It's very important, but it's also very easy to meet. It's so simple that a child can do it. It's so remarkably simple that even an infant can do it! How can an infant do it? They do it by not rejecting the Holy Spirit's gentle embrace. The Holy Spirit is very affectionate, and one of His favorite ways to tenderly touch our heart is through Baptism. What does an infant receive at Baptism? She receives the same thing (Acts 2:39) that all of us receive when we are baptized (Acts 2:38). We receive the gift of faith – belief in the forgiveness of sins and the assurance of salvation (eternal life in the presence of God, which is offered to all people (Titus 2:11 NIV)), and that all of this is accomplished only through the work of Jesus, our Savior. We receive the gift of the Holy Spirit's preemptive strike on our heart. The victory is already won (1 Corinthians 15:54-57). All we have to do is not reject God's gift. That's the one condition. And it's so easy not to reject God's gift…

~

If anyone has the audacity to try to convince you that God's love for us is conditional before His judgment of us, please direct them to Appendices H to H-4, and gently teach them that God's love is a constant flow, and that it's the *assurance of salvation* (our continuing to live in God's love for all eternity) that is conditional (on belief). If you need help gently teaching them this, may I suggest that they read the fortunate and necessary paragraph (Prologue)?

Do not resuscitate

How does an infant know that the Holy Spirit's preemptive strike on their heart is a welcome shock? How does an infant know that God's love is a constant flow? An infant knows because they are instinctively trusting when they encounter loving kindness. It's completely natural for them to trust in God's promises (next section).

We can learn a lot from infants, and one thing they teach us is that death is preferable over anything this world has to offer. The Holy Spirit's preemptive strike is a wondrous force that is aimed to kill. Even an infant knows that it's sweet bliss to submit and be taken out in this way – to be freed from all the empty promises of this world. Why would they not trust the One who created them – the One who gave them life? Why would they not follow their Leader, even unto death? "Do you not know that all of us who have been baptized into Christ Jesus were baptized into his death? We were buried therefore with him by baptism into death" (Romans 6:3-4).

Is an infant really knocked to the canvas when they're baptized? Are older children and adults rendered motionless in the far corner of the boxing ring – limbs askew, down for the count – when they first believe in Jesus as their Savior? Yes and yes, it's really true. They have passed away: "If anyone is in Christ, he is a new creation. The old has passed away; behold, the new has come" (2 Corinthians 5:17).

I invite you to succumb in this way. Do you really prefer to respond to the Holy Spirit's preemptive strike on your heart by kluging your old body parts back together using clumsy, Frankensteinian methods, and then rubbing sticks together, hoping for a resuscitating spark? *That's just plain silly!* Yes, it is, but such a zombiesque existence is precisely what some people prefer over the new life that Jesus freely offers. Throw your sticks to the ground, unscrew the rusty bolts, and "put off your old self, which belongs to your former manner of life and is corrupt through deceitful desires … put on the new self, created after the likeness of God in true righteousness and holiness" (Ephesians 4:22, 24).

~

Most people think that babies can't talk until they're oh, say, about a year or so old. But I tell you that tiny infants surely can talk. We just need to be quiet and listen more carefully. The next time you see an infant baptized, soon afterwards I'd like you to hold her or him in your arms and be very quiet. … *Shh!* … Can't you hear them? I can hear them very clearly. If you need some practice, look at the first picture on the back cover. Now, tilt your head down and stop doubting. Finally, close your eyes, and I'm confident you'll hear me getting louder by the second: "I have been crucified with Christ. It is no longer I who live, but Christ who lives in me. And the life I now live in the flesh I live by faith in the Son of God, who loved me and gave himself for me" (Galatians 2:20). Yes, we can learn a lot from infants. *"Lord, give us such a faith as this"*![1]

Wait! … There's more. … Shh! … Can't you hear them? … "If we have died with him, we will also live with him" (2 Timothy 2:11). … "Put your trust in the LORD" (Psalm 4:5). … "May the God of hope fill you with all joy and peace as you trust in him, so that you may overflow with hope by the power of the Holy Spirit" (Romans 15:13).

God's promises

I'm tired out from saying so much. It has been a big day, and it's time for me to nuzzle in and take a nap, resting in the peace that comes from the assurance of salvation. While you're waiting patiently for Little Bob – that's me – to wake back up, I suggest that you listen to the booming voice of Big Bob as he reminds us of God's sure promises.

Feelings aren't facts

Are you familiar with scrupulosity? … No, it isn't a board game that came out in the 80s, although for many it does feel like a bewildering, never-ending duel to oblivion between our conscience and our shame pit. Scrupulosity is the distressing disorder where the sufferer is repeatedly fearful that God is going to punish them because of something they did, didn't do, said, didn't say, thought, or didn't think. People of all faiths can experience this – Christians are not immune. If you don't consider yourself a professional scrupulosity player, that's my cue to label you a gifted amateur because it's a rare breed indeed who hasn't at least dabbled in this game from time to time. And it's so easy to get drawn in, isn't it? We start on a lazy afternoon, and the next thing we know it has become the dark of night.

Believers are ready players because we easily satisfy the two prerequisites: (i) We know that we are sinners, and (ii) we remember that God sometimes does choose to punish us for committing a sin. What we often forget, however, is that whenever God punishes us before the time of His judgment, it's for our ultimate good, for example to remind us that there are consequences to our poor choices. The next time you find yourself wasting the afternoon playing scrupulosity, I implore you to recite Hebrews 12:10-11 – "He [God] disciplines us for our good, that we may share his holiness. For the moment all discipline seems painful rather than pleasant, but later it yields the peaceful fruit of righteousness to those who have been trained by it" – as you flip the game board off the table. But many of us seem to have poor memories when it comes to passages of Scripture like this.

The stakes of the game of scrupulosity seem high, especially when we fear a harsh punishment that extends beyond this life… Yes, I'm talking about our eternal destiny – the highest stakes. Imagine the distress of worrying that a poor choice you made decades ago might preclude you from being saved. Maybe you don't have to imagine that feeling of gnawing uncertainty because you're very familiar with it – you've been playing this game ever since a certain bad move. You've gone around and around the game board so many times now that what started as a healthy dose of guilt over a mistake has morphed into debilitating shame. Guilt and shame may seem like synonyms, but they are worlds apart. Guilt guides us toward repentance. Shame drops us into an abyss.

This is getting complex. So, it's time for me to explain the rules of the game of scrupulosity.

1) In this fallen world (Genesis 3), our first move is to be tempted / experience inordinate desire / have an intrusive thought. If you're curious about choosing a game piece, here are some common poor choices: covetousness, lewd sexual thoughts, viewing pornography, taking illegal drugs, drinking too much alcohol, overeating, gambling, stealing, profanity, lying, gossiping, slandering, bullying, racism, bigotry, judging. This is a partial list; more game pieces are provided in Galatians 5:19-21 – "Now the works of the flesh are evident: sexual immorality, impurity, sensuality, idolatry, sorcery, enmity,

strife, jealousy, fits of anger, rivalries, dissensions, divisions, envy, drunken-ness, orgies, and things like these. I warn you, as I warned you before, that those who do such things will not inherit the kingdom of God." (If that last sentence made you cringe based on your experience with intrusive thoughts, please read Appendix G – "Thought-action fusion.")

2) Because of our sinful nature, our next move is to submit to temptation / satisfy our inordinate desire / dwell on our impure thought. This feels fulfilling, until it's time for our next move.

3) Because we have a conscience and if we're an avid scrupulosity player, our next move is to feel ashamed about what we have or haven't done, said, or thought

4) Because of our inclination toward independence and if we're a fanatical scrupulosity player, our next move is to withdraw from God because we fear His wrath

   o If this is the move we make, then we have committed to playing the game long into the night; we continue because we see no resolution other than starting around the game board again. Our first and second moves (above) promise to soothe our fears with that familiar game piece, or perhaps this time around with an entirely new one. However, this is a hollow, barren promise – a mirage.

Scrupulosity is a game that cycles around fears, with each player having their own spin on it, i.e., their own negative core belief(s) that lead to fear-inducing thought distortions and a central fear that God is a stern critic, eager to judge harshly. Here are some common negative core beliefs that resonate with scru-pulosity: I'm not good enough; I'm worthless; I'm unlovable; I'm not loving enough; I don't have enough faith; I have too many doubts; I'm a hypocrite; I'm an imposter. Whatever the particulars, it boils down to: *I'm afraid that I don't belong in God's kingdom.*

But feelings aren't facts.

The fact of the matter is this

A distressing bonus level that many players – professional and amateur alike – reach in the game of scrupulosity involves the maladaptive behavior of turning feelings into facts. When we reach this stage (called emotional reasoning), *I'm afraid that I don't belong in God's kingdom* turns into *I don't belong in God's kingdom*. And then every time we have the feeling, we hoard it as further evidence, cementing our biased view that what we're afraid of is in fact true. But our fears don't make it so.

How do we get out of the scrupulosity cycle? How do we put the game board back into its box?

- As an initial step, I suggest taking comfort in knowing that even St. Paul, after his conversion, experienced similar struggles with the first two moves of the scrupulosity game. Here's what he says in Romans 7:18b-19 – "I have the desire to do what is right, but not the ability to carry it out. For I do not do the good I want, but the evil I do not want is what I keep on doing."

- Further comfort is provided by learning that there are alternatives to the third and fourth moves of the scrupulosity game, specifically:

  3) Because we have a conscience, our alternate third move is to feel guilty about what we have or haven't done, said, or thought, and furthermore to allow this feeling to guide us to come out from hiding and confess our sins to God, remembering His promise that we are forgiven: "If we confess our sins, he [God] is faithful and just to forgive us our sins and to cleanse us from all unrighteousness" (1 John 1:9). "Therefore, my friends, I want you to know that through Jesus the forgiveness of sins is proclaimed to you. Through him everyone who believes is set free from every sin, a justification you were not able to obtain under the law of Moses" (Acts 13:38-39 NIV).

  4) Spurning our inclination toward independence, our alternate fourth move is to submit to God's desire to draw us closer to Him, remembering His promise that we are protected:

     He [God] will cover you with his feathers, and under his wings you will find refuge. His truth is your shield and armor. / You do not need to fear terrors of the night, arrows that fly during the day, plagues that roam the dark, epidemics that strike at noon. They will not come near you, even though a thousand may fall dead beside you or ten thousand at your right side. (Psalm 91:4-7 GW)

But what happens when we encounter the first two moves of the scrupulosity game again? Will God give up on us? … There's no need to feel insecure. Rather, remember God's promise that believers will not be abandoned: "The LORD himself … will be with you; he will never leave you nor forsake you. Do not be afraid; do not be discouraged" (Deuteronomy 31:8 NIV). "'For the mountains may depart and the hills be removed, / but my steadfast love shall not depart from you, and my covenant of peace shall not be removed,' says the LORD, who has compassion on you" (Isaiah 54:10).

But what happens when we read Bible verses that pronounce judgment on sinners, such as "Wrongdoers will not inherit the kingdom of God" (1 Corinthians 6:9 NIV)? … There's no need to be scared. Jesus' redeeming work is the end game that gives new meaning to such verses. Believers are no longer seen as wrongdoers, when viewed through the lens of Jesus. "Thanks be to God through Jesus Christ our Lord!" (Romans 7:25).

But what happens when we have doubts? … There's no need to be anxious. No doubt we concoct can negate this promise: "Therefore, there is now no condemnation for those who are in Christ Jesus" (Romans 8:1 NIV). Jesus assures us, *If you trust in Me, you belong in My kingdom* (cf. Romans 8:1-17).

> *Prone to wander, Lord, I feel it; / Prone to leave the God I love.*
> *Here's my heart, O take and seal it, / Seal it for Thy courts above.*[2]

Misquotes of the preposterous kind

I just had the strangest dream: I was in my car seat, and a scary-looking man was driving me to a play date. We were in a cavernous minivan. Occasionally, I would see him look at me in the rearview mirror. I tried to remind him to keep his eyes on the road, but – you know how dreams are – I couldn't seem to get the words out, and all he heard was high-pitched shrieks. Suddenly, he surprised me by abruptly pulling the van over to the side of the highway. I was lurched forward in my seat, and could hear gravel hitting the underside of the van. But the eeriest sound was the passenger door scraping against the already crumpled railing that was the only thing between us and a huge ravine. When we finally stopped, I held my breath and looked for his eyes in the rearview mirror. But all I could see was his bushy eyebrows. We sat there in utter silence for several minutes. Our van occasionally shook violently as eighteen-wheelers went roaring by, coming within mere inches of us. Finally, he slowly turned his head around. Little blue flames came out of his eyes. I was petrified. Then he started bellowing, and thick, white smoke came out of his mouth. His rant was a little hard to follow, but it had something to do with crawling across a quilt to a big bowl. I recognized it from Sunday morning – yes, it looked just like my baptismal font. One of his hands came toward me. His hand was so big that it could envelop my skull and crush it like a peanut shell. I closed my eyes in preparation for this, but then I realized that his arm skimmed past my head. That's when I understood that he was focused on my friends in the back row of the van, who I invited to my play date even though they aren't baptized. I cried out to my friends: "Repent and be baptized every one of you in the name of Jesus Christ for the forgiveness of your sins, and you will receive the gift of the Holy Spirit" (Acts 2:38)! They answered in unison, "We trust the loving kindness of Jesus." Immediately, the driver's countenance became very pleasant and the smoke cleared. He smiled at me, and stroked my hair. I cooed in approval. He asked if I wanted to continue on to my play date, and I answered, "Only if my friends are coming along with me." All he said was, "Of course." He turned around and started the van back up. Before pulling off the shoulder, he fiddled with the radio knobs. The music was faint at first, but I immediately recognized the tune. I started singing, and it didn't take long for my friends to pick up the words:

> *Jesus loves me! He who died*
> *Heaven's gates to open wide.*
> *He has washed away my sin,*
> *Lets His little child come in.*[3]

~

Yes, "*Jesus loves me! This I know, / For the Bible tells me so.*"[4] From these words we're reminded that we need look no further than the Bible to know everything we need to know about the full breadth of God's love for us. As an (I think) interesting way to illustrate this, below I've quoted a few excerpts from the Bible, but then added some additional words after the quotes. As a way to distinguish between them, I've written the additional words inside of brackets, { }, using gray font color, using a smaller font size, and I haven't used quotation marks in those areas that grammatically should have them. If despite such mitigations, you nevertheless feel that this is disrespectful, I ask you to try to see this from another perspective. What I'm doing here is to take some familiar sections from the Bible and demonstrate how ridiculous it is when we take God's love (bullet points with circles) – or the commandment for us to love our neighbors (bullet points with squares) – out of them. Yes, this truly is utterly absurd.

- "God is" (unfinished quote of 1 John 4:8, 16; please look up both verses for the correct ending) {uncaring}

- "I [Jesus] in them [believers] and you [God the Father] in me, that they may become perfectly one, so that the world may know that you sent me and" (unfinished quote of John 17:23; please look it up for the correct ending) {hated them all because they're not as meritorious as me}

- "And he [the Prodigal Son] arose and came to his father. But while he was still a long way off, his father saw him and felt" (unfinished quote of Luke 15:20; please read vv. 20-32 for the correct ending) {indifference, and sulked off to mope about how disappointing it was that his son left in the first place}

- "Humble yourselves, therefore, under the mighty hand of God … casting all your anxieties on him, because he" (partial and unfinished quote of 1 Peter 5:6-7; please look up this passage for the correct context and ending) {has reached the end of his patience, and is tired of hearing you whine about your problems}

- "But a Samaritan, as he journeyed, came to where he was, and when he saw him, he" (unfinished quote of Luke 10:33; please read vv. 33-37 for the correct ending) {passed by on the other side}

- "As you wish that others would do to you," (unfinished quote of Luke 6:31; please look it up for the correct ending) {make them do it, by manipulation, intimidation, and force as necessary, and don't reciprocate because that does not benefit you}

- "So his [Jesus'] fame spread throughout all Syria, and they brought him all the sick, those afflicted with various diseases and pains, those oppressed by demons, those having seizures, and paralytics, and he" (unfinished quote of Matthew 4:24; please look it up for the correct ending) {told them to go away and stop bothering him}

- "And as he [Jesus] was setting out on his journey, a [rich young] man ran up and knelt before him and asked him, 'Good Teacher, what must I do to inherit eternal life?' … And Jesus, looking at him," (partial and unfinished quote of

Mark 10:17-21; please look up this passage for the correct context and ending) {hated him because he lacked one thing}

- ■ "The scribes and the Pharisees brought a woman who had been caught in adultery, and placing her in the midst they said to him, 'Teacher [Jesus], this woman has been caught in the act of adultery. Now in the Law, Moses commanded us to stone such women. So what do you say?'" (John 8:3-5; please read vv. 6-11 for the correct ending). {He said, let's go with that, and step aside so I can throw the first stone.}

That last one made me cry… Yes, the above changes to the Bible are preposterous! Here are a few of the verses that I considered changing in a similar way, but I couldn't bring myself to do it: Psalm 86:15, Psalm 94:18-19, Psalm 147:3, Ezekiel 33:11, John 3:16, John 13:34, Romans 5:8, Galatians 6:2, and 1 Timothy 2:3-4. This is a partial list. Indeed, if we were to remove from the Bible all inferences to God's love and our proper loving response, we would hold an empty book…

But it's not empty, is it? Actually, it's pretty thick, and it could be much, much thicker. "Now there are also many other things that Jesus did. Were every one of them to be written, I suppose that the world itself could not contain the books that would be written" (John 21:25).

Jesus is perfectly empathetic

I just mentioned that not everything that Jesus did is recorded in the Bible. Have you ever wondered what else Jesus did during his earthly ministry? Well, one thing we know that He *didn't* do is sin (2 Corinthians 5:21; Hebrews 4:15; 1 Peter 2:22; 1 John 3:5).

In light of this, one thing I've considered is: *How can Jesus empathize with us when we struggle with sin, since He didn't sin Himself?* Empathy means that we understand how another is feeling / their mood / what they're thinking / what they're going through. But it certainly does *not* mean that we necessarily agree with their point of view. That's true for all relationships, and it's abundantly true for the relationship we have with Jesus. For example, He absolutely does *not* agree with our point of view when we are having sinful thoughts! … OK, He doesn't agree. But does He understand?

Let's consider what Jesus understands about sin.

- Jesus understands very well what it's like to be tempted to sin. Remember, He was tempted by Satan: "Jesus was led up by the Spirit into the wilderness to be tempted by the devil" (Matthew 4:1). We are tempted by our cable TV package, particularly the enticing bundle that takes on shades of blue in the wee hours of the morning. But to be tempted by Satan himself – face to face! … Was this easy for Jesus? *Hardly!* "[Jesus] himself has suffered when tempted" (Hebrews 2:18). It's widely known that Jesus suffered on the cross. Now you know that He suffered also when tempted to sin. Yes, He definitely understands what it means to be tempted. "For we do not have a high priest [Jesus] who is unable to empathize with our weaknesses, but we have one who has been tempted in every way, just as we are" (Hebrews 4:15 NIV). … I didn't realize that Cinemax® was broadcasting way back then… Do you think there were DVRs? … My crass joke here is to make the important point that "every way" means just that – a veritable smorgasbord featuring alluring cornucopias filled to abundance with exotic and succulent fruits of every variety. We already know that not everything that Jesus did and experienced is recorded in the Bible (John 21:25). But the Bible certainly does say that He "has been tempted in every way, just as we are" (Hebrews 4:15 NIV). I'll refrain from getting specific, but I can imagine that Satan got pretty creative when tempting Jesus. Satan's "movie" is not yet rated.

    Shall we be moving along? … OK, here we go… Careful readers of the Bible know that I've left off a few words from the end of the verse I partially quoted not far above – twice! What did I leave off of Hebrews 4:15? … *I'd like one of you to give us the end of this verse. … Yes, please, go ahead:* "One who has been tempted in every way, just as we are – *yet he did not sin*" (Hebrews 4:15 NIV, emphasis mine). When I'm tempted, unless I submit to the Holy Spirit's guidance away from the temptation, my response is always to submit to the temptation – to sin. But when Jesus was tempted, what was His response?

    o Jesus' response that is recorded in the Bible is to quote Scripture; He did this several times as He was being tempted by Satan (Matthew 4:4, 7, 10). Yes, Scripture is the best way to combat Satan. Satan is wily and strong, but Scripture is trustworthy and stronger. What was Satan's response to Scripture? What happened when Jesus said, "Away from me, Satan! For it is written: 'Worship the Lord your God, and serve him only'" (Matthew 4:10)? ... *Go ahead, look at the next verse. ... You're right:* "Then the devil left him" (Matthew 4:11). In this "present evil age" (Galatians 1:4), Satan is wily and strong, and tempts us with many things that are not yet rated, but God is stronger and tempts no one (James 1:13). (God sometimes tests us, but never tempts us.) When we're tempted, we should turn to Scripture and rely on the strength that God provides (Philippians 4:13). In this way, Satan scurries off with his tail between his legs. Indeed, "Resist the devil, and he will flee from you" (James 4:7).

○ Did Jesus have any other response when He was tempted? Well, I propose that He did have at least one other response, and if He didn't have this response during or immediately after His "forty days and forty nights" (Matthew 4:2), I submit to you that this is simply because He already knew this fully, and there was no need to rehash it. I'm proposing that Jesus thought something along the lines of: *I understand what it's like to be tempted by Satan's promises / lies, and I don't want my friends to be misled in this way. I will endure anything to save them from going to where that path leads.*

■ "For because he himself has suffered when tempted, he is able to help those who are being tempted" (Hebrews 2:18)

• What else does Jesus understand about sin? ... *Anyone?* ... I'm seeing some blank stares, so I feel compelled to elaborate. Jesus never sinned, this is true, but just as He understands very well what *leads* us to sin – temptation – He also understands very well the awful *consequences* of sin. Indeed, He understands this far, far better than any of us! In God's perfect mercy (discussed below), while we deserve harsh punishment for our sins, "the LORD [God the Father] has laid on him [Jesus] the iniquity of us all" (Isaiah 53:6). As Jesus endured indescribable anguish on the cross, He certainly understood the consequences of sin... What do you think He was thinking while suffering there? Some words from the cross are recorded (Luke 23:34; Luke 23:43; John 19:26-27; Matthew 27:46; John 19:28; John 19:30; Luke 23:46). I propose – *Here we go again!* – that He did have at least one other thought, and if He didn't have this thought while on the cross, I submit to you that this is simply because He already knew this fully, and there was no need to rehash it. I'm proposing that Jesus thought something along the lines of: *I understand what*

it's like to endure the full brunt of the Father's wrath because of sin, includ-
ing complete separation from Him (Matthew 27:45-46; Psalm 22:1), and I
don't want my friends to experience this! I will endure anything to save them
from the second death (Revelation 20:14-15) and separation from God.

- o "For there is one God, and there is one mediator between God and men, the man Christ Jesus, who gave himself as a ransom for all" (1 Timothy 2:5-6)

When we think of empathy, we think of understanding how another is feeling / their mood / what they're thinking / what they're going through. This isn't always easy for us, but for Jesus this is child's play (for example, Matthew 9:4; Matthew 12:25; and John 4:17-19, 28-29). He takes the concept of empathy to another level altogether. He has what I call preemptive empathy. He understands what it *would be* like for us *if* we were to go all the way down certain paths: specifically, the path lined with *every one* of Satan's temptations / promises / lies, and the path of the *full brunt* of God's wrath because of sin. This is perfect empathy.

Jesus is perfectly selfless

In the preceding section, I mentioned that the Bible records words of Jesus from the cross. Everything that Jesus said and did throughout his earthly ministry reverberates His selflessness. As if this isn't amazing enough through Maundy Thursday, I find it awe-inspiring that even when enduring the agony of the cross on Good Friday, Jesus *still* was being true to Himself – He *still* was completely selfless! Yes, "the Son of Man came not to be served but to serve" (Matthew 20:28), and let us consider Jesus' verbal demonstration of this as He hung on the cross.

- "Two others, who were criminals, were led away to be put to death with him. And when they came to the place that is called The Skull, there they crucified him, and the criminals, one on his right and one on his left. And Jesus said, 'Father, forgive them, for they know not what they do'" (Luke 23:32-34).
  - o Jesus is King, yet He is being treated like a criminal. How does He respond? Does He think of Himself, and become bitter and vindictive? No,

He thinks of others – even the ones who crucified Him – and He forgives them.

- "One of the criminals who were hanged railed at him, saying, 'Are you not the Christ? Save yourself and us!' But the other rebuked him, saying, 'Do you not fear God, since you are under the same sentence of condemnation? And we indeed justly, for we are receiving the due reward of our deeds; but this man has done nothing wrong.' And he said, 'Jesus, remember me when you come into your kingdom.' And he said to him, 'Truly, I say to you, today you will be with me in paradise'" (Luke 23:39-43).
  - Jesus is in agony, and He is tempted by one of the criminals (and Satan) to have it stop immediately (v. 39). It certainly is within Jesus' power to do this. How does He respond? Does He think of saving Himself, and come down off the cross? No, He thinks of saving others, and stays nailed (John 20:25; Colossians 2:14) to the cross to endure still more.
- "Standing by the cross of Jesus were his mother and his mother's sister, Mary the wife of Clopas, and Mary Magdalene. When Jesus saw his mother and the disciple whom he loved [John] standing nearby, he said to his mother, 'Woman, behold, your son!' Then he said to the disciple, 'Behold, your mother!' And from that hour the disciple took her to his own home" (John 19:25-27).
  - Jesus has a lot on His plate at the moment, but He is aware of others who are nearby. How does He respond? Does He close His eyes and think of nothing other than His pain, impatient for it to stop? No, as the eldest son, He ensures that His mother is cared for by one of His "brothers." For this special responsibility, Jesus chooses a spiritual brother – the apostle John. Jesus demonstrates that He is never too busy or distracted to care for our daily needs.
- "Now from the sixth hour there was darkness over all the land until the ninth hour. And about the ninth hour Jesus cried out with a loud voice, saying, 'Eli, Eli, lema sabachthani?' that is, 'My God, my God, why have you forsaken me?'" (Matthew 27:45-46).
  - Jesus is in a very dark place. He is, for a time, abandoned by God the Father. We cannot understand this feeling; the closest thing we can imagine is the rock bottom of severe depression, especially that which is exacerbated by abandonment trauma. When we're depressed, it's common to

shut others out – not to talk unless absolutely necessary. How does Jesus respond to this feeling? Does He shut others out? No, He thinks of us and considers it absolutely necessary that we hear Him – loudly – say this. Why? Because it's a fulfillment of the prophesy of Psalm 22:1, which states: "My God, my God, why have you forsaken me?" He wants there to be no doubt in our heart, in our soul, and in our mind – He is truly the promised Messiah!

- "After this, Jesus, knowing that all was now finished, said (to fulfill the Scripture), 'I thirst'" (John 19:28)
  - Similar to the preceding point, Jesus wants there to be no doubt in our heart, in our soul, and in our mind. In this case, He wants there to be no doubt that He was conscious and alert throughout His suffering on the cross. This was so important to Him that He refused to drink wine mixed with gall just before He was crucified (Matthew 27:34). This was being offered to Him as a small act of mercy – a way to mitigate the pain slightly. "He would not drink it" (Matthew 27:34)! He wants us to know that He really did experience the excruciating – *(You do know that the origin of this word is the same as that for "crucify," right?)* – pain of full payment (next section). He did not file for bankruptcy – He paid the full debt. He refused to drink wine until "all was now finished," and He was not given a divine supply of anesthetic; no, He experienced severe physical pain. He wants there to be no doubt: He is both True God (Matthew 27:54; Colossians 2:9) and True Man (Romans 5:15; Philippians 2:8).
- "When Jesus had received the sour wine, he said, 'It is finished,' and he bowed his head and gave up his spirit" (John 19:30)
  - Again, Jesus wants there to be no doubt in our heart, in our soul, and in our mind. Yes, full payment has been made! "It is finished"! It is finished indeed! Praise be to Christ!
- "Then Jesus, calling out with a loud voice, said, 'Father, into your hands I commit my spirit!' And having said this he breathed his last" (Luke 23:46).
  - In this alternate account of Jesus' last words from the cross, Luke records that Jesus said, "Father, into your hands I commit my spirit!" Did Jesus say this for His own benefit? Did Jesus say this for God the Father's benefit? No and no – He said it for *our* benefit. And He said it loudly! Why? Because He wants to be sure we understand that no matter what

happens, no matter what we experience, no matter what God asks us to endure, we still call our heavenly Father "Father," and we know who to rely on at all times, even as – especially as – we are dying. Through all things and under all circumstances, we trust in Him.

It's truly amazing that the One who is most deserving of our service, came down to earth to serve us! Indeed, "Christ Jesus, who, though he was in the form of God, did not count equality with God a thing to be grasped, but emptied himself, by taking the form of a servant, being born in the likeness of men. And being found in human form, he humbled himself by becoming obedient to the point of death, even death on a cross" (Philippians 2:5-8). This is perfect selflessness.

Jesus is perfectly merciful

What does mercy mean? Mercy is often used almost interchangeably with grace, and that's not surprising. They are closely related.

- Grace means to bless, even though the blessing is not deserved. For example, by God's grace, believers spend eternity with Him in heaven.
- Mercy means not to punish, even though a punishment is deserved. For example, by God's mercy, believers are not cast into hell.

In my two examples, above, I'm talking about when time runs out for us – which generally is different for each of us (Appendices B and J). Specifically, my two examples describe how God's grace and mercy are manifested for all believers at the time of God's judgment.

Now, let's consider unbelievers; and in case I'm not being clear, I mean everyone who rejects Jesus as their Savior. Is God merciful to unbelievers? There are two answers to this question, and it all comes down to the timing. Please take careful note of the timing (given in **bold** font, below), and consider this: Do you know when your time will run out (with respect to God's judgment)? … If you're currently an unbeliever, I'm concerned about you and I very much want you to proceed immediately to Appendix J; please read that section carefully and learn two important lessons: *not* everyone is saved, and *no one* knows when their time will run out. Yes, God will have everlasting mercy on you if you stop rejecting

Jesus as your Savior on your death bed. But do you want to wager your eternal destiny on the assumption that you'll have that luxury?

- **Before the time of God's judgment**, God is merciful to everyone: believers and unbelievers alike
    - "The LORD is good to all, and his mercy is over all that he has made" (Psalm 145:9)
    - "He makes his sun rise on the evil and on the good, and sends rain on the just and on the unjust" (Matthew 5:45)
- **At and after the time of God's judgment**, God is merciful to believers but *absolutely not* to unbelievers!
    - "Whoever believes and is baptized will be saved, but whoever does not believe will be condemned" (Mark 16:16)
    - "Whoever believes in the Son has eternal life, but whoever rejects the Son will not see life, for God's wrath remains on them" (John 3:36 NIV)
        - Concerning those who reject the Son: "Because of your hard and impenitent heart you are storing up wrath for yourself on the day of wrath when God's righteous judgment will be revealed" (Romans 2:5)

It's amply clear that not everyone is saved. Is this "perfect mercy"? The title of this section is "Jesus is perfectly merciful." Did I miswrite the title? No, I didn't. It's perfect mercy because:

- We all are born with a selfish, sinful, human nature that is contrary to God – being "by nature children of wrath" (Ephesians 2:3)
- We all are willfully disobedient – "All have sinned and fall short of the glory of God" (Romans 3:23)
- And when it comes to our physical bodies, our sinful flesh (Romans 7:18), we all are nothing but dust – "All are from the dust, and to dust all return" (Ecclesiastes 3:20)

In light of this, what do we deserve? … We *all* deserve death – "The wages of sin is death" (Romans 6:23a); we *all* deserve eternal separation from God – "You are not a God who delights in wickedness; evil may not dwell with you" (Psalm 5:4). … That's what we all deserve. That's what's fair. It's completely fair that each of us pay the price for our own sins – they are ours, after all. And the price for each sin – every one of them – is death and separation from God.

But God isn't fair to believers. No, He's not! Is He not fair in the sense that He sweeps the sins of believers under the rug, pretending that they don't matter? No, each sin *(every one!)* of each of us *(everyone!)* matters very much. For us to dwell with Him, God the Father's righteous wrath must be completely satisfied – satisfied by justice, which is nothing less than *payment in full*. … It doesn't sound like we're going to get through this by sweeping our sins under the rug. That's right: "Without the shedding of blood there is no forgiveness of sins" (Hebrews 9:22); and we already know what payment in full means: "The wages of sin is death" (Romans 6:23a). … What is to be done? How can we be reconciled with God the Father?

If it's up to us, it's impossible to be reconciled with God. Our making full payment for just one of our sins results in our physical death and eternal separation from God in hell. This is completely fair. This is the punishment we all deserve.

However, I already told you that God is unfair to believers. When we stand before God to be judged – (Don't ever forget, we *all* will stand before God to be judged) – believers actually remain standing! Believers are able to remain standing before God because He sees us as sinless. … *This is unfair – we* all *deserve punishment!* … What's going on here?! Where have our sins gone? Are they under the rug? … Jesus knows full well that *our sins absolutely were not swept under any rug!* … No, God the Father loaded upon God the Son, Jesus, the full weight of every sin already committed, and to be committed, by every person who has ever lived, and who ever will live (Isaiah 53:6; 1 Peter 2:24), and then meted out justice: The Father turned His back on Jesus (Matthew 27:45-46; Psalm 22:1), and for the Father's righteous wrath to be quenched Jesus had to suffer indescribable anguish as He hung on the cross, and after hours of agony – intense physical pain (horrendous wounds [John 19:1; John 20:25; Colossians 2:14], loss of blood [Colossians 1:20; Revelation 1:5], and probably difficulty breathing) and intense emotional pain (abandonment by the Father (Matthew 27:45-46; Psalm 22:1)) – finally did really die (Matthew 27:50; John 19:30, 33-35).

Is this payment in full? Yes, we know that it is most definitely payment in full! How do we know? On what do we place our confidence?

- On Good Friday, Jesus Himself said, "It is finished" (John 19:30)
- Just after He died, "the curtain of the temple was torn in two, from top to bottom" (Matthew 27:51). This indicates that Jesus' sacrifice is acceptable; we now have access to the Father.
- At the end of the previous section, I quoted Philippians 2:5-8. In those verses, we're given a beautiful description of Jesus' earthly ministry. Now read that last verse (v. 8) again and the three verses (vv. 9-11) that follow. This is where we learn God the Father's response: "He [Jesus] humbled himself by becoming obedient to the point of death, even death on a cross. Therefore God has highly exalted him and bestowed on him the name that is above every name, so that at the name of Jesus every knee should bow, in heaven and on earth and under the earth, and every tongue confess that Jesus Christ is Lord, to the glory of God the Father" (Philippians 2:8-11). Yes, Jesus our Savior absolutely made payment in full!
- After His Sabbath rest, Jesus was resurrected (He rose from the dead) on Easter morning. How do we know that He is alive?
  - On Easter morning, Jesus appeared first to Mary Magdalene (Mark 16:9), and she told the disciples, "I have seen the Lord" (John 20:18)
  - That evening, Jesus showed Himself to some of His disciples, gave them His peace, and showed them His wounds (John 20:19-20)
  - Thomas was not there, so the other disciples told him, "We have seen the Lord" (John 20:25)
  - Several days later, Jesus appeared to the disciples again, and this time Thomas was with them. Many of us already know what Thomas said. And all of us should say the exact same thing: "My Lord and my God!" (John 20:28).
  - There are many other appearances (Luke 24:13-35; 1 Corinthians 15:6-8), including: "He appeared to more than five hundred brothers at one time" (v. 6). So, we have the eyewitness accounts of many people!

It's amply clear that this is payment in full indeed! Our sins have not been swept under any rug. Where did they go? … *Wake up! I want you to answer this!* I've given you a lot of important material, and it's time for some interaction. Have you been paying attention? … *Ah! Very good! You're right!* Jesus took them – every one. … We deserve punishment, but who bore the punishment on our behalf? ... *Yes, again, I want you to answer this! ... Oh, you're on a roll now!* Jesus bore the punishment that we deserve. Jesus paid the price in full. Jesus is our redeemer. ... What do we receive instead when we do not receive punishment that is deserved? ... *You're not done yet! I'm looking for a hat trick here!* If you need a hint, please reread the definitions at the beginning of this section. ... ... *Yes, you're right again!* Instead of punishment, we receive mercy. Because of the redemptive work of Jesus, we are reconciled with God. We remain standing before Him at the time of His judgment. By His grace, we dwell with Him forever.

> *In Christ alone! – who took on flesh,*
> *Fullness of God in helpless babe.*
> *This gift of love and righteousness,*
> *Scorned by the ones He came to save:*
> *Till on that cross as Jesus died,*
> *The wrath of God was satisfied –*
> *For every sin on Him was laid;*
> *Here in the death of Christ I live.*[5]

"You have seen the purpose of the Lord, how the Lord is compassionate and merciful" (James 5:11).

And you've learned very well that God's everlasting mercy does not mean that our sins go unpunished. No, severe punishment is meted out! What God's gift of everlasting mercy *does* mean is that *we* do not need to be the ones to pay the penalty. ... Careful readers have noted that I wrote "we do not need to be the ones to pay." Why did I write it that way? I did because someone needs to pay! Believers trust that Jesus has already made payment in full. But what about unbelievers? ... They don't trust this. If they don't trust this, then who's going to pay? ... *Again, I'd like you to answer this for me.* If you need a hint, consider this: Unbelievers have rejected Jesus. They've rejected His redemptive work. They've rejected His payment for their sins. This means payment still needs to be made. ... *Oh, are you saying something? I'm having trouble hearing you... Ah, there you go. Yes, you're right. And, here, let me wipe your eyes.* ... Yes, it is heartbreaking. This is why we should tell everyone about Jesus our redeemer. Without Jesus, it's up to them to pay...

Is this fair? Yes, it is. I already told you that it's completely fair that each of us pay the price for our own sins. And you already know what that means, right? "The wages of sin is death" (Romans 6:23a) and "evil may not dwell with you [God]" (Psalm 5:4). If you want to get what's fair, then reject Jesus as your Savior and accept eternal punishment in hell.

Does God want this? No, let me remind you: "God our Savior … desires all people to be saved and to come to the knowledge of the truth" (1 Timothy 2:3-4). I'm grateful that God wants what is unfair in this case – that He is merciful to us who trust in Him. For a description of this unfairness, let's keep reading further within the verse that I've partially quoted three times already: "The wages of sin is death, but the free gift of God is eternal life in Christ Jesus our Lord" (Romans 6:23). This is perfect mercy and perfect grace. The only one responsible for you not receiving this mercy and grace is you, and this is only brought about by your persistence in unbelief. … *Do not reject this free gift! Do not reject this unfair treatment!*

> *The same love that set the captives free,*
> *The same love that opened eyes to see*
> *Is calling us all by name;*
> *You are calling us all by name.*
>
> *The same God that spread the heavens wide,*
> *The same God that was crucified*
> *Is calling us all by name;*
> *You are calling us all by name.*[6]

We believers – who had a nature that was contrary to God, who were willfully disobedient, and who were controlled by our sinful, dusty flesh – have been transformed by the Holy Spirit: We are recreated with a clean heart and a right spirit (Psalm 51:10); we rejoice to walk in "the obedience of faith" (Romans 1:5; Romans 16:26); and we have the assurance of being raised from the dead, as Jesus was (Romans 8:11). We believers stand in awe before God. Yes, we stand before Him and are deemed righteous. We are not cast into hell – we receive everlasting mercy – all because of the blood (sacrifice) of Jesus, our perfectly merciful Savior.

Jesus is perfectly loving

Love is difficult to define, as I demonstrated very thoroughly in Chapter 1. However, it's clear that important attributes of a loving person are some measure of each of the following: empathy, selflessness, and mercy. And we have just learned that Jesus does not have only "some measure" of these – no, "in him all the fullness of God was pleased to dwell" (Colossians 1:19), and this fullness includes loving qualities. From my vantage point, it's looking like Jesus is setting an entirely new standard in this area. Let's listen carefully to what He has to say on the subject of love.

- "You have heard that it was said, 'You shall love your neighbor and hate your enemy.' But I say to you, Love your enemies and pray for those who persecute you, so that you may be sons of your Father who is in heaven. For he makes his sun rise on the evil and on the good, and sends rain on the just and on the unjust" (Matthew 5:43-45).
  - "Love your enemies"! … *Yes, Jesus is setting an entirely new standard for us. This is unadulterated unconditional love!*
- "Love your enemies, and do good, and lend, expecting nothing in return, and your reward will be great, and you will be sons of the Most High, for he is kind to the ungrateful and the evil. Be merciful, even as your Father is merciful" (Luke 6:35-36).
  - "Expecting nothing in return … kind to the ungrateful and the evil" … *This is full-court-press unconditional love, people! Take note!*
- A lawyer asked Jesus: "'Who is my neighbor?' Jesus replied, 'A man was going down from Jerusalem to Jericho, and he fell among robbers, who stripped him and beat him and departed, leaving him half dead. Now by chance a priest was going down that road, and when he saw him he passed by on the other side. So likewise a Levite, when he came to the place and saw him, passed by on the other side. But a Samaritan, as he journeyed, came to where he was, and when he saw him, he had compassion. He went to him and bound up his wounds, pouring on oil and wine. Then he set him on his own animal and brought him to an inn and took care of him. And the next day he took out two denarii [about two-days' wages for a laborer] and gave them to the innkeeper, saying, 'Take care of him, and whatever more you spend, I will repay you when I come back'"" (Luke 10:29-35).

o   Here we have the familiar story of a Samaritan loving his enemy (a Jew). I've heard some people describe the Good Samaritan as caring. OK, I'll accept that description as a good start, but let me fill you in on many things that the Good Samaritan very much does *not* care about!

   ▪ Does he care in the slightest that the one he is helping is very different from him? … *Not one iota!*
   ▪ Does this journeyer give a whit that they have never met before? … *Bosh!*
   ▪ Is there any translation of the Bible that mentions anything about this uncaring caregiver expecting reciprocation? … *Zilch!*
   ▪ And does he give a Buffalo nickel about the high cost? … *Hooey!* … He's even going to follow up, again with not even a blush of care about the cost!

o   *This is unsullied unconditional love, compadres!*

Have you ever met a teacher or pastor who doesn't practice what she or he teaches / preaches? It's one thing to tell others what to do – and sometimes the advice can be quite good – but it's not very motivating if the teacher / pastor isn't doing such things themselves. Do we have this type of situation with Jesus? Or does He walk the talk? Let us move on from what Jesus said about love to what Jesus did.

• First, let's consider His demonstration of love in miracles. When He healed, raised the dead, drove out demons, fed the masses: Was His generosity based on the ability or willingness of the recipients to reciprocate by fulfilling a need of His? No, what He looked for was faith, which is a gift from God.

• Did Jesus show love only in miraculous ways? No, for example, how did Jesus respond to betrayal, denial, and disloyalty, every one of which He experienced in spades on the night before His crucifixion? We all know that Judas betrayed Jesus (Matthew 26:47-50). Most of us know that Peter denied knowing Jesus as He was waiting for the impromptu trial to begin (Luke 22:54-62). Did you know that all of His disciples abandoned Him when He was seized in the Garden of Gethsemane? Yes, "all the disciples left him and fled" (Matthew 26:56). I have great difficulty forgiving a friend who disappoints me (Chapter 9 of this book), and here we have much more than simple disappointments. These are bitter pills to swallow. How does Jesus respond?

o "When it was evening, he reclined at table with the twelve. And as they were eating, he said, 'Truly, I say to you, one of you will betray me.' … Judas, who would betray him, answered, 'Is it I, Rabbi?' He said to him, 'You have said so.' Now as they were eating, Jesus took bread, and after blessing it broke it and gave it to the disciples, and said, 'Take, eat; this is my body.' And he took a cup, and when he had given thanks he gave it to them, saying, 'Drink of it, *all of you*, for this is my blood of the covenant, which is poured out for many for the forgiveness of sins'" (Matthew 26:20-21, 25-28, emphasis mine).

   Yes, Jesus bled and died on the cross to pay the full price for all sins of all people, even Judas, His betrayer. Full forgiveness is freely given to all who simply believe in Jesus as their Savior.

   Did Judas believe when he killed himself (Matthew 27:3-5)? We are not his judge, but the outlook doesn't look good (Matthew 26:24; Acts 1:25), and his response to his remorse (Matthew 27:3) should have been to turn to Jesus, instead of giving up in despair.

o Similar to Judas, Peter also was remorseful (Luke 22:62) for denying Jesus. How did Peter respond to his remorse? We need look no further than John 21:15-19, where we see that Peter responded by turning to Jesus.

   Did Jesus hold a grudge against Peter, for denying Him three times (Luke 22:57, 58, 60)? No, Jesus wiped the slate clean.

   (*Pop quiz!* … As Peter turned to Jesus, how many times did Peter tell Him, "I love you"?)

   John 21:15-19 ends with Jesus saying to Peter, "Follow me." These words were familiar to Peter, as Jesus said this to him way back toward the beginning of Jesus' earthly ministry, when He was calling His first disciples (Matthew 4:19). … Our God is a God of second chances, not mopey grudges.

o What about the other disciples? What did Jesus say the first time He saw them after the resurrection? Did He chastise them for abandoning Him just a few days before? No, He said, "Peace be with you" … not once (John 20:19) but *twice* (John 20:21)! In case it didn't land the first *or second* time for some of them (for example, we know Thomas wasn't even there), a week or so later Jesus came to them again. Thomas was there this time. Did Jesus say that, on second thought, He had some building resentment that He wanted to get off His chest? No, He repeated Himself: "Peace be with you" (John 20:26).

What does Jesus mean by what He said not once, not twice, but thrice? Does He wear a tie-dye tee-shirt and drive a vintage Volkswagen® van painted with big colorful flowers all around? No, when Jesus says "peace," He is talking about a restored relationship with God the Father. Jesus' sacrifice means that we now have peace with God – we are reconciled with God – provided that we do not reject the redeeming work of Jesus. These slates are not just clean, they are squeaky clean!

- What about the rest of us? What is Jesus' response to our disobedience: our disloyalties, our denials, our betrayals? Every time we sin, we are saying that we know better than God; we are saying that our way is the better way; we are saying that we prefer wandering listlessly over following His will for our lives; we are being disloyal; we are denying; we are betraying. How does Jesus respond to this? Does He say, *I'll get on the cross if you're really, really sorry*? No. "While we were still weak, at the right time Christ died for the ungodly. For one will scarcely die for a righteous person – though perhaps for a good person one would dare even to die – but God shows his love for us in that while we were still sinners, Christ died for us" (Romans 5:6-8).

Let there be no doubt: Jesus walked the talk – He is the embodiment of perfect unconditional love – and He did this for you and for me. How do we know that He did it for us? … I'll quote Romans 5:6, 8 again: "Christ died for the ungodly … while we were still sinners, Christ died for us." That sure sounds like us to me.

~

"Greater love has no one than this, that someone lay down his life for his friends" (John 15:13). Yes, from the cross, Jesus unleashes His preemptive strike on our heart – He calls us His friend. Who does He call friend?

Lord of glory, You have bought us
With Your lifeblood as the price,
Never grudging for the lost ones
That tremendous sacrifice;
And with that have freely given
Blessings countless as the sand
To the unthankful and the evil
With Your own unsparing hand.[7]

Just as I called the man I cast off the bus my friend, Jesus calls each of us His friend. Even if friendship with Him is the furthest thing from our mind at the moment, He preemptively calls us His friend.

How do we respond in kind? How do we call Him friend? Please read the next chapter to learn more about this, but for now a little hint: "You are my friends if you do what I [Jesus] command you" (John 15:14). … What does Jesus command? … *Are you a little nervous?* … Let me assure you – you have nothing to be nervous about. No, rather, be of good cheer as you take Jesus' kind words to heart: "I am gentle and lowly in heart, and you will find rest for your souls. For my yoke is easy, and my burden is light" (Matthew 11:29-30).

~   ~   ~

After-hours

Bob unplugged

Please read the parable of The Prodigal Son (Luke 15:11-32), and then consider the following questions, ideally discussing with a few other people.
- When the son decides to come back home, how far away is he when his father sees him? What does this imply about the father's desire to see his son return?
  - What does this teach us about our heavenly Father's desire to see us turn to Jesus (repent) when we have wandered off?

- Did the father need to hear his son's confession (v. 21) before the father runs to him with feelings of compassion, and greets him with physical signs of affection?
  - What does this teach us about our heavenly Father's love for us? Is it dependent on our confession?
- Just after the father and son are reunited, the son confesses, "Father, I have sinned against heaven and before you. I am no longer worthy to be called your son" (v. 21). What is his father's response to this? What do the robe, the ring, the shoes, and the celebrating represent?
  - What does this teach us about our heavenly Father's response when we turn to Jesus, confessing that we don't deserve to spend eternity with Him?

Now read all of Luke chapter 15. In each of these parables, what is the proportion of "lost" to "not lost"? If you don't understand, I'll get you started: In the parable of The Lost Sheep, it's 1-to-99. I'll let you crunch the numbers for the other two parables.

- How is this proportion changing as we progress through the chapter?
- With the first proportion, what do we learn about the value of each of us as individuals, even when we have wandered off, despite there being countless multitudes of souls already saved? In light of all the others, are we expendable? Does God take notice?
- When we get to the third proportion – which could be argued to be 2-to-0… – what do we learn about God's view of us, even if there were *no* other souls already saved? In such a circumstance, would God simply give up on all of humanity? How many souls does it take for God to take notice? Have you ever wondered how many saved individuals it would take for Jesus to crunch the numbers and reach the conclusion that it was "worth it" to die on the cross? It's clear that not everyone is saved (Appendix J). Yes, Jesus died on the cross knowing full well that not everyone would trust in His redeeming work, and thus be saved. … So, just how many saved souls does it take to make it worth it to Jesus? What's the proportion? Would He die for a billion? Would He die for a million? Would He die for a thousand? Would He die for a hundred? Would He die for ten? If you need a hint for the answers to these questions, read Genesis 18:22-33 and apply the same principle. The analogy

is that if Jesus had not completed His redeeming work, we would *all* be lost, we would *all* be swept away (cf. Genesis 18:23). … Would He die for one? … Deep down in your heart, you already know the answer to this. Deep down, you already know that Jesus died for you, in His infinite, intimate love.

Step up to the microphone

In the "A preemptive strike" section, I pose the question, "Do you think of God as angry or loving?" I then go on to answer that He is both.
- In light of 1 John 4:8, 16 ("God is love"), is my answer reasonable?
- What are potential dangers of overemphasizing God's anger?
- What are potential dangers of overemphasizing God's love?

It's understandable that our human minds often drift toward assuming that God's love for us must be conditional on something. After all, pure unconditional love from the people in our lives is not very common. So, why would God's love be any different? … Consider this: If God's love was conditional, in light of Matthew 5:48, how high would He set the bar on any conditions He would establish?

In the "Misquotes of the preposterous kind" section, the last example is from John chapter 8. This is the familiar story of a woman caught in the act of adultery, and Jesus' amazing reaction to this. When tested by the scribes and Pharisees – who asked Him what should be done, and reminded Him that justice calls for stoning – Jesus has the insightful response: "Let him who is without sin among you be the first to throw a stone at her" (John 8:7). When I have trouble forgiving someone – when I want to start throwing stones – I think back to this verse. It helps me drop my stones back on the ground.
- Who among them was qualified to throw a stone at her? Instead of harsh punishment, what did this qualified person give her instead?
- Justice demands payment, so her sin was not swept under the rug. Who paid for her sin?

  o Forgiving someone is one thing (often a very difficult thing for us), *but to go a step further and pay the price for their sin*: Who does that?

It is certain that the ultimate source of all love is God: "Love is from God" (1 John 4:7). So, it follows that one way God's love for us is made manifest is through the loving actions of people. "If we love one another, God abides in us and his love is perfected in us" (1 John 4:12). Note the "if." While we cannot rely on the actions of people to reveal God's nature to us – because all people have a sinful nature, and even believers often choose not to act in accordance with God's will for our lives – from time to time we do experience manifestations of God's love via the actions of people.

- Think back on your life, and generate a list of memories of when you've experienced manifestations of God's love in this special way
  - o Write these memories down, and put your list where you'll see it periodically, whether that be because you put it on display (e.g., pinned on the bulletin board next to your desk) or you put it in a secret place to revisit once per year

For parents: The preamble to this chapter depicts me interacting very differently with each of two counterparts. The difference is based on me tuning myself to the needs of two different people: one unrepentant and one fearful. When you interact with your child(ren), how's your inflection? For example:

- If you have more than one child, are there (additional) ways that you should be treating each of them differently (although, probably not as differently as in the preamble to this chapter)? For instance, does one have a tendency toward rebelliousness, with another being generally quite timid?
- Similarly, with each individual child, are there (additional) times when you should be treating her / him differently? For example, perhaps one day they are caught shoplifting, and another day they learn that their best friend is moving thousands of miles away.
- Is your love monotonic?

For intimate couples: If you're already familiar with the Bible, I'd like both of you, in turn, to tell your partner *two* Bible verses / passages that are among your favorites, with at least one of these examples being descriptive of God's love for us, and – *You're not done yet!* – tell your partner why these verses / passages are meaningful to you. … If you're not familiar with the Bible, then pick any one of the four Gospels (Matthew, Mark, Luke, or John) and read it together, taking turns reading out loud. When you're done, complete the original assignment, based on the Gospel you just read.

Chapter 3 – Our Love for God

Is there anything as magnificent as God's love for us? No, everything else pales in comparison! His love shines brightly upon us and – unless we resist mightily – we naturally reflect love back to Him; but because of our selfish, sinful, human nature, our reflection is only a faint likeness – as the light of the moon cannot compare to the light of the sun. Surely – "In this is love, not that we have loved God but that he loved us and sent his Son to be the propitiation for our sins" (1 John 4:10). While we are like rocky moons that can merely reflect the love we receive – indeed only a tiny fraction of it – such reflection is "the first and greatest commandment" for us. "One of them, an expert in the law, tested him [Jesus] with this question: 'Teacher, which is the greatest commandment in the Law?' Jesus replied: 'Love the Lord your God with all your heart and with all your soul and with all your mind.' This is the first and greatest commandment" (Matthew 22:35-38 NIV).

So, you can see that we need to take the subject of our love for God seriously!

What is the first thing that pops into your mind when you think about following a commandment from God? For many of us, our first thought is that it must be difficult. But when it comes to following the first and greatest commandment, it is sheer delight, a completely natural and joyous response to receiving what our heart craves most – affirmation that we are loved just the way we are by the One who created us. When we know and feel – deep down – this depth of love, how else can we respond except with awe, obedience, and thankfulness?

Is this difficult? Is this like nothing else we've done? … No, we all have familiarity reflecting this type of love; we all have traveled at least some way down this path – the pleasant way of peace and contentment. How far along are you?

> *I feel warm.*
> *I feel comfortable.*
> *I feel protected.*
> *I hear a steady rhythm that just keeps going and going. … It makes me feel that I'm part of something bigger than me.*

Sometimes I hear other things, but your voice is particularly strong. Sometimes you sing. ... It makes me happy. Sometimes I dance.

I feel a little bit of pressure. It's harder to dance than before. ... But I'm not worried. I'm content.

I feel a lot of pressure! I'm not happy! And suddenly I feel cold! I feel uncomfortable! ... No, wait – I feel warm again. I hear the steady rhythm again, although fainter than before. I hear your voice again, louder than before. I feel comfortable again. I feel protected again.

I feel an emptiness inside. I'm not happy! ... No, wait – I feel sweet satisfaction. Your voice is very close now. I feel comfortable again.

Now, when I hear your voice, I'm starting to see something in that direction. ... I've never seen anything so beautiful.

I feel that same emptiness inside again. ... But I'm not anxious. I know who to ask for help. I reach out to you. I'm satisfied again.

I'm seeing you more clearly now. I can see your smile! ... And I've discovered that I can make you smile and laugh! You do it every time I coo.

I want to be like you. ... I've learned to smile! I've learned to laugh!

I like it when you give me a bath. ... It makes me feel cared for.

I like it when you play with me. ... It makes me feel connected to you.

You are so proud of me! ... I'm starting to let go of furniture and walk toward the center of the room!

I don't like it when you scold me. ... But you've never steered me wrong. I'm learning to trust you. And I'm learning that you still love me.

I didn't like it when you dropped me off at school that first time. ... But now I like to go! I've made friends. And I'm learning many new things. Here's a drawing I made just for you!

You are teaching me about God. ... I always knew that I'm part of something bigger than me!

You explained how babies are made. ... Are you sure that's right?

I have a crush on a boy / girl at school. ... I made you smile.

I'm crying because they hurt my feelings. ... Thank you for listening.

You come to my games. ... I made you cheer.

I'm crying because I made a mistake and we lost the game. ... Thank you for hugging me.

I rolled my eyes when you told me to be home by 10 P.M. I'm sorry for disrespecting you. ... Thank you for forgiving me.

I went to an R-rated movie after all, instead of the one you said I could go to. I'm sorry for disobeying you. ... Thank you for forgiving me. I don't like the punishment you've chosen, but it's fair.

I told you that I had finished my report, so you'd let me go to the beach with my friends. I'm sorry for lying to you. ... Thank you for forgiving me. Again, the punishment you've chosen is hard for me, but fair.

I'm going to the prom. ... Thank you for helping me get ready, and telling me that I'm beautiful / handsome. I made you cry.

I'm graduating from high school. ... You made me blush when you told everyone how proud you are of me.

I'm moving away to go to college. ... Where has the time gone?

I have a new boyfriend / girlfriend – I've never felt this way about anyone else. ... I hope you like them!

We just had our first argument. ... Thank you for the good advice.

We're engaged. ... I made you excited!

Today is our wedding day. ... Let's celebrate!

We just had another argument. ... Thank you for more good advice.

We're going to have a baby! ... I made you excited again!

Here – hold your grandchild. ... Your lullaby brings back memories.

I can't say this without crying. ... I got a job offer. It's a good opportunity, but we would have to move far away.

Merry Christmas! ... It's good to see you again.

You're sick. ... I've come back to take care of you.

Your health is failing. ... I'm here to hold your hand and sing you a lullaby.

It's time for you to go. It's time to say "Goodbye." ... "Don't strain yourself. You know that I already know it. All my memories of you – even my earliest ones – confirm it. I can see it in your eyes, even now. And you know that I've always loved you too."

~

That is indeed a pleasant path of peace and contentment, particularly when we both trust in Jesus as our Savior, in which case we're assured that we'll be reunited in heaven.

Such assurance is the most pleasant Way of boundless peace and contentment. Where are you on this loveliest of journeys?

> *I'm on a trip with my family. I'm seeing a lot of amazing things. Mom said that You made all of this! ... I'm in awe of You!*
>
> *I've learned that You created me too! ... Thank You for giving me life.*
>
> *I've learned that the Bible tells me how much You love me. ... I sang about this in church this morning.*
>
> *I've learned that You love everyone in the whole wide world. ... I memorized a Bible verse about this in Sunday School today.*
>
> *I've learned that You can do anything. ... Look, I drew a picture of You walking on a lake!*
>
> *I've learned that You can even calm storms. The teacher said that You calm the storms in our lives. ... I'm going to tell Mom when we drive home. She's sad because Grandma is sick.*
>
> *Today I learned something new, and a little scary. I learned that You will judge me. My life is in Your hands. ... I fear You!*
>
> *I think the teacher noticed that I got scared. She said that if we believe in You, we have nothing to be afraid about – You save us. ... I'm thankful!*
>
> *I've learned that I'm sinful. ... I'm sorry.*
>
> *I've learned that You forgive me. ... Thank You!*
>
> *I've learned that You died on the cross to take away all my sins. ... You are my friend!*
>
> *I've learned that You rose from the dead on Easter morning. ... It was still dark outside when we got ready for church this morning. We went to church outside, and we saw the sun rise. I've never felt so peaceful.*
>
> *I've learned that if I trust in You, then when I die I'll go to heaven to live with You there. ... Now, I'm not afraid to die.*
>
> *I've learned that in heaven I'll be reunited with others who trust in You. ... I'm happy that I'll see Grandma again.*

I learned a new word today! Compassion. ... I'm learning to be more and more like You!

I have a friend who doesn't know You. They think You are just a regular man who lived a long time ago. ... I told them that You created the world. I sang them a song and showed them a picture.

I've learned that there are a lot of people who don't know You. ... That makes me sad. I'm praying for them.

I asked my friend to come to Vacation Bible School with me. ... They're coming!

The principal at my school has cancer. ... I'm praying for her.

She passed away this morning. ... I cried.

I've learned that there are disappointments in this life. ... But You are always there to comfort me.

I've learned that You supply my every need. ... I'm wholly dependent on You.

I've learned that I don't need everything I want. ... I'm content with what You provide.

You have blessed me with a spiritual gift and unique talents. ... It's sheer joy to use them to serve Your kingdom.

Your kingdom is not of this world (John 18:36). ... I'm included – in Your kingdom.

Some people have disdain for me. ... I belong – to You.

I've learned that there is evil in this world. There are a lot of other voices beckoning, and they seem to be getting louder as I get older. ... But Your voice is still the one I'm drawn to.

You always know what's best for me. ... I trust in You.

I've learned that it's best for me to have no other gods before You (cf. Exodus 20:3). ... The Holy Spirit leads me to put You first in my life.

I've learned that it's best for me not to misuse Your name or to claim Your name in a frivolous way (cf. Exodus 20:7). ... The Holy Spirit leads me to use Your name only in the contexts of worship, praise, thanksgiving, prayer, witnessing, and other ways that glorify You and edify myself and others, and to live my life in accordance with my claim to be a Christian.

I've learned that it's best for me to remember the Sabbath (cf. Exodus 20:8-11). ... The Holy Spirit leads me to set aside ample time to worship

You regularly for the purpose of glorifying You, praying, confessing my sins, partaking in Holy Communion, and in other ways edifying myself and others, and to set aside ample time for rest, trusting in God's provision (Matthew 6:25-33).

I've learned that it's best for me and society to honor my father and mother (cf. Exodus 20:12). ... The Holy Spirit leads me to obey, respect, and, if the need arises, care for my parents and others who have authority over me.

I've learned that it's best for me and society not to harm myself or others, physically or emotionally, whether that be intentionally or based on carelessness or negligence (cf. Exodus 20:13). ... The Holy Spirit leads me to honor God's creation by loving my neighbor as myself (Matthew 22:39).

I've learned that it's best for me and society not to commit adultery (cf. Exodus 20:14). ... The Holy Spirit leads me to be content to wait until marriage to have sex, to think of others only in a respectful way, and to be faithful to my spouse – forsaking all others.

I've learned that it's best for me and society not to take things from others (cf. Exodus 20:15). ... The Holy Spirit leads me to be content with what I have.

I've learned that it's best for me and society not to slander others (cf. Exodus 20:16). ... The Holy Spirit leads me to speak the truth in love (Ephesians 4:15).

I've learned that it's best for me and society not to crave (i.e., desire inordinately) anything that is someone else's (cf. Exodus 20:17). ... The Holy Spirit leads me to be unenvious.

When I stumble at these things, I feel dirty. ... But You wash me. I've learned to place my hope in You.

When I stumble at these things, I feel helpless. ... But You care for me. I've learned to rely on You.

When I stumble at these things, I feel empty inside. ... But You find new ways to provide sweet satisfaction. I've learned to reach out to You.

I don't like it when You discipline me. ... But you've never steered me wrong. I trust You. I know that You still love me.

You have blessed me with Your tenacious love, which is a constant and overwhelming flow. ... The Holy Spirit leads me to love You with all my heart.

You have blessed me with the assurance of salvation. ... The Holy Spirit leads me to love You with all my soul.

You have blessed me with some measure of intellect. ... The Holy Spirit leads me to love You with all my mind.

You have blessed me with some measure of stamina and resolve. ... The Holy Spirit leads me to love You with all my strength (Mark 12:30).

I'm not as strong as I used to be. ... But I'm not anxious. The joy of the LORD is my strength (Nehemiah 8:10)!

I'm becoming more and more forgetful. ... But I'll never forget Your promises.

I'm sick. ... But You are always by my side, taking good care of me.

My health is failing. ... But I know that You are always here to comfort me. You know what's best for me, even now.

It's time for me to go. It's time to say "Hello." ... I hear Your voice – I've never heard anything so refreshing. I'm starting to see something in that direction – I've never seen anything so exquisite. I often wondered what this will be like, but this is like nothing I ever imagined. I often wondered what I'll say to You when we meet face to face (1 Corinthians 13:12). Now I know. "Lord, Jesus, ever since I've known You, there has always been something deep-rooted in my heart and in my soul and even in my mind. Until now, it has been hard to describe. Ever since I've known You, I was assured of Your love for me from the wonders of creation, from all the loving people You placed in my life, from everything the Bible teaches, especially Your redeeming work, and from the assurance of salvation that I have through the Holy Spirit's gift of faith. I was, and still am, in awe of You, and as enabled by the Holy Spirit, I lived a life of obedience and thankfulness. Then, I knew only in part. Now, I 'know fully, even as I have been fully known' (1 Corinthians 13:12). Then, I said, 'I know You love me, and I love You too.' Now, I say, 'We are in love; at last we are intimate.'"

~

This is indeed the most pleasant Way of boundless peace and contentment. If you haven't begun this journey, won't you join us now? Even if you don't draw pictures anymore, or sing songs with or without your Sunday School classmates, until the time of God's judgment it's never too late to hop aboard. If you are looking for a boxcar to jump onto, they all have an open door and plenty of room inside, but if you are an adult I suggest that you start at the seventh boxcar in my list. Why should you start there? Because "The fear of the LORD is the beginning of wisdom" (Proverbs 9:10).

"To love God means that we obey his commandments" (1 John 5:3a GW). This sounds difficult, doesn't it? Impossible even! Yes, it's impossible for us – on our own – to obey God's commandments perfectly. We get a little bit closer day by day as we submit to the Holy's Spirit's guidance along the road of sanctification (becoming more and more Christlike), but we still don't get it right. Does this mean that we can't love God? No, even a child can love God, as I describe above. This person was loving God all the way through their life. How did they do it? They trusted Jesus as their Savior – they had faith – so all of His righteousness became their righteousness (Romans 1:17; 1 Corinthians 1:30; 2 Corinthians 5:21; Philippians 3:9). In this way, they loved God perfectly. They trusted Jesus' redeeming work, and in this way they answered His preemptive strike in kind – in faith, they called Him friend.

> *Lord of glory, You have bought us*
> *With Your lifeblood as the price,*
> *Never grudging for the lost ones*
> *That tremendous sacrifice.*
> *Give us faith to trust You boldly,*
> *Hope, to stay our souls on You;*
> *But, oh, best of all Your graces,*
> *With Your love our love renew.*[1]

"To love God means that we obey his commandments. Obeying his commandments isn't difficult" (1 John 5:3 GW). … We have just discussed why obeying God's commandments isn't difficult. But could it be that you have so soon forgotten His commandments? Our minds do have a tendency to wander, don't they? … No worries. I'll remind you: "'Love the Lord your God with all your heart and with all your soul and with all your mind.' This is the first and greatest commandment" (Matthew 22:37-38 NIV).

"And the second is like it" (Matthew 22:39a NIV).

~   ~   ~

After-hours

Bob unplugged

Is your love for God conditional? It's relatively easy to respond to Him with awe, obedience, and thankfulness when things are rosy. But do you sometimes get bitter at God when things don't seem to be going your way?

- I have a challenge for you: The next time you're in the midst of some kind of difficulty, I'd like you to consciously tell God that you love Him. Rather than doing what comes naturally to our selfish, sinful, human nature when we are faced with a hardship – to slip into discontent, even bitterness toward God – instead tell God that you love Him, come what may. While praying to Him, I'd like you to say: *My love for You is not conditional on anything.*

Semantics bonus colloquium: Note that I do not refer to our love for God as conditional love (I hope you agree that the reason for this is obvious) or even unconditional love. The latter phrase is commonly understood to mean loving a counterpart despite their limitations and flaws. Based on this prevalent usage, I avoid using the phrase unconditional love to describe our love for God.

Step up to the microphone

One theme of this chapter is that our love for God is analogous to our love for our mother, and, likewise, that God's love for us is analogous to our mother's love for us. Analogies often facilitate our understanding of a difficult concept, by drawing a parallel to something we can relate to. However, analogies rarely correlate perfectly with the larger topic being considered.

- In what ways do you think a mother-child relationship is a good analogy to our relationship with God?
- In what ways is it off the mark for all of us?
- In what ways is it far off the mark for a few of us?
  - For instance, consider the likelihood of this analogy resonating strongly for someone with an emotionally abusive mother
- If you learn that your counterpart is troubled or confused about their relationship with God because of challenging interpersonal experiences – for example, they don't trust that God always answers our prayers in the very best way for us because they have never experienced this degree of care from the people in their life – what will you say to them?

Toward the end of the chapter, I provide my thoughts on what I'll say to Jesus when I meet Him face to face. Have you ever thought about what you'll say to Him? … Close your eyes and try to imagine what it will be like. Here's a suggestion: Don't imagine that you're just one of a group, as if your boat just docked at Ellis Island. And don't imagine that you're in a long line, as if church service just ended and you're waiting patiently to have five seconds to shake the pastor's hand. No, it's just Him and you, and His schedule is wide open. So, what are you going to say?

Does 1 Corinthians 13:12 say "face to face" or "faces to face"? Why do you think that is?

Worship is meant to be an affectionate time when the two of us confess our love for one another. Saying this another way, each worship service should include clear expressions of God's love for us, and ample opportunities for our loving response to Him. What will you say to the worship leader(s), if you ever attend an unaffectionate worship service?

For parents: Tell each of your children several of your earliest memories of them. For example, if you are the biological parent(s), describe your feelings when you learned that you were pregnant, when they kicked, when you thought the delivery date would never come, when you started going into labor, and when they were born. Examples relevant to all parents include how you felt when you took them home for the first time, when they first smiled at you, and when they first had a temper tantrum.

For intimate couples: I'd like both of you, in turn, to tell your partner three things: one of your earliest memories of your mother, a specific time when you felt loved by her, and three adjectives that describe her. If, for whatever reason, your counterpart has no such memories, show them some compassion, and ask if they would like to complete this exercise based on another caregiver.

Chapter 4 – Our Unconditional Love for Ourselves

When I was growing up, from time to time at church I was taught about the meaning of "joy." Are you familiar with this? It's j-o-y, for *Jesus* first, *o*thers next, and *y*ou (ourselves) last. Somewhere along the way, I got a little confused about this. I came to the erroneous conclusion – (I'm not sure if a Sunday School teacher ever phrased it this way, but this is how I took it) – that we come last, in *every* way… Let's consider this faux pas from the perspective of love, and let's do this by looking at what Scripture has to say on the topic.

- We are to love Jesus (God) first / most
  - o This makes sense. "One of them, an expert in the law, tested him [Jesus] with this question: 'Teacher, which is the greatest commandment in the Law?' Jesus replied: 'Love the Lord your God with all your heart and with all your soul and with all your mind.' This is the first and greatest commandment" (Matthew 22:35-38 NIV).
- We are to love others next / second-most
  - o This makes sense. "And the second is like it: 'Love your neighbor'" (Matthew 22:39a NIV).
- So, does it follow logically that we are to love ourselves last / least?
  - o *Love ourselves least? Really?* Where's the Bible verse for this? I can't find it.
  - o Actually, if we keep reading past what I quoted above – *(And we don't need to go much further!)* – we realize that we are most assuredly *not* to love ourselves least! "And the second is like it: 'Love your neighbor *as yourself.*' All the Law and the Prophets hang on these two command-ments" (Matthew 22:39-40 NIV, emphasis mine).
  - o It says "as yourself," not *more than* yourself. Many people take "as yourself" to mean that we take stock of our personal preferences and apply these when considering how to treat others (our neighbor); for example, if we like horseradish on rye sandwiches, then we show our love by giving our neighbor horseradish on rye sandwiches. Well, as delicious as that sounds, that's not what "as yourself" means here. For one thing, we obviously should keep in mind our neighbor's preferences (Chapter 6

– "The myth of 'The Platinum Rule' ... " subsection). And more relevant to our discussion here, "as yourself" means exactly that – *to the same degree as yourself.*

Loving ourselves is not selfish

Are any of you uncomfortable with my last few bullet points, above? I suspect that some of you are, especially if you taught Sunday School a few decades back. Even now, I think that's what many people really do think the acronym j-o-y means. Let me clear this up for you: It really is *Jesus* first, *others* next, and *you* (ourselves) last *when the topic is service*. There are *many* Bible verses that speak to this. Yes, we are to serve others (Matthew 20:25-28; Galatians 5:13; 1 Peter 4:10), and as a demonstration of our love for them, in humility, prioritize their needs above our own (Philippians 2:3-4; John 15:13; Matthew 5:38-42; Romans 12:10), provided that they're not injuring us (Appendix Ɔ) and provided that we do not lose our balance and slip into codependency (Chapter 1). But *love* others more? No, that doesn't even make sense. It's crystal clear that each of us is just as inherently valuable as anyone else – each of us is just as lovable as anyone else. Here are the *two* ways that I now write j-o-y: It's *Joy* when the topic is service, and it's *Joy* when the topic is love.

Is this selfishness? No, selfishness comes when we love ourselves *more than* others, and/or when we serve ourselves *as much as or more than* others in such a way that we inappropriately prioritize our own needs relative to theirs.

Why am I going on and on about this? Because much damage can be done to our self-esteem if we think that God wants us to feel less inherently valuable than anyone else – less lovable than anyone else.

For most of my life, I've paid close attention to trying to act in an unselfish way. Somewhere along my path, this became an especially important characteristic for me. I cannot claim that I've always succeeded in being unselfish. Yes, I have stumbled – even fallen down – a few times along the way. Nevertheless, my striving to achieve unselfishness coupled with my prior misunderstanding of j-o-y (thinking it's *Joy*, even when the topic is love) led to some dysfunctional behaviors within a stone's throw of bona fide codependency, as well as an entanglement of dark thoughts: all misplaced stepping stones that enabled my odyssey to the blackness of Love Zero (Prologue).

Due to the importance of this, I've chosen to place the chapter about our unconditional love for ourselves – *(This chapter!)* – ahead of the chapters about our need to be loved by other people (Chapter 5) and our involvement in loving relationships with other people (Chapters 6 and 7).

Loving ourselves, despite our sinfulness

I hope that I've made it amply clear that loving ourselves definitely does *not* equate with selfishness, and that a synonym of loving ourselves is our total – deep down – acceptance that we are just as inherently valuable as anyone else – just as lovable as anyone else.

This appropriate regard for ourselves may seem easy enough to accept when all is going well. But what if we make a mistake? What if we become ensnared in a habitual sin? What if we come to realize that we are disrespecting or injuring ourselves or others in our life? What if it becomes unequivocal that we are doing something wrong and need to change? Is loving ourselves easy then? … I hope that you've noticed that I've been very gracious in this paragraph by repeatedly using the word "if." But you know as well as I do that we make mistakes and poor choices like these more often than we can count. There is no "if" about any of this. Sometimes it's easier for us to see when *others* make a mistake or a poor choice. Sometimes we point fingers and even throw stones. But in our heart we know that we too make such blunders – just like everybody else. That's right – just like everybody else. We're all in the same boat. In the same way that we are just as lovable as anyone else, we also are just as fallible as anyone else – just as sinful as anyone else.

So, how do we respond when we are faced with the horrible consequences of our own sin? … We should respond in the same way that we respond to the horrible consequences of the sin of anyone else who sins against us: we forgive, we facilitate change, we move on in hope – we love. Sometimes it's easier to forgive someone else than ourselves. I discuss this further in the section entitled "What if you are struggling to forgive yourself?" (Chapter 9). In a nutshell, we are to forgive anyone who is remorseful and has an openness to change their behavior, and by "anyone" that includes ourselves. In the same way that we are just as lovable as anyone else, we also are just as forgivable as anyone else.

Positive self-talk when we have a relationship with God

You can see that a theme of this chapter is that we're on a level playing field with everyone else. Just as we shouldn't think of ourselves more highly than we ought (Romans 12:3), we also shouldn't think of ourselves lower than we ought. Nevertheless, for many of us it's not uncommon to have negative thoughts about ourselves from time to time. How do we move past this?

Whenever we feel down about ourselves – whether that be because of remorse over sin (preceding section) or something else, such as comparing ourselves to others (next section) – I agree that we should follow the common advice of engaging in positive self-talk. However, when I do this, I don't talk about myself in isolation, but rather myself in relation to God. What do I mean?

- Instead of saying to myself, *I am inherently valuable*, I say to myself, *God created me, thus I am inherently valuable*

- Instead of saying to myself, *I am lovable*, I say to myself, *God loves me unconditionally, thus I am lovable*

- Instead of saying to myself, *I am forgivable*, I say to myself, *God has already forgiven me because I believe that Jesus is my Savior (Acts 13:38-39), thus I am forgivable*

- Instead of saying to myself, *OK, I'll admit that I'm not perfect, but at least I'm not as bad as many other people*, I say to myself, *"Chief of sinners though I be, / Jesus shed His blood for me"*[1]

- Instead of saying to myself, *I'm happy that I've found Jesus*, I say to myself, *"Love that found me – wondrous thought! / Found me when I sought Him not"*[2]

- Instead of saying to myself, *I am very well-organized and take much care in planning my future*, I say to myself, *I pray regularly and trust that God knows what's best for me in every situation (Proverbs 16:9b)*

- Instead of saying to myself, *I take good care of myself, for example: I practice mindfulness, I don't overwork myself, I have downtime every day, I get enough sleep, I strengthen my body by exercising regularly, I eat a balanced diet (never straying into a fad diet), I drink plenty of water, I don't drink too much alcohol, I don't smoke, I don't take illegal drugs, I go to the doctor regularly for routine checkups and screenings, and I follow doctor's orders*, I say to myself, *God has blessed me with some measure of health, He cares about my emotional and physical wellbeing, and He is pleased when I take self-care seriously (1 Corinthians 6:19-20), for example: ... (same list as above)*

- Instead of saying to myself, *I have strengths, more than some other people*, I say to myself, *God has bestowed upon me a spiritual gift and has created me with other abilities, thus I have a unique blend of strengths that I'm blessed to use to serve others*
- Instead of saying to myself, *I am talented, better than some other people*, I say to myself, *God has a plan for me: He helps me accomplish whatever He chooses; in this way I'm achieving my personal best, and I'm content with that*
- Instead of saying to myself, *There are some people who seem to value me, and that makes me feel good about myself*, I say to myself, *God values me just the way He made me, He has provided me with family and good friends who love me just the way I am, and I will not change myself in any way for the sole purpose of hoping others will value me more than they do now*

Loving our authentic self

Does the last bullet point surprise you? Aren't we supposed to serve others, keep in mind their preferences, and even be accommodating (Chapter 7) to them? Aren't we supposed to change our behavior when we're disrespecting or injuring our counterpart? Aren't we supposed to love each of our counterparts differently (Chapter 1)? Yes, yes, yes, absolutely, and hell yes. ... I want you to look me in the eyes when I say this to you. ... *You're getting warmer. A little further north please. There you go.* ... When you give your love to any one of your counterparts, I want you to serve them, keep in mind their preferences, accommodate them (while never enabling destructive behavior, never neglecting yourself, and never allowing yourself to be taken advantage of), change your behavior if the relationship will benefit from that, and respect them with a unique brand of your love. But answer me this: Who's doing the loving here? ... *You look flummoxed. This is not a trick question. Is my hearing aid on the fritz again?* ... *You* are doing the loving! You, and no one else! Why am I pounding the table when I say this? Because it's impossible for you to truly love anyone if it's not you. True love is authentic. It has to be from you. ... I can tell. ... We can tell. ... It's very easy for us to tell if you're "loving" us without being your authentic self. When you do this, we don't feel loved. Why?

- Because you're holding back – and that makes it challenging for us to bond with you
- Because you're not making yourself vulnerable to us – and that makes us sad
- Because you're not trusting us to love you – and that offends us
- Because you're hoping that we'll truly love an inauthentic version of yourself – and that's impossible for us
  - In Chapter 6, "Loving our representative person" section, I tell you that I love you. (You now have the green light from me to stop plucking rose petals one after another.) I don't only tell you that I love you, I also try to explain how I can love you even though I've never met you, and – *the most difficult concept of all – why* I love you. There's one thing I don't specify in that section – mainly because by then it's well-ingrained in you, and doesn't need to be stated again. *(Far be it from me ever to be redundant!)* By then, it's well understood that I can only love the authentic you. When I close my eyes and see you, I only see the authentic you. I have no view of an inauthentic version of you. I see only the authentic you because I see you in the faces of my loving counterparts – every one of them – and let me assure you, because they love me and I love them, it's only their authentic selves that I know.
  - Does this sound like fluff? Let's consider the counterpoint, and it certainly is not fluffy at all! In that same section, I tell you that you may love me too. There is a contingency stated. When you take that contingency to heart, you know that I'm right and you know that it's not fluffy by any stretch. The contingency is that I've hit you with one of my arrows, and by this I mean that you realize that something I've written is meant just for you. I can assure you that I absolutely did write something just for you. It's up to you to find it. How will you know when you've found it? You'll know by that special feeling you get when you're hit right between the eyes so hard that it sinks deep down into your heart and soul. That far down, there's no room for inauthenticity. Down there is the realm of your authentic self. When you're hit with one of my arrows, not only do you love me, but also – there is no doubt about this – it surely is nothing other than your authentic self who loves me.

- And who are you loving when you are hit with one of my arrows? Could it possibly be an inauthentic version of me that you're loving? … *Preposterous!* … Who would possibly choose to write like this inauthentically? Who would go out of their way to use a word like "preposterous" six – (count 'em) – times in this book? … This is the authentic me, and I cannot be any other way.

On the topic of authenticity in love, so far I've only talked about interpersonal relationships: I can only truly love your authentic self; you can only truly love my authentic self. I see a pattern developing. *Can't you see it?* … I'd like one of you to tell me the next item on our syllabus. … How about you with the goo-goo eyes since midway through Chapter 1. What do you think is next? … Uh, nope… You'll need to wait a little longer for sex; hang in there – only three chapters to go. *Anyone else?* … Here's a hint: We are still in this chapter. … *Yes! Very good!* When it comes to our unconditional love for ourselves, we can only truly love our authentic self.

Is this easy for us to do? For some of us, it isn't as easy as it should be because our authentic self has scurried off! *Where has she or he gone?* … They're frightened… They're hiding… *What are they hiding from?* … They're hiding from judgmental attitudes. They're hiding from criticism. Some of us care far too much about what others think of us – sometimes even to the extent of having social anxiety disorder or avoidant personality disorder. Why are some of us so concerned about the opinions of others? Why do some of us change our demeanor when we're around certain people? Why do some of us get fearful when we interact with people we've never even met before? … All such anxieties arise because we know that we're different from others, and at times in our past we've sensed a judgmental mindset or have even been openly criticized. Simply the memories of such events are enough to cause fear – enough to cause us to change. If it gets bad enough, we're rarely ourselves – we're constantly trying to be someone else, with the elusive goal of pleasing others.

When we do this, we are idolizing others – placing them at a higher level than God. God created us in a certain way – with specific strengths, specific characteristics, a specific personality – for a reason. Far be it from us to segregate our God-given authentic self because of our perception of the opinions of others.

When we discriminate against ourselves in this way, we're saying that we care more about such opinions than we do about our God!

The only time we should change is when God wants us to change, for example: if we are disrespecting someone (including ourselves), if we are injuring someone (including ourselves), if we are not doing something that God wants us to do, if we are ensnared in a persistent, habitual sin (1 John 3:4-10), and if you do not yet believe that Jesus is your Savior.

God certainly does *not* want us to change based solely on the opinions of others or on our apprehension when we compare ourselves to others. God provides parents, teachers, pastors, and others whom we should emulate when appropriate, i.e., when they are trustworthy and God-pleasing mentors. However, when we compare ourselves to others who don't have this special role in our life, and furthermore when we aspire to be like them, then our authentic self is hiding under a rock. Self-improvement initiatives have their place, and that place is only when such actions are helping us achieve a change that God wants for us.

If you find yourself trying to become like someone else, please ask yourself why you're doing this. Is it because they are a trustworthy and God-pleasing mentor? Or is it because you see them as successful or popular? Don't forget: God created you the way you are on purpose, He loves you that way, and He wants you to love yourself that way. Why would you ever want to change from this? Why would you ever want to seclude your authentic self?

Some people would answer this by saying that they don't like to be different from others – they would rather just blend in. But blending in is not God-pleasing! If He wanted us to blend in, He would have made us all the same. But He didn't do that, did He? No, even so-called "identical" twins are surely not truly identical, and this is based on differences – as subtle as they might seem – in their upbringing, experiences, and, more importantly, differences in God's plans for them. Each of us is unique because God values diversity (1 Corinthians 12:4-30). God values our one-of-a-kind role. Each one of us – *No one can replace us!* – has a special place within His plan. Only He knows where this is, until we have the joy of experiencing His plan unfold. He takes pleasure when you – *No one else!* – help a counterpart who needs what God provides through you. He takes pleasure when one of your counterparts – *No one else!* – helps you, when you need what God provides through them. Similarly, He takes pleasure when two of us learn and grow based on the differences between us; He takes pleasure when two of us share our thoughts, feelings, fears, and aspirations with one another; He takes pleasure when two of us form an emotional bond; He takes pleasure when two of us desire one another in a God-pleasing way, and expand our special friendship into becoming husband and wife. He takes pleasure when we love one another.

And He takes pleasure when we stop hiding our authentic self. Let His pleasure be our pleasure. We do this by loving ourselves, just the way He made us.

Strengths

I have a homework assignment for you! I want you to make a list of your strengths and – *That's not all!* – talk about your list with at least two other people. … Does this make you a little nervous? … Why? … We just discussed that everyone has strengths, and that God gave us these strengths for a reason. It's very beneficial for each of us to identify our strengths, as this helps us broaden our perspective on how God will be using us to serve His diverse kingdom.

Here are some hints about good ways for you to identify your strengths.

Feedback from others

When you talk about your strengths with at least two other people, *before* you tell them any that you've identified, ask each of them to tell you at least three strengths they see in you. Take notes!

Spiritual gifts

Consider your spiritual gift(s). Everyone who believes in Jesus as their Savior has at least one spiritual gift (1 Corinthians 12:7; 1 Peter 4:10). Such gift(s) are certainly strengths. Spiritual gifts are discussed in Romans 12, 1 Corinthians 12-14, Ephesians 4, and 1 Peter 4.

Don't get discouraged if some spiritual gifts seem too "lofty" or intimidating for you to have.

- Some spiritual gifts may sound reserved for large-scale miracles, but I don't agree. For example, I consider people who are good at helping others feel better emotionally to have at least some measure of the spiritual gift of healing. Similarly, I consider people who have strong active listening skills to have at least some measure of the spiritual gift of interpretation of tongues.

- And other spiritual gifts may sound daunting but they really aren't. For example, the spiritual gift of prophesy includes straightforward application of God's Word to a given situation. Also, the spiritual gift of exhortation may sound a little intimidating to a mild-mannered person, but the same gift is sometimes referred to as the spiritual gift of encouragement, and I like the sound of that.

An important point is that we don't need to see evidence of consistent "success" in order to have a particular spiritual gift. What do I mean? Let me draw an analogy. When we witness to someone – I mean share our Christian faith with someone – the receptiveness of our listener to the Holy Spirit's message is not our responsibility. Some reject and some do not. This may cause us to draw the conclusion that we have inconsistent "success" in our ability to witness. Despite any discouragement we may feel, we are surely called to witness to everyone in our life, using our own unique trowel and/or watering can (cf. 1 Corinthians 3:5-9). In a similar way, when we serve others with our spiritual gift(s), there may be cases where, as far as we can tell, there's no tangible impact. This could be due to our not being aware of the impact; another possibility is that God has other plans in this circumstance. This may cause us to draw the conclusion that we don't have a particular spiritual gift. But that's not necessarily the case.

How can we know which spiritual gift(s) we have? Generally, we'll feel a desire to serve in those way(s). Maybe more importantly, especially since it's possible to be gifted in areas that we haven't really considered before, we should listen carefully to the feedback we receive from others. For example, even if not everyone we talk to always seems to feel better emotionally after our conversation, if several people have told us that they often experience such a benefit after talking with us – bonus points given if they say that this sometimes occurs simply by being in our company – then we have evidence that we have at least some measure of the spiritual gift of healing.

Notice that I wrote several times above, including in my previous sentence, "some measure." To be sure, let's not fall into the trap of thinking that we need to achieve a sufficiently oxygen-depleted height of giftedness in order to state confidently that we have a particular spiritual gift. For example, we don't need to be Mother Teresa or Fred Rogers to have the spiritual gift of mercy. Similarly, we don't need to be Billy Graham or Luis Cortes to have the spiritual gift of evangelism*.

Pray. Ask the Holy Spirit to help you identify your prominent spiritual gift(s). Once you identify one, *own it!* Keep up the good work! Pray for the Holy Spirit to empower you further. Feel the joy of your spiritual gift(s) continuing to develop for even greater edification of others.

> *Note: There seems to be some controversy about whether there is such a thing as the spiritual gift of evangelism. Those who say there's not such a gift like to emphasize that we should all be evangelizing. I don't understand the controversy. It is clear. There certainly is a spiritual gift of evangelism (Ephesians 4:11-12). We are all to *witness* (share our faith: plant and/or water seeds); we are not all gifted in *evangelism* (the gift of helping others stop rejecting the Holy Spirit). The key is to understand the difference between the meaning of the words "witnessing" and "evangelism."

~

I feel compelled to add that if anyone ever asks you to demonstrate a spiritual gift, as a way to "prove it," they are false prophets led by the spirit of the antichrist (1 John 4:1-6) and are to be avoided because they erode our spiritual health.

~

In this subsection, I've mentioned a few specific spiritual gifts, but there are more! After reading Romans 12, 1 Corinthians 12-14, Ephesians 4, and 1 Peter 4, if you're still a little muddled about the full list of spiritual gifts and which one(s) are prominent for you, then I suggest taking a spiritual gifts test, such as the one found at https://gifts.churchgrowth.org/spiritual-gifts-survey/, and supplementing your thoughts and prayers with what you learn there.

Generalized personality type

Speaking of tests, to help you identify your strengths, I also recommend that you take a Myers-Briggs Type Indicator® (MBTI®) test. Actually, I recommend that you take several versions of the test, each at least a few days apart, to establish a consistent result for yourself. If you're unfamiliar with MBTI tests, today is your lucky day because you can peek at Appendix M, where yours truly provides tips about how to take these tests in an unbiased manner.

Your MBTI test result – your generalized personality type – will come back as four letters, with each of these four letters representing one of two possibilities (two ends of a spectrum), as detailed below. Keep in mind, however, that it's possible for any of your letters to be essentially a "tie" between the two possibilities (meaning you're near the center of that spectrum).

If you remember a little math, or prefer to count on your fingers and toes, you can see that there are 16 possible four-letter combinations. Each of these 16 combinations refers to a generalized personality type, and each of these is characterized by general strengths and weaknesses common for that type. Each version of the test you take typically will provide descriptions of the 16 generalized personality types, including correlated strengths and weaknesses. For a more in-depth treatment, you can read the granddaddy of them all, *Psychological Types* by C.G. Jung,[3] or, for lighter reading, *Gifts Differing: Understanding Personality Type* by Isabel Briggs Myers with Peter B. Myers.[4] You may not identify with every one of the strengths and weaknesses listed for your generalized personality type, but many people are surprised at how familiar the description sounds, in light of their personal experience.

Below, I summarize what each of the eight letters represents.

- 1st letter
  - I (Introversion) – energy is expended when interacting with others, or
  - E (Extroversion) – energy is gained when interacting with others
- 2nd letter
  - N (iNtuitive) – prone to abstract thinking and future possibilities, or
  - S (Sensing) – prone to more concrete thinking, focused on present realities
- 3rd letter
  - F (Feeling) – more weight given to personal and social considerations, or
  - T (Thinking) – more weight given to logic and facts
- 4th letter
  - J (Judging) – prefer structure and order, or
  - P (Perceiving) – prefer a flexible lifestyle

The nice thing about the MBTI test is that you don't need to study for it. And, provided that you take it in an unbiased manner, you'll get an A+! I know that I don't need to tell you that there are no "preferred" personality types. All 16 general types are equally awesome. When you're confident that you've obtained an unbiased MBTI result, read descriptions (from several sources) for this generalized personality type, consider the parts of the descriptions that resonate with you, and thank God for making you this way!

Weaknesses associated with our strengths

Any guesses as to my MBTI generalized personality type and my prominent spiritual gift? ... *No one?* ... By now, I would think that some of you have surmised that I'm an INFJ (although that F is a close call) with the spiritual gift of mercy.

And how about my strengths? Below I list my prominent strengths (bullet points with filled circles), and for each I include way(s) that I sometimes misuse, misapply, or overemphasize this attribute such that it's a weakness (bullet points with open circles). While doing your homework, please do similarly as you consider your list of prominent strengths.

- I am compassionate – very much wanting to help others in need and ease their pain
  - I am often overly sensitive, easily offended, and for such reasons hesitant to make myself vulnerable (open up) to others
  - I avoid conflict, and have a hard time being firm with others, even when the situation certainly warrants it
- I am patient
  - I am patient 99% of the time which – when combined with avoidance of conflict – means that when the stars align I suddenly explode in anger with little to no warning
- I am generally unflappable, not easily flustered or discouraged
  - I am slow to react, which is especially not helpful in urgent, emergency situations
- I am empathetic – (usually) able to see the perspectives of others
  - My mood is often swayed by the moods of others in my vicinity, even people I don't know, especially in the negative direction...

- I am thoughtful
  - I often get lost in my thoughts, at the expense of interacting with others
  - Sometimes I overthink things, dwelling on situations and building houses of cards in my mind
- I am insightful and creative – usually thinking outside the box
  - I have so many ideas that this can lead to indecision and even waffling
- I am an idealist – (Yes, I think this is a strength) – generally hopeful and looking for the best (silver linings) in any given situation
  - I used to be a full-blown perfectionist, but I've made such great progress that I'm pleased to announce that I've reached the category of merely having strong perfectionist tendencies
  - I am often overly critical of others
- I am detail-oriented – (I'm not sure if this is really a "strength," but I'm very good at this!) – and in the process often notice nuances and trends that many others miss
  - It's easy for me to identify trifling imperfections in my counterparts, and sometimes this causes them to feel hurt
  - I tend to take things literally (precisely as they are stated) – not in a flexible, idiomatic manner – so I often manage to find a way to be offended by how people phrase things
- I am hard-working
  - I often go overboard and slip into workaholism
- I am trustworthy, fair, and reliable
  - I get very angry when someone else is not any one of these things; often this is appropriate anger, but sometimes I prematurely shut such people out of my life, and sometimes I lose my temper
- I am persistent, so I finish what I start
  - I am persistent, which is often incredibly annoying to others

This is a pretty long list! I'm a thorough person – *(Oh, darn it! I wanted to include "thorough" in my list!)* – so I tried to think of everything. I encourage you to do similarly when creating your list, and don't forget to include feedback from others. Don't rush through your homework, falling into the trap of thinking that you need to be perfect at something for it to be a strength. If I included only those things that I never falter at, my list would be very short… Oh, I just faltered again! The Holy Spirit just reminded me that indeed my list of strengths would be completely blank.

My sinful nature is a good shot – a *very* good shot… He takes pleasure in lining my strengths up on fence posts. After adjusting his wide-brim hat, he stares down my bullet points, daring them to make a move – even a twitch. … Seconds turn to minutes. … If on this particular day there happens to be a breeze, a tumbleweed drifts by. … Without warning and with no provocation, he pulls his six-guns out of their holsters, and with no time to aim nevertheless shoots a hole right in the center of each of my bullet points. If he happens to miss one – very rare – he has one bullet left to finish the job – this time taking careful aim… This is my fate, whenever my sinful nature rides high in the saddle.

~

With so many disappointing ways that I misuse, misapply, and overemphasize my strengths, such that they become real weaknesses, can I still love myself? … At times in my past, I was often sorely tempted to focus on my weaknesses. It's such a temptation for me because it soothes my perfectionist side. Why? Because I get the satisfaction of coldly cataloguing the evidence and reaching a "logical" conclusion – and I highly value logic. In such instances, my logic convinced me that even my strengths are weaknesses – and from there I didn't need to travel far to conclude that I have little value. In the past, such an odyssey was strangely satisfying to me because it felt accurate – and I highly value accuracy. On the coldest, darkest days, my desire for utmost accuracy led me to reach the self-imposed verdict of worthless. All felt right, except I had just told myself that I am unlovable, and that I am incapable of loving.

When thinking only of myself, this is as far as I could travel – stuck at Love Zero and not even able to have the satisfaction of loving others. What led me to take my focus off my weaknesses, come to peace with my imperfections, and love myself just the way I am? … Two things:

- First, the Holy Spirit reminded me that God already loves me this way, and who am I to disagree with Him?
- Second, the Holy Spirit reminded me that several of my counterparts also struggle with their own evidence, and this made me sad. When thinking of myself, it was strangely satisfying to perform the (seemingly) accurate

analysis and reach the (seemingly) logical conclusion. But when thinking of others, I could not bear to watch them apply this self-analysis and reach this conclusion about themselves; from this vantage point, I could finally see that such distorted thinking is harsh and cruel. ... (Are you like me – harder on yourself than you are on others? If you often find yourself falling into that trap, please read this bullet point as many times as it takes for the message to sink into your heart: It's *Joy*, not *Joy*.) ... I remembered that their lives are not meant to be spent coldly cataloguing and reaching logical conclusions – and from there I didn't need to travel far to conclude that it's also harsh and cruel for me to think this way about myself. This was a short journey because, fortunately, I also highly value consistency. Because it's harsh and cruel for my counterparts, it follows that it's harsh and cruel for me. It's distorted and inappropriate thinking for all of us because it ignores the fact that we have access to the overwhelming flood of God's forgiveness – His "illogical," refreshing, and compassionate forgiveness.

God wants us to stop relying on ourselves, and instead become wholly dependent on Him. Reliance on ourselves has only one logical conclusion – one gloomy destination – and that is not a good place to be. Submit to God, and He will take you to a new place – giving you a new heart and putting a new spirit within you (cf. Ezekiel 36:26).

Our sinful nature causes even our strengths to be manifested, from time to time, as real weaknesses. But God is infinitely stronger than our sinful nature, and by His power even those things that we consider to be weaknesses do not hinder His kingdom and, from time to time, may even play a role in expanding it. How is this possible? It's only possible when we fully submit to Him, allowing Him to use all of ourselves – our strengths *and our weaknesses* – as He sees fit.

Diversity in groups

I'd like to close this overall section by considering group dynamics when we have people with different sets of strengths (for example, people with different generalized personality types). Let me start with the question that is surely on everyone's mind: *Shouldn't our "polar opposite" generalized personality type (for example, ESTP is the polar opposite of INFJ) be our arch-nemesis?* I hope the answer surely on everyone's mind is: *No, not at all. It's just someone very different from us. And what's wrong with that?* That's right – what's wrong with that? Maybe your polar opposite is lying in bed next to you right now, and isn't that wonderful?

I already mentioned that no generalized personality type is preferred over any other. Let me be clear that I mean this from the perspective of the individual. From a group dynamic perspective, however, there are circumstances where certain generalized personality type(s) are preferred. Allow me to elaborate with a couple examples, as I hope such considerations will help you identify ways to put your particular set of strengths into good use in group settings.

- Let's say our congregation or workplace is struggling with internal conflict; several troublemakers are stirring the pot and creating a real lack of unity. We need someone to step up to the plate and lead us out of this cesspool. We need someone who calls a spade a spade. We need someone to stand up to the bullies and tell them that their behavior will not be tolerated. We need someone with thick skin – who won't be intimidated by strong personalities. We need someone who can think on their feet – react quickly as new information gets thrown at them, for example during meetings. We need someone who can tick all these boxes, and get a good night's sleep because they're not replaying these events over and over in their mind. In such a scenario, should we be looking for an INFJ to do all of this? The Lord works in mysterious ways, but generally we're not going to get this type of leadership from an INFJ.

- Let's say our congregation or workplace seems to be going fine from one perspective (for example, there's not much internal conflict) but from another perspective seems to be in a rut. We form a committee whose purpose is to energize the group by developing a five-year vision and a specific plan to achieve this vision. An INFJ is identified as the chairperson of the committee. They start jotting down the names of some folks whom they are considering to ask to join them on the committee, and they show the list to you. You see that everyone on the list – and it's a long list… – is an INFJ as well. (You know this because they are all in an INFJ club together. *What fun!*) What should your recommendation be? … *Hello?* … Your recommendation should be to dump this pitiful, sorry excuse for a list, and start over to create one with diversity. Yes, the strongest teams are ones that are diverse. I'm not so controlling that I'd suggest conceiving a 16-member committee, and then embarking on an ambitious quest to find one member from each of the 16 generalized personality types. As tempting as this may be to some of us – *I would be quick to dub them The Magnificent Sixteen* – let us refrain from drifting toward such levels of perfectionism. OK, so if we're not going to strive to achieve absolute perfection, what's the general idea? What's the take-home message here? … For each team that you're a member of, consider the strengths that are already present. Are there any strength gaps? Most teams have some… Once the gaps are identified, find people with these particular strengths and ask them to join your team! And as you're looking for ways that you can serve, for example in your congregation, please don't submit to the temptation to join a group that is very like-minded to you. How is that helping diversity? I challenge you to fill a gap.

Balance

I just asked you to consider your strengths, and such reflection is typically an uplifting experience. Identifying and honing our strengths can help us live a more purposeful and fulfilling life. However, it's possible to go too far and get out of balance, even fall down.

One way we can go too far with strengths is to become arrogant about them. Arrogance is unloving because it diminishes others. A more mature perspective about our strengths comes in the form of confidence. Confidence is the healthy attitude that we know what we're capable of – we know what we have to offer. When used in a loving way, confidence helps us identify how we can best build others up, and then carry this out.

Another way we can go too far with strengths is to rely on them disproportionately as a way to make ourselves feel worthwhile. Such imbalance is especially likely when we have low confidence / low self-esteem. A common form of this occurs in the workplace, where the workaholic feels worthwhile only when excessively productive in his chosen field of expertise. Workaholism is not at all loving to ourselves – (we are disrespecting our time and need for proper balance in our life) – and of course it has a negative impact on our family – (neglect and setting a bad example, implying that to have value, to be loved, they need to accomplish much or be the best).

Please read the following story of a man obsessed to be the best, with the underlying issue being his negative feelings about himself, exacerbated by not being able to meet the inappropriately high expectations of his hypercritical, unsupportive father. The narrator's unloving disposition toward himself spilled over into an inability to love others. If this story resonates with you, I implore you to unstrap yourself from the grindstone and seek your balance point!

"Can you help me?"

I heard her, but I assumed she was talking to someone else.

"Oh… sorry… but can you help me?"

So annoying... Doesn't she know we're supposed to be quiet in the library?

She coughed and tapped her pen on the table. "I recognize you from biophysics, and I was wondering if you could answer a question I have about our homework."

I looked up to give her a glower, and that's when I realized that she was looking at me. "Oh, are you talking to me?"

"Yes, I'm having trouble with number 6, and I know you're pretty good at things to do with neurophysiology."

"Yes, I am, but I'm too busy to help you." I looked down and focused on number 7 in our homework. As usual, I was doing each problem twice. So far, everything checked out – as usual.

"Oh, OK. Sorry to disturb you."

I ignored her, and wished she would go away. After about half an hour, she finally did. She said goodbye, and that really distracted me. I was almost done double-checking the last problem, and she made me have to clear my calculator and start over. I hate that.

I hate it anytime someone distracts me. There was that spelling bee in third grade. The word – I'll never forget this – the word was "xylophone." I knew it was an "x." My dad had pounded that into my head beforehand. But someone coughed. I looked up, hesitated, and spelled it with a "z." My dad was in the front row. He stood up and said to me – not very loud, but loud enough for some others to hear – "I spent a lot of time teaching you all the words, including that one, so you'd be the best. I guess I didn't spend enough time." And he walked out.

My heart sank, and I felt bad for disappointing him. I promised myself that I would try even harder next time. As I sat there thinking about this, it was difficult not to cry. I was proud of myself for not crying, which became more and more difficult as I heard all the simple words that the other kids were getting. Finally, it ended. Some kid misspelled "thought." I went out to the parking lot, but my dad's car was gone. So, I walked home. It was four miles. When I got there, all he said was that I am a disappointment, that he was not going to spend any more time helping me with spelling, and that since I lost I had to redo all my homework a second time – to check my answers – until he told me I could stop. He never did.

As long as I could focus on my work, with no one distracting me, my dad seemed satisfied. One time, after I got straight As all through fifth grade, he even told me that I could buy a package of Ding Dongs® when I went inside to pay for the gas. When I came back to the car, I made a special point to thank him, but he didn't even look at me as he gruffly said, "Where's my change?"

The next day, he blew a gasket because I didn't put the trash cans back into the garage before he got home from work. I told him that I was waiting for it to stop raining. He yelled that I was a big baby. He stormed into my room to get what was left of the Ding Dongs, ridiculed me for already eating one, took the rest, and told me to follow him outside. The neighbors across the street had just pulled into their driveway; they saw and heard the whole thing. He yelled at me to hold my hands out. He slammed the package down into my hands and called me a _____ing idiot. He opened one of the trash can lids, and told me to throw the package away. At first I hesitated, and he yelled, "Throw the _____ing package away! ... I never should have let you have this! I give you a reward and you get lazy! ... And get these trash cans inside the garage. If you ever forget again, I'm going to make you throw your dinner away!"

After I took the trash cans in, I went inside, closed my bedroom door, lied on my bed, and stared at the ceiling fan until I finally fell asleep well after midnight. We never spoke of that incident again.

I tried so hard and made it almost a year, but then I slipped up again. It was my first chess tournament in middle school. I was in sixth grade, and I easily made it to the quarterfinals; all the others remaining were eighth graders. If only that teacher hadn't been wearing that crazy sweater. It had a bunch of red and black squares, and said something about "king me." *So annoying...* I could not focus, and when my opponent went with the Queen's Gambit, I hesitated to go with the French Defense. I hesitated for just one move, but that was enough... I lost control of the center squares, and from then on it was slow death. Halfway through that my dad stood up in the middle of the room and said – loud enough so everyone could hear – "I've seen enough," and left.

When it was finally over, I went into a bathroom stall and cried in silence. After that, I went out to the parking lot, and was not surprised to see that my dad's car was gone. So, I walked home. It was six miles. When I got home, all he said was that I am a disappointment, that he was not going to spend any more time helping me with chess, and that since I lost I was no longer allowed to play with my friends (he called them "a distraction") until he told me I could again. He never did.

I brought this story up during my speech at high school graduation. This is ingrained in my memory. I said, "If you're not the best at something, you cannot think about anything else until you are. For instance, in sixth grade, I lost the middle school chess tournament in the quarterfinals. So, I have practiced chess for at least one hour a day every day since then. I have never lost another chess match. I ignored everything in my life except schoolwork and chess, and now I am the best." There were a few audible gasps from the crowd.

I was relieved to be done with my speech, and I thought I did pretty well. But then as I was sitting there, having to wait for all the other kids to get their diplomas – *so annoying...* – I remembered that I completely forgot to tell the story about beating Hildegard out for top spot in English class. I handily beat her in every other class, but English was a close call. Oh, the teacher was so excited about Hildegard's essays – something about "voice," whatever that is. She even got some token award at graduation. But when I found out that I was two percentage points behind her in class, with only one week to go I did every extra credit assignment we could do, and I beat her out by a tenth of a percentage point. I was so proud of myself. *Best in every class!* I was so mad at myself for forgetting to tell that story in my speech! That would have been the icing on the cake. Speaking of which, at the reception after graduation, Hildegard congratulated me and asked if I wanted a piece of cake. It did look good, and I had been looking forward to it, but since I forgot that part of my speech I couldn't allow myself to have any. My dad taught me that if you fail at something, you need to discipline yourself to improve your focus. And over the years I found denying myself food was an effective way to stay focused. The empty feeling in my stomach made it easy to remember that I had done something wrong.

Oh, I was so glad to finally be done with high school. Ugh… high school… – the worst three years of my life! All those lazy, big-baby kids with low aspirations. This is what happens when they get rewarded for "doing their best." How can it be their best, if they have time to hang out talking to each other? And some of them are even talking about going to college! I don't get that. I mean, if you can't go to a Top 5 college, why bother to go at all? Even Hildegard, the second-best student in school – second best is right… – was quivering about whether she could get into even a Top 10! I'll never forget that conversation.

One day after calculus class, she came over to me – *so annoying…* – and said, "I'm really having trouble with all these college application essays. How's it going for you?"

"I've already gone through them all twice. I'm done."

"Oh, really? Where are you applying? I know you're really smart. Do you think you'll go to an Ivy League college?"

"Well, that's all I'm applying to. So, yes…"

She gasped. "What about backups?"

"Oh, there are a few backups in there."

"Well, uh, you know the acceptance rates are pretty low. I mean, they don't have room for everyone who's qualified."

"I know that! I'm more than 'qualified'!"

Her jaw kind of dropped, and she just looked at me for a moment. Then she finally turned and walked away. I never saw her again after graduation, so she obviously didn't go to Princeton.

I remember my first day at Princeton like it was yesterday. I hadn't even visited before I moved into my dorm. My dad wouldn't drive me. He told me to take a bus. The walk to the bus station took longer than I thought it would. I couldn't carry all my bags at once, so I kept moving half a little ways, and then I would go back to get the other half and go a little beyond the other half. This jagged approach was taking quite a while, and I started to worry that I was going to miss my bus. Thankfully it was a few minutes late, and I did barely make it. After a few transfers, I finally arrived in Princeton. I was disappointed to learn that it was quite a long walk to the dorm. I had allowed myself to eat a granola bar on the bus, so to compensate I couldn't allow myself to take a taxi. As I walked, again in overlapping bits, carrying half and then the other half, I remembered those walks home from school after the spelling bee and the chess tournament. It was dark by the time I got to my dorm building.

When I started college, I had no idea what I wanted to major in or what I wanted to do after I graduated. But it didn't take me very long to figure out that a lot of my competition – I actually had some now – were planning to go to med school. So, I figured I should do that. When it was getting close to the time to start applying, there was this "med school fair" – *so annoying...* – where representatives from various schools came on campus to give us their dog and pony shows. I looked at the schedule, and it seemed like the schools were presenting more or less in reverse order of their ranking. The whole crazy thing was hours and hours long, so I figured it would be efficient to just go to the last half hour. I only needed to hear the top three anyway. I had just finished my P. Chem. problem set – the redo checked out – and I went down the hall to go to the bathroom. I was wearing clothes – (usually on the weekends I just shuffled around in my bathrobe) – so a girl from across the hall was taken by surprise.

"Oh, are you headed out?"

"Uh, yeah, there's this med school dog and pony fair thing that I'm going to check out."

"Sounds interesting. Are you hoping to go to med school?"

"No, I'm not hoping to go. I'm definitely going."

She paused a second, and then kind of chuckled. Then she said, "Well, that sounds pretty tough, but it must be motivating to be able to help people in that way."

Now it was my turn to pause. I had never thought of it that way. I finally said, "Oh… yeah… I guess."

I'll never forget my interview at Johns Hopkins. They seemed really impressed with me, and we were obviously starting to wind down to the end of the interview. But then came a question unlike any I had heard before. It really came out of left field for me. They asked, "If a parent is heartbroken about their young child who has recently been diagnosed with leukemia, and they come to you to ask if you can help, what would you say?"

I sat there for about ten seconds, trying to think of how I could possibly answer such a question. Then my mind went back to my high school graduation speech. So, I said, "I would tell the parent that I have learned that if you're not the best at something, you cannot think about anything else until you are. So, I have put everything aside except my schoolwork, and now I am the best. I would tell the parent that they can feel good because they have found the best."

They didn't say much after that answer. They just kind of wrapped it up, and said they'd let me know.

I didn't think I had much to worry about, but then came the letter. My roommate brought it in as I was cooking my dinner. … I'll never forget that feeling. … I had never been turned down by a school before. I taped the rejection letter to my bathroom mirror, threw my dinner into the trash can, went to my bed, and stared at the ceiling fan. I thought back to that night my dad yelled at me about the trash cans; I didn't cry that night. But this night I did.

The next morning I got a phone call. It was Pastor from the church back home. I hadn't seen him in years. He told me that my dad had a bad heart attack the night before and didn't make it. My mind immediately went back to the morning my dad told me that my mom had died the night before. Both times no warning. With my mom, I didn't even know what it meant to die. I guess they knew I didn't really understand, and that's why neither of them told me ahead of time, even though they knew it was coming. That time, I was shocked. This time, I was relieved. Yes, I felt a wave of relief wash over me when I heard that my dad was gone, and not coming back. I didn't want to admit this feeling to Pastor, so I just thanked him for contacting me and asked when the funeral would be. He said that he was going to ask me the same question… and he wanted to know if I could come home in the next day or two. That's when it dawned on me – as the only child, I was expected to manage the funeral arrangements. My short-lived relief was quickly overshadowed by this burden. I stammered that there was no way I could come home before Friday afternoon, but that I would do that and be there all weekend.

He helped me make the funeral arrangements. I didn't belabor over any decisions. I just picked all the easiest or cheapest things. When he asked if I wanted to say a few words during the funeral, I immediately said "No."

He said that he understood. Then he asked if there was any particular Scripture passage I thought should be emphasized during his short message during the funeral. I said, "I don't care – just pick anything."

The next weekend I went back for the funeral. As I was waiting for it to start, I was sitting there relishing the sweet relief that I was finally able to enjoy again – knowing that this whole distraction would soon be over. I was so lost in my mind that I didn't even realize anything had started until we were almost done with the first hymn. It sounded vaguely familiar – "Amazing Grace" I think it's called. I heard people sing "wretch," and I thought to myself, *That describes Dad all right…* My mind went back to my childhood: the high expectations, with little encouragement; the stern requirements, with few rewards; the verbal abuse; the unpredictable anger that seemed to come out of nowhere; the neglect – all with no apology. I previously tried to avoid thinking about those things, but I now found it strangely soothing to allow myself to consider a perspective I never could before – the perspective of looking back, realizing that it was finally behind me. I was lost in thought, when suddenly I realized that Pastor seemed to be starting his message. Something he was reading took me back to when I was a very young boy. I remembered this story from Sunday School. Mom used to take me. (Dad never did.) It was the story of The Lost Sheep – how the shepherd left 99 sheep to find the one who had wandered off (Luke 15:1-7). I knew enough about the story to wonder what the heck this had to do with my dad. Pastor kept harping on "This man receives sinners" (Luke 15:2). I thought to myself, *Well, at least one of those words applies to my dad...* Not surprisingly, there weren't very many people there (mainly some extended family and a few people from my dad's work). But I still found it strange that every time I looked up, Pastor was looking right at me.

Afterwards, Pastor told me that he knew my dad was challenging to live with, and that he hoped I would be able to move on from my difficult childhood and learn that most others are more loving than my dad was. The last thing Pastor said to me was, "Don't ever forget that while some people in our life might neglect us, God never does. And if we ever feel lost and alone in the world, we should remember that Jesus is right there to take us back home – just like He was for the one sheep in today's parable."

That gave me something to think about on the bus ride back to Princeton.

~

The first thing I was going to do when I got back to the dorm was to double-check all my homework for the week. I had finished the first pass on Friday. But on the bus it occurred to me that I rarely found any mistakes on my second check, so it didn't seem to be a very efficient use of my time. So, I made a rash decision: For the first time since third grade, I was *not* going to double-check my homework! So, instead, the first thing I did was to knock on the door of the girl across the hall – the one I had talked to before the med school fair. She looked surprised to see me. I said, "Oh, hi, maybe you don't recognize me on a Sunday evening without my bath-robe."

She smiled and asked me what was up. I answered, "Remember how I said I'm going to med school? But I've been rejected by my first choice, and I'm starting to get nervous about the other two. I've never been re-jected before, and I want to talk to someone who knows what that's like. So, I figured I'd come to you."

She stared at me with no expression. … Then, suddenly she literally dropped down onto the floor and started laughing hysterically. She finally caught her breath and said, "Oh, buddy, you need more help than I thought! You have been a recluse so long that you don't even know how to integrate back into society! If that's your attempt at a come-on, I have to tell you that it's never going to work!"

I said, "Uh, yeah, I guess… So, does this mean you can help me?"

"Yes, I can help you. Give me a few minutes to get ready, and then why don't we go to the corner and share a small pizza?"

Once there, the first thing she asked me was what I did over the week-end. She had noticed that I wasn't around. I said I had gone home, but I didn't give the real reason. I said that I had no choice but to go home because this was the weekend of the annual Velcro® convention, and I couldn't miss that. She just sat there and smiled, and told me that I'm funny. She asked if I was the grand high exalted mystic ruler of the con-vention. All I said was, "Of course," and she just started laughing again.

She said, "I spent most of the weekend studying. I had thought that was bad, but at least it didn't have anything to do with Velcro."

I surprised myself by saying, "Studying is overrated. It's bad for the eyes, and seldom requires me to get out of my bathrobe, which is also bad for the eyes."

She laughed again. I continued, "And it doesn't seem to have helped me get into med school."

I told her about my interviews, and how I was surprised that they kept asking about how I would talk to patients – the other two even more than Johns Hopkins. "I thought med school was for students who are top of their class, not for students who have time to talk to people."

She asked, "Then why are you taking the time to talk to me?"

"I guess I'm at the end of my rope."

She put her head down on the table and laughed and laughed. Finally, she composed herself enough to say, "So, what happens next? Are you thinking to apply anywhere else?"

"Uh, well, I think all the deadlines are past."

Then she said that she knew of a good med school near her hometown, and she thought it had rolling admissions. She knew about it because several members at her church taught or went to school there.

I asked (knowing the answer, and so I smiled as I asked it), "Is it Top 5, or at least Top 10?"

She smiled and said, "No, but they are known for their strong program that trains doctors to serve in developing countries. It's a Christian med school."

"I didn't know there was such a thing."

"It's not that uncommon, especially since a lot of Jesus' miracles were healings. It's a natural fit."

I just kind of sat there, looking at her. Then she continued, "You don't know much about Christianity, do you?"

"No, not really."

"Then why don't you come with me next weekend? There's a church that meets on campus, and it's mostly students."

"Well, that's good because I wouldn't want to shock any old fogies when I show up in my bathrobe."

She smiled, and reached out to touch my hand. That made me feel a way that I barely remembered ever feeling before. I hadn't felt this way since my mom was alive. It was the feeling that someone cared about me.

The next Sunday morning, I knocked on my friend's door at the time we agreed to leave for church. When she opened the door, we both did a double-take of surprise. I went first: "I didn't expect you to wear a dress."

She was very quick with her response: "And I didn't expect you to wear pants, so I guess we're even!"

When we arrived at the so-called church, I did another double-take. This was not what I was expecting at all. I said to her, "Where's the other team? Isn't this a volleyball court? Where are the pews and worn-out hymnals? Where's the organ? Where's the pulpit? And I guess you must be trying to start a new trend with your dress. Looks like you've got a lot of girls to convince… Speaking for myself, I'm finding their current tendency toward shorts and tank tops very acceptable – very acceptable indeed…"

She quipped, "We're not here to look at that. Let me introduce you to the pastor."

That led to my third double-take of the morning – definitely a record for me. This guy looked like he just strapped his surfboard on top of his surf wagon – you know, the kind with the wood paneling. As I shook his hand, it struck me that he looked me in the eyes and smiled. He seemed genuinely happy to meet me. I expected him to ask about my church background – I had been rehearsing my response to that – but he just asked what year I was in college, where I grew up, my family: stuff like that. I soon found myself telling him that both my parents had passed away, my mom when I was a kid and my dad fairly recently. I usually don't like to tell people about my mom dying – I hadn't even told my friend yet – but somehow it just seemed natural to tell him. We were still talking when all of a sudden there was this incredibly loud sound. I was very startled. I'm sure Pastor noticed, but all he said was, "Oh, is it already time to get started? We get going with a few praise songs."

I thought to myself, *Praise songs? Sounds more like a Led Zeppelin concert…*

My friend and I gravitated toward some of her other friends. They were all very welcoming to me. As I looked around the room, I was struck by the lack of uniformity, not only in the people themselves but also in what they were doing: coming, going, coming back, eating, talking, drinking, hugging, squealing with delight, singing, even dancing a little, hands in the air, eyes closed, swaying to and fro… My first thought was that some of it seemed a little disrespectful, but then I thought back to how I usually spend my Sunday mornings and I realized that these people have the right idea.

I was expecting a little downtime supplied by a rote liturgy, but right after the last song – well, some of us needed a little more time for a few more hugs and squeals – Pastor got up there and dived head first into his message. And, wouldn't you know it, the topic was again Jesus our Good Shepherd. Pastor said that this week's memory verse – (In subsequent weeks, I realized that this is a regular thing with him) – is Psalm 95:7, and he had us recite it together a few times: "For he is our God, and we are the people of his pasture, and the sheep of his hand." He then stressed that the theme of the day is that Jesus calls us personally, just like a shepherd calling his individual sheep. He quoted John 10:3 – "The sheep [us] hear his voice, and he [Jesus, the Good Shepherd] calls his own sheep by name." The next thing that Pastor did was very impactful for me. He, speaking as Jesus, said several times, "I am calling you, __ ," each time using a different specific name. He did this about four or five times, and the last time he used my name. We had just met, but he used my name. And I have a very unusual name! I had never met anyone else who has my name. I was self-conscious about that. My name made me feel like an outsider – unconnected. When Pastor said my name in that way, it was the first time that I associated my name with feeling connected.

Pastor then went on to talk about the Good Shepherd leaving 99 sheep to find the one who had wandered off (Luke 15:1-7), and that reminded me of my dad's funeral. Pastor said that sheep are prone to stray, and that one way we can stray is to become so downtrodden by hardships in life that we give up on God, coming to the conclusion that He doesn't care about us. He gave examples of abandonment, abuse, and unloving parents. Pastor went on to say that all such hardships are in one way or another a result of humanity's sinful nature – failures of people, not of God – and that God wants to rescue us from the consequences of sin. He wants us to stop relying on ourselves – we will only wander and get lost – and instead rely solely on Him, submitting to His will that we be laid on Jesus' shoulders (cf. Luke 15:5) and carried back to His fold. Pastor started winding things down by saying that one of Satan's tricks – one of the ways he wants us to wander – is to try to convince us that we know better than God, that we should give up on God and rely on ourselves. Pastor finished by saying that Satan is wily, but God is greater. Satan lures us to wander, but God's call and will are stronger – "no one will snatch them [His sheep] out of my hand. My Father, who has given them to me [Jesus], is greater than all, and no one is able to snatch them out of the Father's hand" (John 10:28-29).

After the sermon, we sang a simple song that was familiar to me. I hadn't heard it since I was in Kindergarten. Yes, it usually is thought of as a children's song, but everyone seemed to be focused on it, especially after hearing Pastor's message. I had this strange feeling that seemed to be a mixture of sadness and elation. I had never felt this way before. My eyes started to tear up a bit, and my first thought was that I didn't want to cry. I noticed out of the corner of my eye that my friend was looking at me. When I turned to look at her – I guess my eyes had teared up more than I thought – a teardrop was jostled out of my eye and it rolled down my cheek. I was embarrassed, but then I saw her smile at me, and then she reached out to touch my arm. I felt a surge of relief that she wasn't put off by my reaction. She seemed to understand. I then felt comfortable to cry freely. It was hard for me to actually sing the words because I was too emotional. I mostly just listened.

> *I am Jesus' little lamb,*
> *Ever glad at heart I am;*
> *For my Shepherd gently guides me,*
> *Knows my need, and well provides me,*
> *Loves me ev'ry day the same,*
> *Even calls me by my name.*

Day by day, at home, away,
Jesus is my staff and stay.
When I hunger, Jesus feeds me,
Into pleasant pastures leads me;
When I thirst, He bids me go
Where the quiet waters flow.

Who so happy as I am,
Even now the Shepherd's lamb?
And when my short life is ended,
By His angel host attended,
He shall fold me to His breast,
There within His arms to rest.[5]

~

When I got the acceptance letter from the med school that my friend recommended, there was no doubt in my mind. I felt God's call to go there. The first person I told was my friend. The first thing I said was that I was accepted. Her expression didn't change much – other than to look a little anxious – and she said, "Well, of course you were... So... are you going to go?" I barely started telling her when – I guess she could tell from my smile – she lunged at me, gave me a big hug, and even kissed me on the cheek!

I was a little embarrassed and joked, "Maybe I should change my mind and stay with you!"

She turned a little serious and said, "Oh, no, God has important work for you to do, and don't let anything distract you."

She smiled again and went on to say, "There's something I've been wanting to tell you, and now's the perfect time. I want you to know that I've never met anyone like you. When I first saw you around the dorm, I agreed with everyone else that you were a big jerk. When I first actually met you, I was introduced to a whole new level of annoying. In our first few conversations, I was astounded again and again at your awkwardness and total lack of social skills of any kind. But in time I learned that there's something about you that is very endearing. It's hard to describe, but it has something to do with a sweet boy who wants to be accepted for who he is and to stop trying so hard to live up to the expectations of others. I'm so glad that you've found peace in knowing that this is God's calling for you. You are perfectly suited for this! You still have a lot to learn about bedside manners, but I've seen enough to know that with some effort – and heaven knows you have never shied away from effort – you'll eventually get there. God has great plans for you! I'm so happy that you've learned that and … [She hesitated a bit] … and that He loves you. … And I just want to say that I … [Again, she hesitated, and looked at me intently, as if to see if I was holding up OK; her voice broke a little] … I … love you too. I'm happy that we've become friends."

She took my hand, kissed me on the cheek again, and said, "OK, so that means I'm definitely going to visit you not long after you get started! I want to hear all about it!"

Sure enough, just a couple months into med school, she came to visit me. I told her about my courses, my new friends, my new church – *(Yes, it meets on a volleyball court!)* – the intramural sports that I was inept at but doing anyway…, but I was most interested in telling her about a one-day workshop I had recently attended.

I said, "It's designed to help healthcare workers empathize with patients. When I learned about it, I immediately thought of you! In my mind, I saw you wagging your finger at me and saying, 'You'd better go to this, or I will know the reason why!' So, I went, and let me tell you about this instructor! She is over-the-top bubbly like you've never seen! She had us sharing, story-boarding, role-playing – the whole nine yards. I was hesitant at first, but then I really threw myself into it. I was head nurse! Oh, you can't imagine my performance! Oh, and you'll like this: You know how I'm a little dense when it comes to bedside manners. She asked us what we would do if we have a child patient who is scared of us. For some reason, she was looking right at me the whole time she was talking about this, and sure enough she called on me to answer. I thought for a moment and then said, 'I would tell them to grab hold of their mom and shut their eyes, really really tight.' The instructor stared blankly at me for a few seconds, and then she said – get this – oh, this is good – she said, 'If I was to close my eyes, I would be even more scared of you. … Here's a better idea. If you have a patient who is a child, sit down next to them and ask them to tell you about their toys. If they have some with them, ask them to show them to you, and then actually play together.' My eyes were like saucers… *Genius!* The things I'm learning here… You have no idea…"

My friend just smiled at me.

I continued, "Do you want to see the notes I took?"

"Like nothing else!"

"Oh, I know you're going to like this… I've been looking forward to showing you."

I handed her my notebook and said, "Take a look!"

She opened up my notebook about halfway through the sheets, but the pages were blank. She flipped to some earlier pages – but they were blank too. She eventually made it all the way to the first page, and finally there was something. There was a clumsy drawing of a little girl, eagerly pre-senting to all interested a stuffed animal in her outstretched arms; that was all there was, except underneath this work of art I had written, "Hug a unicorn."

My friend looked up at me, smiling widely but with her eyes watering up. I said – a little choked up myself – "And I didn't double-check my work."

That made her tears fall, and we hugged. I said, "I want to thank you for so many things: for becoming my friend against all obstacles I threw in your way; for listening to me, even when I was annoying and clumsy; for inviting me to church; and for encouraging me to go to this school. I'm so happy here, and I can't wait for what's next. … I want you to know that you are by far the best friend I've ever had. … [I hesitated a bit.] … I've never felt this way about anyone else. … I [Again, I hesitated, and looked at her more intently, to make sure she was holding up OK; my voice broke a little] … I … love you."

The whole time I was talking, she had this glow about her. She had never looked so beautiful. When I was done, she closed her eyes, and … we kissed.

~

I'm almost to the end of my story, but let me tell you just one more thing. We need to flash forward a few years. It was the end of my first day of residency. I was exhausted, and just wanted to go home and crash. I got into the elevator, and already inside were a woman and her young son. She looked like she had been crying. When I got in, for some reason her son decided to push the button for every floor between us and the ground floor… That's a lot of floors! I looked at him and my jaw literally dropped. He just stuck his tongue out at me. I thought about what to say to them about this, but I came to the conclusion that it was best not to say the first few things that popped into my head. Instead, I asked his mom, "Is every-thing OK? You seem upset about something."

She said, "I just learned that my son's test results came back positive for leukemia. … Our doctor's out of town at a conference, and we were just told point blank by some flunkie lab rat. … I'm confused and anxious." Then she looked at me and asked, "Can you help us?"

My mind went back to my interview at Johns Hopkins. Sometimes we learn best from our mistakes. I definitely knew how *not* to answer her! Instead, I said, "I know your doctor. She has experience treating leukemia. You're in good hands. When I get home, I'll send her an email and ask her to take a look at your son's results and set up a meeting with you as soon as possible. I think she'll be back in town in a couple days. I'll tell her that you're confused by results you just received, and I'll ask her to prioritize meeting with you. And I will be praying for you and your son. What are your names?"

She was visibly comforted by what I said, and she thanked me for my help. She told me their names, and I did a double-take when she said her son's name. I guess she noticed, because she said, "Oh, you've probably never heard that name before. It is unusual."

I said, "Yes, it is unusual, but I've heard of it. You see, that's my name too."

I reached out and put my hand on her son's head, scrunched his hair a little bit, and said, "God loves you, Nahum, and I'll be praying for you."

I'd like you to take home at least two messages from this story.

- We shouldn't judge people by how they come across. We don't know their full backstory. And we don't need to know all of that to help them look forward, like his friend did in this story.
- I've often heard it said that we need to learn to love ourselves before we can love others. I suppose there's some truth to this, but there's a step before this. We need to learn that God loves us before we can truly love ourselves.

~   ~   ~

After-hours

Bob unplugged

I mentioned that self-improvement initiatives have their place, and that place is only when such actions are helping us achieve a change that God wants for our life. When we do find that God wants us to make a change, more often than not we find said change to be difficult. … Is this surprising? … No, because when making any change it takes time to learn a new way; it's typical that things will get harder before they get easier. This common phenomenon is sometimes referred to as the J-curve of change.[6]

- I have a challenge for you: The next time you identify a change that you feel called to make, or you learn of someone else in your life going through a necessary change, pray about this daily from the time you become aware of this until you or your counterpart have learned the new way sufficiently well such that it's feeling natural, for example a new habit has formed
  - What should we pray about during the oftentimes difficult transition?
    - Pray for patience and stamina, trusting that with sustained effort the day will come when the benefit being sought will finally be realized
    - Pray for protection from Satan, knowing that he will try to discourage us and tempt us back to the comfort zone from whence we began our difficult journey
    - Pray for an openness to ask others for assistance, when it will be beneficial
    - Pray for a positive disposition, one that celebrates all the milestones along the way, not only reaching the final destination
    - Pray for a selectively good memory, one that recalls prior difficult changes that we've made successfully in the past
    - Pray for a selectively poor memory, one that doesn't discourage us by reminding us of past failures
    - Pray for peace, resting assured that God has a plan for us, and resting assured that we're on the brink of experiencing the special joy of learning what our next role is

God doesn't ask us to change without a good reason, so we should be excited when it's our turn to grow.

Step up to the microphone

Let's talk about margins. … First, look at the pages in this book. Would it have been better for the words to be crammed to the edges? Think of how much more I could say! … Now, look at your schedule. Is it crammed to the edges? … Just as we need plenty of sleep to function properly the next day, we also need sufficient downtime during our waking hours to function properly throughout them.

It's important for our physical and emotional health that we not overtax ourselves.

- What can you do to widen your margins?

To help you with your list of strengths, I asked you to get input from others and to read about strengths typically associated with your generalized personality type. I hope that you learned some new things about yourself!

- Which of your strengths surprises you the most?
- How will you next make use of this "surprising strength"?

I mentioned that even those things that we consider to be weaknesses do not hinder God's kingdom and, from time to time, may even play a role in expanding it. Think of an example where an apparent weakness of yours, or of someone you know, was used by God to edify someone else.

When it comes to seeking a balance point, keep in mind that we cannot achieve "perfect" balance in any area of our life, at least not for longer than it takes to blink our eyes. This is the whole nature of balance! We continuously need to make adjustments. So, don't get discouraged when you feel out of balance – just take note, and start leaning the other way.

- What area in your life is most out of balance?
- What are some ways you can restore balance in this area?

Consider the story at the end of this chapter. The narrator was an overachiever for years, before he finally saw his inherent value and learned how to love himself.

- Is there anyone in your life who has blinders on when it comes to seeing their inherent value?
- Can you think of ways to help them take their blinders off?
  - To this end, what can we learn from the narrator's friend?

For parents (1 of 2): Ask yourself if you're pushing any of your children too hard in any areas. Pray about this, and ask God if you should dial anything back a notch or two.

- If you identify something to adjust, where do you think your original expectations came from? Was it something your parents expected of you? Does it relate to something you regret about your past? Please keep in mind that we should not be projecting our past hardships or failures onto our children.
- Regardless of whether you identified anything to dial back, please look for opportunities to tell your children – when they're not the best in the group (for example, they were in a race and they didn't win) – that you're glad they tried their best, and you're proud of them

For parents (2 of 2): In the coming month, I'd like you to tell each of your children at least three things about them that you consider to be strengths or gifts. If you have more than one child, please don't tell them all at once as a group – rather, tell each one individually. If they no longer live with you, don't forget that you can call them on the phone, have a videoconference, or send them a written message.

For intimate couples: I'd like both of you, in turn, to tell your partner at least three things about them that you consider to be strengths or gifts. … After both of you have done this, then I'd like both of you, in turn, to tell your partner at least three additional things about yourself that you consider to be strengths or gifts.

Chapter 5 – Our Need to Be Loved by Other People

So far in this book, I've focused on love for ourselves (previous chapter) and the one-on-one loving relationship each believer has with God (Chapters 2 and 3). But there's so much more to cover because I haven't said much yet about our one-on-one relationships with other people. (Although, I did give a little sample, the tippy top of the iceberg, in the story at the end of the previous chapter.)

I feel like a preteen waiting for the rope to drop at Disneyland®! Where will I go first? *Space Mountain*®? *Winnie the Pooh*®? *Frozen*® *Sing-Along*? … I'll never tell!

While I'm very anxious to get to Chapters 6 and 7 because there I finally get to take a deep dive into our giving love to others – so much of what brings joy to our life – I first want to say a few words about our *receiving* love from others. This also should be a continuous source of joy in our life.

Yes, it should. But is it? When we look at the brochure for Disneyland, it sure seems like it is. Everyone is smiling. Everyone is laughing. Everyone is enjoying time with family and friends. No one is left out. No one is alone. But not every day is a trip with our family and friends to an amusement / theme park, filled with exhilarating sing-alo… – I mean clamorous rides… In real life, we get busy with our day-to-day activities, and spend an inordinate amount of time not smiling, not laughing, and not feeling connected to others – not feeling joy. Yes, while there are many people all around us, we often struggle to feel meaningfully connected to any of them. If this becomes a way of life for us, we can come to feel lonely.

If you often experience loneliness, I'm sorry, and my best advice is for you to bring it to God, pour out your frustrations, and ask Him to help you change the situation. May I suggest the following prayer?

- *God, I'm so thankful for Your love – words cannot express – and I'm thankful that You made me the way You did. I know I have quirks, and more importantly I know there are (other) things You want me to change in my life. But even during that journey of change, I do love myself, and I accept that I am an inherently lovable person. But there's still an empty space in my heart. I have some family and friends, but nevertheless I often feel lonely and isolated, and that makes me sad. I crave to be more connected to people. So often, when I reach out, everyone seems so busy and preoccupied with their own problems. It makes me feel like they don't care very much about me, when they spend more time talking about their latest "crisis" than they do asking about how I'm doing. And then they rush off laughing about how busy we all are. I'm not that busy... I have some spare time on my hands... God, help me find someone who wants to spend time with me – someone I can talk to. I have so much I want to say, but there doesn't seem to be anyone who wants to listen. I know You listen to me, but I also want someone else with whom I can share the simple, day-to-day things of life. God, please help me find a friend like this.*

Yes, Jesus wants to help you. He knows what it's like to feel lonely – even beyond the loneliness that comes from mild neglect (as alluded to in the above prayer). He is familiar with the feeling of outright rejection: "He was despised and rejected by men, a man of sorrows and acquainted with grief; / and as one from whom men hide their faces he was despised, and we esteemed him not" (Isaiah 53:3). What did He do about it? Did He change anything about Himself to make others feel differently about Him? No, He didn't do that, and neither should we – at least not for the express purpose of trying to make any specific person love us. When we feel lonely, we shouldn't try to remedy the situation by muting our inherent characteristics (our inherent preferences – our personality) to fit the expectations of others. Maybe we should change something about the way we *interact* with others – (Lots of good tips in Chapters 6 and 7! Plus a few teasers toward the end of this chapter) – but we shouldn't try to inhibit anything about our personality. God created us the way He did on purpose. Why would we want to change that?

God also created us to be social, and while a little downtime is healthy, we all benefit from interacting with others. So, it's natural that we become sad and lonely when we don't get enough positive interaction. And it's also natural that God places people in our life to help alleviate our loneliness.

But it isn't always so simple, is it? Sometimes the people in our life aren't very loving. Yes, in many ways this life is not what God intended it to be. So, before I take this chapter in the direction of recovery from loneliness, I'm going to take a few more steps the other way. ... There is a dim and serpentine path, with loneliness being one of the stepping stones, that leads to the heartache of feeling unloved or even all the way to the misery of feeling unlovable. Other stepping stones that may be on this path include:

- Considering ourselves unattractive / undesirable / uninteresting
- A poor self-image / low self-esteem
- Chronic depression
- Our being the victim of a traumatic event (for example, rape) or more prolonged abuse (emotional, physical, sexual)
- Suicidal thoughts

If one of your stepping stones is suicidal thoughts, please turn right now to p. 333, and pray that prayer and read the surrounding paragraphs.

Four gray stepping stones

Whatever our particular stepping stones, if we walk down such a path, we start to generate a list in our head of who we think doesn't love us. If our evolving and oscillating list ever hits the ocean floor of every single person and God (we are unloved by all), and even to the lowest ebb that this cannot change (we are unlovable), then we have reached the full depth of Love Zero. I describe this in the Prologue, and there I include a prayer for you if you occasionally have this thought distortion. Here, I'd like to address the healthier, but still dire, situation where:

- We know that God loves us, although our understanding of this may be immature (for example, we may have a distorted view of the nature of His love) and/or we don't feel God's love in our heart
- We have some degree of positive regard for ourselves, although this may be underdeveloped
- *But* at times we come to the conclusion that few or no others love us

If you ever feel this way, please know that part of God's love for you includes His desire for you to be loved by other people. Keep this in mind as you ask God to help you experience more love in your life.

Below, I've written prayers – I call them prayer-testimonies – that give us a peek into four specific scenarios. These prayers are cries for help – laments of hurting and flawed people – so we can relate. Note that there's little to no indication within the prayer that the pray-er has come to realize that there's an "answer" that they will then try to actualize. Many times, that's exactly what our prayers are. We cast our anxieties on Him, knowing that He cares for us (cf. 1 Peter 5:7). The answers come in due time; certainly, this is the case with God and our real prayers, and to a lesser extent I hope you find some of my commentary after these prayer-testimonies useful.

- Here's a prayer-testimony of someone who feels very much unloved, and perhaps unlovable, because of low self-esteem and being in one or more relationships that are emotionally abusive.

  God, thank You for loving me. You never disappoint me, but sometimes I can tell that I disappoint You and others. When I make someone get angry with me, my first feeling is shame. I'm so ashamed of myself for disappointing them again. How can You and they forgive me? Next, I try to figure out what it is about me that made them get angry this time. I keep trying to change, but nothing seems to work. No matter how hard I try, the cycle continues. When I'm useful to them and I don't make a mistake, they treat me OK. But if I screw up, one way or another they let me know that they're not happy. Some people – the ones I don't know very well – just scowl and give me the silent treatment. Others get really angry with me, and give me a piece of their mind! And sometimes, especially lately, my husband gets so enraged that he tells me I'm stupid and says other mean things that make me feel worse about myself. I don't know how to keep anyone happy with me. I've tried everything! What should I do?

  o Before I answer your question, let's get back to first principles. You are surrounded by unloving people and are being emotionally abused, at least by your husband and possibly by others as well. Unfortunately, you're blaming yourself, and you keep trying to change yourself to make the situation better.

    ▪ This is a common conclusion we come to, especially for those of us with low self-esteem. *It must be my fault. What should I do differently to make others happy with me?* When we find ourselves thinking such things, we should stop cold. If you learn nothing else from this book, learn this: God loves us just the way we naturally are, God wants us to love ourselves just the way we naturally are, and God wants others to love us just the way we naturally are. (Extra credit! There's one more similar statement to take to heart. What is it? … If you're stuck, read Chapter 6!)

There are no exceptions to any of this. So, one of the main messages of this chapter is that if someone doesn't love us just the way we naturally are, then we should cut our losses and find others who are more compatible with us. If we happen to be in a close relationship with our unloving counterpart (like this woman and her husband), such cutting of losses is still advisable in the form of a timeout – which is meant to be a time for both parties to let the dust settle and then consider how best to reinvest in the relationship.

Only when we're already in a loving relationship should we consider trying to change something about ourselves for the sake of the relationship. Do you see the distinction between this and what the woman was trying to do? We should never change to try to make an unloving counterpart happy, or to "make them love us." We should only change when our counterpart already loves us anyway, and both agree that a change will create a better relationship.

- Here's a prayer-testimony of someone who feels unlovable, possibly approaching Love Zero, because they can't get past their feelings of shame and they have a distorted view of God's love and forgiveness.

God, we're at that time when we're having a moment of silence before Communion. As usual, there won't be enough time for me. It's awkwardly long for everyone else, but for me it was another awful week and I don't have time to rehash it all now. But You know all of it anyway. A part of me knows that You have to forgive me, but another part of me doesn't understand why You keep on forgiving, especially since my list of sins is the same as every other week. I feel so sorry, but I must not be sorry enough because I thought true repentance means I'll stop. But I can't stop! This proves that I'm an awful person. And these people around me – they think I'm normal, just like them. They have little sins like driving a few miles an hour over the speed limit and saying a mild swear word now and then. Little do they know the depth of my depravity, which is highlighted by greed, envy, discontent, and lust. How can I look them in the eyes? If they really knew me, they would hate me. I guess they can somehow tell, though, and that explains why no one here talks to me. I come to church most Sundays, but my thoughts are despicable, even when I'm here. I don't contribute much time or money because I'm self-ish. I so much want the good life that most other families here have. I guess You love them more – yes, that makes sense. I don't like this pastor. He reminds me of my boss, and I don't like him either. I don't like my job. I don't like my apartment or my roommate. Everyone in that building drives me crazy. Speaking of which, with any girl I'm attracted to, even the ones here in church, the next thing I know I'm thinking about her in ways that are inappropriate and disrespectful. It happens every single time. Why can't I be normal?

- o My friend, you are normal! At least in the nature of your sins, you are normal. You do have a few things to learn about the nature of God's love for you, though. God wants you to move on from your feelings of shame, and accept – deep down accept – the forgiveness that Jesus provides. You have plenty of time during the moment of silence before Communion. It doesn't take very long to pray and take to heart: "God, be merciful to me, a sinner!" (Luke 18:13). And it's OK that you need to pray this every week. So do I; so does everyone, and not just for things that you might happen to notice, like driving a few miles an hour over the speed limit and saying a mild swear word now and then.

- Here's a prayer-testimony of someone who's very self-conscious and feels unloved, at least by those in this particular circle, because of being very dif-ferent from others.

  God, there's no one at all like You – that's for sure. But sometimes I feel like there's no one at all like me either! It's one thing to be unique, but this is ridiculous! God, why am I like this? I don't seem to have anything in com-mon with anyone. Just yesterday, at the company picnic, I had nothing inter-esting to say. Fantasy football… what the heck is that?! Sounds pretty screwy to me. After the picnic, some of the guys went out for another round of drinks. But of course no one invited me. And the girls in Sales – did You hear the way they laughed when I asked if I could get them wine spritzers? I didn't know that no one else liked those anymore. There go my chances with the new hire. Even after the wine spritzer debacle – Stupid me! – I was delusional enough to think that she was looking my way, but then I saw her turn toward the others and laugh, and I think she even rolled her eyes. I'm glad I didn't hear what they were saying. I can't stand being rejected... My chartreuse ankle socks probably didn't help. Oh, God, why don't I like football, drink beer, talk to girls who laugh with their friends, and wear long white socks?!

- ▪ Similar to the first prayer-testimony in this set, but in a more light-hearted way, here we have another case where someone feels they should change to be more like others
- ○ *No! Don't change!* Well, at least don't change a thing about the football, the beer, and the socks. On the other hand, it wouldn't be such a bad idea to tighten the belt on your self-confidence and start talking to more women, especially ones who laugh with their friends.

- And my final example in this batch is a prayer-testimony of a woman who feels unloved, probably by a wider circle of people than our friend in the previous example, because she feels undesirable and uninteresting.

    God, every morning I look in the mirror and I see my flaws. I feel ugly. I try to camouflage with makeup and the clothes I pick, but there's only so much I can do... I go to work, and I feel so plain next to everyone else, especially that new girl. And I think my officemate has a thing for her. He used to talk to me most days, and I liked that, but it has been less since she's come on the scene. I guess my stories of going to the mall with my mom and taking my nephews to the two-dollar movie theater aren't as interesting as her yoga classes and "hobby" of giving massages – (Give me a break...). Oh well, one more dream to let go of. Every night when I get ready for bed, I look in the mirror again and see the same things that I started my day with. I hate the way I look. Why am I stuck with this body? What man would ever want to be with me? I'm fat... and getting fatter... I don't really fit into half of my pants anymore. Time to transition to the next size up. I keep telling myself that I should exercise, but I don't have the energy. And what would I wear?!

    - ○ Before I answer your last question, first things first: I don't need to see you to know that you are a beautiful woman. Don't let anyone, or any society, cause you to think otherwise. You are beautiful because God made you. And when you look in the mirror, maybe take a step or two back and put away the magnifying glass. No one is perfect; we all have our flaws. I didn't say you are flawless – I said you are beautiful.
    - ○ Now that we've got that settled, regarding what you will wear to exercise: *Wear whatever it takes!* Your health is more important than what you're

going to wear, and what anyone might think of that. And you seem to have fallen into the trap of thinking that exercise will make you even more tired. *No!* A proper amount of exercise will give you *more* energy. Don't believe me? Give it a whirl, and just try to prove me wrong!

One black stepping stone

Yes, there are so many different ways that we can feel unloved and even unlovable. I've provided four scenarios, but these are just the tip of the iceberg. These four examples are relatively easy to talk about. Other examples lie deeper, way down below the surface, where few have been and know how dark it gets. Maybe you know… all too well… Oh, I can't tell you how sad it makes me to think of such things!

As an example of how dark it can get for some, I feel compelled to go down a little deeper – actually, a *lot* deeper. What I've written three paragraphs down is not so much a cry for help as it is a heartbroken retrospective. This is a woman scarred for life because she was raped as a child by her uncle. She has had difficulty for years feeling loved by others because of trust issues exacerbated by this traumatic experience. Yes, appalling events that last only a few minutes can leave horrible scars that last a lifetime. What I've written below is not graphic, but some readers may find it more disturbing than they would like. But it's important for all of us to realize how bad it can get for some. Yes, I do want you to feel uncomfortable. It's natural that such stories make you uncomfortable – and angry! If you suspect that anything like this is occurring in the life of someone you know, you must follow up, ask questions, and take the child seriously. The instant you know or strongly suspect that anything like this – I mean even the warning crimes (sexual harassment) in my story – is occurring, take action immediately. Support can be found 24/7 at the National Sexual Assault Hotline (800-656-HOPE (4673)) or by visiting www.rainn.org. But, as always, call the police or 911 if help is needed urgently.

To be clear, this is not based on a true story. But in another sense, it is… Unfortunately, there are countless girls and women – and boys and men – who have been the victim of such abuse, and have abhorrent stories like what I've written below etched in their memories. To each of them, I want to say: I sincerely apologize to you for not getting it right – for not capturing the true depth and darkness of your awful experience. I ask that you forgive me, and find it in your heart to accept my meager attempt to capture a glimpse of your nightmare, as my way of trying to teach others about the pervasive impact of such atrocities.

Before I get started, it's important to say that anyone who harbors internal thoughts that resonate with the actions of the uncle in this story must seek help immediately. This is serious. This is not a slippery slope. No, this is free fall along the jagged walls of a cliff of unconscionable height. If you find yourself plummeting in this way, reach out to a professional counselor – they have the rare combination of training and a nonjudgmental mindset – and with their help pull the ripcord of your parachute.

I've written this as a prayer (another prayer-testimony), which may strike some readers as a little odd. Most of us don't pray like this, but it would be OK. God wants us to open up our hearts to Him. And even though He already knows all the details, it can be therapeutic for us to let it all out. He has all the time in the world to listen to us – so why not include all the background, all the specifics?

- *God, I wish that everyone would just leave me alone! Like just today – I can't believe how nervy it was for all those people at work to ask me what my plans are for the weekend. I don't ask them such personal questions. Can't they take a hint? Every Friday it's the same thing! And every Monday I have to figure out something to say that I did. I don't know them well enough to talk about things like that. And so I don't! It took a lot of trial and error over the years, but I finally figured out that the best way not to have to open up to people is to laugh and smile – I've been told that I have a nice smile – and to say as little as possible. When I smile, people usually stop probing for infor- mation. They see I look happy, and that usually is enough to make them go away. I've noticed that if people think I'm upset about something, they talk to me more. So, now I never show that I'm upset. I used to get angry a lot, but then I learned it's best to push it back down and not say anything. When I was a young girl, I talked a lot – mainly to my girlfriends. I'd go over to their house, or they would come to mine, and we would laugh and play for hours. We talked about our pets, collectible mini-toys, princess movies – as the years went on, taking more and more notice of their love interests... – nail polish, boys at school – You know – girl stuff. Then I hit puberty – a little earlier than my friends – and all of a sudden boys started looking at me funny. At first, I kind of liked the attention, but it got a little creepy when older guys, including some of my teachers, the dads of some of my friends, and even my own uncle, sometimes looked at me the same way. The leering was bad enough, but it got worse. Let me tell You about my "dear" uncle… – no Prince Charming, that's for sure. He wasn't married, and he used to visit us for a couple weeks every summer. That last summer, the first thing that seemed weird was I noticed him showing up in my room more often than before. He always had some excuse. At the time, his explanations seemed somewhat reasonable, but looking back those were pretty lame excuses… That time I caught him open, slowly and only slightly, my bathroom door when I was taking a shower – he said that my parents were wondering where I was, and he just wanted to help them find me. And when I caught him digging through my dirty clothes – "Helping your mom with the laundry" – yeah, right! Now I know how I lost certain private items… I wish this was all there was to tell. I partially blame myself for what happened next. I believed him – stupid me! I should have told my parents. But how do you tell your mom, "Your brother saw me naked"? How do you tell your dad, "The best man at your wedding was pawing around in my laundry basket this morning"? The summer before, I told my parents about that time in the pool when he started touching me in places I didn't think he should; but they said I should be grateful that he was taking the time to teach me some new swimming strokes, and that I must be mistaken. Boy, were they mad at me! They said it's wrong to accuse someone without proof. I learned my lesson! That's right, I didn't say anything about that time when I woke up and realized my sheets were pulled back, because all I saw was my uncle leaving my room as he quietly closed the door. I think he touched me, but then again I might have dreamt that, and I certainly didn't have any kind of proof of anything. But then there was that last morning, just before he left. He touched me that morning, all right. The first thing I remember is I was having a dream that I was roller-skating and suddenly slipped backwards, and then I realized that my uncle was lying beside me in bed. Before I had fully come to, he put one of his hands over my mouth. I was so scared! He seemed to be in a hurry. At first, I didn't know what he was trying to do – he seemed awfully intent on something – but then… – it's too horrible to describe – he… raped me. It hurt. I was terrified and mortified, and wanted nothing else than for it to stop. One thing I couldn't understand is why he wouldn't stop, even though he knew he was hurting me. He had never physically injured me before. I think it lasted a couple minutes – the whole time I was desperate for it to stop. I was completely mute, but he seemed worried that I was going to scream; his hand over my mouth got tighter and tighter. When he was done, he seemed pretty panicked; he told me not to tell anyone and that he had to go right away. I buried my head under my pillow, and he left me like that. I was in shock. I don't know how long it was before I stumbled into my bathroom. I stood there for a few minutes, leaning on the countertop and looking into the mirror at myself – at first in silence and then I cried. Then I got dressed, and went out to tell my parents that he had hurt me. They asked me how, and I was too embarrassed to say. They started getting a little agitated, and I finally blurted out that he hurt me in my private parts. My parents didn't really seem to believe me, and I was too ashamed to show even my mom any kind of proof. It was only later that day, when the doctor said something had happened, that they finally believed it. I learned a lot of things that day, not the least of which is you never know when you're going to be hurt by someone familiar to you and who has never hurt you that way before.*

~

This woman needs love, and needs it now…

~

The four – no five – people I describe earlier in this chapter before her: They all need love, and they all need it now. Yes, we all have our stories that we could place alongside theirs. We're all in the same boat. We all need to be loved, and I have yet to meet anyone who would not be helped by more love in their life.

We will revisit our six new friends shortly. In the meantime, it's important to emphasize that anyone who experiences escalating sexual harassment, rape, or any other trauma should seek professional help to provide Godspeed on their road to recovery. Trauma should not be taken lightly. Do not expect its influence to simply fade away with time. See the "What if you have experienced trauma?" section (Chapter 9) for more on this topic.

Repaving our path

So, now comes the tricky part. How do we receive more love in our life? By now you should know that this is kind of a trick question. For one thing, it's impossible to make any specific person love us, and what's more we shouldn't try. You already know my stance on trying to change our personality – (if indeed that is even possible) – or anything else about ourselves with the express purpose of trying to make any specific person happy / like us better / love us: That is absolutely not allowed! No exceptions! I'm a stickler on this… Why? Two reasons: (i) Anyone who loves us unconditionally would never set such a condition on their love for us, and (ii) we should never change for anyone who does not love us unconditionally. That brings us full circle! Are you with me?

In light of such an edict, how does someone come up from such depths of feeling unloved and even unlovable? If you're reading the chapters of this book in sequence, then you already know an important part of the answer: Despite any negative feelings we struggle with or dark experiences we've had, not only are we lovable, we are already loved unconditionally; even if no one else loves us this way, God does. This is a life-changing message, but I submit to you that even this is not enough for us to feel whole. There still is an empty space in our heart, if we are not being loved by other people.

Don't believe me? God's design is for every infant to be loved by their mother and father, or under some circumstances by only one of them or by some other loving adult(s). If a child grows up without receiving such love, not only is that a travesty of a childhood but also how will they understand God's love? Being a parent or guardian is an awesome responsibility, but this responsibility is fully met if we are a loving parent or guardian. How important does God think this responsibility is? To answer this, we need look no further than to Jesus' birth and childhood. He came down to this earth as an infant, and while I'm sure that Jesus could have somehow grown up OK on His own, His Father in heaven had better plans and provided Him with a loving mother and father down here.

Yes, parents loving a child is an example of another important part of the answer to my question (repeated again here): How does someone come up from such depths of feeling unloved and even unlovable? God places in our life people who should give us love. First, it's our parents or guardians. Then, it's other family members and friends. Yes, even those of us who will never be a parent or guardian have an awesome responsibility, and that is to love those whom God places in our life. If you're reading the chapters of this book in sequence, then you do *not* yet know all my thoughts – *(I guarantee you – you don't!)* – on the subject of how we can show love to others. *It's coming soon! You're almost there!* One thing I'll say now on the subject is that God wants to use you to help others come up from feeling unloved. By loving others, you are giving them such an amazing gift! Such a blessing!

But what if *we* are the ones feeling unloved? Is there anything *we* can do? I know that I don't need to remind you about my edict. … Right? … *Oh, come on! It's just a few paragraphs up!* … All right, I'll wait for you to catch up. … … OK, now that you remember that, there are a few things we can change about the way we *interact* with others that you may find helpful on your journey of experiencing more love in your life. Here's a little warning: I'm going to ask you to take some risks. I never said there would be no risks! And I'm going to say some things that might offend you. I never said I would hold back on what I say because I might offend you!

- Don't assume the worst about others. Just because some others hurt you in the past doesn't mean that everyone will. There are many upright, honorable, and trustworthy people. To assume that someone you don't know is not upright, honorable, and trustworthy is not being loving to them. You are judging them – already a no-no – and doing so without all the facts.
    - I understand that we need to be careful. There is evil in the world, and unfortunately some people, some even familiar to us…, do want to hurt us. Be aware of your surroundings, and the circumstances. I said don't *assume* the worst about others. If you have good reason to be suspicious, then you must take that into account. It's a balance; don't swing too far either way, and keep an open mind. Ultimately, it's more damaging to live in fear and assume the worst about everyone than it is to keep an open mind.
- When you find someone to be trustworthy – *(Be careful – this condition must be met!)* – take another step and make yourself vulnerable – open up – to them. I know this can be scary. If you don't know them particularly well, then make this a small step. A simple example of making yourself vulnerable in a small way is to tell your counterpart that you visited your grandmother over the weekend (and it's probably a good idea to ask your counterpart what they did). An example of a slightly larger step is to tell them that your

grandmother has not been feeling well lately, and you're starting to become concerned. An example of a still larger step is to say that when you were a girl, your grandmother would brush your hair while you would read a book to her, but you recently learned that she doesn't remember this anymore, and that made you cry. To whatever depth we feel comfortable going, making ourselves vulnerable is a way to let our counterpart know we trust them, and that's an expression of love. More importantly for the discussion in *this* chapter, you're also giving them a good opportunity to love you back. If they take this opportunity, then you're on your way to making a friend. Keep in mind that their expression of love for you may be as simple as listening attentively and showing some measure of concern / caring. Give it a try, and see who responds in a nonjudgmental and loving way. Gravitate toward such people. They are loving you! Don't miss it or take it for granted. Make yourself a little more vulnerable to such people, and see how far you can go!

- Tell your spouse and/or your close friends your needs in the relationship. None of us are mind-readers. (Believe me… I've tried the silent treatment, and it doesn't work… When we expect our counterpart to read our mind, both of us are in for a heaping plateful of disappointment and frustration.) We all have needs, and it's natural that we'll begin to feel unloved if more and more of these needs are not being met. So, instead of sulking – (I already told you, that doesn't work; I'm an expert on this topic) – it's best for our relationship for both of us to make our needs clear. It's totally natural for us to tell our spouse or close friend (and for them to tell us): *I'm upset, and need to talk with you*; or, *I'm depressed, and I don't understand why – I'm hoping you can help me come out of this*; or, *I'm apprehensive about something, and I'd like your support*; or, *I'm overwhelmed, and need a break*; or, *I'm sad, and need some compassion*; or, *I'm happy, and want to share something exciting with you*. In a marriage, from time to time it's natural for us to go further and tell our spouse (and for them to tell us), using body language, and words if needed: *I desire you, and would like to make love. If right now is not a good time, is this evening OK for you?* or, *That feels wonderful, and, if you don't mind, like this would be even better*.
- If you're spending time gazing at your navel – feeling sorry for yourself, stuck in the labyrinth of blaming others for all your problems – look up and think of others first. Give some form of love to others. This on its own should

help you feel better. And chances are that at least a little bit of love will come back. You may need to be patient, and it may not be as much as you give, but love does have a way of growing on itself – the momentum builds. It may not even come from the same people you're showing love to, but when we stop gazing at our navel we're more open to receive love from anyone. Maybe there's someone trying to give you love now, and you're not even aware of it.

    o   On the topic of not gazing at our navel, please refer back to my "week of true love" in the Prologue – and note especially that the "deluge of love started with me reaching out to a friend"

- Avoid the common temptation to isolate yourself from others: physically, emotionally, or spiritually. All of these can be addressed by finding a church that expresses a loving attitude (not all do – don't get me started…), and once found: attend regularly, get involved, get to know people, and put the above pointers into practice!

- Ask people to pray for you or for someone you know (family member, friend, classmate, coworker). The act of praying is an expression of love – the prayers are showing that they care about you. And oftentimes they will follow up, to ask you how it's going – another expression of love. If you're a little hesitant to ask individuals to pray for you, you might find it easier to make your request known to a prayer group or "prayer chain." Most churches have something like this. (If yours doesn't, ask them to start one!)

Yes, being loved by others is a fundamental need, and if that need isn't met there's an empty space in our heart. If you feel such an emptiness, I'm sorry, and I ask you to try such approaches as listed above. While we can't make any specific person love us, and shouldn't try, there are things that can be done to help us feel more loved overall. Surround yourself with loving people, distance yourself from hurtful people (Appendix Ↄ), stop brooding over your past, and ask God to help you transition to a more positive future.

Six rising paths

Oh, if only it was always as simple as I just described! When we feel unloved, it means that we've been hurt in the past. In turn, this means that it's not always easy to make such changes. How can we not assume the worst about people? How can we trust people and open up to them? How can we think of others first?

Sometimes the damage is so severe that these changes are simply not possible for us. Things that are easy and second nature to some of us, to others of us are impossible. But I should say impossible *on our own* – without help from others. Yes, we are to "Bear one another's burdens" (Galatians 6:2). When we find someone who has been beaten down to the point of feeling unloved, and maybe even unlovable, let us be moved to help them with their burden. ... Is there anything sadder than knowing that another feels unloved? Is there anything more joyous than giving love to such a person?

It truly is a joy to love others, and we're almost to the part of this book where I finally get into that, and not in a small way! But before we go there, let's revisit our six friends from earlier in this chapter. Let me take you places where such people can go, with God's help. I apologize if these transformations seem a little "too easy," but such changes are indeed possible if we all look out for one another. And I do think it's best to remain optimistic no matter how dire the circumstances seem to be. So, without further ado, let's take a peek into our friends' prayer journals / diaries – *(How's yours going?)* – for six prayer-testimonies of thankfulness, based on such an optimistic viewpoint.

- *God, I'm so thankful for Your love – words cannot express, but I'll try! ... You did it again! You knew I wanted to make a friend – a close friend who wants to spend a lot of time with me and get to know me well – and now I have one. I feel so much better. There's nothing I can't tell her. We talk about everything. You know that I so much wanted someone who would listen to me, but I've come to realize how much I enjoy listening to her too. She often says how much she appreciates being able to confide in me. I'm so happy to have such a good friend!*

- *God, thank You for the changes I'm starting to see in my husband and in our relationship. The first few times I told him how I feel when he says mean things to me, he got mad and I felt ashamed for bringing it up. But You gave me the strength to come out of that and say it again when there was another opportunity. Lord knows I had lots of opportunities! ... Looking back on it, the biggest change in him came when I told him that I couldn't take it anymore and I was going to go to my parents' house the next time. That's when he finally agreed to come with me to counseling. I explained that I had to talk to someone. I said I'd go by myself, if he wouldn't come with me. God, thank You for giving me the courage to be more assertive. You know I struggle with that. It still feels a little weird to me – to tell people what I want – but I'm finding it easier as time goes on and as I do it more.*

- *God, I'd like to say thank You for the changes that I've felt in my life over the last few months. I think it started when Pastor – he's not such a bad guy after all – started that Bible study for young adults. At first, I went because I wanted to showcase my Bible knowledge. But I've learned so much from others. Where do I begin? I guess the thing that has struck me the most is how much others are struggling with sin in their life. We usually don't get too deep into the specifics, but I can tell that others have the same kinds of failings that I do. And I thought I was so different. And we don't only talk about struggling with sin; we also talk about how You forgive, and how we are to forgive each other, and sometimes we even talk about forgiving ourselves… I used to think that I had to stop a sin in order to really be forgiven for it. Now I know that God keeps forgiving – completely – over and over, and we are to do the same. I've started to make some friends and, yes, one of them is a girl. And I think she likes me! Does she? ;o) Well, anyway, I like her a lot, and the only thing I feel bad about is sometimes I think about her in lewd, boorish ways that I know are inappropriate. I'm sorry. Please help me have more respectful thoughts about her, in line with a more God-pleasing desire – and in this and other ways be a better friend to her – and, finally, thank You for forgiving me. Again!*

- *God, there's no one at all like You – that's for sure! Who but You could have changed my life like this? And I'm so relieved that I didn't have to join a fantasy football club, start drinking beer (Yuck!), and wear ridiculous scratchy socks! The girls in Sales are still laughing amongst themselves – (So immature!) – but I don't care about any of that anymore. You know that I've taken a shine to the woman in Accounting – (the ONLY woman in Accounting!) – who for some reason I had never really noticed before the monster truck rally. She really DID roll her eyes at me – after I said that I was surprised there was anyone from work besides me who liked to spend their Saturday evenings this way. For a moment, I felt three inches tall. But instead of turning to her friends and laughing, she introduced me to her younger sister and brother, and explained that she was helping them live their lifelong dream of being sprayed with mud from the rear tires of a grossly oversized minivan. I joked that that was my dream too, and ever since then we've been spending more and more time together. We're still just friends, but who knows? I've never met anyone like her. I think about her all the time... Every time I see her, she seems to perk up, and she flashes that amazing smile and of course that means there's also that little laugh that makes my heart melt. I have an extra ticket to the ice capades this Sunday afternoon, and I'm trying to muster up the courage to ask her to come with me. I'm thinking to hide the ticket under a cinnamon bun, and she'll discover the ticket while she's eating. She liked that the last time I did it – a ticket to the roller derby under a blueberry muffin – even though I learned that she hates blueberries... and roller derbies... Yes, I'm doing it!*

• *God, thank You so much for helping me turn my life around. It took several years, but when I look back I can see such a difference. I have so much more energy, and a more positive outlook on life. My doctor says I'm in great shape. And it actually has been fun! I really enjoy my exercise classes; I'm so glad that I added yoga – I've met lots of good friends there. And on the weekends, I like to squeeze in at least one jog on the beach. Some of my friends and I enjoy biking together. Next weekend, we're biking 30 miles up the coast! I couldn't have made it three miles five years ago. I remember how out of shape I was, and how bad I felt about my body. Now, I'm comfortable with my full figure; it suits me, and serves me well. I used to stare at myself in the mirror every day. Now, sometimes I forget to look long enough to brush my hair, and I show up at work looking like a French Poodle! God, really, thank You for helping me feel better about myself, physically and emotionally. There were times when I thought no one really liked me. Thank You for the friends I've made recently, as well as the old ones I've reconnected with – they were wondering how I was doing... And You know there were times when I thought no man would ever want to be with me. Now I've learned to set aside my fear of rejection and live for myself. I learned this at my counseling sessions. You know that I started going because I wanted to figure out how to change myself in order to attract a partner, but I learned that all I really needed to work on was my self-esteem, and that I'm already a beautiful woman, outside and in. And I've noticed that more than a few guys agree with my new outlook in this area. Like the new hire in the Patents department at work – I find him quite attractive, and it didn't take long for it to be obvious that the feeling is mutual. After a few weeks of playful flirtations, he finally asked me out. But by then I had noticed that he often doesn't treat the women in his department very respectfully, so I respectfully declined. And during last month's bike ride with some of my friends, we stopped at that frozen yogurt stand – You know, the one at the end of the pier – and it was hard not to notice that guy in an undersized tank top, displaying more than a few muscles and looking around to see who was taking heed. So sophomoric… Then I caught him checking out my new biker shorts and everything else in that general vicinity, and I thought to myself: Well, at least he has good taste. Naturally, I couldn't help but give him a nice view as I climbed back onto my bike; and I thought to myself as I rode off: In your dreams, buddy.*

• *God, thank You for helping me begin to trust people again. It took a lot of time and therapy for me to learn that there are some people who can be trusted. Thank You for putting such people in my life! One thing that happened – it's a little embarrassing – that helped me see who these people are was at last summer's company picnic, well actually after the picnic. When I got home, I realized that I had forgotten to fasten a couple buttons on my blouse, so kind of a lot was showing… My first thought was that I must have done that toward the end, but – no – I knew I hadn't done anything with my buttons the whole time. Hmm… I couldn't understand it – all those guys there, and not one of them gave me that funny look. They didn't leer at me! I'm usually so careful not to show much of myself, but this time I had slipped up. Well, but this has helped me see that these men are different. I know this may seem like a small example, but it made me feel respected. I like that. And I began to notice other things. For example, one time in the lunchroom one of the guys was getting something out of the refrigerator when he accidentally brushed up against my – well, You know – my pants…; he stepped back, looked me right in the eyes, and said he was sorry. I liked that. I smiled and laughed, as usual, and started to walk away, as usual, but then I turned around and told him that I understood it was an accident. And then there was the time when that VP sent that email to the group – the whole group! – saying that I had missed the deadline for getting those invoices to our biggest client. I made a beeline to my boss and told him that the VP was wrong – I had sent them on time, and I was going to dig up the time-stamped copies to prove it. But he said I didn't need to bother to dig those up. He believed me! I really liked that! And he went straight to the VP to give him a piece of his mind! (I must admit I was a little embarrassed by that.) Anyway, maybe the biggest thing relates to the older guy I have to work with on the budget every quarter. He reminds me of my uncle… not just the way he looks but even some of his mannerisms… At first, I was revolted by my coworker and often experienced a trauma trigger when seeing him; so, I did everything I could to avoid him as much as humanly possible. And that made it even more surprising when – after I got back from my trip to Grandmother's funeral – there was a card on my desk, and it was from him… Inside it says that he's sorry for my loss and that he wants me to take comfort in knowing that she's in heaven. (When I told him the reason for my trip, he asked me if she was a Christian. I thought that was a little forward at the time.) I now look at him differently. He actually seems to care about me… I like that. And I'm realizing that when people ask me other questions, like what I'm doing over the weekend, those really aren't too personal after all. Like yesterday, instead of just laughing and smiling and making something up, I was bold and said that I don't have any plans at all. So, the next thing I knew I was invited to the zoo; this afternoon a group of us are meeting there to spend some time together. I think I'm going to like that.*

~

Such changes are indeed possible if we love the people God places in our life. We may not know their full backstories – actually, we usually don't know the half of it – but love always brightens the way, no matter how dark the path behind has been.

~   ~   ~

After-hours

Bob unplugged

Sometimes in life, we may come to the conclusion that we aren't particularly lovable because we haven't done anything that may be considered outstanding or impressive.

- But remember those who have loved and encouraged you at any time in your life. Think about this person / these people for "one silent minute."[1]
  - ○   …
  - ○   Now answer this: Did this person / these people care for you because of something outstanding or impressive that you did?
- Especially if there's any doubt in your mind about the answer to the above question, please spend at least one more silent minute contemplating another quote of Fred Rogers, someone who knew more than a thing or two about unconditional love: "You don't ever have to do anything sensational for people to love you"[1]
  - ○   …
- Now that that's settled, please change one word in the above quote. (I know Mister Rogers would be OK with this…) Change "people" to "God." That's it – that's the only word to change. Think about that for at least one more silent minute.
  - ○   …

Step up to the microphone

One theme of this book is that we often don't know people's backstories, and we shouldn't judge based on appearances. For example, the full backstory of the woman who had been raped as a child is not known by most people in her life, and we shouldn't be quick to judge Nahum's awkward behavior (first-person narrative toward the end of Chapter 4).

Think about the people in your life. Consider that (with rare exception) you don't know their full backstory, and there may be something about their history, largely or completely beyond their control, that for whatever reasons has led to their current behavior rubbing you the wrong way.

- Think of specific counterpart(s) who rub you the wrong way – anywhere from the mild abrasion of an odd quirk to the deep excoriation of willful, destructive sin – and consider this: If you were to learn that there's something about their backstory that's directly related to their current behavior, would your feelings toward them change?
- When should we give our counterpart the benefit of the doubt? When should we not?

In light of the numerous modes of communication now available to us, and the plethora of online social networks at our disposal, do you think loneliness is becoming less or more common?

Consider your counterparts. Are there circumstances where our modern devices and networking options are helping them or us feel *less* lonely? Are there circumstances where they or we are feeling *more* lonely now than before?

In one of the prayer-testimonies, the pray-er admits that she knows she should exercise, but she's worried about what she'll wear. Imagine that she's a friend of yours, and she's asking for your support. Further imagine that you just happen to exercise daily at a gym not far from where our friend lives, and you've agreed to meet her at the gym to help her get assimilated into an exercise regimen. You don't need to use any more of your imagination to know that you are in remarkably great shape – I already told you that you exercise daily.

That's all well and good, and here's my question for you: What will you wear when you go with our friend to the gym? (Recall that I advised that our out-of-shape friend wear "whatever it takes.") … While you're obviously free to wear whatever you want, if you're looking for some advice, I'd like to remind you to consider our friend's feelings. I'm not going to go so far as to say that you should wear nothing other than a replica of whatever it takes for our friend. However, in such situations, my recommendation is to lean toward something that dials-down the contrast between you and our friend, at least until our friend forms their new habit.

- Do you agree or disagree with my advice?
- If you generally agree, can you think of exceptions?

For parents: Remind each of your children that there's nothing they can't tell you. Tell them that if they ever have any question about the appropriateness of anything anyone does to them or says to them, or to anyone else, they should ask you or, if you're not available, another responsible adult. When a child talks to you, listen attentively and take them seriously – even if you don't want to believe what they're telling you... Ask follow-up questions to keep the dialogue going.

For intimate couples: This *should* be a very easy homework assignment for you, but some people find it difficult to express everything that's in their heart. ... I'd like both of you, in turn, to look your partner in the eyes and tell them that you love them. You have to use their name (I will accept pet names) and the L-word. There is no synonym that can satisfactorily replace it. And if I hear the phrase "love you too," I am giving you an F.

Chapter 6 – Unconditional Love Between People

The previous chapter ends with the stories of six people, each of whom is beginning to experience more love in their life. These influxes of love may seem small, but that's the wrong way to look at it. There's no such thing as a small bit of love. Love is always on a grand scale. Oh, sure, it can grow and grow without bounds from whence it begins, but even the first hint of love cannot be contained – we are drenched from head to toe.

This is helpful to remember when we're contemplating how to give our best loving to our counterpart. If you ever find yourself thinking that some gift of love that you're considering to give is too small to have an impact, I'd like you to go surfing. That's right, wax down your surfboard and get out there! If you're a newbie, let me fill you in on what surfers spend an inordinate amount of time doing. We spend an awful lot of time waiting. What are we waiting for? … We're waiting for a wave that will drench us from head to toe. From whence come such waves? … They come from a faint breeze – a gentle breath of wind. No hurricanes needed! A soft whisper is enough to immerse us completely.

Keep this in mind as you form your new habit. Yes, I'd like you to stop ruminating about how to give love, and just give it! When you're an old, leathery surfer dude like me, you've waited long enough for the perfect wave. I learned long ago that in this life there are no perfect waves – just a wondrous cavalcade of delicate sighs that sustain recurring percussions that can only be described as sweet submersion.

When we stop philosophizing (synonym for ruminating), stop rehearsing (synonym for procrastinating), and just go ahead and give our counterpart our soft whisper of love, we find that it's especially fun when we catch them off guard. … The look on their face when their peaceful day at the beach – strolling carefree, barely knee-deep in the calm water – is abruptly disrupted by an epic wave toppling them head-over-heels into the swirling foam!

Now, it's hard to surprise our counterpart when they're lying on their surfboard, waiting and waiting. Loving our counterpart when they're anticipating it is the topic of Chapter 7, because that's where we talk about conditional love relationships. Conditional love can give us some sweet rides on bodacious waves, but there's nothing quite like sweeping our unsuspecting counterpart off their feet with unconditional love.

How do we surprise our counterpart in this way? Well, first of all, we need to meet them at the beach. Meeting them at the beach is very simple – it means we've discovered that they're in our life. That's pretty easy. The next step is to choose our timing carefully – give our soft whisper at just the right time. ... *How do we know when it's just the right time?* ... That's a good question, and here's my good answer: *Just the right time is precisely when they least expect it!* That's pretty easy too. When we give unconditional love to our counterpart, including one with whom we have a conditional love relationship, maximum impact is achieved when they are unsuspecting* – blithely unaware that our tsunami of unconditional love is approaching.

> *Note: In interpersonal relationships, my view is that we generally should not "expect" to receive unconditional love, and that's because our counterpart is (like us) a fallible human being. Fallible human beings sometimes disappoint; for example, our counterpart may choose not to love us unconditionally. So, whenever we *do* receive unconditional love, we should *always* be refreshed and delighted that our counterpart has chosen, in the face of all our flaws, to give us their unexpected soft whisper. We should never take unconditional love for granted.
>
> - An exception for most – (I wish I could write "all" here…) – of us is the unconditional love we receive from our mother when we are a fetus and an infant. We all experience a startling tsunami of unconditional love from our mother that begins at our conception. For the vast majority of us, this continues in an unwavering fashion through birth and its immediate aftermath. Then, most of us can rest assured that our mother's towering waves will continue to crash down on us as we think of nothing else than playing in the wet sand. After all, it does take a long time to learn how to surf. Until we learn, we should expect to receive unconditional love from our mother and other loving caregivers. (Mothers and other caregivers: Don't let us down!)
> - Another, similar, exception is if we are disabled and are fortunate to have at least one loving caregiver. Surfing does require good balance, and I understand that sometimes this is just not possible for us.

> If this is the situation we find ourselves in, we should expect to re-
> ceive unconditional love from our loving caregiver(s). (Loving care-
> givers: I know this is not always easy… Thank you for your persist-
> ent love.)

- So far, this note pertains to interpersonal relationships. Standing in
  stark contrast is the unconditional love we receive from God, who
  never disappoints. Without exception, we should all always (until the
  time of God's judgment) expect to be continuously pummeled by
  His unconditional love – unable to escape His "gentle whisper" (1
  Kings 19:12 NIV). … But do we ever take it for granted?

I'm an expert on the element of surprise when it comes to soft whispers. I
have vast experience as a stealth lover. What's my secret? My secret is that over
the years I've become extremely sensitive to the signs of being unconditionally
loved. … And every time, I am astonished. … In the Prologue, I play the violin
a bit, opening up to you that there was a time when I doubted whether I am
unconditionally loved by people in my life. Since then, I've become more and
more aware that of course I am. … *How do I know?* … I know because I've been
drenched! So, since that time I've simply been mimicking my sneaky counterparts – mainly by surprising *other* counterparts – and now I'm an expert too.
What's the secret handshake? What's the code word? It's remarkably simple:

- We love our counterpart just the way they are – not how we wish they were.
  We love them "as is," excrescences and all. We remind them that they are
  inherently valuable – they have nothing to prove.
  o   This is a startling dunking of staggering proportions!
- We love our counterpart for no particular reason (other than their benefit, for
  example, addressing one of their needs) – not as an act of reciprocation or
  because we are expecting something in return. We love them just because.
  o   This is a thunderous crash of cold, cold water!

As we begin to explore such surprising love in greater depth, let me start by
considering our love for no one in particular…

Loving our representative person

When I was younger, I'd sometimes ask myself: *Is it possible to love someone we don't know?* Early on, in ignorance, I actually was leaning toward *No.* However, as I thought about it more, I realized that there are cases where we absolutely do love people unbeknownst to us. One early case I considered was the love a mother has for her developing child during pregnancy. However, I concluded that this isn't a good example because I consider her developing child to be a person – *(This is certainly true! About this, there is no debate!)* – whom the mother *already knows*. I cannot claim that *I* would know my counterpart in an analogous situation (which is science fiction, to be sure). I don't have the heart of a mother. But a mother knows…

So, I set that example aside. But I did think of some other examples: Maybe we are a teacher who doesn't know all our students (due to a very large class size, or perhaps it's a web-based format). Maybe we help develop a drug that benefits patients we never meet. Maybe we are a public servant who doesn't know everyone in our jurisdiction. Maybe we are preaching on *The Lutheran Hour*, in which case we obviously don't know everyone listening to our radio broadcast. Maybe we hear about an emergency or tragedy on the news, and we pray for those directly impacted. Maybe we financially support mission work that saves lost souls on the other side of the world, or the other side of town.

Is this love? Didn't I say that the apex of love – ecstatic love – is intimate, which means two, and only two? *Yes, I did say that* (Chapter 1 – "Semantics 101, Fall Semester" section). *Thank you for remembering.* Not only are the examples in the previous paragraph expressions of love, but they are bona fide expressions of *intimate* love when we see our recipients as they truly are – precious individuals – not as a mass of fuzzy faces. But how do we do this, since we don't know them?

As I begin to answer this, let's consider the perspective of a more profound example of loving people unbeknownst to us – an act of heroism where the hero doesn't know at least some of the people she or he is helping. How does the hero do this? I'm no hero, and if I ever am one, it would only be due to God working through me. Furthermore, my willingness to love in this special way would only be made possible by the love I've already experienced in my life. If I had never experienced love, what would motivate me to act altruistically?

~

I'd like to take a moment to thank every loving counterpart of a hero. You played an important role in your friend's or loved one's heroic act. She or he was motivated to give love to others based on knowing what it means to receive love. Thank you for giving love to your friend or loved one. They were remembering this when they were heroically serving others.

~

The preceding paragraph illustrates that we're motivated to love people we don't know by the love we share with our counterparts – every one of them. In Chapter 8, "Love is … kind" section, I briefly describe how the love I've shared with each of my counterparts has helped me write this book. Everything I've experienced with them has taught me what it means to be loving, and what it means to be unloving. If it weren't for them – every one of them – I wouldn't have been able to write this book the way that I have. And I wrote it this way because, dear reader, I love you. I don't know you, and yet I love you.

How is it possible for me to do this? … It's a little hard to explain; I'll do my best. … If you're reading this particular paragraph, then I assume that you're reading most, if not all, of this book. If that is indeed the case, then I assume that you have an interest in this book's topic. If that is indeed the case, then I assume that you're aware of a need to experience more love in your life, whether that be love for yourself, love within relationships with other people, or, most importantly, love within a relationship with God. Whether your need is in only one of these areas, or all of them, I want to help you. But how can I help you? I don't know you! Sure, I could try to give general advice – do this, do that, don't do this, don't do that – but that's like throwing mud and hoping it sticks to your particular wall. Such mudslinging is not particularly motivating to me, which means that I'm not very effective at doing it. What is motivating to me is touching your heart with a specific image that really hits home for you – an illustration that resonates strongly. More than mud that sticks, I want it to be an arrow that penetrates. You already know that I loathe generalities and I adore specifics. Why is that? It's because generalities are muddy, splotchy, and not always sticky, while specifics are sharp, focused, and sometimes on the mark. I started this book with a large quiver stuffed with arrows; I'm shooting often, and aiming for you. Did I hit you with one of my examples, one of my prayers, one of my stories? Does one seem like I wrote it just for you? … It should, because I did. And that was easy because even though I don't know you, I know others who are just like you (having similar challenges, needs, hopes, etc.). When I close my eyes and think of you, I can see you. I can see you in the faces of my counterparts – every one of them – and you are the most beautiful creature I have ever seen. I love every one of them, and so it follows naturally that I love you.

And you love me too, if I've already hit you with one of my arrows. … *Thank you! (I'm blushing…)* … If you don't love me yet, there are many more arrows to come. Please be patient. And who knows? Perhaps, in time, you'll find that you have indeed fallen head-over-heels in love with me.

Above, I describe how it helps me to consider all my counterparts simultaneously. I refer to such a conglomerate as my "representative person." They are a very flexible person, to be sure. When I want to write about someone hurt by infidelity, I close my eyes and my representative person's spouse or boyfriend / girlfriend has cheated on them. When I want to write about someone who has been unfaithful, I close my eyes and my representative person has made an awful mistake. When I want to write about someone who is being abused, I close my eyes and my representative person's innocence and/or vulnerability is being taken terrible advantage of by someone they trusted. When I want to write about someone who struggles with their own abusive behavior, I close my eyes and my representative person has low self-esteem and tries to compensate by controlling and demeaning others. When I want to write about someone struggling to forgive, I close my eyes and my representative person has been hurt very deeply and needs time to process how to proceed. And so it goes.

I told you that they are just like you.

~

How does this relate to the topic of a hero? I already told you that I'm not a hero. So, it doesn't relate that way. How it does relate is that when a hero is faced with the decision to act or not to act, she or he closes their eyes (at least figuratively) and sees who they can help. Even if the hero doesn't know these people beforehand, even if they *never* meet, it doesn't matter – the hero sees them clearly in their mind. They are a conglomerate of all the loving counterparts the hero has ever known. There are people in need, thus the hero's representative person is in need. That is enough for the hero to choose to act in love.

This is intimate love between the hero and their representative person. The hero is not loving a mass of fuzzy faces. The hero is closing her or his eyes and making tender love to the most beautiful creature they have ever seen.

Humility

For some reason that I can't fathom, many people have difficulty with the concept of humility. While I can't fathom it, I do know that it's all because of egoism. When left to our own devices, we all drift toward egoism, which is when our values are based on self-interest. We become so wrapped up in ourselves that when a new concept enters our mind, the first thing we consider is: *How does this impact me?* And when that new concept involves us being humble, from the perspective of egoism the impact we see is that we are diminished – we feel lowered relative to others.

But there's a better way to look at the very same scenario. Have you ever been in a glass elevator that's near another one? I have, and I've even stumbled when mine wasn't moving at all… Why did I stumble? Because mine was still loading and the other elevator suddenly went up quickly; seeing that tricked my mind into thinking that my elevator was going down (and I stumbled because it happened at a time when I wasn't expecting movement). My mind told me that I was being lowered below the people in the nearby elevator – but my mind was playing tricks on me.

When we serve others, or in other ways express humility, it may seem like we're lowering ourselves. But that's not how we should look at it. Instead, we're flying at altitude and our humility is lifting others up. What's so diminishing about that? … *Nothing!* … There's nothing diminishing about humility, when viewed from the perspective that is contrary to egoism – and this is the perspective of altruism, which is when our values are based on the interests of others.

Consider a case where one provides the ultimate service to others – even others they don't know – sacrificing themselves as a true hero (previous section). This is an act of resplendent humility, and of course none of us would refer to this as diminishing to the hero, or anyone else for that matter. No, the hero was flying at altitude – a truly breathtaking altitude (oxygen masks required!) – when she or he was buoying others up to magnificent heights.

Opportunities for such dazzling humility don't present themselves to us every day. In the meantime, let's strengthen our humility skills in down-to-earth ways such as these, that I'd like you to complete – *I'm serious* – over the next twelve months.

- Tell each of your counterparts at least three strengths that you see in them
  - When someone tells you about a strength they see in you, thank them for their feedback, and tell them you'll look for more opportunities to use this strength to serve others
- Unless you never collaborate with them in any fashion (very rare), tell each of your counterparts at least one way that the group (team, family, etc.) is stronger because of their involvement
  - When someone tells you how you make the group stronger, thank them and tell them you're happy that you're able to contribute in this way
- When you find that someone has a specific type of personal need (for example, they just learned that they have ovarian cancer and they're scared), or there is a particular nonpersonal problem that needs to be addressed, identify who is most capable to help in this situation, and ask them to help. Don't be mysterious; tell them specifically why you're asking them.
  - When someone asks you to help in a specific way, because you're just right for the situation, thank them for asking you and tell them you'll be happy to do it again if a similar situation occurs in the future
- Look for opportunities to praise others for something they've done well and … *(This isn't rocket science, people)* … go ahead and praise them! Be specific!
  - When someone praises you for something, thank them and tell them you're glad that they were positively impacted; and praise God!
- Look for opportunities to encourage others who are facing a challenge, whether this be a long-term struggle or simply a bad day. Tell them that they're special, and that you're praying for them – lifting them up to the throne of God.
  - When someone encourages you, thank them and tell them they've just made your day!

Nothing here diminishes us – nothing here is self-deprecating. Everything here lifts others up and, if truth be told, in the updraft we're lifted up – at least a little bit – ourselves. And what's wrong with that? … *There's nothing wrong with that!* It's completely natural that our heart is buoyed by lifting others up in true humility. This is not selfishness. This is not egoism. This is not our mind or heart playing tricks on us. This is simply what it feels like to live in love.

Empathy

I just told you that it's natural to be buoyed ourselves when we lift others up in true humility. Does this surprise you? It shouldn't when you consider that to live in love we are to be empathetic with our counterparts. When we're empathetic, at least when we throw our heart and soul into it, we experience at least some small measure of what they're feeling. So, of course we should be buoyed when we lift up our counterparts!

If I've lost you, let me explain immediately what empathy is. In its simplest form, empathy means understanding / appreciating / acknowledging / considering another person's feelings or perspective, and it does *not* include that we necessarily agree with them. The topic of empathy may seem complex because of the following points that you may have encountered somewhere along the way.

- You may have heard that empathy includes yourself literally experiencing a large measure of another person's specific emotions (although, again, not necessarily agreeing with their reasons for feeling this way)
  - o Sometimes this is the case, and I refer to such experiences as "hardcore empathy." However, you certainly don't need to be hardcore (i.e., you don't need to be a so-called "empath") to show empathy to another person…
- You may think that empathy means essentially the same thing as compassion and the most common definition of sympathy
  - o The latter two are familiar terms that generally refer to a feeling of sorrow / concern about another person's hardship. Empathy encompasses this, but is a much broader concept because empathy is not only useful when interacting with someone who's feeling down. Empathy also helps us resolve conflicts, and it further strengthens bonds when we're feeling up.

- Some marshmallowy descriptions of empathy stray beyond the simple rendering that I've provided above by adding that our being empathetic requires that we have actually experienced what the other person is experiencing, or at least something pretty close to it
  - I don't agree that this is a requirement. My view is that having such a background makes empathy *easier* to achieve and to a *deeper* level. For example, someone who has experienced the suicide of a family member will generally be able to empathize more profoundly with another who is going through this heartache, than will someone who has not known this grief.
    - Be that as it may, I don't ever want to hear any of you use lack of specific experience as an excuse not to be empathetic. This is a cop-out to the ultimate degree!

Why should we be empathetic? Is it so we get a boost when we humbly lift someone else up, as I describe in the preceding section? That is a good reason, but there are at least two better reasons.

- Empathy is a trusty advocate when we encounter someone with whom we disagree or don't have much in common. Empathy reminds us to think twice and consider why our counterpart has their point of view, and that we almost certainly have more in common than our first impression tries to convince us. How do we better understand their point of view? How do we discover common ground? … *Anyone?* … OK, you there, with the black lipstick. What do you think? … … Uh, no… we don't dust off our ouija board and seek messages from the great beyond. … Anyone else have a better idea? … From the dazed looks on your faces and the notable increase in fidgeting, I can tell that you're overthinking this. Empathy is not all about interpreting facial expressions and other subtle clues. *The best way to understand someone's point of view is to ask them to explain it to you. The best way to find common ground is to have a conversation.* One of the best ways that we can empathize with someone is to make use of our communication skills, not the least of which is active listening. Did you know that you can have an engaging conversation without saying very much? Sometimes our counterpart has a lot that they want to get off their chest, and a powerful way to empathize in such a situation is to listen to them. And by listen, I don't mean sit there with all the expression of a fossilized horseshoe crab and with an attention span that conjures up images of a cnidarian drifting to and fro with the current. I mean listen actively; in other words, do the opposite of our sleepy friend here who I moved to the front row on the first day of class. Active listening means that we don't allow ourselves to become distracted with our smartphone or similar gadgets, but instead give our undivided attention, maintaining good eye contact and showing interest in such ways as occasionally nodding our head and saying "uh huh" or similar, and better yet paraphrasing to make sure we're on track. By clearly demonstrating our engagement in the conversation, we're showing our counterpart that we care about them and want to understand their point of view. We may not agree with their point of view, but understanding it is one step closer to resolving a conflict (if there is one) and locating the common ground that surely is there, waiting to be discovered.

- o   What do we do if we find ourselves in a conflict and our counterpart isn't being empathetic toward us? The first thing to try is to initiate empathetic behavior ourselves, and our counterpart usually will follow suit. If they don't, then we should get a third party involved, for example a mutual friend, a coworker, our pastor, another church-worker, a social worker, or a professional counselor.

- In this section, my points are moving from least to most important. When considering why we should be empathetic, I started with the good reason that it gives us a boost when we humbly lift someone else up. I then moved on to the better reason that it helps us discover common ground with our counterpart, and reach resolution when there's a conflict. Now, let's consider the best reason to be empathetic.

The best reason is that – when we submit to the Holy Spirit – empathetic behavior points others to Jesus. How does it do this? Please allow me to elaborate. When we believe that Jesus is our Savior, we find ourselves on a journey called sanctification. Throughout this journey, the Holy Spirit leads us to become more and more Christlike. What is the purpose of this? Is it for our own personal benefit? There may be something to this, but my view is that the larger benefit is for others who are observing our behavior. When they see more and more of us being "little Christs" – *They're everywhere!* – others will be more likely to think to themselves: *I get it.*

What are behaviors that lead us to become more Christlike? In the Prologue, I state that Jesus is perfectly empathetic, perfectly selfless, and perfectly merciful, and in Chapter 2 I elaborate further on each of these three attributes of Jesus.

o   Can we be perfectly merciful? No, but as guided by the Holy Spirit, we take on more and more of a forgiving nature.

o   Can we be perfectly selfless? No, but as guided by the Holy Spirit, we delight more and more in humbly serving others – lifting them up!

o   Can we be perfectly empathetic? No, but as guided by the Holy Spirit, we seek to understand what others are going through to more and more depth.

When Jesus came to earth, He literally put Himself in our sandals. Why did He do that? Well, at least two reasons are to make the following clear to us.

o   He understands firsthand – to the deepest level – what we go through when we are tempted to sin. "Jesus was led up by the Spirit into the wilderness to be tempted by the devil" (Matthew 4:1). "[Jesus] himself has suffered when tempted" (Hebrews 2:18).

o   He understands firsthand – to the deepest level – what we *will* go through *if*, at the time of God's judgment of us, we reject Him as our Savior. On Good Friday, Jesus endured on the cross the punishment that we deserve – the full brunt of the Father's wrath because of sin, including complete separation from Him (Matthew 27:45-46; Psalm 22:1). He endured this, so we don't have to; all we need to do is trust in Him as our Savior.

Don't miss the important point that both of these ways in which Jesus perfectly empathizes with us relate to His suffering. He suffered when tempted and He suffered when He bore our sins on the cross.

Similarly, we should put ourselves in other people's shoes because our struggles help us relate to their struggles and, when we are a believer, this connection lends itself naturally to witnessing opportunities – opportunities to point them to Jesus. How does empathy do this? The details will vary for each of us, depending on our unique backgrounds and the individual counterparts we have the joy of sharing our life with, but below I give some general examples, all of which follow the template of (i) identifying with another person's feelings or perspective, (ii) stating a biblical truth, and (iii) providing some form of encouragement or offer to help. (Don't forget that lack of specific experience doesn't give us a pass from being empathetic. We all have sustained struggles of various kinds, and are adept enough to apply our experiences to our counterpart's current situation. We all have vivid imaginations, so why not put them to good use?)

○ Many of us who are believers have been tempted to minimize our sins; and a subset of us, in our past, have even pretended that our sins don't matter – that there are no consequences. So, when our counterpart's indifference to their sins becomes apparent to us, we know firsthand what they're going through. This enables us to tell them: *I know what it's like to think that my sins aren't that bad when compared to the sins of others. I can relate to the opinion that there's no downside to a life of sin. ... But there's a God who created us, and we will meet Him when we die – to give an account. He is not only a God of mercy – He is also a God of justice. Can't you see that someone needs to pay the full price for our sins? I remember what it felt like for these truths to sink in – deep down, sink in. And now I want you to know that you too are a sinner in dire need of forgiveness.*

○ Most of us who are believers know the awful weight of our own sin. So, when our counterpart is ashamed and distraught over their sin, we know firsthand what they're going through. This enables us to tell them: *I know what it's like to accept that I'm a sinner – totally unable to stand before God based on my own merits. I can relate to feelings of guilt and utter unworthiness. ... But our God is not only a God of justice – He is also a God of mercy. Jesus paid the full price for our sins, and we're forgiven because of His redeeming work. I remember what it felt like for these truths to sink in – deep down, sink in. And now I want you to know that you too have access to this flood of forgiveness.*

○ Most of us who are believers know the sting of being sinned against by someone we trusted. So, when our counterpart is hurt in this way by someone else in their life, we know firsthand what they're going through. This enables us to tell them: *I know what it's like to be severely disappointed and even mistreated. I can relate to the feelings of having been betrayed and even wanting to retaliate. ... But God forgives every one of our sins when we place our trust in Him, and He wants us to forgive those who sin against us, and furthermore to demonstrate our willingness to work together with them toward reconciliation. God wants us to be merciful to others, just as He is merciful to us. I remember what it felt like for these truths to sink in – deep down, sink in. And now I want to pray with you and in other ways help you on your journey of forgiveness and, if God wills it, reconciliation.*

○ A few of us who are believers know the blackness of feeling that we are unloved and unlovable, applying the verdict – that it's impossible for anyone to love us – to all of our aspiring courters, even God Himself. So, when our counterpart is tormented by such feelings, we know firsthand what they're going through. This enables us to tell them: *I know what it's like to think that no one cares about me. I can relate to the feeling that even God Himself can't love me. ... But it's God's nature to love, and He considers us inherently valuable. God places loving people in our lives, and His design is that we live in love with one another. I remember what it felt like for these truths to sink in – deep down, sink in. And now I want you to know that you too are already loved – both by God and by me.*

○ Several more of us who are believers know the dark gray hue of chronic depression. So, when our counterpart is distressed by such feelings, we know firsthand what they're going through. This enables us to tell them: *I know what it's like to feel deep sadness day after day, sometimes for no apparent reason. I can relate to the feelings of hopelessness and indifference – that nothing matters. ... But God wants us to experience more joy in our lives, and He provides ways for us to achieve this – definitely by reaching out to people we already know, and possibly also by seeking professional help. We matter to God and to the people who love us. I remember what it felt like for these truths to sink in – deep down, sink in. And now I want you to know that it's your turn to blossom, and I'm here to help you.*

○ Most of us who are believers know the heartache of the death of a loved one or friend; and a subset of us have not always known the assurance of salvation. So, when our counterpart is troubled by such a loss, we know firsthand what they're going through. This enables us to tell them: *I know what it's like to lose someone close to me. I can relate to feeling deep sadness that they're gone, and even wondering what happens next – both to them and, when it's my turn, to me. ... But Jesus is preparing a place for all who trust in Him as their Savior. God wants you, me – all people – to be His forever. I remember what it felt like for these truths to sink in – deep down, sink in. And now I want to pray with you and in other ways help you – as empowered by the Holy Spirit – to place your hope in God's sure promises.*

And so it goes. In a nutshell: Our showing empathy to each of our counterparts demonstrates very clearly that we hear them and care about their background, their point of view, their feelings, their needs, and their struggles. ... Why be so demonstrative? ... Because we expect something in return? ... No, it's because we care about them as an individual. Being empathetic is a powerful way to connect with another person – to be a positive influence. And this influence is especially constructive as we seek to connect via our struggles, as this allows us – both of us – to see Jesus more and more clearly.

~

Before we leave the section on empathy, I'd like to expatiate on one of my other favorite words and on one of my least favorite phrases.

One of my Top 25 words is vicariousness. I like this word because of the way it rolls off the tongue. As if that's not enough, I also like it because of how it relates to empathy. As if that's not enough, I like it because I tend to root for underdogs. Vicariousness is a true underdog word. It gets a bad rap because people associate it with one of my least favorite phrases, to be disclosed in the next paragraph. (Please wait patiently.) In the meantime, bask in the glory that is vicariousness! ... Some of you are not basking... at least not in line with my standards associated with true basking. Could it be that you don't know what this glorious word means? ... I think I'm right, and I've just given you a hint about the meaning of vicariousness. To be more clear, vicariousness means that we imagine what someone else is experiencing / feeling / thinking. Does that seem creepy? ... *(I did it again, didn't I? At this point, it's better to stop fighting it, and just accept it.)* Vicariousness is not creepy at all when properly applied.

What's creepy about surprising our friend with a gift, and getting that special feeling when we see how delighted they are to have received it? What's creepy about thoroughly applying Dr. Bob's sex advice (Chapter 7), and getting that special feeling when we give our spouse prodigious physical pleasure? What's creepy about forgiving someone who has hurt us deeply, and getting that special feeling when we see their tears fall? These are simply expressions of empathy, and there's nothing creepy about that.

That is, there's nothing creepy about it unless we misapply vicariousness and turn it into one of my least favorite phrases. To wit, in the Top 25 of such phrases is "living vicariously." LV means that we are neglecting our own fundamental needs and have become obsessed with others, and the details of their lives, to the extent that – if they are aware of it – we are making them uncomfortable because of the degree of attention from us. This is far afield from our best loving. Even our spouses need some space to enjoy a measure of autonomy. Part of being empathetic is sensing when our level of involvement is putting a strain on our relationship. Like all things in life, there is a proper balance, and each of our relationships will have its own balance point when it comes to the appropriate amount of vicariousness to apply.

My quest to slay two mythological beasts

Unbeknownst to you, very many times while writing this book I've been struggling mightily to stop myself from climbing onto a soapbox – *one of my favorite places!* Sure, I've allowed myself to climb up – ever so slightly and ever so briefly – here and there. But truth be told, I've been holding myself back. *I can't take it anymore!* I must climb up where the air is thinner. And now's the perfect time.

The myth of "The Platinum Rule," as told by yours truly from high up on a soapbox

We've all heard of The Golden Rule: "As you wish that others would do to you, do so to them" (Luke 6:31), or similarly: "Love your neighbor as yourself" (Matthew 22:39). Some eggheaded individuals have gone down rabbit holes in their attempts to try to sound more enlightened than Jesus by introducing a "new concept" that they've branded The Platinum Rule. But let me assure you that this is not a new concept by any stretch. The gurus of TPR emphasize the point – which is such an obvious point... – that we should not literally (based on our preferences) be treating others as *we* would want to be treated, but as *they* want to be treated; in other words, we should keep in mind that our counterpart's preferences are probably different from ours. ... *Well, duh!* ... What can "As you wish that others would do to you, do so to them" possibly mean other than we each keep in mind our counterpart's preferences? That *is* exactly what we wish others would do for us! *Of course* we want to be treated based on *our* own preferences, not our *counterpart's* preferences!

Consider the following scenario:

- We have a friend, and he lov... – likes very much beef brisket open-faced sandwiches. He likes them so much that his special gift for us, his vegan friends, is such a sandwich – *No, wait!* – he has gone the extra mile and deep-fried it in the one thing that he lov... – revels in even more than beef brisket open-faced sandwiches: hand-extracted lard.

  The so-called logic of TPR ruminators is that because our friend would be tickled pink to receive such a scrumptious snack from anyone, it follows that by giving his masterpiece to anyone he is surely acing The Golden Rule with flying colors, and they smugly go on to say that we need "enlightenment" in the form of a new and better rule, namely TPR...

  I do not use the word asinine lightly, including here. I also do not change the names of rules lightly, but take careful note that I am officially renaming TPR *The Golden Rule for Dummies*.

(Now you know that my tallest soapboxes are reserved for lectures to anyone who thinks of themselves as more enlightened than Jesus. Proponents of TPR are certainly in this category.)

~

A calm summary given from off the soapbox is: Proponents of TPR, when badmouthing The Golden Rule, are focusing on the preferences of the giver, and they're doing this from a worldly perspective that assumes selfishness and inflexibility – that the giver is of course only considering their own preferences. In stark contrast, Jesus is not stating The Golden Rule based on an assumption of selfishness and inflexibility; and this is logical because His topic is how to love others. How can He establish guidelines about how to love others from the perspective of selfishness and inflexibility? It doesn't make sense…

The myth of "tough love," as told by yours truly from a slightly (only slightly …) lower soapbox

I already told you (Chapter 4) that I tend to take words very literally – precisely as they are stated. This sometimes causes me to despise phrases that others somehow live with. Whenever I hear or read such a phrase, it's like the unfortunate soul responsible for the anathema is scratching their chalkboard with their fingernails. In the Top 25 of such phrases is "tough love." It's hard for me to write that myself. I will henceforth abbreviate it as TL.

What the hell can TL possibly mean?! … I think some misguided individuals accept this as a satisfactory phrase to describe that we love under all circumstances and if, for example, the recipient of our love needs a firm talking to about their need to change because they are hurting themselves or others, then we tell them that in no uncertain terms. … *Of course we do this, but what's tough about it?* … In the big picture it's not tough for us to give, and in the long term it's not tough for our recipient to take to heart. … What's that? You think I'm cheating by adding the provisos "big picture" and "long term"? … No, I'm not cheating. Of course it may be difficult for us, when we're the messenger, to muster up the courage to say what needs to be said, and to supplement this with a healthy expression of on-point anger. Of course it may be unpleasant and even painful for us, when we're the recipient, as we are hearing the message that we need to change, and as we start to process this. But love always looks far beyond the short term. Even in the midst of uncomfortableness and pain, love maintains a broad, long-term vision. From this perspective, there's nothing tough about love; love is always gentle.

- For example, in Appendix A, I tell all readers who are rejecting Jesus as their Savior that they should be terrified (Hebrews 10:26-31) because if they persist in unrepentance and unbelief they'll be left with a wrathful God (John 3:36) who will surely punish them (Revelation 19:15). How can I be more tender than that? And taking such a message to heart can only be described as sheer bliss.

- Similarly, in Chapter 8, I tell all readers that we should completely impale any of our counterparts who do not accept the fact that they are a sinner with the Holy Spirit's heavy and barbed lance. With our hand never relinquishing its firm grip on that mighty weapon, our beloved counterpart writhes in blinding pain, lying exposed for 40 blazing hot days and frigid nights; but when they start to glimpse the truth, we find ourselves conjoined in an ecstatic coupling.

I've heard many people claim that they're giving TL in this or that situation. When I'm aware of the circumstances, often the so-called TL is actually misdirected anger or even abuse. This is why the phrase TL upsets me! It's so often used as a rationalization by a bully or an abuser. Bullies and abusers don't care about unbelievers and people who don't accept the fact that they're a sinner. So, instead of giving big-picture, long-term love in the gentle ways that I wrote above – what I refer to as Challenging Love – they pass "by on the other side" (Luke 10:31, 32), i.e., ignore such counterparts. Instead, bullies and abusers are on the prowl for their next victim, who often is a trusting counterpart who should be loved, but instead gets so-called TL and a flimsy rationalization.

The next time you find yourself claiming to be a giver of TL, I'd like you to remember that we must all give an account to God (2 Corinthians 5:10; Hebrews 4:13). If your so-called TL was actually mistreatment or abuse, and if your account to God does not include your sorrow over your sin in this regard, then you are in real danger of facing a wrathful God (John 3:36). Indeed, at the time of God's judgment, if you deny your sinfulness and reject Jesus as your Savior, then you'll know how tough God can be, and it won't be love by any stretch. "Tough" and "love" do not mix.

~

I'll close this subsection by quoting Ephesians 4:15-16. For some reason, the beginning of this quote is sometimes used as a rationalization to give TL. However, I searched high and low for a translation that uses the word "tough" and I couldn't find one. "Speaking the truth in love, we are to grow up in every way into him who is the head, into Christ, from whom the whole body, joined and held together by every joint with which it is equipped, when each part is working properly, makes the body grow so that it builds itself up in love."

Forgiveness

I hope you can forgive me, but much of this large topic is covered in Chapter 9, especially in the sections entitled: "What if someone sins against you?" "What if you are struggling to forgive yourself?" and "What if someone disappoints you?" In those areas, forgiveness is discussed in some detail from the perspectives of both unconditional love and conditional love.

For the sake of brevity – *(We can all try new things, can't we?)* – here I'd like to focus on the special impact we can have on our counterpart's life by surprising them with forgiveness. The biggest surprises I've given my counterparts have come when I've submerged them in the cool, rejuvenating water of forgiveness that comes from out of the blue. Forgiving our counterpart after they apologize is refreshing – no doubt – but here I'm talking about those opportunities that lend themselves to forgiving them before they have the time to get on their surfboard of remorse and wait for the anticipated wave of forgiveness to come. I'm talking about *preemptive forgiveness*. Some people think that we should always wait until our counterpart demonstrates remorse before we forgive. However, from the perspective of unconditional love, we don't forgive our counterpart because they're remorseful, we forgive them because we love them unconditionally. Such surprising forgiveness has the biggest impact – this shows our counterpart their inherent value in an unanticipated way.

How did I learn the tremendous impact that such preemptive forgiveness brings? I first learned this from the biggest surprises I've received from my counterparts.

When we're surprised in such a way, it's life-altering – we can't help but be changed. Our authentic self is not static – we evolve throughout our life. Yes, "The people you love will change you."[1] Some people think that we should always wait until our counterpart demonstrates a willingness to change before we forgive. However, from the perspective of unconditional love, we don't forgive our counterpart because they're willing to change, they change because we shock them with unconditional love.

Authenticity

Back in Chapter 4, in the "Loving our authentic self" section, I go on at some length expounding upon our need to love our authentic self. In my enthusiasm, despite the main topic of that chapter being our love for ourselves, I do include some points directly related to our giving love to others. Given the possibility that you haven't memorized that entire section quite yet, I feel compelled to provide an important excerpt here: "I can only truly love your authentic self; you can only truly love my authentic self." Note that this is referring to the authenticity of the one *receiving* love. Now, I'd like you to tell me a corollary that's related to the authenticity of the one *giving* love. … Yes, you there, with the wistful glances since the beginning of Chapter 2. … Uh, no… Any iambic pentameter is purely coincidental until Chapter 9, and even then I'm absolutely *not* singing from below your balcony! That's not the corollary I'm looking for here. … Anyone else? … *Yes, very good!* Only your authentic self can truly love me; only my authentic self can truly love you.

How can you tell if it's my authentic self? … *It's easy!* You can tell in the same ways that I can tell if it's your authentic self. … I can tell by your dumbfounded faces – *(Very authentic, by the way!)* – that it's time for me to provide some examples.

- Here's a good one: When you give me food, if you want to startle me with a seismic sea wave, then may I suggest that you take the time to prepare the food yourself? I do like to be tangled in seaweed, and this is accomplished in a very simple way: When you prepare food for me, all I ask is that you consider my preferences in this regard. In a nutshell, I don't care what particular food you make, but whatever it is I'd like you to prepare it with your own bare hands – I mean, get way down in there – and, if I'm honest, break a sweat. I do want it to be intimate. When I eat it, I want to be able to tell that the only one who could have made this is you.

- Here's a better one: When I receive a card from you, if you don't write anything in your own words, then how can you expect me to be drenched? I want a thorough soaking, and this is accomplished with remarkably few words, provided that those words are from your heart – no one else's – and are only for me – no one else. I do want it to be intimate. When I read it, I want to be able to tell that the only one who could have written this is you.

Seeking our balance point in the contexts of conditional and unconditional love

From time to time, for example as we're handwriting a card or making food with our own bare hands, we may start to fret about an apparent lack of balance. What do I mean? As we pause to wipe our brow, it may occur to us that it sure does seem like we are putting a whole lot more sweat into a particular relationship than is our counterpart. What should our reaction be?

- From the perspective of conditional love (next chapter), we should assess how balanced the relationship is and, if appropriate, dial back our efforts a notch or two. ... Does this answer surprise you? It shouldn't, in light of the first six words of the answer. A conditional love relationship should be roughly balanced with respect to reciprocation. It may not be like-for-like, and there may be periods where it's a little bit askew, but overall neither individual should be significantly outdoing the other, as that would be an unhealthy conditional love relationship. Conditional love should be a friendly pseudo-competition of sorts, with both counterparts seeking to keep the "score" close. We should not be seeking to "win," and we certainly never want to win by a landslide.

  Winning by a landslide is a clear indicator of an unbalanced conditional love relationship, and something needs to change. If the relationship is a marriage, then couples therapy is in order. With other unbalanced conditional love relationships, it may be as simple as acknowledging in our heart that the friendship is not going to be as close as we had hoped it would be. However, before coming to this conclusion, it's probably best to have a conversation with our counterpart, to see if we may be misunderstanding something. For example, we may learn that their primary love language (Chapter 7) is physical touch, and that explains why they've started to whack us on the shoulder every time they see us; it's their way of saying that they love us.

  Sometimes we are so busy wiping our furrowed brow that we become bitter – not a good place to be. If you feel out of balance in this way, slow down a bit and – instead of curling up in a ball to sulk – lie on your surfboard and wait patiently. Chances are, someone in your life is whispering softly.

- From the perspective of unconditional love, we should *never* assess how balanced the relationship is. Rather, we should *always* be seeking how best to dial up our efforts a notch or two. ... Does this answer surprise you? It shouldn't, in light of the first six words of the answer. Unconditional love never considers balance from any vantage point, one of the most mundane of which is the vantage point of reciprocation. Every now and then, our unconditional love for one another is relatively balanced, for example in a soul mate relationship (below). However, balance is never what we set out to achieve via unconditional love. When we happen to stumble upon balance in this context, it's entirely due to the unforeseen circumstance of two exquisite gifts – one from each of us, one for each of us – both unexpected and both given for no reason (other than the benefit of our counterpart, for example, addressing one of their needs).

Our gifts of unconditional love are always exquisite, always unexpected, and always given for no reason. Can you think of a better reason to give a gift of love? If you ever find yourself waiting to give any gift of love until "an opportune time" – until there is a reason – stop riding the brakes, dial it up a notch, and give your love immediately! There's no greater joy than astonishing our counterpart with a tidal wave of love. Why wait for a reason?

If what I've written so far in this section seems a bit confusing – too extreme one way or the other (*too much* attention to balance, or *not enough* attention to balance) – I hope the following closing comments will clear things up.

- Most relationships are a *blend* of conditional and unconditional love and, as such, within these relationships our eyes are not glued to the scoreboard but neither are we clueless. The need for balance with respect to reciprocation is balanced – *(Are you with me?)* – based on the unique blend of love in each of our relationships. It's in our close conditional love relationships where it's most important to maintain reasonably well-balanced reciprocation. And keep in mind that our closest conditional love relationship is our marriage.
  - (An interesting exception occurs when a married individual becomes disabled, and their spouse rises to the occasion by becoming their caregiver. In such cases, the relationship evolves such that conditional love takes a back seat to unconditional love.)
- With some of our counterparts, however, we don't have a conditional love relationship. In such cases, it's not uncommon for our unconditional love for them to be completely one-sided. If it is, then what I've written above (second bullet point of this section) stands on its own. We always amp it up,

astounding our counterpart again and again (of course not making them feel uncomfortable or burdened) – and we never expect anything in return.

What's that? Isn't this out of balance? ... *Yes! You've got it!* It is extremely unbalanced, just as it should be in such a scenario. We give and give, of course all the while attending to our own needs – never neglecting or exhausting ourselves.

Am I asking for too much? Isn't this difficult? ... Sometimes it's very difficult to unconditionally love an unresponsive counterpart. But no matter what, there is always one way that we can dial up our one-sided unconditional love and find rest for our souls: Praying for a specific individual is an excellent way to love them unconditionally. It's generally best to tell our counterpart that we're praying for them. But if for whatever reason we don't tell them this, of course we proceed undeterred! When God's answer comes, we can still smile when we see them startled by the overwhelming crash of water, even though they're unaware that our soft whisper played a role in giving rise to this crest.

360 degrees of reciprocation

The preceding section is unbalanced. I've written it from the perspective that we're the ones giving more love than we're receiving. It often feels this way, doesn't it? And sometimes it doesn't just feel this way but is absolutely true, as we continuously flood others in our life with unconditional love.

Is there anything wrong with this arrangement? From the perspective of unconditional love, there's nothing wrong, and one reason why is that while we may not experience much reciprocation from a particular counterpart, this doesn't mean that their loving attitude is not being amplified. When I give a counterpart unconditional love, I consider myself to be doing two things: Primarily, I'm reminding them – for no reason – that they're inherently valuable, and secondarily, I'm teaching them how to love unconditionally. When they are a diligent pupil, they will experience intensified unconditional love for others, and this will shine forth in all directions. Yes, I am blessed as I enjoy some of their glow personally, but my heart is also filled with joy as I vicariously know that much more of my counterpart's warmth is radiating to others. I refer to this glow as 360 degrees of reciprocation. (By the way, the similar but scaled-down concept of "paying it forward" ranks highly in my list of Top 25 least favorite phrases because it infers unidirectionality and no amplification.)

I will now give an example, and the simplicity of this is intentional; this is to show you how easy it can be to spark such wide-sweeping reciprocation. Imagine, if you will, that I'm on a hike, and out of the blue I send my counterpart the following text message: *Hey! I just saw an iguana on my hike, and I immediately thought of you! Here's a picture. Shall I inform the Iguanuban Society about this sighting? If I have indeed discovered a new species, I'm naming it after you, and you can't stop me!* ... After experiencing this, my counterpart has no choice but to embark on a previously unimagined junket of 360 degrees of reciprocation. They have no choice because now they know how good it feels when a friend thinks of them for a funny reason, and lets them know about it. Henceforth, they can't help themselves from doing similarly with their counterparts, as opportunities arise.

Don't like my example? Well, just for that, my homework assignment for you is to spark one junket of 360 degrees of reciprocation sometime in the next three months, and this must be under circumstances where you know your recipient will feel loved and energized, but you don't expect very much reciprocation (to you personally). How will you know if you've aced my assignment? You'll know when all you get from your counterpart is a huge smile.

~

This section is just as unbalanced as the previous one! Are we always giving more love to our counterparts than we're receiving from them? Absolutely not, thus I must make an adjustment and seek my balance point on this topic. Sometimes – despite our giving constantly – we nevertheless are drenched with more love from someone in our life than we happen to be giving them at that particular time. I will address this wondrous perspective without delay!

Basking in unconditional love given to us by another person

In this life, there are a few feelings that are uniquely beautiful. I'm going to be bold and try to list them. Did I miss anything?

- Knowing God loves you
- Knowing you are saved
- Learning, usually as a young child, that you are loved by the members of your family
- The first time you fall in love with a "sweetheart," and it's reciprocated
- Your first kiss
- Your proposal of marriage being accepted / you being proposed to, and accepting
- Various parts of the marriage ceremony, for example when you are pronounced husband and wife
- The first time you are sexually intimate with your spouse
- Every other time you are sexually intimate with your spouse
- Confirmation of pregnancy
- Birth of a child
- Surprising someone with forgiveness
- Being surprised by forgiveness
- Basking in unconditional love given to us by another person (distinct from God) (this section)
- Being in a soul mate relationship (next section)
- Giving unconditional love to another person (this chapter and Chapter 10)

Some of these feelings are easier to describe than others. I find basking in unconditional love given to us by another person to be one of the harder ones to describe. I'll do my best.

One reason I find it hard to describe is because it's one of the relatively few things on this list that doesn't involve a choice we make. We don't choose to be loved unconditionally; someone else chooses to love us this way. In this regard, we submit to them.

The idea of being submissive is another reason I find it so hard to describe. When we grow up in a western culture, we're told from Day One to be assertive, not to be passive; we're told to be proactive, to take charge of the situation, to make choices for ourselves; we're told to become independent, to stop being a baby and grow up. But to bask in unconditional love we should – figuratively speaking, and with respect to the unconditional love we're receiving from our counterpart – be passive, allow our counterpart to choose, and grow down. Yes, we should – from the perspective of our counterpart's unconditional love for us – submit to them.

Being submissive usually has a negative connotation, and that's largely because of the possibility that we'll be taken advantage of. That's certainly not uncommon in our sinful world. But when an individual is unconditionally loving us, they've proven themselves to be trustworthy, so we can trust them not to take advantage. In other words, it's safe to be submissive to them.

What does it feel like to submit in this way? To what can we compare it?

I can compare it to specific examples of unconditional love that we may be familiar with, but in each case there are caveats.

- For example, it's like being forgiven when we're *not* seeking forgiveness. However, of course I'm not suggesting that we purposely sin, and furthermore not seek forgiveness, just so we might be loved unconditionally. For one thing, that's manipulative – which of course is unloving to our counterpart. For another thing, that will almost certainly cause major damage to our conditional love relationship! Saying all of this another way: We do not lay plans to receive unconditional love; it finds us.
  - o Note that when we're aware of our sin and we respond properly by confessing / apologizing, we're involving (asserting) ourselves in the forgiveness. It becomes an exchange of sorts. But receiving unconditional love is not an exchange by any stretch.
- A better example is an infant loved by her mother. Yes, we soak it in – we bask in our mother's love. However, here I'm talking about receiving – from anyone in our life – unconditional love as an adolescent or an adult.
- The best example is our basking in the unconditional love of God. I even wrote an entire chapter about that! However, here I'm talking about receiving unconditional love from fallible human beings.

In the Prologue, I describe an experience where I craved unconditional love from fallible human beings. The main lesson I learned is that I was already being loved this way but I wasn't seeing it clearly because I was too inwardly focused – too selfish. To experience the full weight of unconditional love – which is a prerequisite for being able to describe it – we need to be outwardly focused and selfless.

Enough background! Now I'll try to describe the feeling of basking in unconditional love given to us by another person.

- I'm always surprised – it's always unexpected
  - o In interpersonal relationships, unconditional love is, by its very nature, surprising and unexpected (with rare exceptions – see the preamble to this chapter)
- Even if it doesn't involve emotional healing – *(Sometimes it does!)* – I still feel "healed" from the perspective that I'm cared for
  - o An analogy is an infant being fed by her mother
- Even if it doesn't involve forgiveness directly, I still feel "forgiven" from the perspective that I'm accepted for who I am – even though I'm inherently sinful
  - o I'm loved despite my flaws, which is an incredible relief. Sometimes we might feel that we need to become "flawless," for example in our behavior, in order to be deserving of love. To be loved without becoming flawless means that *I* am loved, not my behavior.
- I'm affirmed because I'm not being asked to change
- I have a sense of freedom because I know that I'm not judged
- My experience has been that unless my counterpart verbalizes their unconditional love for me – and does this at an early stage – by the time I become aware of it, it's apparent that it has been there for a long time
  - o Maybe I could be more perceptive, but another reason I'm a little slow in realizing it's there is that unconditional love inherently means that my counterpart is not expecting me to appreciate or reciprocate. In other words, while they're not deliberately hiding their unconditional love for me, they're not showboating it either.
- When I do become aware of it, I feel a constant effect of oxytocin and/or similar hormone(s) for much longer than normal – I'm talking days
- This may surprise you: In contrast to my reaction when receiving conditional love, when I become aware of unconditional love my initial reaction is *not* to consider how I'm going to reciprocate. Phase 1 is basking. I bask until the "happy hormones" taper off. This may sound selfish, but this is part of being submissive to the choice of my counterpart. Of course I express thankfulness in whatever way(s) are appropriate, but even mild reciprocation such as this is entering the realm of conditional love, and wading any deeper into that

pool can wait. Let me submit to their unconditional love – let me bask a little longer…

o   Having said this, throughout my basking I'm storing up more and more trust and affection for my counterpart. If my growing love includes a fair measure of unconditional love for them – (It's not as easy as it sounds, because anything that is in reciprocation for their unconditional love is conditional love) – and if by God's design we're compatible in the way I describe in the next section, then I have an exquisite journey ahead of me, and my counterpart is coming along!

Earlier in this section, I mentioned that we cannot choose to be loved unconditionally. That choice is entirely our counterpart's to make. However, we can choose to shut ourselves off from it. If my list above sounds great but these feelings are unfamiliar to you, maybe you're shutting yourself off from receiving unconditional love from others. We should all open our doors a little wider – some of us a lot wider. We should all spend more time frolicking on the beach, knee-deep in the calm water. Opening our door and going out to frolic in an utterly unsuspecting way is done by becoming more outwardly focused, more selfless, and more submissive to the unconditional love that comes our way.

Soul mates

At an even higher level than what I just tried to describe is the "elusive" soul mate. Right up front, I'd like to say that I don't agree that soul mates are particularly elusive. And, yes, I mean "soul mates," plural, even for any one of us at any given time. We often hear about "a soul mate," singular, with the implication being that we can have only one, and furthermore that there's one ideal person out there for each of us – with each of our lives being a quest to find this person, with some of us finding and others of us not. But life is not a fairytale, and rarely is it truly a tragedy.

In my life, I've gone to great lengths to pursue many different things, but I've never considered myself to be on a quest for a soul mate. And looking back at the few soul mate experiences that I've had, one thing is clear: I never could have "found" these people on my own – God placed them in my life. For one thing, the way that they helped me, and me them, couldn't be discerned early in the relationship. If you are on a quest to find a soul mate, get off your steed and drop to your knees. Yes, pray to God, and ask Him to bless you and your future soul mate(s) by bringing you together to experience, in time, this special type of love.

If you're beginning to wonder what the heck I'm talking about, never fear! It has been a very long time since I've crafted a definition, and now's the perfect time to compose another!

- Succinct definition of a soul mate relationship:
  - Two counterparts, with the first having a unique characteristic – I'll call it a gift – that complements a weakness – I'll call it a need – in the second, and with the second having a gift that complements a need in the first
- Here I provide further commentary on what a soul mate relationship is:
  - The two gifts are inherent – not skills that can be learned
    - They may be spiritual gifts
  - The two needs are long term and significant – not just short-term minor difficulties
    - Each need represents a real weakness that many others have difficulty tolerating, but that the counterpart in the soul mate relationship accepts unconditionally
  - Despite this unconditional acceptance, some degree of mitigation – I'll call it healing – spontaneously occurs
    - Here we have a good example of the amazing heights that can be reached with full-blown unconditional love – the healing is not required, and yet it occurs
  - The word "mate" is fitting because, at least from the perspective of the two needs, the two people are whole / complete only when they are conjoined (figuratively)
  - It doesn't take a genius to see that a soul mate relationship is truly an exquisite thing
- Here's what a soul mate relationship is *not*:
  - It's *not* finding a likeminded person
  - It's *not* finding someone who helps you, but receives little from you. (That's covered in the previous section.)
  - It's *not* finding someone whom you should seclude from the world – keeping all for yourself. (That is both selfish and inhibitory to your counterpart.)

- And here's what a soul mate relationship *might not* be:
  - It's not necessarily a marriage
  - It's not necessarily a sexual relationship
  - It's not necessarily a relationship where the two counterparts are compatible in ways beyond the two gifts and two needs
  - It's not necessarily the only such relationship that either counterpart has
    - Yes, it's reasonable for one person to have multiple soul mate relationships occurring simultaneously. However, we always need to be wary of becoming too close to someone who is not our spouse; we must not slip into an emotional affair.
    - Most commonly, if a person has more than one soul mate relationship at a given time, they're having different needs met in each
  - It's usually not a parent-child relationship, although of course that is possible, for example if a parent has a profound need to learn how to express caring to others

You can see that a soul mate relationship is about as close as two people can get to a perfect portrayal of mutual unconditional love. (Another peak that's more or less at the same lofty height is a mother-infant relationship.) And, let's face it, if two people are having this much of a positive impact on one another, there's a pretty good chance that they're going to be very close friends. Why am I stating the obvious? I'm a very thorough person, and one of the themes of this book is that there are many scenarios where unconditional love is not necessarily appreciated or reciprocated. But here we've found – no, stumbled upon – no, been blessed by God to encounter – a synchronism where our unconditional love for someone is balanced, in a special way that transcends traditional appreciation and reciprocation, such that both counterparts are positively impacted in a spontaneous way that words can hardly describe. Yes, it is a mountaintop experience. I wanted you to see this. And while we're up here, you can also see that there are some other peaks almost as high – clearly, way up here above the timberline there is plenty of room for friendship. Again the obvious! OK, OK, let me explain. Here's the kicker – a traditional friendship is a conditional love relationship. Conditional love relationships can be beautiful – even part of this mountain range – but they very frequently get complicated. All those conditions! What I've tried to describe here – a soul mate relationship – on its own doesn't have any conditions. Love is freely offered in both directions; both provide benefit to the other without requiring benefit back. It is truly exquisite. There is no other feeling quite like it. This is true love between people. To admit that there probably is also a traditional friendship is like remembering that at some point we need to start climbing back down this mountain.

~

The next chapter focuses on conditional love and, yes, we'll experience some more heights. I advise at least crampons and an icepick. I have a feeling that some of you are also going to need an oxygen mask – indeed, Dr. Bob's sex advice is surely coming. But also surely coming are slippery upper slopes and warning signs about precipitous drops over the edge, where the air is thicker and shadows predominate. Don't be misled – conditional love is often challenging and some-times even dangerous. But if we're equipped properly, conditional love can be marvelous and sometimes even beautiful. Even then, however, it still can't hold a candle to a soul mate relationship or to the love between a mother and her infant. Without doubt – here on earth, in this lifetime – unconditional love is the most exquisite form of love possible between people.

~ ~ ~

After-hours

Bob unplugged

In the preamble to this chapter, I provide my viewpoint that in interpersonal relationships we generally should not "expect" to receive unconditional love (and I give a couple of exceptions). I go on to say that the reason we should not expect it is that our counterpart is (like us) a fallible human being and, as such, they sometimes disappoint, for example they may choose not to love us uncondi-tionally. Were you surprised that I place the "blame" on our counterpart? Do you think it makes more sense to point the finger squarely at ourselves, rationalizing that we should never expect unconditional love because we are not worthy of receiving it?

Before you even try to wrap your brain around that last question, let me inform you that your recurring bad dream has come true: Yes, you really did forget that you registered for Semantics 201, and the final exam really is today! Lucky for you, there is only one question, and on the surface it doesn't seem too hard. Here it is: *Are we worthy of unconditional love?* ... I teach this course in my sleep, so I can give you a hint to get your syrup pouring: There are two correct answers to this question, and it all comes down to our definition of worthy.

- If we define worthy as the quality of having excellent merit, then of course we are never worthy. For one thing, based on our thoughts, words, and actions, none of us (other than Jesus) on this side of eternity have "excellent merit." More importantly, the concept of unconditional love is not even relevant if the receiver is not flawed or otherwise in need; on this basis, the question on your final exam is self-contradictory, if we define worthy in this way.
- If, on the other hand, we define worthy as the quality of having high value, then of course we are worthy of unconditional love! No one (not our counterparts, not ourselves, and not God) loves us unconditionally because we deserve it. We are loved unconditionally because we are worth loving.

Because I helped you with your final exam, I'm compelled to assign you summer-homework, and here it is:

- In Chapter 7, I write about some thoughts that led "me to conclude ... that I'm not worthy of being given compassion." ... Am I worthy of being given compassion?
- How would you define unlovable? (If you're stuck and want to peek at my two-word definition, see the fortunate and necessary paragraph [Prologue].)

Step up to the microphone

I did my best to describe the feeling of basking in unconditional love given to us by another person. Please consider:

- From your own experience, which of my points ring true, and should anything be subtracted or added?
- Go through the list again, including any revisions based on the prior bullet point, and consider what rings true when we now view it from the perspective of God's unconditional love for us
- Go through the revised list again, this time imagining what the wounded man experienced when he received unconditional love from the Good Samaritan (Luke 10:25-37). For example, was the wounded man surprised? Did he expect to receive unconditional love, especially from this particular counterpart?
  o It can feel good to be surprised, especially when we're surprised by unconditional love. Does this mean we should not express our needs?

Imagine that your friend confides in you that they are feeling unloved by other counterpart(s). Your friend concludes that the other(s) would care about her if she was somehow different. She's sad, and has an unfavorable view of herself. … What would you tell your friend?

(Imagine that) you are feeling unloved by other counterpart(s). You conclude that the other(s) would care about you if you were somehow different. You're sad, and have an unfavorable view of yourself. … Is it fair to tell yourself something incongruent from what you would tell a friend?

One thing I've noticed over the years is that college campuses tend to have a strong culture of interpersonal acceptance. (I do not consider it a coincidence that I started to draft this book while on the UCLA campus for several days, attending a conference [that had nothing to do with love, by the way]. I was already feeling growing motivation along these lines, and the students inspired me further.)

- Have you noticed the same thing?
- If so, what do you think the reasons are? And why does it start to fade away, at least for many of us, when we graduate?

For parents: Think of specific ways that your child(ren) have helped your representative person evolve. You may never have the opportunity to serve others heroically, but how have your child(ren) motivated you to be willing to do so – I mean, even if the people served are unbeknownst to you?

For intimate couples: It's possible that you're not soul mates, and that's fine. Many couples become soul mates later, as the relationship evolves. Maybe this prompt will help with such an evolutionary process.

- I'd like both of you, in turn, to tell your partner at least one way that they've helped you in a tangible way. (In this exercise, there's no need to try to associate their help with any particular strength of theirs.)
- After both of you have done this, then I'd like both of you, in turn, to tell your partner what you consider to be one of your most significant weaknesses, and it needs to be something long term and impactful – not just a short-term minor difficulty.

Chapter 7 – Conditional Love

If you just finished Chapter 6, you know many of my thoughts on the exquisiteness of unconditional love. Does this mean that I'm going to give conditional love short shrift? …

Now, you know better!

Even though I just told you (at the end of the previous chapter) that conditional love can't hold a candle to unconditional love, conditional love can still make my heart melt. Why? Let me illustrate it this way. While it goes without saying that conditional love is inherently imperfect (because it's based on conditions), it can also be tremendously fulfilling. If conditional love was a person, I'd refer to them as endearing – imperfect but very lovable. Think of your partner or think of your best friend; now think of some flaw in them. *(You could have at least* pretended *to take more time to think of it!)* Let's say your partner has some physical "imperfection," for example a birthmark, or let's say your best friend has a "quirk," for example they stutter when they get nervous. Many would point to the birthmark and consider it less than beautiful, possibly even unsightly; many would draw attention to the stuttering and say it's ineloquent, possibly even clumsy. But you love your partner, you love your best friend, and you consider such things endearing – and rightly so!

I like analogies, and I just set one up. Conditional love is analogous to our partner or best friend with the flaw we just considered, and unconditional love is analogous to our partner or best friend without that flaw. Which is more beautiful? Well, at least from an idealist / perfectionist viewpoint (often mine), without the flaw is more beautiful, possibly even exquisite, and with the flaw is not as beautiful, and certainly not exquisite. But I got you a little angry, didn't I? How dare I disparage your partner or best friend because of such things?! That's exactly right… How dare I… (This type of treatment is an example of how perfectionism can be a tremendously annoying trait. I'm an expert on this topic – as any of my counterparts can substantiate.)

Yes, conditional love personified is truly endearing, and I must give her the generous attention she deserves.

Bonding

I find the most endearing thing about conditional love to be the formation of a bond between two lovers*.

> *Warning: I like to use the word "lovers" when referring to the two counterparts in *any* conditional love relationship, not only sexual relationships. Similarly, because these two people are in a loving relationship, I like to say that they are "in love." ... Does such wording make you uncomfortable? ... If so, that's good because it means you're becoming aware that you have preconceived notions about what it means to be lovers, and what it means to be in love. I like to call such preconceived notions "semantic bias." You may like to call my tutelage something else, such as "Bob being a pain in the a$$," and that's fine with me. You see, I have no semantic bias, that is unless you disagree with me on any point.

Now, where was I? ... Ah, yes, bonding between lovers – *one of my favorite topics!*

One of the most beautiful experiences in life is forming a bond with a lover, whether they be our one sexual partner, and/or a friend or family member. Forming such bonds is beautiful because:

- As with our snowflake (Chapter 1), there is no other bond like the one we have with our lover
- Our bond isn't static – it's constantly evolving, and ideally always becoming stronger and stronger
- And finally – *(This one's my favorite!)* – even our strongest bonds are simultaneously very delicate. Are you surprised? You shouldn't be. You shouldn't be surprised when you consider what our bonds are made of – myriad delicate strands. Below I provide just a few example strands. These are selected from an inexhaustible list.
  - *Thank you for listening to me last night – I'm becoming more and more comfortable making myself vulnerable to you*
  - *Thank you for comforting me when I told you what was troubling me – I'm finding you more and more compassionate*

- *Thank you for understanding how I feel – I'm finding you more and more empathetic*
- *Thank you for asking how I'm doing today – I'm finding you more and more caring*
- *Thank you for telling me about that memory – I'm finding you more and more endearing, and I'm glad that you are more and more comfortable making yourself vulnerable to me*
- *Thank you for remembering the anniversary of when we met – I'm finding you more and more thoughtful*
- *Thank you for telling me how much you cherish me – I'm feeling more and more inherently valuable*
- *Thank you for the gift – I'm finding you more and more generous*
- *Thank you for remembering my preference – I'm finding you more and more considerate*
- *Thank you for cooking that for me, with your own bare hands – I'm finding you more and more nurturing*
- *Thank you for eating what I cooked for you, with my own bare hands – I'm finding you more and more daring*
- *Thank you for running that errand for me – I'm finding you more and more kind*
- *Thank you for serving me in countless ways – I'm finding you more and more selfless*
- *Thank you for letting me serve you in countless ways – I'm finding you more and more accommodating to my wishes*
- *Thank you for holding my hand – We're becoming more and more connected*
- *Thank you for warmly embracing me – We're becoming more and more affectionate*
- *You looked especially handsome / beautiful when we were walking along the beach yesterday evening – I'm becoming more and more physically attracted to you*
- *Thank you for kissing me – I want to be closer to you*
- *Thank you for making love with me last night – We're becoming closer and closer*

o *Thank you for being faithful to me – I'm finding you more and more honorable and trustworthy*
o *Thank you for the pet name that you call me – I'm finding you more and more fun*
o *Thank you for not freaking out when I decided on a pet name that's just right for you – Are you finding me more and more fun?*
o *Thank you for standing up for me when no one else did – I'm gaining more and more respect for you*
o *Thank you for telling me that I upset you – I'm finding you more and more honest and transparent*
o *I'm sorry – Thank you for forgiving me*
o *Thank you for apologizing – I forgive you*
o *Thank you for talking about how we can do better next time – We're becoming more and more flexible and open to change*
o *Thank you for staying with me all these years – We're becoming more and more committed*
o *Thank you for telling me that you love me – We're becoming more and more expressive*

I could go on forever with more examples, but these are sufficient for us to see that our bonds are made up of lacy strands. Each strand on its own is very delicate, but together such strands can form a bond so strong that the two lovers can withstand any adversity under the sun.

Each of the above lacy strands is beautiful (very delicate). Below I list example strands that are exquisite (most delicate). I waited until this chapter to discuss bonding because it naturally fits a conditional love relationship. However, as I already told you in Chapter 1, a conditional love relationship should include some measure of unconditional love. Saying this another way, a bond between two people – two lovers – should include some strands that are *not* based on thankfulness, appreciation, desire, reciprocation – attributes of conditional love – but rather on pure unconditional love. These are strands that one counterpart extends to the other, even though the giver has no presumption that the receiver will take hold of the strand and pull it taut. Such strands are already exquisite when we extend them; the bond is strengthened, at least a little bit (our loose, exquisite strand becomes entwined in the taut, beautiful strands that we've already established with our lover), even though the receiver may not be particularly aware of this at the moment. Such an exquisite strand can become a stronger component of our bond in one of two ways: The more common, very strong (but not strongest), way is when our counterpart comes to appreciate our exquisite strand, takes hold of it, and pulls it taut. The less common, strongest, way is when our counterpart extends – *not* as a form of reciprocation for our exquisite strand – their own, unrelated, exquisite strand to us. We now have two exquisite strands that naturally conjoin to form the strongest strand possible. These are the kinds of taut strands that are within the bond of a mother-infant relationship and a soul mate relationship.

The air is getting pretty thin up here, so let me climb down a little bit and give examples of exquisite strands that we should be extending to all our current lovers as well as others in our life, to see who else we will fall in love with.

- *You're in my life, and that makes me happy*
  - Note that even an infant can express this and, for them, under all circumstances this is an exquisite strand
  - For the rest of us, to be an exquisite strand our expression of this must come from completely out of the blue – that is, given for no reason – and "backsies" (our counterpart expressing the same to us within a reasonable time limit … oh, let's say one month) are strictly not allowed!
- *You need someone to help you, and I'm happy to do it*
- *You're having trouble falling asleep; I'll read your favorite book to you*
- *You're hurting; I'm praying for you*
- *You're struggling; hang in there, and don't forget that I'm proud of you*
- *You made a mistake; it's OK*
- *I see that you're worried; here, let me hold you*
- *You seem depressed; I want you to know that you are inherently valuable*
- *Are you doing OK? It seems that something's troubling you. Do you want to tell me about it? … Oh, you're fine? Well, OK, but I want you to know that I care about you and am always available to listen. You can talk to me about anything.*
- *I can see that you don't get close to others easily, but, if it's OK, I'd like to get to know you better*

- *I remember that you told me that you get anxious in social situations. Would you like me to come meet you before the party, so we can go together?*
- *I heard about what happened at yesterday's meeting. That must be very frustrating. I would be quite upset. How are you handling it?*
- *Are you nervous about giving that oral presentation to the group next week? I would be happy to help you practice.*
- *You seemed embarrassed during our ice-breaker, when you admitted to the group that a quirky thing you do is practice your speeches in the bathtub – using little duckies to represent the Board of Directors. I'm defending my thesis next week, and I've been worried sick! But tonight I'm going to try your approach. I have a fuchsia duckie that is a ringer for Dean George!*
- *Here's a picture of an iguana that I saw on my hike this morning. It made me think of you! I know you lov… – very much like iguanas, so I wanted to share this with you.*
- *Many people find you harsh, but I understand that you have difficulty remaining calm when under stress. Would you like to go on a walk and tell me what's been troubling you?*
- *Many people find you uncaring, but I understand that you have difficulty expressing emotions. Is there a time you'd feel comfortable talking to me about it?*
- *What you did annoyed me; I'm choosing to let that go*
- *What you did hurt me; I'm choosing to let you know, and I want to wipe the slate clean – I want to give you another chance*

It's a lovely thing to extend such exquisite (most delicate) strands. We extend them for no reason other than the benefit of our counterpart. We are surely blessed to have opportunities to love in such ways.

And sometimes we are blessed in another lovely way. Yes, sometimes we feel that special tug – indicating that the strand has become taut.

Preferences of our lovers

By now, you know that I like specifics, that I like to zoom in to see the fine detail, and that I like to consider individuals instead of groups. Such things comprise a subset of my general preferences, and I think such perspectives do provide good vantage points when viewing the grandeur of love.

At this point, however, I'd like to begin the discussion on the preferences of our lovers – (And please remember that I'm using this word for our counterparts in all our conditional love relationships) – from a perspective that's more general. Similar to the concept of our generalized personality type, Gary Chapman has taught us well that there are five generalized "love languages." His book, *The 5 Love Languages: The Secret to Love That Lasts*,[1] is helpful for any pair of lovers and is an absolute must-read for everyone who is dating or already married. Gary Chapman's book helps us learn our preferred love language, and – especially when we also learn the preferred love languages of our counterparts – this guides us toward building stronger, more loving relationships.

The five love languages are: gift-giving, quality time, words of affirmation, acts of service, and physical touch. … Any guesses as to my primary love language? … *No one?*

- I've given more than a few hints along the way, and here are more hints about what it isn't: I appreciate receiving gifts, and I very much like to give gifts to my lovers. I appreciate it when my lovers spend time with me. I appreciate it when my lovers help me out in tangible ways, and I enjoy that special feeling that comes when I know I've helped them. I'm not the most affectionate person, but that certainly doesn't mean that I don't savor physical touch, even of a nonsexual nature.

- But what makes my heart sing when I hear or read them? What drives me to despair when I don't remember them or my voracious appetite for them is not satisfied? And what do I give when I try to give my best loving to my counterpart? … What I crave most, and what I give you when I'm madly in love with you, are words of affirmation. As I've already alluded to (Chapter 6), and as I'll elaborate upon further shortly (Chapter 8), I'm writing this book to a "representative person" – a conglomerate of all the individuals I know and love. I'm madly in love with my representative person, and this book is my love letter to them.

Gary Chapman teaches us that it's beneficial to know the primary love language of each of our counterparts because this helps us give them love more impactfully. Please see his book for more and better particulars, but I can't help myself from providing just a little bit of commentary on how we can show love to others, using their primary love language.

- **Gift-giving**: Don't give gifts only when it's common to do so (birthday, anniversary, Christmas). Also give gifts at other times and for *no* apparent reason! Pay close attention to your counterpart's preferences, and remember these when choosing your gifts for them. Try to have your gifts somehow symbolize your relationship. To the extent reasonably possible – and without going overboard, such that they begin to feel uncomfortable – give high quality gifts and in other ways be generous, as this is a way to express how you feel about your counterpart.

- **Quality time**: Make it clear that you're prioritizing your time with them. For example, when you're with them, don't keep checking your email and phone; turn such things off, and focus on your counterpart. Give them the gifts of active listening and your undivided attention. When doing an activity with them, add extra time, to ensure that the two of you won't feel rushed. The activities don't all need to be showstoppers. For example, it would be meaningful for you to set aside time each weekend to go on a walk in the park with your counterpart.

- **Words of affirmation**: Don't worry about the exact words, the grammar, the eloquence, and such minor details; it's much more important that you express yourself in your own words. Be authentic – especially counterparts in this category don't like it when there's a lack of sincerity, and they can tell. Be specific – they long to know the what, the how, and especially the why; it's totally fine if you can't really explain it – it's your trying that touches their heart. They also crave hearing that you're praying for them.

- **Acts of service**: Always be on the lookout for the specific types of help that your counterpart appreciates. On the one hand, these may be things that they don't like doing themselves, and they feel loved when you handle it for them. On the other hand, these may be things that they *do* like to do, and the scope of the activity is large enough that they feel loved when you do it *together* with them. In either case, why not give your counterpart the special treat of surprising them? For example, wash the dishes while they go for a walk with a friend. Or when they're getting ready to leave to serve dinner at the homeless shelter, tell them that you'd like to come along with them. If the clues for how we can help are not coming in fast and furious, there's no harm in asking our counterpart how we can best help them. Although, when doing this, I like to give some specific suggestions, while at the same time showing an openness to change. For example, "I know that you're going to be very busy this week. Can I bring a meal one evening? Or would it be more helpful for me to do something else, like run an errand?"

- **Physical touch**: (Here, my commentary on this language is from the perspective of nonsexual situations. I cannot guarantee that I can limit myself in this manner for the duration of this chapter.) Before whatever touch you'd like to give your counterpart, look for clues that they're comfortable receiving it. If you're unsure, either ask them directly or make a gesture related to what you'd like to do. For example, if you'd like to give them a hug, you could hold both of your hands out slightly and look at them inquisitively. If that's not clear enough, it may be sufficient to add simply, "Is it OK?" With whatever touch you provide, plus-it by looking your counterpart in the eyes, smiling, holding the touch for at least a couple / few seconds (so they don't get the impression that you're anxious to end it), and somehow vocalizing your feelings (doesn't need to be words). If you're fortunate enough to have become emotionally close with someone whose primary love language is physical touch, when you greet them and when you say goodbye, take the opportunity to touch them in some way: a kiss, a hug, a touch on the shoulder.

I'm getting antsy with such generalities. (To me, these are generalities.) I must get back to detailed specifics. Let me provide you with some specifics of how I tailor my love for my lovers depending on their primary love language. *(Say that ten times fast!)* As you're filing back into the bus (after our field trip to visit Gary Chapman), let me remind you that while we are of course to keep our counterpart's preferences in mind, to give our best loving we also need to be true to our authentic self. Don't forget that important component of my 103-word definition of love between people (Chapter 1). This means that when I'm making love with one of my lovers – *(There's no reason to raise your eyebrows... Are you slipping back into semantic bias?)* – I'm keeping *both* of our preferences in mind. Below are examples of what I just might do... when you least expect it!

- If we are in love and your primary love language is gift-giving, then on a day as ordinary as any other you just might find a gift bag on your desk, and

inside, next to a stuffed animal – *(an iguana, of course!)* – is a card within which I've handwritten how happy I am that you're in my life
- If we are in love and your primary love language is quality time, then during our hike in the mountains I just might tell you memories from my childhood, and ask if there are any memories that you'd like to share with me
- If we are in love and your primary love language is words of affirmation, then I just might suggest that we write a poem together (Chapter 9)
- If we are in love and your primary love language is acts of service, then after I wash your car, with my own bare hands, while you definitely will notice that I missed a few spots, you just might find on your seat an envelope, within which is a photograph of us, and on the back of it I've handwritten why you are special to me
- If we are in love and your primary love language is physical touch, while my hug may be clumsy, I just might whisper in your ear that you are beautiful, *je te chéris tellement, e tu sei il mio amato*

How's that for specific? … Guess what I'd like you to do now? … *Did you seriously think that I was going to say all of that and let you off the hook?* … I'd like you to be just as specific as you consider how you'll make love with each of your lovers – (Translation: how you will show your love to each counterpart in your life) – for each of them keeping in mind their primary love language as well as your own. If you're not sure of theirs, ask them, if it's not awkward; otherwise, make a guess. Here's your assignment:
- Right now, create a list of at least one plan per counterpart, and make a commitment that you'll actually do these things over the course of the next twelve months

While you're working on your assignment, I'm going to be writing on the whiteboard at the front of the bus. … Oh, let me erase this… *Who's been doodling?! I want to see you at the next bio-break.* … OK, now, who thinks it's hard to speak in two love languages at once? … Come on, raise your hand if you think it's hard. … Hmm… That many of you think it's hard? Wait – leave your hands up, so I can write down your names. I want to see each of you at the next bio-break as well. … *Two measly love languages… Child's play, I say!* I'm going to write down on the whiteboard an example of how we can speak in *five* love languages at once! I'm going to teach you how to be penta-lingual! Am I setting the bar too high? … *No, I'm not setting the bar too high!* … We may be more fluent in one language or another, but with each of our lovers let's strive to be penta-lingual – I mean, when we are the giver. (When we are the receiver, expecting penta-linguistic treatment from any single counterpart puts us squarely in the category of high maintenance.) Certainly don't limit yourself by giving in your primary love language only, and, similarly, don't limit your counterpart's experience by having them receive in their primary love language only. Receiving their primary is like taking a warm shower after a jog or walk on a cool autumn morning, but let's aspire to deliver a more thorough drenching than that – think Niagara Falls in the spring. Here's a simple example. Let's say your wedding anniversary is coming up. You can't expect to get away with making love in only one or two languages. Here's what you should be doing.

- **Gift-giving**: I hope you didn't forget an anniversary present!
- **Quality time**: May I suggest a getaway – a couple days at least – without the kids?
- **Words of affirmation**: I like the way you wrapped your present, but why not plus-it by attaching a card? And don't forget to whisper in her ear…
- **Acts of service**: Do you think a trip plans itself?
- **Physical touch**: To be penta-lingual, you need to know more than one word in each of the five languages. You're not linguistically skilled in a language if you only know one word, especially when that word is so short – *(only three letters!)* – and ends with one of the least frequently used letters in the alphabet. Even in a sexual relationship, physical touch should be far more than a one-word language. Here are some other words that you should be using more often, and certainly on your anniversary trip: hold her hand, warmly embrace her, stroke her hair, look her in the eyes, and … *Well?* … Go on then… … *Kiss her, you fool!*

~

I hope you agree that I've amply provided sufficiently elaborate specifics for how we can express our love. However, I'm not finished yet because the title of this section is "Preferences of our lovers." What do we do if one of our lovers is not comfortable being as expressive as I have portrayed? For example, someone who has what I refer to as a flower (others would use the unnecessarily long word "wallflower") personality (Chapter 9) likely has preferences that do not resonate with their waxing poetical in my ear, or vice versa, at least not early in our relationship. In a nutshell, a person with this personality type is relatively quiet, passive, and doesn't express feelings or emotions very openly. There are two general characteristics of a flower lover that are important for the present discussion.

- The first is that they are simply waiting for another to initiate. How should we react in such a situation? ... *Well?* ... Go on then... ... *Initiate, you fool!* ... Just as a simple kiss is often a prelude to something more intimate, our initiation should be subdued compared to some of my examples above. For instance, before we whisper sweet nothings in French or Italian, let's start with something less ethereal, for example a casual conversation during our lunch break: "Is there anyone sitting here? ... May I join you? ... So, what do you think of this training session so far?" With a low-key opening such as this, we may soon find that our quiet counterpart is fluent in many languages, and even has a few new phrases to teach us.

- Another general characteristic of a flower lover is that they are typically quite accommodating to others, sometimes to a fault. Being accommodating – being subordinate – is such a beautiful way to express love within a healthy relationship. We should *all* be striving to be subordinate to *all* our lovers who are trustworthy and treat us fairly. But when our counterpart doesn't have these important characteristics, then we should be looking for other ways to express our love for them – (Yes, we should at least love them unconditionally) – being careful not to become overly accommodating, as that is unloving to both our counterpart (we are enabling their behavior) and ourselves (we are discounting our inherent value). I have more to say in the next section about healthy and unhealthy subordination, but for now I'd like you to be candid with me. ... Do you doubt that we should *all* be striving to be subordinate to *all* our lovers who are trustworthy and treat us fairly? Are you thinking: *Our flower lovers are themselves relatively subordinate by nature, so are we really to be subordinate to them?* ... My answer is an emphatic, *Yes! Especially to them, yes!* ... This may sound difficult, but it really isn't that hard. Below are a few straightforward examples of how you can subordinate yourself to a naturally subordinate person in a healthy way.

- At least half of the times when the two of you have a choice to make – (It could be as simple as where to go to eat, or which movie to see) – ask them their preference – (They may be reluctant to give it… But be persistent!) – and go with that
- Ask for their advice about something specific, and thank them for it
- Praise them for something they do well and, if it's true, add the point that they are more capable than you are in this area
- If it's true, tell them that they inspire you in some specific way – be explicit
- Speak highly of them to others
- Give them a gift for no reason
- When having a conversation, don't dominate and certainly don't interrupt them
- If they say something self-deprecating, counter this without being disingenuous, and explain why you have a different point of view. Be specific, or it won't stick!
- Tell them something personal about yourself, which also shows that you trust them
- From time to time, mimic them in some way, which is a subtle way to show that you like or respect them, or agree with what you're copying
- Thank them for their friendship, and tell them that you care about them, or better yet go all out and tell them that you love them – (Yes, I mean use the L-word!)

Here's an important point to keep in mind; here's why I said, *Especially to them, yes!* While we should subordinate ourselves in a healthy / balanced way to all others who are trustworthy and treat us fairly, who's going to be impacted the most by our behaving in this way? It's a subordinate person! They're not used to being treated like this! They'll take notice! This is a powerful way to show love to a naturally subordinate person. They'll see their inherent value in a new way – part of my 103-word definition of love between people (Chapter 1) – and hopefully in the process get a tangible boost to their self-esteem. And this is just what they need to take a step away from their tendency to be overly accommodating to untrustworthy counterparts…

Prognosis: subordination

Be honest. When I tell you to be subordinate to all your counterparts who are trustworthy and treat you fairly, what is your reaction? What is your prognosis? … If your assessment is that we should amputate the thought from our mind – *stat!* – then I beg to differ, and allow me to elaborate immediately.

You have already learned very well that sometimes a concept is better understood when considered against the backdrop of its opposite (Chapter 1 – "Antonyms of love" section). For this reason, I'll begin this discussion with a description of the opposite of healthy subordination.

- **Unhealthy subordination**: This occurs when we consistently accommodate others who disrespect us and treat us badly. That is – at a minimum – borderline abuse; indeed, unhealthy subordination is often one early step toward an outright abusive relationship. For example, an aggressive man may intimidate his timid partner so easily that the two of them form a habit of him making all decisions – even the small ones. It starts to feel natural – *(to both of them!)* – and a real concern is raised if he's so enamored by the feeling of power and control that he's easily angered when this arrangement is threatened. This is like a freight train rumbling down a mountain toward a railroad switch. The train is going one way or the other, and either way it's not going to be pretty (sharp turns ahead). One direction it can go is extreme subordination of his partner becoming a way of life. This already qualifies as emotional abuse. The other direction it can go is for emotional abuse to evolve such that it encompasses physical abuse. The overall issue here is that the aggressor is generally going to keep pushing the envelope more and more… and more… Who's going to stop him? … If the growing sense of entitlement to wield power and brandish modes of intimidation makes him feel better about himself – strokes his fragile ego – then we've got a real problem on our hands. If you have a friend whom you suspect may be in such a relationship, it can be difficult to learn more and figure out if help is needed, but you have to try. Pray for your friend and for opportunities for you to help, if help is indeed needed. Look for the warning signs of abuse, which include:
  - Change in mood or behavior
  - Increased absenteeism
  - Change in clothing typically worn (for example, tight collar / long sleeves, even on hot days)

- o   Overly anxious to please their partner / fear of disapproval
- o   Comments about their partner making all decisions, being in control of all the finances, being jealous, having a temper, etc.
- o   The above are especially concerning when coupled with warning signs of dependent personality disorder because many sufferers are susceptible to being abused. Symptoms of dependent personality disorder include:
    - ▪   Difficulty making decisions independently
    - ▪   Extremely passive demeanor (lack of assertiveness)
    - ▪   Fear of being alone / abandoned

If you notice such signs, address it with your friend. When doing this, tell them specifically what you noticed. In the rare event that this would legitimately be inappropriate (with the only example I can think of being something related to a part of their anatomy that we should not be looking at, but we inadvertently saw briefly), then say that we notice a difference in them, and ask if everything's OK. If she says that everything's fine, make a point to say that you are her friend and are available whenever there's something she wants to talk about, and that you will of course keep any sensitive topics between the two of you. Even if she tells you nothing initially, she'll appreciate your willingness and this may lead to her opening up later. If the signs continue, ask again, and in my opinion it's often better for any specific concern you raise to be at least somewhat different than what you asked about previously. Obviously, an exception is if there's a particular thing that's especially concerning.

- **Healthy subordination**: In stark contrast to the above, healthy subordination is where both parties in the relationship essentially compete with one another to be subordinate to the other. This is analogous to the first principle of Dr. Bob's sex advice. It's a very simple point: Healthy subordination is when both parties subordinate themselves to the other because of their love for one another; unhealthy subordination is when one of the pair regularly subordinates themselves to the other, with little to no reciprocation from their counterpart.
    - o   In a healthy / balanced relationship, we subordinate ourselves to lift our counterpart up (as described above, where I explained why we should

subordinate ourselves especially to a counterpart having a flower personality)

o In an unhealthy / unbalanced relationship, our counterpart comes to expect our subordination, and in such a way pushes us down

If you're going to irritate me by quoting a fragment of Ephesians 5:24
("Wives should submit in everything to their husbands") out of context, all
I'm going to say – *(You are right to doubt me…)* – to that is: *Keep reading.*
Or do you not want to be reminded that the very next verse says: "Husbands,
love your wives"? *Oh no!* Where's the verse that says wives are to love their
husbands?! *I've searched Ephesians 5 and surrounding chapters, and I can't
find it!* Does this mean that wives are not to love their husbands? No one is
so unreasonable that they would answer "yes" to this (especially in light of
Titus 2:4). Likewise, no one should be so unreasonable that they would say
that husbands should never subordinate themselves to their wives (especially
in light of Ephesians 5:21). Husbands, if my last sentence made you cringe,
you need a timeout. … … OK, you've had ample time to look up Ephesians
5:21, so by now you should know that we are to be "submitting to one another
out of reverence for Christ." … OK, let's move on – *(Again, you are right to
doubt me…)* – but keep thinking about that.

And think about this: Ephesians 5:25 says, "Husbands, love your wives,
as Christ loved the church and gave himself up for her." How did Christ love
the Church? In a nutshell, He came to serve (Matthew 20:25-28; John 13:3-
9). Husbands, we are to love our wives the way that Christ loved the Church
– we are to love our wives by serving them. Healthy / balanced subordination
is an impactful way to serve, to love. And it's really not that hard! I just gave
you a lot of easy ways to do it a few pages ago! If you do such things as I've
listed – and I'm confident you can think of better ways that fit your personal
relationship – then you are surely loving your wife. And when you love your
wife in this fashion, it's natural that her love for you will continue to grow
and be expressed in such ways as her honoring Ephesians 5:24, and I'll now
give that whole verse! "Now as the church submits to Christ, so also wives
should submit in everything to their husbands." Naturally, not only should
she respect you (Ephesians 5:33 GW) and submit to you in everything, but
she *will* respect you and submit to you in everything if and when – (Yes, I

said *if and when… Did you forget that your marriage is a conditional* love relationship?!*) – she knows that she is truly loved by her trustworthy, faithful husband, who always supports and encourages her, always looks out for her best interests, always treats her fairly and with respect, never abuses or otherwise takes advantage of her, and submits to, i.e., meaningfully serves, her "out of reverence for Christ" (Ephesians 5:21), in ways that are fitting to the manner a husband should love his wife.

> *I once heard a pastor say – in public! – during a sermon! – that spouses should love each other "unconditionally, *not conditionally*" (emphasis his). … This is wrong. … In this life, God has set up marriage to be a conditional love relationship (next section and Chapter 10). While spouses should also love one another with a large measure of mutual unconditional love – (making their marriage a cocktail of conditional and unconditional love) – it's *more important* that spouses love one another conditionally. Those who demand 100% unconditional love – with 0% (no) conditions – from their spouses are abusers and/or whiny crybabies. (I told you that I like soapboxes.)

Dichotomies in our rulebooks

In case you missed it, I just mentioned that all healthy marriages are based on conditions being met, and that this is *more important* than the spouses' unconditional love for one another. … *That's right. You heard me.* … Don't believe me? Do you think that a perfect marriage should have no conditions? … I'm an idealist by nature, but even I know that this is nonsensical. Why? Because the world we're living in is saturated with sin, and it's impossible for any two of us to live in harmony with one another with no rules. They may be unwritten rules, but they are established nonetheless – and for good reason! With no rules, we're going to be hurt by our counterpart, and – let's face it – we also know that we're going to hurt them.

Is it a hopeless situation? … No, it's not, because the game of conditional love does come with a rulebook, and when we get married we have entered the big leagues. In the big leagues, we should be following the rulebook with scrupulous attention! When we don't follow the rules, our wholly sensible game of baseball could decompose to the disarray of cricket. To avoid such catastrophes, let us study our rulebook in meticulous detail!

The first rule in the big leagues' rulebook is that each married couple makes up their own rules. What do I mean? There is a template that provides the groundwork, but each couple prioritizes the various dichotomies and sets the boundary within each individual dichotomy. … *Have I lost you?* … *Allow me to explain immediately.* … In the preamble of our template, the purpose of the rulebook is made clear: We live in a sinful world, and when left to our own devices we all drift toward the antonyms of love (Chapter 1). God provides us with loving counterparts – including the special counterpart we love the most (other than God), our spouse – and with each of these counterparts we are to stop such drifting and, instead, together find a safe haven where we are mutually protected from these antonyms. Our protection comes in the form of conditions that, when met, allow sinful people – *That's us!* – to experience love between one another. God does not need such protection, and thus loves us completely unconditionally. But we can be hurt by one another, and we benefit from the protection that conditional love provides.

In our template, standard dichotomies are provided for us (some are listed below). Each dichotomy represents two extremes within which we decide where to draw our boundary, and this location establishes a condition that must be met for there to be harmony in our relationship. In every one of our conditional love relationships, most importantly our marriage, the two of us prioritize the dichotomies and set the boundaries related to each. Even if we don't talk about these things specifically – *(We should!)* – the prioritization and specific boundaries are clearly established. Such things are clear because we know when we've stepped over a boundary… This occurs when healthy conflict emerges. Such conflict not only makes the boundaries clear, but can also cause boundaries to shift – and dichotomies to be reprioritized – in appropriate ways as our conditional love relationship evolves.

If you're confused, the easiest way to get back on track is for me to stop philosophizing and present to you some common dichotomies. I've listed several below. Actually, I've created two lists. The first has those dichotomies for which we should set our boundary all the way over at one extreme end – in my vernacular, the white end – of the spectrum. These are what I call black-and-white dichotomies because *any movement* toward the black end of the spectrum is unacceptable! I'm not saying that a conditional love relationship cannot, in due time, withstand such sins, but I am saying that these sins put the relationship into a crisis, and positive resolution comes only via a timeout period, professional counseling, dedication of both counterparts to work hard toward reconciliation, and renewed pledges that there will be no such breaches in the future.

- Kind and respectful behavior ↤ Abuse
- Sexual faithfulness ↤ Physical intimacy of an erotic nature with another

Yes, my list of black-and-white dichotomies is very short. If you disagree with the brevity of that list, and want to place some of my gray-area dichotomies (listed below) into your list of black-and-white dichotomies, that's totally fine with me. … *Never forget – Rule #1 in all rulebooks is that each pair of counterparts gets to make their own rules!* … Why have I placed all the following into my list of gray-area dichotomies? Isn't the black end of each spectrum unacceptable? Yes, of course, each black end is unacceptable. But above I said that *any movement* toward the black end is unacceptable. Here, I'm saying that a movement toward the black end – while always not our best loving, and in many cases a sin – typically does not place our conditional love relationship into crisis mode. Such intermittent migrations into light gray territory usually don't send us into a tailspin, and that's because we both should have a forgiving attitude and a willingness to strive to do better in the future. Saying this another way: Despite my perfectionist tendencies, even I can see that occasional falterings are to be expected and should be tolerated within a healthy conditional love relationship. Why should these kinds of stumblings be tolerated? Because we have a bond that can withstand such flickering, and we have some measure of mutual unconditional love for one another.

- Kind and respectful behavior ↤ Insensitivity and disrespect
- Sexual faithfulness ↤ Lustful thoughts about another / Obsessive, sexual fantasies / Chronic, flirtatious behavior
- Forming and maintaining healthy friendships outside of our relationship, including with others of the opposite sex ↤ Emotional affair
- Balanced reciprocation ↤ Neglect
- Support ↤ Neglect / Indifference
- Selflessness ↤ Selfishness
- Amenability ↤ Stubbornness

- Reliability ↤ Irresponsible, capricious behavior
- Trustworthiness / Honesty ↤ Chronic lying
- Transparent communication ↤ Manipulation
- Transparent communication ↤ Withholding of important information
- Openness with respect to our feelings and emotions, including discussing things we think should change about our relationship, differences of opinion, things that cause us to feel angry, and the like ↤ Passive aggressiveness
- Gentleness, especially when one makes themselves vulnerable ↤ Harshness
- Comforting ↤ Cold-hearted / Insensitive disposition
- Tolerance ↤ Bigotry
- Tolerance ↤ Judgmental attitude
- Forgiving attitude ↤ Mercilessness
- Remorse over our sin that has hurt our counterpart / weakened our relationship, and our willingness to make a change from that sinful behavior ↤ Hardened heart

Does thinking about such dichotomies disturb you? That's not a surprising reaction because they are a reminder that in this sinful world, interpersonal relationships can get complicated – they do take on shades of gray. But for exactly this reason, establishing appropriate conditions is important. In each of our rulebooks, we find that some conditions go without saying (they become clear simply through the process of bonding), some are formed during our periodic check-ins (Appendix Q), and still more conditions are fleshed out via healthy conflict. Whichever way they are created, suitable conditions provide the framework of our sanctuary – our special place where the two of us protect one another from the antonyms of love.

The sanctuary of marriage

When we're unmarried and in the exploratory stages of building a sanctuary with a counterpart, sometimes we begin to see that it's a comfortable place indeed and that it includes mutual desire for physical intimacy. In such cases, it's natural that we start to develop more elaborate designs for our safe haven. In simpler terms, in such cases it's natural that we begin to consider marriage.

In the preceding section, I make it amply clear that marriage is, first and foremost, a type of conditional love relationship. And in the transition from Chapter 6 to this chapter, I expound in no uncertain terms that conditional love cannot hold a candle to unconditional love – about this, there is no doubt. … *In light of all this evidence, have I disparaged love within a marriage?* … Careful readers already know that of course I have not disparaged love within a marriage! They remember that my definition of conditional love (Chapter 1) states that such relationships should include some measure of mutual unconditional love. So, yes, we can – *and should!* – climb higher than the altitude established by our rulebook. This goes for *every* conditional love relationship. And in the most important type of conditional love relationship of all – a marriage – we should be setting our sights above the clouds.

In marriage, Priority One is to live harmoniously, and to do this we **must** follow our rulebook! When we both have duly demonstrated – as empowered by the Holy Spirit's guiding hand – our unwavering commitment to strive for this, then we are acclimated and equipped to climb higher in our mountain range. Exerting ourselves to make such ascents above the basecamp defined by our rulebook is as close as we can get to a perfect marriage.

~

But before we get out of breath, let's retrace our steps and go back to first principles: Before we become engaged to be married, we should of course take the time and emotional investment it takes to establish a special friendship with our counterpart. If engagement is indeed in our future, somewhere along the way of our splendid journey of mutual discovery (a journey that some blandly refer to as dating), we begin to work together on blueprints for our distinctive sanctuary of marriage. One extension to our sanctuary that we are especially eager to complete is that most private wing of physical intimacy. This portion of our layout brings us to entirely new dichotomies and boundaries within. You are currently unaware that this serves as a perfect segue to my next section!

Should we have sex before marriage?

I was tempted to have this be a one-word section. Any guesses as to what this one word is? … In case you need a hint, it has only two letters. … And these letters just happen to be the first and second letters of the second half of the alphabet.

The answer to this section's question is – *No!* We should *not* have sex before marriage. Why? Because it is God's will that we wait until male-female marriage to include sex in the relationship (Genesis 2:24; 1 Corinthians 7:2; Exodus 22:16; Matthew 5:27-28; Hebrews 13:4).

That's easy for me to say – *I'm married!* … When we're dating, it goes without saying that there's mutual physical attraction. And it also goes without saying that the vast majority of us naturally have sexual desire. We're designed this way, and it's a beautiful design. It's beautiful because God is the designer. Yes, God wants us to enjoy sex as a wonderful expression of love and intimacy between husband and wife (Song of Solomon); and – oh, that's right – on occasion there is conception, another wonderful expression of love and intimacy.

So, with all the benefits of sex, shall we promptly marry the first person we're physically attracted to? From a very limited perspective, that may sound logical – but obviously this is a half-baked idea because becoming husband and wife is a huge commitment that we need to take very seriously, based on much prayerful consideration. A successful marriage needs considerably more than mutual physical attraction. We need to be compatible on many other levels, which can be boiled down to our becoming close friends. I've looked at this from every angle, and I always reach the same conclusion: A close friendship is a prerequisite of becoming husband and wife. Establishing a friendship like this takes time.

We seem to be at a crossroads here. So far in this section I've told you that we should not have sex before marriage, that it's ill-advised to get married before we've taken the long time it takes to fully bake a close friendship – of course with someone we're physically attracted to, and they us – and that by design we both have sexual desire. So, the 64-thousand-dollar question is: *What are we supposed to do in the meantime?*

In my opinion, the best course of action is:

- Only date one person at a time, and this needs to be someone we're attracted to *both* physically *and* emotionally

- If we take the time to establish a friendship and we both are interested in beginning a physical relationship, express our desire to do so with words and, if both are comfortable, with very simple forms of physical affection (holding hands, kissing, *hands back on the waist, mister*)
  - If we take more time to establish a closer friendship such that we both are willing to talk sincerely about what it would be like to be married to one another, then, if both are comfortable, increase physical affection a little bit more – a *very little* bit more (*Dude! I already warned you!*) – being careful that any advancement from one encounter to another is extremely limited.

    Importantly, before marriage, any step toward an increase in physical intimacy should be vanishingly small so we don't get overwhelmed and submit to temptation. Before venturing down an unfamiliar path, the new boundaries must be crystal clear – and *absolutely* respected.
  - If we become engaged to be married, then, if both are comfortable, increase physical affection a little bit more (taking small, clear steps, as above), of course still refraining from intercourse and anything on the brink of this (see below).

    Engagement should not be taken lightly. Do not become engaged unless only an unforeseen circumstance (large surprise) would cause you to change your mind. You should both spend much time in prayer before agreeing to become engaged.

Throughout this time, are we sinning? My view is that it's possible to do all of the above without sinning. (I hope by now you know that I would not suggest anything that I thought would of course be sinful.) Is it possible that we *are* sinning? *Absolutely!* Even before our first kiss we're sinning if we're having lewd, disrespectful thoughts about our counterpart. So, of course we may be sinning throughout this process. But if we can set lewd, disrespectful thoughts aside, the reason I think physical affection beyond hands on the waist can be done without sinning is that – in the way I described it – our degree of physical intimacy is progressing slowly, in parallel with our emotional closeness. In every physically intimate relationship, it's always important for physical intimacy not to rush ahead of – but rather remain balanced with – emotional closeness. And I already told you (in the first bullet point) that each of us should be on such a journey with only one other person. To be pursuing this type of special friendship with two people simultaneously is definitely not our best loving; yes, we are sinning against both of our counterparts. We should have no more than one physically intimate relationship at a time. (This is discussed further in the "Exclusive, intimate bliss" subsection, later in this chapter.)

There still is something that hasn't been addressed; I'll call it the elephant in the room. ... (Yes, we need to talk about this. It's a common question of Christian singles.) ... What if we're in a dating relationship and we can't function properly without a sexual outlet beyond the limited physical affection described above? ... We shouldn't short circuit the process; we shouldn't shorten the timeline. Nope, it's best to remain patient. ... Throughout this journey, we shouldn't directly involve our boyfriend / girlfriend in the intimate degree of physical affection inferred by the elephant in the room. Nope, that would be on the brink of intercourse, already causing both counterparts to sin (physical intimacy rushing way ahead of – not in balance with – emotional closeness), and that's unloving. ... OK, elephant, I'm finally going to address you... Here goes... ... *Oh, I'm definitely doing this; don't you have any doubt about that!* ... If we're in a dating relationship and we truly can't function properly without a sexual outlet beyond the limited physical affection described above, then the most loving thing we can do to resolve the situation is pleasure ourselves. It's so easy to sin when doing this, in light of Matthew 5:27-28; however, I consider there to be at least two scenarios where doing this is not a sin. (The first isn't directly relevant to this discussion, but it sets up the second scenario nicely.) In my opinion, it's not a sin if we're married *and* thinking only of our spouse *and* when they're unavailable for more than a limited time (1 Corinthians 7:3-5). (I consider "limited time" to mean at least a few weeks. If they'll be available in less time than this, it's better to wait.) That settles that, and now let's move on to the second scenario. We're much more likely to be faced with this because now I'm talking about a dating relationship. And guess what that means? ... *It means that our counterpart is most definitely* NOT *available!* When we're in such a relationship, in my opinion, it's not a sin to pleasure ourselves if we're thinking only of our counterpart, and only in a respectful and loving way. I consider this not to be committing adultery in our heart (Matthew 5:27-28) because we're in a special relationship with our counterpart. Importantly, however, our thoughts should not be lewd and disrespectful, as that is sinful.

Guys – the above paragraph applies to you as well.

Shall we be moving along? … Any requests for further elaboration? … *No?* … OK, I will submit to your wishes – that is, after the following four-part dénouement.

- Historically, the elephant in the room has been considered by many to be always sinful – even shameful. However, I don't agree. If we're thinking only of our boyfriend / girlfriend, and not in a lewd, disrespectful manner, then what do we have to be ashamed about?

- Furthermore, such a sexual outlet provides a way to supplement, privately and individually, the slow progression of our special friendship, helping us remain stalwart in our respect of boundaries when we are together. If this isn't being loving to our boyfriend / girlfriend, then I'd like to hear you explain to me why that is.

- How can I say that the elephant in the room often is not sinful in the context of a dating relationship, and also say that we should not directly involve our special counterpart in the elephant? Isn't that inconsistent? … Good questions, and here is my good answer: Before marriage, the elephant is a private and individual matter. Why? Because when two are involved, the elephant is standing on the brink – indeed, he's at the very threshold – of intercourse, and an unmarried couple should not be this close to the edge for *both* of the following reasons: It's out of balance (already enough of a reason) *and* if we do submit to temptation – fall off the edge (so easy to do) – we are being exceedingly unloving to one another; what has happened cannot be undone.

- Finally, I understand that a dating relationship may disintegrate and that both people may go on to marry others. Even if this happens, I think it's reasonable that the first two individuals would have the type of background described above. They waited until marriage to have intercourse; and they waited until marriage to directly involve a counterpart in the intimate degree of physical affection inferred by the elephant in the room. You already know that I like analogies, and here's another: Having engaged in physical affection that progressed beyond hands on the waist – in balance with emotional closeness – with someone we never marry, then moving on to other dating relationships, and eventually marrying one such counterpart is a reasonable background because the physically affectionate experiences are analogous to the sexual experiences within a first marriage of someone who goes on to marry a second time (based on either their first spouse dying or a divorce for a legitimate reason, such as unfaithfulness [Matthew 5:31-32] or, I would add, abusive behavior without resolution [Appendix Ɔ]).

~

I'd like to end this section with words of encouragement to those of you who are single. Take to heart the following blessings of waiting until male-female marriage to have sex.

- Ladies, please don't go further than you are comfortable, no matter how persistent your counterpart is. If he's worth continuing to date, he'll respect your wishes to go slowly and have boundaries. He needs to learn to be patient. Two (of many) attributes you should be looking for in a man you would consider marrying are patience and respect for your wishes. At some point in your journey of getting to know him better, why not tell him that these are attributes you consider to be important? If he's a good friend and wants your friendship to grow further, he'll take this very seriously.
  - o (The above bullet point is a generalization. Guys, please do similarly if your girlfriend is persistent.)
- Guys, please don't push it. A girl or woman who doesn't want to go fast with anyone is beautiful and worth waiting for. While you initially may be disappointed, don't forget that you're blessed to be establishing a close relationship with a lady who's virtuous and trustworthy. Isn't that the type of woman you want to marry? *(Guys, your heads should be nodding up and down now… Yes, that's it…)*
  - o (The above bullet point is a generalization. Ladies, please don't push it either.)

In summary, attributes of people who are willing to wait until marriage to have sex are exactly the attributes we should be looking for in a potential spouse: patience, virtue, respect, and trustworthiness.

Dr. Bob's sex advice

Here's the part of the book that many of you have been waiting for! I like to call this section "Dr. Bob's sex advice," but you might end up calling it "Is that all you've got?" If that's your attitude, then I think you're looking at sex as only a means to physical pleasure. But it's meant to be much more than that.

Choosing our personal pronoun wisely

Let me start with a question for you, and as you can see I'm diving right into the deep end of the pool here: When you are having sex, how much of your attention is devoted to your pleasure? Many sex advice books go on at great length – sometimes even with intriguing pictures! – providing an abundance of compelling ideas for how you can achieve even more pleasure. It might surprise you to learn that I'm not so prudish that I frown upon such guidance. Actually, my only issue with these suggestions is the personal pronoun that's often emphasized – and in case I'm not being clear, I mean: *you*. That's right – you're turned 180 degrees off target if you're focused on achieving more pleasure for *yourself*. My guidance for you – sorry, no pictures… – is to focus on *your spouse* achieving more pleasure! Good sex requires good communication (more on this below), and I can't think of anything more pleasing for your spouse to perceive than you are going to focus on their pleasure. And if you're persuasive enough such that you can convince them to give this a try as well – *(If you take the first step, then I'm confident that you'll be very persuasive!)* – then all I can say is you are about to embark on a beautiful journey, and I wish you well!

Holding our horses

Second of all, what's our hurry? We've got lots of time, and what better way to spend it than being intimate with our spouse? I have a time challenge for you, and this doesn't have anything to do with how *often* you are intimate. (Please wait patiently for my words of wisdom on that.) It has everything to do with the amount of time *per intimate rendezvous*, what I refer to as the whole enchilada. Obviously, it varies somewhat from one enchilada to another, so let me put it this way. Whatever your average intimate rendezvous time has been over the past year, I challenge you to increase this average by at least 50% over the coming year, and then another such increase the year after that. So, I'm giving you lots of time to improve! And to be clear, I'm *not* talking only about the amount of time when you're literally one with your spouse (intercourse); I'm talking about the amount of time for the whole enchilada of being physically intimate (including foreplay, etc., and cooldown). Yes, I know who I need to talk to…

- Guys, huddle up. … Here's the deal. I can't help but notice that some of you are quite intent on scoring that touchdown – yes, even winning the game… But look at the clock! It's still only the first quarter! We've got 100 yards of turf, and plenty of time on our hands. Don't worry – you'll score that touchdown. But before you do that, you need to make sure that your challenger knows you mean business! If you think I'm going to tell you that winning is everything or the only thing: take a lap, hit the pine, and listen up! I don't want you to just lose the game… oh, no… I want you to lose the game in impressive fashion! Even if she doesn't score any touchdowns this time, I still want her to win by a landslide based on field goals and safeties. (Safeties are especially fun…) If you start looking down the field toward that goal line before the fourth quarter, I want you to signal for a timeout and draw up a different play. Here's a good call – another unconverted third down followed by a punt – and then another and another. I want to see grass stains all over your punter! And I want her punter to be bored silly. … And after you finally score that touchdown, on the last play of the game, there are still two things left for you to do: First, with tender affection, gently and unhurriedly show the victor what a good sport you are. … Lastly, … Oh, excuse me, I'll keep waiting. *You're learning exceptionally well!* … … OK, lastly, I want you to lie back on the turf and look up at that scoreboard; know that I'm proud of you for losing – yes, I'm proud of you for that – but if you lost by less than double digits, then it's time for you to tighten the laces on your Keds® because you're looking at ten laps buddy!
- And now a few words for the ladies: Your husband desperately needs your help! I think some of these guys don't even know what a safety is… And from what I've seen of their cooking skills, many of them don't know much about cooking an enchilada, let alone the whole enchilada. So, they'll need some guidance. Give it! And while you're at it, tell them that you want them to hold their horses, and take their time. If they give you any trouble, send them to me – and I'll make it twenty laps!

Keeping it crisp

Yes, enchiladas can be hard to cook. So much is dependent on good communication. None of us are mind-readers – we all need guidance. And everyone is different. I don't care how detailed the descriptions are in the enchilada book you have, or how many compelling pictures therein, your spouse is unique and deserves custom attention.

Some of us are a little embarrassed to talk about such things, even with our spouse. One thing to keep in mind is that words may not even be necessary – body language can speak volumes. If nevertheless you find yourself too timid to speak in any language about this subject matter, the first step is to create a safe environment where the two of you are comfortable making yourselves vulnerable to one another in this way. The one in the pair who is more comfortable expressing themselves should set the example, first by making some simple clarifications, then, importantly, asking their spouse some simple questions. If this still isn't enough for new ideas to emerge, then my suggestion is to set aside a time once a year (for example, near your anniversary or near New Year's) for the two of you to have a conversation about new things that you want to try in the coming year. I like to call such a meeting of the minds and bodies: *Our binary vision of consensual sex under the next 12 moons*. When I preside over such meetings, I'm a stickler about both having equal time – even the same number of suggestions. But something tells me that I will not be presiding over any of your annual meetings, so you're on your own in this regard. But at least give me the satisfaction of knowing that neither of you will be dominating the conversation. Keep in mind that the suggestions the two of you bring forth shouldn't be limited to specific ways to engage in foreplay or intercourse; rather, they can also relate to things like timing, venue, clothing, etc. – any of the ingredients of the whole enchilada.

- You have to agree ahead of time that you'll respect your spouse no matter what they suggest. The two of you are already as physically intimate as you can get, so I think you can handle a simple suggestion.
- Of course your spouse has veto power. This may play out in either of two ways. Your spouse may say, *"Absolutely not!"* in which case you need to respect that (don't whine or try to bargain). Alternatively, your spouse may say that they're not really sure, and need time to think about it or take it slow with preliminary steps.

- ○ (In my opinion, a suggestion that is vetoed counts as a "turn" – I told you I'm a stickler – but you're more than welcome to make up your own rules… *How gracious of me!*)

Dr. Bob's inflexible definition of fair game

So far, I've talked about focusing on your spouse instead of yourself, slowing down, and good communication to keep things fresh. Underlying all of these is respect for your partner. I did allude to this in the preceding filled-circle bullet point about veto power. That really goes without saying, but it's so important that I'll say it again, although in a slightly different way: In a healthy sexual relationship, pretty much anything is fair game, provided that both partners are emotionally stable, treat each other as equals, respect the seclusion of their sexual activity (i.e., don't supplement in any way that involves anyone else – not only literally [as in an open relationship], but also in such contexts as sexual fantasies and viewing hardcore pornography), and are truly OK with doing it; but if either partner doesn't want to do it – does not consent – then a line has been drawn that should *not* be crossed! Rule #1 in sex is: Both are to respect their partner! There are more than enough ideas out there, and you both should be content doing only what you *and your partner* are comfortable with. That is the loving way to be.

Dr. Bob's inflexible definition of natural abundance

With so many good ideas to try, even after narrowing them down to the ones that both partners are comfortable with, it's obvious that married couples should be having sex often. An even more important reason for spouses to have sex often is that this is such a meaningful part of bonding. Yes, the strands related to sex are very delicate indeed, thus yielding strong, enduring bonds.

So, what are my words of wisdom related to the frequency of sex? What's my definition of "often"? … Am I going to make it mandatory that you buy an oversized wall-calendar and a vast selection of colored pens, one hue per good idea to try? Well, for one thing, I'm not sure I can assume that your budget and/or storage space can accommodate buying that many pens. And, for another thing, as tempting as it may be to storyboard each and every intimate rendezvous for the upcoming week, let us not overlook the benefits of spontaneity. I like to plan as much as the next person, but when it comes to sex let us throw our planners out the window. Having said that, there is one small bit of planning – no planner or wall-calendar needed for this – that I do recommend to ensure that we meet my definition of "often." Oh, have I not defined that yet? My apologies. Let me correct this immediately. My definition of often is very often. Married couples: To ensure that you have sex very often, make a goal with your spouse to have sex at least once by the end of each time cycle that you agree upon. For example, some couples on their honeymoon may be able to establish bihourly cycles, a.k.a., essentially continuous activity – a blurring of cycles, let us say. For the rest of us, I do suggest a longer time cycle than this. ... Are you waiting anxiously for my recommended time cycle? ... After much internal deliberation, I've decided to allow you to establish between yourselves your own time cycle – your own definition of very often. ... *You're welcome!* ... If you're not sure how this works, let me provide an example. If you and your spouse agree upon the (what some of us would consider an agonizingly long) time cycle of weekly, the next step is to agree upon when this time cycle ends. Let's imagine that you've agreed that it ends each Saturday night. This means that if you haven't had sex spontaneously all week long – *all week long!* – then you will be having sex on Saturday night, or I will know the reason why (Translation: you owe me an explanation).

- In all seriousness, I really do recommend that married couples agree upon a recurring timeframe within which both partners will make a good effort to be sexually intimate with one another at least once. In my view, the agreed-upon time cycle should be sufficiently long such that spontaneous sex usually occurs at least once before the time cycle ends. My opinion is that spontaneity is the ideal, and I consider the time cycle approach to be "Plan B" in the unfortunate (and hopefully rare) event that spontaneous sex is not part of your recent history.

  I do understand that sometimes there are good reasons why an entire time cycle will go by without physical intimacy. Except for extreme circumstances (for example, illness or extended time away from one another), empty time cycles should be infrequent, and – please – at least give me the satisfaction of knowing that you'll do your best to more than make up for this glitch the next time you are both healthy and together!

- A potential downside to establishing a time cycle is the possibility that sex could start to feel routine or even burdensome to one or both partners. This is an important point, and I have a little more to say about this in the next main section. *Stay tuned!*

Exclusive, intimate bliss

Last but certainly not least, I want to say a few words about loyalty. At all periods of our life, there should be only one other person with whom we are physically intimate. Never cheat on your partner! Your partner may change for one reason or another as you enter a new chapter in your life, but this change in partner should be clear cut. Never cheat on your current partner! This is certainly true if we're married, but I'm adamant that this is the case even if we're not. Why? When we're physically intimate, we should be totally focused on our partner. Of course, at most times in our life we're not making an enchilada, but every time we are we should be going back to that same comfortable place – that place of intimacy that we share with the one person we love the most. At such times, for us to be totally focused on them – to be truly one with them – it's inconceivable that the thought of anyone else would be distracting us. An intimate relationship infers two, and only two. The person we love the most deserves to be the only one we are physically intimate with – any breach in this is nowhere near our best loving.

All the sex advice in the world, including mine up until this point, pales in comparison to this: When you marry someone, you're telling them that they're the person you love the most and that you're committed to maintaining a loving relationship with them; be loyal to the person you love the most – be sexually intimate only with them – and you have achieved bliss.

Slippery upper slopes and sheer drop-offs related to sex

Well, that's the extent of my sex advice – all the rest are details, which you can work out on your own!

But there are a few more things I want to say on the topic, in a broad sense. Let me continue with some commentary on the good, the bad, and the ugly about sex.

The good thing about sex is that it's intimately private and prodigiously pleasurable. The bad thing about sex is that it's intimately private and prodigiously pleasurable. The ugly thing about sex is that it's intimately private and prodigiously pleasurable.

What do I mean? Simply this: The features that make sex so great are the very things that can trip us up. For example, in a healthy sexual relationship, the intimate privacy allows both partners to experience such emotional and physical closeness that they literally become one; and of course they give one another the gift of prodigious physical pleasure. But sometimes our sinful hearts and minds get so caught up in the fervor that we twist this beautiful experience into an unattractive burden, or possibly a disfigured hardship, or sometimes all the way to a warped nightmare.

Where do I begin? Let me start with mere falterings, move on to the moderately atrocious, and finally work my way down to the depths of the truly heinous. In the following subsections, a large component to most if not all of these malfunctions is our desire for physical pleasure, but for many of these there is also the desire in some of us to control and – I'm sorry to say – sometimes even demean others, and underlying all of these is our selfishness, which is one opposite of love (Chapter 1). Yes, it's obvious that the flaws and dysfunctions described in each of the following subsections are not our best loving.

Cooling our jets

I don't need to remind you that sex is pleasurable. So, it's not surprising that many of us like to do it a lot! But, wait, sex requires two… And sometimes our partner is not in the mood, or is tired, or for whatever reason doesn't want to have sex right now. It's unloving to expect our partner to flip a switch just because we happen to want to turn the lights out.

I hate to break this to you, but if this is the situation you find yourself in, then the best course of action is to cool your jets and wait. I don't think I need to convince you that sex is most enjoyable when both partners desire it. When one partner is not desiring it, then we should be patient. If you're concerned with how long the wait will be, there are ways to reduce it… Do something else to please your partner, keeping in mind their primary love language. And literally tell them that you love them. I doubt that you'll have to wait too terribly long for their flower to bloom…

If, despite my pleas for patience, you make your intentions clear – so abundantly clear that your partner feels guilty and goes ahead and tries to "flip their switch" as best they can – the danger is that sex might be starting to feel like a duty to them. Frequent sex is great, provided that it doesn't turn into mere routine or, worse, seem like a burden to either partner. It's better to wait until both are enthusiastic and motivated.

- In all of this, keep in mind the time cycle I recommended in the previous main section

  o On the one hand, remembering that a time cycle has been established provides a way for the more eager partner to remain patient – they know that the wait will probably be no longer than what has already been agreed upon. Also, either partner may experience a growing sense of anticipation as the current time cycle ticks down, and we all know that anticipation is an effective aphrodisiac.

  o On the other hand, if we find ourselves regularly waiting until the end of each time cycle to finally have sex, then we should ask ourselves if sex is starting to feel routine or burdensome to either of us. If yes, then a longer time cycle may be appropriate for us. However, that's a slippery slope that I'm hesitant to suggest starting to slide down. A better suggestion is for the two of us to talk about it openly and honestly, and consider supplementing this with couples therapy, as there may be some underlying issues that a counselor can help us resolve.

    Married couples: This is important and deserves full attention, as regularly giving our spouse the gift of intimacy is part of our marriage commitment (1 Corinthians 7:3-5). That may sound a bit stodgy, but not all commitments need to be a burden to fulfill. Jets are built for flying, after all – let's give them a chance to soar in pairwise fashion. And don't forget that the twosome flight is not all about physical closeness – it's a time for emotional closeness as well. Why not start the evening by simply telling your spouse specific, nonsexual reasons why you're happy to be with them at the end of the day, and see what clouds begin to nucleate? My experience has been that excellent flying conditions tend to develop during an intimate conversation. And don't fret if it takes a few conversations for your favorite cloud formation to appear; we all know how unpredictable the weather is.

Harmful distractions

Yes, sex is pleasurable and some of us want to do it a lot. If we're not patient as we look to the skies for suitable conditions, then we might start to look elsewhere for other ways to satisfy our desires. A common example is turning to pornography, which unfortunately is so easy to access these days because of the internet. Another common example is sexual fantasies about others, possibly even others we know personally. Turning to pornography or internal sexual fantasies is extremely disrespectful and emotionally hurtful to our partner, we're committing adultery in our heart (Matthew 5:27-28), and, if we're married, we're not respecting our marriage.

If we find ourselves ensnared with such distractions, we should talk to our partner about ways to become closer.

If you are at times distracted with pornography, I want you to think seriously about how damaging this behavior is to so many people, not only yourself and your partner, but also consider that you are supporting an industry that is a deep chasm entrapping so many, in and behind the scenes. This is not what God intended sex to be! God wants us to enjoy real sex as a private time of emotional and physical closeness with our spouse. If, instead, you're slipping down into the crevasse of pornography, I'd like you to pray the following right now.

- *God, I know that it's unhealthy on so many levels to look at porn, but I just can't stop going back to it. I'm realizing that I might be addicted to it. First of all, forgive me. Second of all, help me put it aside once and for all. I remember that You have promised that You will not let me be tempted beyond a point that I cannot be rescued by Your provision; yes, I know You will provide me with a way to escape the temptation (1 Corinthians 10:13). I don't seem to be able to find a way of escape on my own. So, I'm asking You to please show me the way! If I truly am addicted, please motivate me to get professional help. I love my partner, and enjoy being intimate with them, but at other times my mind has wandered and I've desired others. Help me focus on my partner, and completely forsake all others at all times.*

Privacy, please

Sex is intimate, which means two, and only two. With all distractions behind us, we naturally find ourselves intensely focused on our spouse. With no one to disturb us, both of us naturally find ourselves uninhibited. The time for even a hint of restraint is long past. Throughout the breathtaking voyage, we are comfortable because we are alone with the person we love the most. We are free to express ourselves in ways no one else would understand.

Privacy related to our sexual practices is a gift we give each other at *all* times. Even when we're not together, the specifics of what we do when we are together stay between the two of us – it is our secret. If one partner tells or, God forbid, shows any specifics to anyone else, that is being exceedingly disrespectful and emotionally hurtful to the other partner. This is a severe breach of trust. (Of course, an exception is if the two of us agree to discuss such specifics with a counselor.)

We should never tell a secret to someone we don't trust. … How do I know that I can trust my wife? I know because when I ask her to hang the "do not disturb" sign on our hotel room door handle, after doing that she closes the door… and locks it… and latches the chain… She knows that I'm not going to tell her any secrets until I'm sure that we're not going to be disturbed by anyone: not her best friend across the hall, not the dutiful maid, and not even the curious bellhop. When I'm telling a secret, do you seriously expect me to hear a knock on the door? A flimsy sign is not enough. The door must be bolted and latched.

Unprotected exposure

When we're intimate with someone – when we're telling them our special secret – we make ourselves vulnerable to them. Sex is as physically intimate as we can get, and it should also include a good measure of emotional intimacy. Such vulnerability inherently means that we can be hurt. For example, if our partner criticizes our physical appearance, our emotional response (or apparent lack thereof), our intimate preferences, our "sexual performance," or similar personal things, this is profoundly upsetting.

If you experience this, immediately tell your partner how this makes you feel. If they respect you, they'll stop. If they don't stop, then you're in a close relationship with someone who isn't being at all loving when they ignore your appropriate admonishment, and instead continue to say things that disrespect and emotionally hurt you.

We should never lock ourselves in a hotel room with someone who makes a habit of throwing things. And when they throw our secret back in our face, we need to have a serious conversation that includes the potentiality that we'll be checking out early.

Unfaithfulness

Worse than any of the above is cheating on our partner – being physically intimate with someone else before ending the first relationship. For the one cheated on, this gashes a deep wound that leaves a lifelong scar. This is especially true if the first relationship is a marriage.

Yes, reconciliation is possible after one cheats on the other, but this calls for a great deal of couples therapy* and time to reestablish trust. After one has cheated on the other, the couple is at a crossroads, and must choose between ending the relationship or working closely together to try to restore it. It's not a loving option to continue the relationship when cheating has occurred and nothing substantial is done to address it. Cheating is the reddest of flags and cannot be swept under the rug.

- In the "What if your partner is unfaithful to you?" section (Chapter 9) is a story that describes a husband struggling to forgive his wife who was unfaithful one time

*Note: Several times in this book, I recommend professional counseling. I understand that sometimes this is a financial hardship for us, especially if we don't have health insurance that includes substantial coverage for the type of treatment that would be most beneficial to us. When paying for therapy out of pocket would be a real financial burden, we have entered the realm of a gray-area issue.

If you are struggling with something that is impacting your life in a relatively light gray way, then an option is to make use of a mindfulness / meditation app, such as Calm® or Headspace®, and/or cognitive behavioral therapy (CBT) app, such as Moodfit®, Sanvello®, Daylio®, or TalkLife®. I recommend supplementing this with regularly scheduled (weekly is typically a good frequency) discussions of your progress with someone you trust, such as your spouse, another close friend, pastor, other church-worker, social worker, or a support group.

If, on the other hand, your life is being impacted by a red flag, a black flag, or a flag of any other color that can only be described as dark gray, then I implore you to find a way to get professional help. Your best friend has pitched well for eight innings, but even from the steps of the dugout you can see that it's time for some relief. Loosening-up in the bullpen is a professional non-judger (a rare combination) who has been in such situations before. They are paid the big bucks for a reason, and they are duly warmed-up and ready to throw their patented change-up.

Now's the time to dig deep with one hand and wave them in with the other.

Sexual abuse in an adult relationship

I just called cheating the reddest of flags. There is another flag that is the blackest of black – and that is the flag of abusive behavior. Any type of abuse is abhorrent, but sexual abuse has its own disgusting twist to it. Here I'm talking about sexual abuse within an established couple whose lives otherwise appear relatively normal. This is an example where the intimate privacy inherent to sex is being used to hide a secret – a dirty secret of one using intimidation, manipulation, and sometimes even physical force to control the other. In a nutshell, sexual abuse occurs when one humiliates the other in a sexual manner, or when one coerces the other to perform any sex act that they don't want to do, at least not at that particular time, and it's often something that is physically hurtful and/or that most people would consider degrading.

(Recall Dr. Bob's inflexible definition of fair game: Pretty much anything is fair game in a healthy sexual relationship, provided that both partners are emotionally stable, treat each other as equals, respect the seclusion of their sexual activity, and are truly OK with doing it. But if either partner doesn't want to do it – does not consent – then a line has been drawn that should *not* be crossed!)

One of the sad aspects about sexual abuse is that the victim is often very reluctant to tell anyone about the abuse – for one thing because they might be embarrassed, possibly even to the extent of deep shame – and for another thing because they might be scared of their partner's reaction. Another sad aspect about sexual abuse in an established relationship is the complicated nature of the relationship; yes, the victim may still love their partner, despite their abusive behavior, in which case the victim may not see leaving as a viable part of a solution.

If you're in a sexually abusive relationship, words cannot express how sorry I am, and I'd like you to pray right now. I suggest starting with the following prayer-testimony of a wife who is being sexually abused by her husband, and then customize it to fit your circumstances as you take your own story to our heavenly Father.

- *God, I'm very confused right now. When my husband and I started having sex, I was happy to be close to him in that way. But when the newness wore off, he seemed to keep wanting more and more from me. At first, that seemed like a natural progression as we became more experienced in lovemaking. But some of the things he wants me to do make me uncomfortable and cause me to feel bad about myself. I've tried to talk to him about it, and sometimes he seems to understand and back off, but then the next time he wants it again, and even gets angry if I say I don't want to. He says I should do it, if I love him. I'm so confused! I still do love him [or, I sometimes feel that I still love him], but what he's doing doesn't seem right to me. I so much want to talk to someone about this, but it's embarrassing. Who can I talk to? What should I say to my husband? God help me!*

I've purposely ended this prayer-testimony without an implication that the woman starts to realize some answers to her questions. I did this for two reasons. First, this is exactly how many of our prayers are; they are cries for help, and the answers come later. Second, good answers to such questions are so specific to your situation. So, all I can do is give some general recommendations. My best advice is that you really do need to talk about this. Talking to God is the best place to start. You also need to find others to talk to: perhaps a close friend or pastor, but more importantly you should talk to a professional counselor or social worker to help you create a safety plan. In these conversations, please don't be embarrassed! Obviously, you don't need to get into the specifics. It's enough to say that your partner is expecting things that you're not comfortable with, and you don't know how to deal with it. Such conversations should help you identify a path forward, including generating a safety plan and identifying a safe haven (friend's home, family member's home, shelter) where you can go if needed; don't tell your partner where this is.

At some point, the path forward includes addressing the situation with your partner. Every couple is different, and you both should be talking together with a counselor to get their advice for your particular relationship. If you are seeing a counselor periodically but your partner is not yet accompanying you, I do have some general advice about how to ask them to do so. In my opinion, a good time for such a conversation is very soon after having sex, or perhaps the following morning. Your partner may be most open to a change in their sexual behavior at such times. Below I give two scenarios where a conversation seems like a good idea, provided you're confident that you're safe; I also give a third scenario where I advise initiating a timeout period before having such a conversation.

- If your most recent sexual encounter was abusive, you love your partner anyway, you do enjoy being physically close to them when it's not abusive, and you're confident that you're safe, then I suggest:
  o Tell your partner that you love them and that you enjoy being physically close to them, except there are certain things that you really don't like doing – be sure to give the specific example that just occurred – and for the sake of the relationship you want to talk to them about it, and that the best way to do this is to talk together with a counselor
- If your most recent sexual encounter was *not* abusive, you love your partner, you do enjoy being physically close to them when it's not abusive, and you're confident that you're safe, then I suggest:
  o Tell your partner that you love them and that you enjoy being physically close to them, except there are certain things that you really don't like doing – be sure to give a recent specific example – and how thankful you are that this most recent time something like this did not occur; nevertheless, for consistency in this and for the sake of the relationship you want to talk to them about it, and that the best way to do this is to talk together with a counselor
- If you're not sure you really love your partner anymore, or you don't enjoy being physically close to them anymore, or you feel in danger, then I urge you to follow the advice in the "What if you are being abused?" section (Chapter 9)

Unfortunately, the victim of sexual abuse has the additional burden of being the only one who can blow the whistle on the dirty secret. This is a private sin, and the abuser isn't going to stop on their own. Yes, the abuser needs help, and the most loving thing the victim can do – for themselves and for their abuser – is blow the whistle one way or another. A soft blow may be enough, if the abuser will agree to go to counseling and take it seriously. Otherwise, a loud blow is needed, and this may take the form of staying at a safe haven for an extended period, filing for divorce, and filing charges of abuse. It takes courage to blow the whistle, but I know you have it in you. When you say, *Enough is enough!* you are surely giving your best loving to *everyone* in your life, not the least of whom is yourself.

And now for a few words of admonishment and, yes, comfort for you if you're the one being abusive to your partner. First things first: I want you to know that God still loves you. And it's for this very reason (Hebrews 12:5-11; Revelation 3:19) that He commands that you stop this behavior! You must stop hurting those around you, especially the one who because of love and physical intimacy has made themselves most vulnerable to you. Stop taking advantage of them! I understand that there are circumstances in your life that have caused you to struggle with this, and that it may be difficult to change on your own. All I'm asking is that you take this seriously, read the "What if you are struggling with the sin of your own abusive behavior?" section (Chapter 9), ask God to help you, and get help from friends, your pastor, and a professional counselor. Such people should not judge you. (If they do, give them a copy of this book!) True friends and mentors really do want to help you wipe the slate clean. And when progress is made in your own disposition, focus on the ultimate goal, which is to work together with your partner so you can reconcile and establish a more loving relationship.

Sexual abuse of a child

Even worse than what I describe above is sexual abuse of a child. Example warning crimes – sexual harassment – are in the heartbreaking story that ends in the rape of a child (Chapter 5 – "One black stepping stone" section). If you suspect that any such crimes are occurring in anyone's life, you must follow up, ask questions, and take the child seriously. The instant you become aware of any such crimes occurring now or at any time in the past, you need to take immediate action for the sake of the child's physical and emotional wellbeing – not only now but for the rest of their life. If they live with you and the abuser, for example you are their mother and the abuser is their father, then leave the home immediately with the child to take them to safety, and don't come back until the situation has resolved one way or another. Support can be found 24/7 at the National Sexual Assault Hotline (800-656-HOPE (4673)) or by visiting www.rainn.org. But, as always, call the police or 911 if help is needed urgently.

Regarding the perpetrator, the most loving thing we can do for him is to file the full gamut of charges and do everything we can to make sure he's punished to the maximum extent permissible by law. Doing any less is enabling his behavior, which is not loving him at all. Pray that this punishment may motivate him to turn his life upside down, to start living in a loving and caring manner, 180 degrees off course from his heinous crime(s). In all of this, let us remember that final judgment isn't ours (Psalm 75; Matthew 7:1-5; John 5:22; Romans 2:1-3; 1 Corinthians 4:5) and that God's incredible love is capable of bringing about changes we can't imagine.

And even if there is such a miracle, let us never forget the lasting impact the crime(s) have on the victim. We should pray for them often, actively nurture and support them, and never let them forget that there are many trustworthy people who love them very much.

~

As I warned you at the beginning of this overall section, sex is intimately private and prodigiously pleasurable, and unfortunately these features lead some to take harsh advantage of another's vulnerability. This is the opposite of what God intended sex to be. He designed sex to be an intimately private, prodigiously pleasurable, and frequent expression of love between husband and wife, with both being comfortable harmonizing their vulnerabilities.

Further reflection on the sin of sex before marriage

Some of you may be upset that I'm not hammering harder on the sin of sex before marriage. Several of my statements have actually acknowledged that such shenanigans are taking place! While it's absolutely correct that God intends sexual intimacy to be reserved only for male-female marriage relationships (Genesis 2:24; 1 Corinthians 7:2; Exodus 22:16; Matthew 5:27-28; Hebrews 13:4), it has come to my attention that sex before marriage is a common sin. Yes, it is a sin. Nevertheless, instead of ignoring it or lobbing fireballs, when I speak of the important topic of the dysfunctions that can occur in sexual relationships, I've decided to include in the conversation everyone who's partaking. In many cases, single people who are in a sexual relationship are at least considering marrying their partner somewhere down the road. Whether an unmarried, sexually active couple is consciously considering marriage or not, I'd like them to be thinking along with the rest of us about how to respect and honor one another at all times – during *and before* marriage. I'd much rather approach it this way, as opposed to lecturing them in a sidebar conversation that boils down to lobbing fireballs of judgment, most likely prompting a staccato of defensive rationalizations. Let the one who is without sin lob the first fireball (cf. John 8:7).

But don't mistake my acknowledgment with endorsement. Because it's God's will that we wait until male-female marriage to include sex in the relationship, in the portions I've written that speak directly to having sex in a healthy way, I generally make reference to a spouse, as opposed to a partner. I usually use the broader term, partner, in areas that deal with the potential for dysfunctions in sexual relationships.

And for a description of the blessings of waiting until male-female marriage to have sex, please see the last portion of the "Should we have sex before marriage?" section, earlier in this chapter.

The beauty of vulnerability

We've been talking about sex for quite a while now, and aptly so. It's called making love for good reason. In a healthy marriage, we share our love with one another in countless ways, and sex is a marvelous part of this. It's natural that we have strong desire for our spouse, especially when they make themselves physically vulnerable to us. They are very handsome / beautiful indeed.

And it's beautiful anytime anyone reveals to us something about themselves that makes them vulnerable – provided that it's something appropriate with respect to our relationship. This is true not only when we're making love with our spouse, but also when we're sharing our love with any of our counterparts. Of course, vulnerability of a physically amorous nature is only appropriate with our boyfriend / girlfriend / spouse, and vulnerability of a genuinely sexual nature (intercourse, or anything on the brink of this) is only appropriate with our spouse. But I'm moving on from the topic of sex – *(In this world, all good things must come to an end)* – and now I'm talking about emotional vulnerability of a non-erotic nature.

As C.S. Lewis wrote, "To love at all is to be vulnerable."[2] That is certainly true, for one thing because we are demonstrating to our counterpart that we trust them enough to make ourselves vulnerable to them. But it is also true that we demonstrate our love to our counterpart by our felicitous response to their vulnerability. I address both perspectives in turn.

- When we make ourselves emotionally vulnerable to someone, we are taking a risk. We're pulling aside our veil, at least a little bit, and allowing our counterpart to see something about our authentic self that we're not comfortable showing many others, or possibly *any* others, if our counterpart is our spouse. We're telling a "secret" – revealing something we hold very dear. We don't do this nonchalantly. This is like telling a new love interest, for the very first time (and without a prompt from them), "I love you." Our heart is fluttering and our mind is reminding us that we might be crushed by our counterpart's reaction, but we're compelled to proceed nevertheless. Love that swells to this amplitude within us cannot be contained by fear or logic.

- When anyone makes themselves emotionally vulnerable to us, the first order of business is to remind ourselves that someone has just taken a risk – someone's fearing that they'll be crushed by our reaction. ... So, what should our reaction be? ... We must calm their fears. To this end, we *must* treat them with respect and not judge them, no exceptions! ... Oh, I see a hand up. ... Do I mean even when we have no relationship with this person? ... That's a good question, although technically it's a nonsensical question. It's nonsensical because, under all circumstances, if someone makes themselves emotionally vulnerable to us – even if we've never interacted with this person before – by definition we have now entered into a relationship with them. Their vulnerability toward us has established this.

  And we must not reject their advances. They are showing that they trust us and are looking to us for support. What an excellent opportunity for us to give them love! And, no matter what they're revealing, it's remarkably easy to love in such a situation. Even if we literally cannot find what seem to us to be the "right" words, we're clearly loving them by our active listening with empathy and kindness: not judging, not rejecting, not reacting harshly. If we later think of additional right words to say, we'll have plenty of opportunities to say them because our loving response has furthered the development of a close relationship.

I have addressed both perspectives in turn, but we're not done yet. We can't leave the situation hanging like this – with only one counterpart making themselves emotionally vulnerable to the other. That would be as unsatisfying as the following scenario, the end of which I have no familiarity with: Imagine, if you will, that on an evening as ordinary as any other, we crawl into bed and our spouse initiates no small degree of physical vulnerability, in no uncertain terms and with clear intent of a long-term nature (at least 30 minutes); and further imagine that our response to this is nothing short of meaningful and sustained interest in said vulnerability; and further imagine that, despite our indisputable ability to make ourselves physically vulnerable to our spouse in likewise manner, we nevertheless decide to roll over and go to sleep. … This is not satisfying. In a similar way, it's not satisfying within any relationship if one counterpart makes themselves emotionally vulnerable and the other doesn't make themselves at least somewhat emotionally vulnerable to the initiator in likewise manner. To achieve satisfaction, we should be striving to achieve mutual empathy.

- When we make ourselves emotionally vulnerable to someone, and our counterpart demonstrates meaningful and sustained interest but nevertheless doesn't make themselves emotionally vulnerable to us, I suggest thanking them for listening, and doing this in such a way that they're encouraged to open up as well. This may be accomplished simply by our saying that we'd like to return the favor. A more proactive approach is to follow up on something specific from the conversation. For example, if our counterpart seemed able to relate to something we told them, then why not say that we noticed this and we're curious about what made it relatable to them?

  It's comforting to have someone listen to us, but let's not stop there. Being heard makes us feel loved – for good reason – but a true dialogue is even more satisfying.

- When anyone makes themselves emotionally vulnerable to us, we should not need to be coaxed into returning the favor. They may be saying many other words, but by making themselves emotionally vulnerable to us, what they're really saying is "I love you." … How do we return the favor? What do we say in response to such a clear declaration? … Well, the circumstances may warrant something other than the four words we commonly say in response to this, but here's a little hint, if you need one: Often, a good way to tell someone that you love them is to mimic their behavior. Mimicking is one of my favorite ways to say "I love you too." And what better time to mimic than when our counterpart has made themselves emotionally vulnerable to us?

  Our counterpart is surely comforted when we listen to them, but let's not stop there. Remember, they took a risk by making themselves emotionally vulnerable to us. The ultimate way to calm their fears is to demonstrate that we're not only happy to listen, but we love them so much that we have something (appropriate with respect to our relationship) to reveal to them too.

Fear of vulnerability

I've decided that we've gotten to know each other well enough that I'm going to make myself more vulnerable to you. This section is hard for me to write, but my love for you has grown to sufficient amplitude that this wave must break – it has become imminent.

In writing, I seem to be fairly comfortable making myself vulnerable – *(How many people do you know who are willing to address the elephants I've been addressing?)* – but when it comes to personal interactions, both in group settings and one-on-one, I have had much difficulty allowing myself to be vulnerable. Until fairly recently, this was one of my most significant weaknesses, and it hindered my ability to express love and form bonds.

I struggled with fear of vulnerability for as long as I can remember, and in my adult life there are two incidents – both occurring years ago, but still ingrained in my memory – where my making myself vulnerable to a counterpart caused me to experience intense emotional pain.

- The first I cannot discuss, other than to say that every time I read Genesis 50:15-21, I think to myself: *What an incredibly merciful reaction in the aftermath of willful sin.* That's what I think. Here's what I know: I'm no Joseph.
- The second I can discuss at a high level: I opened up to a friend and told them about an experience that caused me deep emotional pain in my childhood, and how I felt this hardship has impacted my life since that time. Most people cry when I reveal such things. And even if they don't cry, some degree of a sympathetic response is natural. However, my friend has never expressed to me one morsel of compassion.

Perhaps some of you are thinking that while the second example doesn't exactly lend itself to any of my "Let us do it this way" lists, is it really *that* painful? We should have thick skin, right? Well, maybe so, but it turns out that my skin is not particularly thick in general, and in this case an especially fragile area was chafed. In the immediate aftermath of receiving no reaction from my counterpart, my reaction was for my self-esteem to be temporarily shattered – to feel not only unloved by this person (a feeling that lasted weeks to months) but also unlovable with respect to most people (a feeling that lasted several days).

Did I overreact? Yes (see the next two bullet points for what I learned during my pity party), and I haven't even told you my whole reaction yet. My over-reaction went even further: I felt ashamed for telling my friend my "secret." … That should never be. Maybe I should have made it more clear to my friend that I was craving support and affirmation. Maybe I could have used our experience as a teaching opportunity – at an opportune time gently telling my friend what most people would appreciate when they open up to them in such a way. Maybe it would have been better to wait to tell my friend something so personal until we developed a closer relationship. Maybe, if I felt that I couldn't wait to express what I was feeling, it would have been better to choose someone else to tell – someone more likely to react in a compassionate way. Maybe I could list a thousand maybes, but no matter what: We should never be *ashamed* to tell a counterpart something we feel in our heart*, provided that what we're disclosing is appropriate based on the scope of our relationship.

> *Note: This is true even when confessing a sin, when our confession is in the spirit of repentance: expressing our remorse for what we did wrong and openness to change our behavior. Sin can lead to feelings of deep shame, but it's never shameful to confess and repent. If you feel ashamed because of a sin, confess in the spirit of repentance – at least to God, if it's a private sin – and allow your shame to be drowned in forgiveness. If you confess a sin to your counterpart and they're not spiritually mature enough to forgive you, even in light of your repentance, be patient with them and, if you trust in Jesus as your Savior, take comfort in knowing that God has already forgiven you.

It's easy to say that we should never be ashamed to open up to a counterpart in a proper manner, but what if they don't react the way we were hoping? In my case, my pain taught me two valuable lessons that are related to this question.

- I learned that we should not base our self-worth on the opinions of others – neither on what they say, nor on what they *don't* say. In my example, I was clearly allowing the lack of a compassionate response from one person to have *way* too much of an effect (namely, leading me to conclude, temporarily, that I'm not worthy of being given compassion). We should never give others this much control over our self-esteem. Rather, our self-esteem should be based on our own intimate relationship with our authentic self – no others (other than God Himself) should be allowed to disturb our privacy.

- I also learned that we should not assume that the world revolves around us. In my example, I took my friend's lack of expressed compassion too personally; I assumed it was meant to convey the message that they don't care about me. However, I eventually heard a different message. As I continued to interact with my friend, doing my best to love them and coming to appreciate the ways that they do show love in return, over the years I came to realize that they have profound difficulty – more than anyone I've ever known (although I do know several close contenders…) – expressing emotions in general. So, while we may not be the greatest match for one another (I, craving words of affirmation, and they, not very adept at giving them), I still love my dear, inexpressive friend, and I know that they love me.

~

When we have fear of vulnerability, what are we afraid of specifically? … Don't forget, I'm an expert on this topic. So, I know very well what we're afraid of. Allow me to provide the briefest of summaries: We're afraid of allowing our love to swell to sufficient amplitude such that our wave breaks. We're afraid of what people will say – or not say – in light of such a splash. We're afraid that when our veil is pulled aside, our counterparts will be repulsed. We're afraid that people will think less of us, once they know our secret. We're afraid that we'll stand out as being different from others – and judged harshly for that. We're afraid that people will use what we give them as ammunition – bringing it up later in a hurtful manner. We crave affirmation, but we're afraid to ask for it because that would make the silence even more painful. We crave inclusion, but even when it's offered we cannot accept it because nothing is worth the risk of being abandoned again. We're afraid of rejection. … That's a lot to digest, but can you see how we're being selfish when we have such thoughts? In much, if not all, of my list, we're thinking more about our fears than we are about connecting with our counterparts. Yes, when we're afraid to be vulnerable, we're prioritizing our doubts, and this is far afield from our best loving.

- We're not giving our best loving to God. We're idolizing others. We're telling God that we care more about what one or a few people think of us and our feelings than we care about His point of view: which is nothing less than boundless love for us, just the way He made us. We're telling Him that we're ashamed of who we are – forgetting that we are one of His dear offspring.

- We're not giving our best loving to ourselves. We're allowing the opinions of others – or our fear of what their opinions might be, if they only knew our authentic self – to erode our confidence and discount our self-esteem. This is mistreatment of ourselves. Our estimate of our value may oscillate (unfortunately), but all the while our inherent value – i.e., we are cherished by God – cannot be altered, no matter if we hear clear ridicule or if we simply conjure up misunderstandings or assumptions in our anxious mind.

- We're not giving our best loving to the people in our life. We're prioritizing our fear of their reaction over their (and our) need to be loved. If we don't open up to our counterpart, it's true that we won't be hurt by them – at least not based on all that we're withholding – but it's also true that we've given up on having a close relationship with them.

~

I don't know if you've figured this out yet, but something I've picked up on is that none of us are perfect. ... I will give you a moment to recover from this revelation. ... OK, now I'd like to go one step further and reveal to you the corollary that no two people are perfectly compatible. ... Here, sit down and breathe into this paper bag. There you go. ... But let's look at the benefits of this level playing field. Just as we should not be on a quest for a soul mate – (Remember, God places soul mates into our lives) – we also should not be wringing our hands about our counterpart's every reaction (or lack of a reaction) to us being... well... us. Sometimes they'll be annoyed by us, and that's OK. Sometimes they'll become angry with us, and often when the dust settles we realize that they had good reason. Sometimes there will be misunderstandings, resolved when we remember that the world does not revolve around us. And, yes, occasionally there will be willful sin against us. All such things are part of this life. Let's not be so scared of encountering a willful sin, or a misunderstanding over a few careless words or careless lack thereof, that we prioritize living in fear over living in love with each of our dear, imperfect friends.

Opening the door for our emotionally disabled counterpart

For some of us, it's easy to shift our priorities in the way I just described, but for others of us we have a deep-rooted emotional disorder that is not so simple to overcome. For those of us with post-traumatic stress disorder (PTSD), abandonment trauma (a.k.a., PTSD of abandonment), borderline personality disorder, avoidant personality disorder, social anxiety disorder, or a similar challenge, bland advice to get thicker skin, take a risk, or become more confident simply ring hollow if expressed to us in a neutral way. Why is that? Because we interpret neutral comments / advice as criticism, which only validates our fears and makes us feel worse. Ironically, and sadly, those of us with such disorders actually do strongly crave close relationships, but we have trouble forming bonds because we're holding back due to a heightened fear of rejection, often induced by some kind of traumatic experience in our past.

So, what can be done? … If we have a counterpart with thin skin, fear of vulnerability, low self-confidence, or all of the above (usually the right answer, if any of these attributes apply), we should treat them in a similar way as we treat someone with a physical disability. In other words, we should treat them just like everybody else, and offer assistance when it's needed. How do we offer to open a door for an emotionally disabled counterpart? We smile, brighten our eyes, and say in a distinctly non-neutral way that we're glad to see them.

Is opening a door easy? For some of us, it's remarkably easy. But for others of us, we occasionally do need assistance, and we're looking for you to help us.

Handpicked adornments

I ended the previous chapter with a description of the dazzling exquisiteness of unconditional love, and how it is more beautiful than conditional love. I started this chapter with an analogy of how conditional love is like a partner or close friend with some defect. It's certainly true that conditional love is not perfect.

However, one thing that I've (slowly) learned in life is that something, and more importantly someone, doesn't need to be perfect to be beautiful.

When is conditional love beautiful? I see several attributes that are essential for conditional love to rise to the level of true beauty.

- For a conditional love relationship to be beautiful, there needs to be a good measure of mutual unconditional love. At a minimum, both counterparts need to accept that they both will continue to have flaws throughout this life, and that this is never a reason to stop loving one another.
  - In my opinion, for this attribute to be most impactful, initially we need to clearly see the flaws that we are choosing, based on love, to turn a blind eye to (i.e., accept as part of our loved one's inherent self)
- Both counterparts need to have a forgiving attitude. At a minimum, as explained in the "What if someone sins against you?" section (Chapter 9), each *always* offers forgiveness, under *all* circumstances.
  - In my opinion, for this attribute to be most impactful, initially we need to feel real pain associated with the sins that we are choosing, based on love, to wash away (i.e., forgive and "forget," which in my vernacular means we remember that we have chosen to let it go (Chapter 9))
- Both counterparts need to be open to changing their behavior whenever it benefits the relationship and, importantly, behavior *must* be changed whenever one counterpart is harmed – physically, emotionally, psychologically, or spiritually
  - In my opinion, for this attribute to be most impactful, initially we need to experience arduous difficulty associated with the change we are choosing, based on love, to complete for the benefit of our counterpart, ourselves, and our relationship
- There needs to be emotional closeness, with both counterparts being comfortable making themselves vulnerable to one another
- Both counterparts need to be trustworthy, and both need to trust one another
- Both counterparts need to be respectable, and both need to respect one another
- Reciprocation, not necessarily like-for-like and not necessarily without some transitory skew, overall needs to be well-balanced. The two counterparts need to treat one another fairly – neither dominating the other in any way.

- Both counterparts need to communicate with one another openly and transparently
- Both counterparts need to affirm positive feelings for the other, demonstrated through actions and – my favorite… – expressed with words

With all these adornments, conditional love is very beautiful indeed. It's hard to take our eyes off of her. It's natural that we desire a relationship such as this.

~

Have you ever experienced having more desire for the less perfect of two alternatives? Sometimes perfection is not what gives us the most satisfaction. Allow me to make an analogy – and for this to land properly I need to introduce you to my acquaintance, Natas. He's a backwards fellow who makes a good first impression, and he'll latch onto us if we get to know him better. For example, if we – ladies or gentlemen – accompany Natas as he's walking on the sidewalk downtown, he just might point out to us, using merely the corner of our eye, the photograph of a professional model with the utmost degree of masculinity or femininity and adorned with – *How do I put this?* – not necessarily very much, but just enough for us to consider him or her alluring. Especially with professional photography, lighting, air-brushing, and the like, he or she is perfe… – no, let's phrase it this way – without noticeable flaw. But do we desire him or her as much as our boyfriend or girlfriend or spouse, even without proper lighting and with no air-brushing of any kind? … *Guys, I can tell you've got it. … Ladies, you shouldn't need to think about this… Give me some kind of a reaction… There you go…* That's absolutely right! We always desire our boyfriend or girlfriend or spouse more than anyone else, even those who have no noticeable flaw. Why is that? Because our special friend is a real person with whom we have a connection, they too are handsome / beautiful – (There are infinite manifestations of human attractiveness / beauty) – their flaws make them endearing to us, and their adornments are handpicked for us only, based on our preferences, not the preferences of every slack-jawed troglodyte gawking at a magazine rack.

Considering the possibility that my analogy may not have made it clear enough, I should say a few more words about why there are circumstances where conditional love sometimes feels more satisfying than unconditional love be-tween people:

- Unconditional love is *always* exquisite – no doubt
  - o It's *always* exquisite to receive. However, while God's unconditional love for us is a constant flow, we have no say about when we receive unconditional love from people. (If we have any direct involvement in when we receive love, then it's in the category of conditional love.) We receive unconditional love when a counterpart chooses to give it to us. Sometimes, it may feel like a long time between one of our receiving experiences and the next.
  - o It's *always* exquisite to give. However, sometimes this is very painful for the giver, for example, if our counterpart is unresponsive, unappreciative, or unremorseful. Indeed, *giving unconditional love may be the most difficult thing that we do in our life*.
- For such reasons, conditional love, when beautifully adorned, sometimes feels more satisfying, as further elaborated upon here.
  - o We receive love back, and we have some influence on when this will be
  - o We have a bond with another human being, and that's a beautiful thing
    - We're happier together than apart
      - What we have in common with our counterpart is often what helps us connect early in the relationship
      - What we *don't* have in common with our counterpart helps us grow and leads us to truly cherish them
    - It's affirmed, again and again, that we matter
      - We see, again and again, tangible evidence that we're having a positive influence on someone else's life
      - We see, again and again, tangible evidence that someone else genuinely cares about us

To be loved is a fundamental need of each of us, as amply discussed in Chapter 5. Unfortunately, in this sinful world, it's common for people to choose *not* to love us – to conclude that we do *not* satisfy the conditions that they require. With this general lack of acceptance as our backdrop, we more easily see the grandeur of someone choosing to love us. To be sure, it's beautiful and satisfying when another person chooses to enter into a conditional love relationship with us, with handpicked adornments.

~

But I must end this chapter with a warning. Let us not become so enamored by the beauty and satisfaction of a well-adorned conditional love relationship that we forget what is more beautiful and more satisfying. Whatever we do, we must *never* be completely satisfied with conditional love relationships. To live a meaningful life, we must experience a greater love than this! The relationship that each of us should desire most – above *all* others – is the intimate relationship that God wants to have with us. Submitting to God's choice to love us unconditionally – with all our imperfections, all our flaws – is, without doubt, the most exquisite and most satisfying experience of this life.

~   ~   ~

After-hours

Bob unplugged
    Please reflect on my warning at the end of the chapter, and consider circumstances where it's not beneficial for us to have things *too* good, whether that be wealth, fame, or – *(Are you surprised that I add these?)* – a long list of friends or a "perfect" spouse. With these latter examples, think of specific ways that being comfortable in the present may not be best in the long term.
*   Could anything like this be happening in your life?

    On the one hand, we should seek to improve our interpersonal relationships; but on the other hand, this always needs to be in proper balance with our spiritual life, which is ultimately more important.

If you're sensing a lack of balance – too much focus on interpersonal relationships, to the detriment of the intimate relationship that God wants to have with you – think of ways to meld the two. For example, deepen your relationship with your otherwise perfect spouse by sharing a devotion every morning. Invite your friends – the whole list – to Easter service, followed by a get-together at your home. The next time you write another big check for the homeless shelter, why don't you go there – with your spouse and some of your friends – and see what the shelter has done with the money you've donated over the years, and then roll up your sleeves and help them spend some more.

Everything we have comes from God, including the people in our life. Let's not allow such blessings to distract us. Let's use our material blessings to equip us for our spiritual journey, and let's invite our counterparts to be sojourners with us.

Step up to the microphone

Consider your counterparts, and for each think of at least three specific strands in your emotional bond with them. (If this seems difficult, look back at both of my lists of strands, and I think you'll find that this exercise really isn't very difficult after all.) Now, compare and contrast each set of strands.

• Based on your assessment, are any two snowflakes alike?

I describe our emotional bonds as being made up of delicate, lacy strands that together can form a strong bond. While delicate strands are beautiful, they are also fragile. They can be quickly and easily frayed by careless words or selfish actions.

• Have your words or actions frayed any strands lately?
• What can you do to repair the damage?

Near the end of the chapter, I say that what we have in common with our counterpart is often what helps us connect early in the relationship, and that what we don't have in common with them helps us grow and leads us to truly cherish them. ... Think about several of your loving counterparts, and for each consider what the two of you do and don't have in common.

*   Is one category (do or don't) more impactful for you than the other?
*   Does it depend on the counterpart?
*   Does it change over time, either within a relationship or as you age?

To help you become penta-lingual (i.e., become linguistically skilled in each of the five love languages), I give an explicit example related to going on an anniversary trip. Now, I'd like you to lay plans for being penta-lingual with your spouse or close friend on a weekend as ordinary as any other, except that it has the point of distinction of being in the near future. As you orchestrate your preparations, keep in mind that a gift doesn't need to be something wrapped with ribbons and bows, although it does need to be something special, given freely (without "payback"), and, for your assignment, not better described by one of the other four love languages. In my opinion, examples of true gifts are making a pie from scratch and tickets to a Broadway show (while preparing an ordinary meal is an act of service, and tickets to a two-dollar movie theater are ... well ... I'm going to say physical touch).

*   Is it difficult to be penta-lingual?
*   Which love language is the most challenging for you to speak?
    *   What can you do to become more linguistically skilled in that language?

For parents: Have a conversation with each of your unmarried children about what we should be looking for in a potential spouse. Emphasize that attributes high on our list should be patience, virtue, respect, and trustworthiness. If your child already knows what the birds and the bees are up to behind closed doors, then add that another attribute high on our list should be commitment to remaining a virgin until marriage. Finally, tie it all together by explaining how these five attributes are interrelated.

For couples:

- For dating couples: Both (guys, you need to do this too), in turn, thank your counterpart for respecting your wishes to have boundaries related to physical affection before marriage. Thank them for being patient, and for supporting your decision to remain a virgin until marriage.
- For *married* couples *only*: This week, in and/or out of turn, explore at least two (each of you choosing at least one) new ways by which you will actualize Dr. Bob's sex advice. (If you're reading this at 11 P.M. on a Saturday night, then you'd better get moving!)

Chapter 8 – Love Is …

If you've ever been to a wedding – and I'm going to go out on a limb with the bold assertion that you have – then I'm going to go out on another limb that you've heard 1 Corinthians 13:4-13 applied to marriage. Both limbs have about the same degree of sturdiness. Yes, it's common for this passage to be used during the wedding ceremony, and otherwise applied to marriage. And for good reason! This is a beautiful description of love. I might even call it a definition of love… Indeed, it does capture so many facets of what it means to love.

But does it only apply to marriage? *Heavens no!* What comes immediately before and after this passage? … *No one?* … I'll wait for you to look it up. … *You're right!* Paul inserts this beautiful description of love within a large section on spiritual gifts – 1 Corinthians chapters 12-14. Yes, 1 Corinthians 13, often called the love chapter, is smack dab in the middle of an elaborate discussion on spiritual gifts. Is that a coincidence? *Hardly!* You see, spiritual gifts aren't edifying to others unless those gifts are used in a loving way. In the first three verses of 1 Corinthians 13 (what I call Paul's love chapter "windup"), Paul explains that even the "higher gifts" (1 Corinthians 12:31) are worthless if not accompanied by love: "If I speak in the tongues of men and of angels, but have not love, I am a noisy gong or a clanging cymbal. And if I have prophetic powers, and understand all mysteries and all knowledge, and if I have all faith, so as to remove mountains, but have not love, I am nothing. If I give away all I have, and if I deliver up my body to be burned, but have not love, I gain nothing" (1 Corinthians 13:1-3). Paul makes it clear that love is a crucial component if we're going to use our spiritual gifts to serve others. (And can you think of any other relevant use of spiritual gifts? I can't.) Paul makes his point clearly, but please indulge me to draw an analogy. I think of it as love and a spiritual gift being a pilot and a copilot, both needed for the spiritual gift to land properly (to edify someone else). Which is the pilot and which is the copilot? … Love is the pilot (1 Corinthians 12:31b).

Paul then proceeds in the remainder of 1 Corinthians 13 to define love. This is not an easy task, as I discovered when writing Chapter 1 of this book, but Paul gives a beautiful definition. In 1 Corinthians chapters 12-14, Paul is discussing spiritual gifts, but does his definition of love only apply to the use of spiritual gifts? No, this is how we are to love even when doing so in ways that we're not particularly gifted. Without love, we can't meaningfully serve others with our spiritual gift(s). In contrast, without particular spiritual gifts, we can meaningfully love, even in ways normally associated with gifts that we don't have. For example, we don't need to have the spiritual gift of mercy to be compassionate; we don't need to have the spiritual gift of exhortation to be encouraging; we don't need to have the spiritual gift of healing to make someone's day. (If I ever hear you say that you can't love someone because your spiritual gift(s) aren't a good "fit" to them, you have to run five laps and give me 25 pushups, and then I'm giving you a stern tongue-lashing.)

We have already established that the definition of love in 1 Corinthians 13 doesn't apply only to spiritual gifts. That's what makes it applicable to marriage – we love our spouse this way, regardless of our set of strengths and weaknesses. Are we to love this way only in marriage? No, this is how we are to love in all our relationships. (Married couples, if you're disappointed because you don't have a love chapter all to yourselves, I have good news for you. You have a whole "love *book*" to apply! Read Song of Solomon, and have at it! Yes, much of Song of Solomon is only to be applied by married couples – I mean, when the application is in a literal fashion.)

OK, where was I? Oh, yes, Paul's definition of love. Much of this definition is a series of statements about what love is and what love is not. I've listed all these facets of love below and, as you might have guessed by now, for each I've provided additional commentary. My commentary is not meant to "explain" each facet, but rather to establish a launching pad from which your own thoughts can project further. As you read each of these sections, please think and pray about how you, with the Holy Spirit's guidance, will apply this particular facet of love not only as you bless others with your spiritual gift(s) but also as you love in ungifted ways. Furthermore, please consider how you will pursue application not only with your spouse or boyfriend / girlfriend, but also in *all* your relationships.

"Love is patient" (1 Corinthians 13:4)

In several of the sections after this one, I describe scenarios where we are called to forgive ourselves and others. That's not surprising, because forgiveness is such an important part of what it means to love a fallible human being. For example, a moderately difficult scenario is discussed in the "Love bears all things" section – we become annoyed with our counterpart, or they become annoyed with us. Much more difficult scenarios are discussed in the "Love … keeps no record of wrongs" section – our counterpart commits a grievous sin and hurts us very deeply, or we commit such a sin and hurt them very deeply. I've already specified that forgiveness is an important aspect of love. And here I've alluded to another important aspect of love. *Who would like to tell us what it is? … Yes, just shout it out. … Very good!* Love is often difficult – sometimes *very* difficult!

Can you think of anything more difficult than continuing to love another person who has hurt us very deeply by their grievous sin against us? … *Anyone?* … I can think of four things:

- The first is the feeling – no, it's not so much a feeling as it is a realization of truth – that all unbelievers will surely experience when they finally realize that they're wrong about who Jesus is. Without doubt, there will be much grief on Judgment Day. On that day, each unbeliever will commence an excruciating odyssey of indescribable anguish that can't be resolved in any way other than eternal regret.

- The second is the thought distortion of Love Zero. I try to describe this in the Prologue. It's utter blackness, to be sure, but fortunately it resolves for those of us who do not reject the Holy Spirit's gentle embrace. Thus, the thought distortion of Love Zero can be infinitely shorter-lived than the truth of the utter, eternal blackness of the preceding bullet point; I've cleverly named that truth: Love Minus Infinity. You may have heard others refer to this never-ending distress as hell. Whichever name you choose, let there be no misunderstanding – hell is the complete absence of love for all eternity. I don't know the temperature, but in the absence of love such details are not important – the pain is the same regardless.

- The third is the pain of realizing that we've deeply hurt someone who trusted us, by our grievous sin against them. This deep-down heartache takes much time to resolve… This generally takes much longer than coming out of Love Zero. Yes, it takes time for us to see the pain in our counterpart's face, to realize that we are the cause of it, to admit that we were wrong, to confess with tears our sin against them, to accept that we need to change, to start the long journey toward change, to prove ourselves trustworthy again, to rediscover that our counterpart loves us, and what's more to learn that what seemed impossible is true – that our counterpart *never* stopped loving us, despite our previous, grievous sin against them. It takes patience. ... This is a difficult journey, to be sure, but you can see that it has a lovely destination.

- And there's something that requires even more patience. Yes, there's one more thing that's more difficult than continuing to love another person who has hurt us very deeply by their grievous sin against us. *Who would like to tell us what it is? ... Yes, just shout it out. ... No, that's not it, but good try! ... No, it's definitely not that – no comment. ... Anyone else want to give it a shot? ...* I gave you a hint when I said it requires more patience than what I describe in the previous bullet point – the difficult journey with a lovely destination. What could possibly require more patience than that?! What requires more patience – what is more difficult – is when our counterpart continues to sin against us in ways related to what made the journey necessary in the first place. What is our reaction to be when the difficult journey with a lovely destination has detours that cause us additional pain? ... Jesus makes it clear that we are to forgive our counterpart again and again (Matthew 18:21-22). ... Now, of course there are circumstances where we continue to forgive and love unconditionally, and yet it's appropriate to distance ourselves from our counterpart for our physical and/or emotional wellbeing; and sometimes this distancing may need to be permanent, if we find reconciliation (i.e., restoration of a healthy relationship) to be impossible (Appendices Ɔ and D). OK, fair enough, but I don't consider the following scenarios to be so dire that we conclude that reconciliation is impossible.
  - o Imagine that our partner sinned against us by being sexually unfaithful.

    Somewhere along the way of our – *Remember, the two of us are traveling together!* – difficult journey with a lovely destination, we discover that they are regularly accessing pornographic websites. We confront them about this, and they admit that, while they haven't been physically intimate with another since their infidelity was disclosed, they have since become addicted to pornography and in such a way frequently desire others and fantasize about having sex with them.

    What is our reaction to be?
  - o Imagine that our counterpart sinned against us by physically abusing us.

    Somewhere along the way of our difficult journey with a lovely destination, they start to exhibit new traits: They're even more easily angered

than before, they're starting to throw objects – not at us, but pretty close…
– and they're starting to say mean things to us.

What is our reaction to be?

o Imagine that our spouse sinned against us by deceiving us with chronic lying about their whereabouts – with regular trips to casinos coming to light, along with considerable debt.

Somewhere along the way of our difficult journey with a lovely destination, it becomes apparent that our spouse has initiated an emotional affair with one of our mutual friends. Early signs are that, from time to time, our friend inadvertently tells us things about our spouse that we didn't know ourselves. Some of the examples are related to recent events. It becomes especially concerning when our spouse claims that they haven't communicated with our friend for the last several months, but our friend told us yesterday that the two of them have been meeting for lunch at least once per week for a while now.

What is our reaction to be?

These last three scenarios are not as inspiring as my first description of a difficult journey with a lovely destination. My first description is the way it's supposed to work. That's how God wants us to react to such challenges that we encounter in our relationships. But my later descriptions are, unfortunately, more in line with our experience in this fallen world. Why? Because we're sinful, and it's natural for us to replace a sin we set aside with another. Yes, our selfish, sinful, human nature responds to one positive development with yet another roadblock – yet another detour. So, what is our reaction to be to such detours? We are to pray, we are to persist in love, we are to remain patient and hopeful, and – yes – we are to aspire to forgive (Chapter 9).

In each of the three detours I describe above, it has become abundantly clear – *(Wasn't it clear enough already?!)* – that professional help is the right call, and well-worth the investment. With the help of such counseling, the two counterparts will need to be working hard on such things as proper ways to fulfill our need for physical intimacy and affection, effective communication, increasing self-esteem, anger management, honesty, transparency, trust, and proper ways to fulfill our need for emotional closeness.

As I wrote in the first paragraph of this section, love is often difficult – sometimes *very* difficult! On our own, we can't persist in love in the ways I describe. Even with professional help, on our own we don't have good reason to be patient and hopeful. And forgiveness and reconciliation? On our own, it's hopeless… There's only one way that such difficult journeys reach the lovely destinations that God desires for us. That one way is to rely on His guidance – to submit to His will. So, we pray, and wait patiently for Him (cf. Psalm 37:7a).

"Love is patient."

"Love is … kind" (1 Corinthians 13:4)

Is it just me, or does the world seem to be getting meaner? For example, I used to enjoy reading the posts at the end of online articles because I would find people's opinions interesting and sometimes helpful or amusing. But more and more, it seems that many people who make such posts just want to vent into the wild blue yonder, and create an opportunity to beat the drums of their agenda, no matter how distant that agenda is from the article we're supposed to be commenting on. And some of the posts get nasty! Do they think this is Facebook®? Whether it be nytimes.com® or Facebook, some people write things that I hope they'd never say. But that's part of the problem, isn't it? Apparently, some feel comfortable posting nasty notes – feel comfortable posting things they'd never say – because they're protected by the void between us: the void formed by the inherently impersonal internet. We sit all alone, staring at our monitor, typing as fast as we can – *We must post next!* – blasting away at usernames or little pictures or drawings. We often don't even know the people behind these names and icons. Maybe we even forget that there are real people behind those bubbles.

Living in such bubbles is natural – we feel a need to protect ourselves. But from what I can tell, our bubbles are getting bigger, even when we're off of our computers and out in the real world. Our bubbles are getting bigger because the world is getting nastier. And the bigger our bubbles get, the more comfortable we feel being nasty back. Don't you see? It's a positive feedback loop. What is to be done?

Back in the Prologue, I summarize the scope of this book, and in so doing I even provide a short list of things I have *not* written about. Then, in Chapter 1 it becomes amply clear that my view of love is generally zoomed in; for example, the apex of love – ecstatic love – is intimate, which means two, and only two. Based on such statements, and everything else in this book, you can see that I'm not writing very much on the topic of group dynamics. There have been a few jaunts here and there that brush up against the topic, but these are mere junkets – bio-breaks on our main voyage. Why have I chosen not to say much on the topic? Isn't it important? Isn't there a lot to be done to improve how we all get along with one another, especially when we disagree? Yes and yes, but I'm not writing very much about group dynamics because – *I'm now giving my answer to the question at the end of the previous paragraph* – the way we make a difference is to change our behavior and be kind to our counterpart.

That's counterpart, singular. When we're speaking or writing to a group of people, we should either be thinking of each of them individually (which is not difficult, if the group is not very large and we know everyone) or having in our mind one representative person. Yes, such a representative person is a very complex and diverse person, if we're making a good effort to speak or write effectively to a broad audience. As I've written this book, I've never considered myself to be writing to a group of readers. I've always had only one reader in my mind. This reader, this representative person, is a conglomerate of myself and everyone I've ever had a relationship with. Everything I'm writing, we already know – I'm simply writing it down in our diary. At any given point in this diary, I'm focusing on a certain characteristic of this complex and diverse representative person, and at that point I'm writing as if that portion is intended only for the specific individual(s) who define this characteristic in my mind. It's very personal – very private. It's as if I'm handwriting my cherished counterpart a special card, and I want only them to see it. Occasionally, what I'm writing resonates strongly and literally with specific individual(s); and occasionally, one of the specific individuals is me. For example, this is the case in the "Backstage pass" subsection of Chapter 9, and that area also resonates strongly and literally with my mother. That is a very private passage. I'm writing to myself as a boy and to my mother. We're saying "Goodbye." We're saying "I love you." This is very personal. I don't feel comfortable writing such things to a group of people. I can only write this in our diary. Sometimes, the resonance is with another particular individual; if you recognize yourself, thank you for your contribution to our diary. Most often, I embellish greatly as I create characteristics that are a stew of tiny bits from each of a long list of individuals, and resonate with none of us (or resonate with all of us, depending on your point of view…). For instance, I don't know anyone who has sexually harassed or raped their niece or anyone else for that matter, but my representative person is capable of committing such atrocities. I cannot bring myself to write despicable things like this to a group of people. But I must include this in our diary… Why? Because my representative person may be mistreated in this way; I need to tell her story; I want to provide her with some comfort – to encourage her with the forecast that she has a bright future, even with such a dark history.

But I digress… Why did I digress? To make the point that when we interact with groups of people, we shouldn't treat them as usernames or icons, or fuzzy faces in a crowd. We need to remember that any group, no matter how big, is made up of individuals, each of whom is unique and valuable. So, when we interact with our counterpart – who is typically an actual person but should be a representative person when we're interacting with a group unfamiliar to us – we should pop our bubble, make ourselves vulnerable, and encourage our counterpart to do likewise. How do we encourage them to pop their bubble? We make them comfortable. How do we make them comfortable? We shower them with kindness. The world has taught them to expect nastiness, harshness, discrimination, or at best indifference, but we surprise them with kindness. Below I provide several examples of the contrast between the expected reaction and kindness.

- We are a kindergartener attending Vacation Bible School for the first time. We're in a large class, with more than 20 others, none of whom we know. On the first day, we're asked by our teacher to file into the sanctuary for opening chapel. All our classmates walk in as they were asked, but when we enter the sanctuary, we freeze and can't move another inch. The reaction we expect, the reaction we fear, is: *Get moving! Keep up with your classmates! Can't you see that we're on a tight schedule here? Can't you see that I have many other kids to keep track of? And some of their name tags have fallen off already!* But kindness says: *Would you like to hold my hand and walk up with me?*

- We are a middle school student, and we're being bullied by another student on the far corner of the playground, near the school library – which is usually empty at this time of day. In the midst of this, another student happens to come out of the library. We don't know them, nor them us (we're not in the same grade). The reaction we expect, the reaction we fear, is: *I'm just going to walk right on by. I'm staying out of this. I don't know either of you, and I don't want to get involved. I might get hurt or ridiculed.* But kindness says: *Hey, knock it off! I know your homeroom teacher, and I'll let her know what I've seen here. And I'm going to stand in between the two of you for as long as it takes to make sure there's nothing more for me to tell! You – what's your name? OK, now scram! ... I hope he knows that he's looking at detention for this. He'll find out soon enough. And are you OK? What's your name?*

- We are a junior in high school, and we just transferred from the public school across town to a Christian school. That's all well and good, except for one thing – we're Muslim. Our parents are changing our school because the Christian one has a great basketball program, and we just happen to have obtained the very apt nickname, "Chairman of the Boards." On our first day at our new school, we see a lot of pale-skinned kids who all seem to know each other. We see some of them hug as they greet one another. We see a small group praying together in the hallway. We see, and very easily hear, seemingly every other student enthusiastically singing praise songs during morning chapel. We are very uncomfortable, and everyone seems to be picking up on this. The reaction we expect, the reaction we fear, is: *You look different from me and my friends. You sound different from me and my friends. I don't understand how you can believe what you do. Don't you know that this is a Christian school? Why are you here? Some terrorists are Muslim, so I think I'm better off keeping my distance.* But kindness says: *I remember my first day at this school. I knew absolutely nobody! I had just moved in from out of state the summer before. What classes are you in? ... Uh oh. For AP Bio, I hope you don't have Mr. George... It's a long story.*

- We "borrowed" our father's car, and went out with a group of friends. Maybe we got distracted, but the bottom line is we've had an accident. The reaction we expect, the reaction we fear, is: *How dare you take my car without asking! I'm never letting you go out again!* But kindness says: *I'm glad no one was hurt. Next time, you need to ask before taking my car, and we need to talk about who's coming with you and where you're going. And we have plenty of time to talk about this because you're grounded for a month.*

- We are participating in a fund-raising activity, and we ask our family and friends if they'd like to donate money to help the cause. The reaction we expect, the reaction we fear, is: *You've made me feel obligated to give* *something. And this thing you're doing – why does that concern me? I don't have any connection to that. I want you to see that I'm irked to give this $5. I hope you'll remember this, and leave me off your list next year.* But kindness says: *I'm proud of you for participating in this. Thank you for including me in your network of supporters. I'm happy to sponsor you and contribute financially to this cause that's important to you, and thus is important to me too. I wish I could give more now; please ask me again next year.*

- A group of us are preparing to leave work for the day, and several of us are in the kitchen to grab our leftovers from lunch. (We had gone out together. Most of us had leftovers, and stored them in the fridge.) We go first. As we're pawing through the various containers, we accidentally drop one of them, and its contents go flying all over the floor! The reaction we expect, the reaction we fear, is: *Why are you so clumsy? That was going to be my dinner!* But kindness says: *Oh, please don't worry about it. This fridge is too small, and we all jammed our stuff in there. Here, let me help you clean it up.*

- We read an online article on the topic of building one another up emotionally. This article edifies us so much that we decide to post a comment, saying that the article has motivated us to handwrite an encouraging card to each person in our extended family and to each of our friends. In the card, amongst other things, we're going to tell our recipient the strengths we see in them, and specifically how they've inspired us. Shortly after our post, a few people respond positively, but a few others make fun of our idea. One concludes that we must not have very many friends, since we can consider doing such a thing. Several new people post their agreement that we're obviously a loser, and desperate for attention. The reaction everyone expects, and the reaction some (the people who responded positively) fear, is: *You have just declared war! You started it, and I'll finish it! Who are you to make fun of my idea?! You are all big jerks! I saw your posts yesterday... Outrageous! I disagree with everything you write!* But kindness says: *If some of you don't want to write such cards, that's fine. But I'm still going to do it, regardless of anyone's opinion about it and regardless of how long it takes me. And I know that each of my recipients will be pleased to receive their card.*

- We look in the mirror and see some bulges that weren't there before. And, coincidentally enough, every pair of pants in our closet seems to be mysteriously shrinking, little by little. The reaction we expect, the reaction we fear, is: *You don't look like I remember, and I don't want to be as affectionate with you as I used to be.* But kindness says: *You're still beautiful / handsome, and I'm going to delight you with the same tenderness and passion that we enjoyed early in our marriage.*

- We are on a difficult journey with a lovely destination (described in the previous section), and we cause a most unexpected detour – a long gravel road with lots of potholes. The reaction we expect, the reaction we fear, is: *I'm so disappointed in you. I thought you were making progress! I've lost my patience with you, and this time I'm really giving up on you.* But kindness says: *I'm still hopeful. We did make progress and, because of that, now we know that we can recover from this. Yes, this is a challenge I wasn't expecting, but I forgive you. I still love you.*

- We commit a grievous sin against our spouse, for example we were sexually unfaithful or an argument turned violent and we physically hurt them. The reaction we expect, the reaction we fear, is: *I hate you. You're an awful person who can't be trusted. I never want to have anything to do with you again. I'm leaving you forever.* But kindness says: *You've hurt me very deeply. I'm very angry. I can't be around you right now. I need time away from you to think and pray. ... ... We need to talk. But I don't want to do this one-on-one. Let's make an appointment with Pastor or a therapist. ... ... I'm glad that we've been having these sessions. I think I might be starting to heal a little bit. But there's still such a long way to go. I can tell that you regret what you did. Thank you for telling me how sorry you are that you hurt me, that you want to change, and that you'd like to try to get back together. I'll keep praying about this. I think it will be at least a few more weeks before I'm ready to think about living together again. ... ... I'm beginning to see a real change in you. Do you see it too? I'm feeling a change in myself as well. A few months ago, I thought we should probably get divorced. But I've been regaining my trust in you, and I've been remembering more and more why I fell in love with you. ... ... I miss you. I want to be with you again. ... ... I ... I forgive you. And, yes, I still love you.*

A thread running through the above examples is that most of us fear what our counterpart's reaction will be. The world has taught us that we should expect a nasty, harsh, or biased reaction, or, at best, indifference. When someone is

fearing *our* reaction – whether this is someone we've known for years, or someone we've just met, or even a representative person for a group – let us calm their
fears. Let us give them one pleasant surprise after another.

"Love is kind."

"Love does not envy" (1 Corinthians 13:4)

Are you content? We might feel reasonably content on an average day: we
like our car; our apartment is pretty nice; our job is not too boring and it pays the
rent; we have recently decided to brush off our rusty vocal cords by joining the
choir; a few heads turn when our boyfriend / girlfriend or husband / wife walks
in the room. But some days, we might feel a little differently about such things.
… What about the day our neighbor drives up in his new sports car? How do we
feel about our car now? What about the day our boss invites us to her home for
a get-together, and we see her mansion… and pool… and tennis court… and
maid? How do we feel about our apartment now? What about the day the new
guy at work gets promoted over us? How do we feel about our job now? What
about the choir practice where the choir director informs us that she has the title
role in the Metropolitan Opera's upcoming performances of *Aida*, and she proceeds to belt out her favorite aria, "*Ritorna vincitor*," in magnificent fashion?
How do we feel about our vocal cords now? What about the day our friend's new
boyfriend / girlfriend walks in the room and a *lot* of heads (ours?) turn?

On days like these, we can become envious. Envy is unloving because we're
being selfish – we're looking at the situation through the lens of what we don't
have. Also, at least in the examples I've given so far, we're focusing on material
things, special talents, and outward appearances. Such things do easily come to
mind when trying to describe the feeling of being envious.

The next time you get this feeling, please pause and look at the situation differently. Let's take our eyes off physical things, and instead focus on spiritual
things. St. Paul writes, "We look not to the things that are seen but to the things
that are unseen. For the things that are seen are transient, but the things that are
unseen are eternal" (2 Corinthians 4:18). In the big picture, does it really matter
whether we take our journey to our heavenly home in coach or first class? We all
– at least all of us who trust in Jesus as our Savior – are going to the same place.
When we get off our plane, all having reached the same destination, are we really

going to care whether we ate caviar or pretzels on the way? … What kind of car we drive? *Who cares!* Our apartment? Let's be thankful for a roof over our head and a pillow to sleep on. Our job? Let's keep up the good work, in proper balance with other aspects of our life, and ask God if we should stay or make a change. Our singing voice? I advise one or both of the following: Close your eyes and envision a special filter that makes each of our voices sound magnificent to God, and/or close your car windows and belt it out. Your boyfriend or husband? Perhaps we're not going to find his cardboard cutout in the sporting goods store, but consider all the ways that he's just the right man for you. Our girlfriend or wife? Perhaps she's not going to make the cover of the swimsuit issue, but consider all the ways she's more beautiful than any cover can display.

And our friends from my first paragraph of this section? Are we being loving to them when we're envious? Obviously we are not. We're being selfish, and essentially saying that we want what they have. … Our neighbor with the fancy sports car? Let's ask him to take us on a drive; maybe we'll start a friendship. Our boss with the mansion? Let's not worry about the surroundings, and just have fun with everyone at the get-together. The new guy at work? Let's keep an open mind, and maybe he can teach us a thing or two; and what's wrong with that? The choir director with the magnificent voice? Carpool with them to the next choir practice, roll up the windows, and see what develops. Our friend with the head-turning boyfriend / girlfriend? Let's pray that they develop the kind of loving relationship that we've found with our partner.

~

So far in this section, I've focused on envy of material things, special talents, and outward appearances. But there's another way we can become envious. Have you ever been envious of friendships our friends have with *others*? I have – multiple times. I like to get emotionally close with my friends, and that's fine, but associated with this, at least for me, is becoming envious when they get close to others. This is an example of what I call emotional envy.

When I feel this way, I remind myself – no, the Holy Spirit reminds me – that love is not a limited resource, with my friend's love for me decreasing more and more as they find more and more others to love. No, the needle on love's gas gauge is always above the "Full" mark, no matter how long we've had the pedal to the metal.

The Holy Spirit also reminds me that I love my friend, and that means I want what's best for them, and what's best for them is a diverse network of friends. We all have something unique to offer. Yes, I do have something unique to offer my friend. But others also have unique qualities to offer my friend. How audacious is it when I even think of wanting to limit that? Exceedingly! It's the audacity of emotional envy.

"Love does not envy."

"Love does not ... boast" (1 Corinthians 13:4)

The preceding section discusses envy, which is wanting something that someone else has. Boasting is somewhat similar, in the sense that it's bragging that we have something that others don't. By boasting, we're essentially saying: *Aren't you envious of me? You should be! And here's why!* Whether or not we are actually envious of a boastful person, we're not being loved by them when they speak to us in this way.

When we speak to others, we should be thinking about how we're coming across. If we're talking about something that our counterpart doesn't have, it's fine to talk about it, but let's be careful with our words. For example, a boastful person might say: *I've been sinking my annual bonus into the back yard for years now. Early additions were just a pool and a spa – hardly worth mentioning; most people in this neighborhood have those. Then came the outdoor kitchen – pretty nice, but not the biggest on the block. What really got me to stand up and take notice was the gazebo I had put in a couple years ago – it's even bigger than Bob's, and that's saying something! Mine's so big that I've put inside a couple poofy recliners, a huge, wrap-around sofa, and an 80-inch HDTV. Instead of watching Sunday's game in your apartment, we'll be more comfortable if you come to my place.* Under the same circumstances, a more humble and loving way to express this would be: *Would you like to watch the game at my place this Sunday afternoon? I'd enjoy seeing you. I'll barbeque something for lunch and, oh yeah, don't forget to bring your swimsuit.*

"Love does not boast."

"Love is … not arrogant" (1 Corinthians 13:4)

This is very similar to the preceding section. What's the difference between being boastful and being arrogant? When I think of boasting, I think of the words people say to puff themselves up, with such assertions usually being expressed only periodically. When I think of arrogance, it goes beyond occasional words to a chronic, distasteful attitude that boils down to entitlement / inherent superiority, with such expressions being made not only in words but also in more subtle ways like cliquism (social exclusivity) and body language. I think of boasting as an attempt people make to puff themselves up because they feel small on the inside. I think of arrogance as a way people make it clear that they really do think highly of themselves – more highly than they ought (Romans 12:3).

I've already amply explained in Chapter 4 that we are to love ourselves. When we love ourselves, we are to think highly of ourselves. What's the difference between this and arrogance? When we think highly of ourselves in a proper way, we're confident in our strengths, knowing that it's the Holy Spirit Himself who has given us these abilities, and we're bold in our use of them for the benefit of others. When we think highly of ourselves in an improper way, we ostentatiously showcase our strengths, are boastful about our role in having these strengths (for example, our "natural" ability and/or our effort), and we use these strengths primarily to benefit ourselves and rarely to benefit anyone outside of our clique.

Proper love for ourselves allows our strengths to be used mightily and humbly in lifting others up. Arrogance diminishes others.

"Love is not arrogant."

"Love … is not … rude" (1 Corinthians 13:4-5)

In the "Love does not … boast" section, not far above, I provide an elaborate narrative of what a boastful person might say to their less fortunate – at least from the perspective of worldly possessions – counterpart. I then provide a suggestion for a more modest approach, one where we are more careful about our choice of words. Why should we be careful about the words we use? One reason, especially relevant to boasting, is so we don't cause our counterpart to become envious. This is a very good reason because envy can lead to covetousness, which is clearly a sin (Exodus 20:17) – and far be it from us to cause our counterpart to sin! But I can think of two additional very good reasons that are applicable *anytime* we communicate with *anyone*.

- We should always remember to be respectful to our counterpart. We've all heard that whenever we communicate, it's important to consider our audience. Well, in addition to considering their demographics, their history with us, their demeanor at the present time, and other utilitarian factors such as these, let us also consider that our counterpart is an inherently valuable human being, regardless of their demographics, their history with us, and their demeanor at the present time. ... Do their demographics hardly overlap with ours? *So what?!* Is their history with us a little mottled? Let's be the one to take the first step toward putting the past into our rearview mirrors. Does their present demeanor bring to mind a snarling beast? Let's face up to the challenge of giving them a tangible reason to try on for size a different disposition. Is it difficult to be tolerant of the differences between us? Is it difficult to come to peace with the past? Is it difficult to smile when our counterpart is frowning or even growling? ... Sometimes such things are very difficult, but here's a good place to start: Let's treat them with respect.

- Being respectful is one thing – a very important thing – but there's another step we should all be taking. We should always remember to keep in mind our counterpart's feelings. I'm not talking so much about their present demeanor or mood – I mean how they will react emotionally to what we say to them. Yes, I'm asking you to look into your crystal ball and predict the future. Specifically, *before* speaking, I want you to ask yourself: *How will my counterpart feel about what I'm eager to say?* If the answer to this question is: *This will probably make them feel worse*, then only say what's on your mind if it's truly edifying to them, and – as always – be careful about your tone, specific choice of words, and give them a chance to voice their opinion / reaction. In this way, we clear up misunderstandings before they have an opportunity to fester. Even when it's appropriate to give so-called tough lov... – no, I cannot write that – TL (Chapter 6), to be authentic love it must be a respectful dialogue that, by the end, has lifted our counterpart up because they know we love them, and want only the best for them.

How do we form the habit of consistently communicating in this way? It all boils down to remembering the inherent value of our audience, and that we are to humbly serve them with unselfish communication. Far be it from us to say: *I know what it takes to be successful. For you to achieve anything, you need to focus and apply yourself for more than the short haul. I'm sorry, but I'm just not seeing it. When are you going to surprise me by pulling up your boot straps?* … Now, that's just plain rude! … Let's practice choosing our words more wisely, for example: *Visualize what you want to achieve, pray about it, get advice from trustworthy and God-pleasing mentors, put the parts of their advice that resonate with you into practice, make a commitment to apply yourself consistently over the long haul, celebrate the milestones in your progress, and soon you'll find that you're on your way toward accomplishing what you set out to do. And that's when you know that you're already successful.*

"Love is not rude."

"Love … does not insist on its own way" (1 Corinthians 13:4-5)

Being selfish is so rude (prior section)! I was incredibly rude when drafting this book! Yes, I was. If only you could have read my early drafts! It's so hard to choose, but let me give you just a few examples: The first version of my analogy to explain intimate love (Chapter 1) rendered it impossible to assign an R rating to this book; I was undaunted. Then there was my first attempt to describe human-animal bonds, and I was neither gray nor light-handed (also Chapter 1); I felt my harangue was justified and on point. 1,178 exclamation points! No, 1,178 exclamation points. There, that's better. 576 occurrences of "should." Now, that just shouldn't be! And, last but most, the elephant in the room (Chapter 7) was not only addressed, but he was addressed in unequivocal detail, guaranteed to make every reader blush; I was proud of such an achieve-ment. Oh, if only you could have read each and every word – I would have been so pleased! … And you would have hated it…

How did I learn that you would have hated it? My representative person told me. In this case, my representative person was quite clear in my mind's eye. You see, I had several very real people review my very real early drafts. Without exception, each and every very real reviewer reacted to such self-misguided excursions with, *"Oh, my! Please reconsider such follies!"* or something to this effect, with the underlying message being, *"Please respect your audience. From our vantage point, most readers would appreciate an adjustment."*

Sometimes we let our own preferences get out of hand. Just because I want to touch the whole elephant doesn't mean that you want to hear my unrated description of this. And, more importantly, I might like to *think* that I've touched the whole elephant, but shock without value and heavy-handed smugness only serve to make it abundantly clear that I'm just another man with his eyes closed, describing the parts I've touched thus far in my experience. How presumptuous of me to think that I've touched the whole elephant![1]

My representative person reminded me to open my eyes and consider my audience – not only your preferences but also your points of view – and not to insist on writing as if only to clones of myself. ... After a moderate amount of internal deliberation, I learned that they are absolutely right. Being true to my authentic self is essential – (That is what I was deliberating about) – but just as essential is respecting the preferences and points of view of my counterparts. Both essentialities are possible to achieve simultaneously. Just as we put on a swimsuit – as skimpy as it may be – when we go to the beach, in this book you can see the authentic me just fine, and all the while feel no need to shield your adolescent child's roaming eyes as I sashay by, with nary a towel or coverup of any kind.

Many times in life, we want to do something a certain way, and if we pause for a moment to consider the reason why, we realize that it boils down to nothing other than it feels good to us. It's generally fine to proceed in this way if we aren't breaking any local laws – or any of God's laws – but there are times when we should adjust our straps a smidgen. How do we know? There are no mirrors on the beach. ... Our loving counterparts are our mirrors, and they have a good view from all angles. When a trustworthy counterpart tells us in a gentle and loving manner that our G-string is revealing too much information, then we should go back to our van to put on something with a little more coverage. How do we know what to pick from our duffle bag? We should bring our friend into our van, so they can help us choose something more appropriate for this particular day at the beach and – of course, as always – it needs to be something that necessitates a *lot* of sunscreen and is flattering to our figure – our special, one-of-a-kind, awesome figure.

Bring them into our van? Really? ... Yes, when we are in intimate love (Chapter 1) with someone who loves us unconditionally, we are comfortable showing them our authentic self, in all its glory. One of the reasons we make ourselves vulnerable in this way is it helps us learn how best to evolve. Our authentic self continues to develop / evolve throughout our life. This evolutionary process is driven, at least partially, based on feedback from others who love us unconditionally, as they point out what we should flaunt, what we should tone further, and what areas we should treat more modestly. As I mentioned earlier (Chapter 5 – "Repaving our path" section), we should *never* change for anyone who does not already love us unconditionally. But when we have found a counterpart who has demonstrated that they *do* love us just the way we are, then we should invite them into our van so they can help us – with their gentle suggestions – choose our beachwear for the day.

~

I will close this section with a reminder that I love you. I already told you that – *twice!* – but you may have doubted it. Now, you know for sure that I love you. … How do you know for sure? … Because I went back to my van – invited a few mentors to join me inside – and, after some deliberation, I revised my early drafts…

"Love does not insist on its own way."

"Love is … not easily angered" (1 Corinthians 13:4-5 NIV)

In the Prologue, I make the comment, "I felt that it's unfortunate that God doesn't talk to us directly and in such a way tell us what He thinks of us." Every time you read that, I hope you're thinking: *Oh, come on! Of course God "talks" to us in countless ways, not the least of which are: the wonders of creation; our study of the Bible; the instruction of our trustworthy, God-fearing pastors, teachers, and other mentors; many of our day-to-day interactions with our loving counterparts; our time spent in prayer, including our frequent request that we learn to be patient as we await God's guidance.* Yes, I hope you're thinking that – because it certainly is true. But when it comes to literally talking to us directly, I think most of us can agree that God is generally on the quiet side (at least with those of us on this side of eternity).

One advantage of being quiet is that people perk up when we have something to say. It's like when Yellowstone's Steamboat Geyser erupts – people stop and take notice!

Did you know that the Bible does record quite a few times when God literally talks? Yes, it does – and when we come upon such verses, we should stop and take notice. Several such occurrences involve God talking to Moses. What did God say to Moses? Well, amongst other things, God literally spoke the Ten Commandments (Exodus 20:1-17) before they were recorded on tablets, not once (Exodus 31:18) but twice (Exodus 34:27-28)!

Why twice? Wasn't once enough? Well, once should have been enough, but something happened… Looking back on it, it was clearly an overreaction… But isn't that so often the case when we look back on those times when we've allowed ourselves to be swept away by the swift current of our anger? In Moses' case, it went like this. When he saw the Israelites' most recent relapse into idolatry, he got angry – fair enough – but was a little hasty when he allowed his anger to escalate into a hissy fit that included smashing the first set of tablets: "As soon as he came near the camp and saw the calf and the dancing, Moses' anger burned hot, and he threw the tablets out of his hands and broke them at the foot of the mountain" (Exodus 32:19).

Moses' anger was certainly justified, but he was a mite hurried when it came to choosing how to react to his initial feelings of anger. From this, we can all learn a lesson: While many times in life our anger is justified, let us refrain from throwing things…

Since Moses' anger about what the Israelites were doing was justified, then wasn't God angry too? … *Oh, yes, God was very angry!* …

> The LORD said to Moses, "Go down, for your people, whom you brought up out of the land of Egypt, have corrupted themselves. They have turned aside quickly out of the way that I commanded them. They have made for themselves a golden calf and have worshiped it and sacrificed to it and said, 'These are your gods, O Israel, who brought you up out of the land of Egypt!'" And the LORD said to Moses, "I have seen this people, and behold, it is a stiff-necked people. Now therefore let me alone, that my wrath may burn hot against them and I may consume them, in order that I may make a great nation of you." (Exodus 32:7-10)

But did God start throwing things in a temper tantrum? No, He slowed things down. Instead of letting things escalate too quickly, He let things percolate. He took the time to reflect back on His promises…

> But Moses implored the LORD his God and said, "O LORD, why does your wrath burn hot against your people, whom you have brought out of the land of Egypt with great power and with a mighty hand? Why should the Egyptians say, 'With evil intent did he bring them out, to kill them in the mountains and to consume them from the face of the earth'? Turn from your burning anger and relent from this disaster against your people. Remember Abraham, Isaac, and Israel, your servants, to whom you swore by your own self, and said to them, 'I will multiply your offspring as the stars of heaven, and all this land that I have promised I will give to your offspring, and they shall inherit it forever.'" And the LORD relented from the disaster that he had spoken of bringing on his people. (Exodus 32:11-14)

I told you that God never breaks His promises!

From this, we can all learn a lesson: While many times in life our anger is justified, throughout our reaction to it – not the least important time of which is when we first sense those initial feelings of anger – let us slow down and zoom out to see the big picture. Are we really going to overreact to our anger by severing our bond with our counterpart in one rash moment of passionate ire? Didn't we make promises to our counterpart, whether specifically stated in public – for example, at our wedding ceremony – or implied by our privately calling them friend? Like our God, we should be reflecting on our promises to our friends and loved ones, even when – especially when – we are angry with them.

What else did God say to Moses? Well, amongst other things, God had quite a bit to say between the production of the first and second sets of tablets. Did God slip into the conversation that Moses' moment of rage had caused a lot of extra work? No, God moved on from that, and instead had an intimate moment with Moses – passing before him and proclaiming His name.

> The LORD descended in the cloud and stood with him [Moses] there, and proclaimed the name of the LORD. The LORD passed before him and

proclaimed, "The LORD, the LORD, a God merciful and gracious, slow to anger, and abounding in steadfast love and faithfulness, keeping steadfast love for thousands, forgiving iniquity and transgression and sin, but who will by no means clear the guilty, visiting the iniquity of the fathers on the children and the children's children, to the third and the fourth generation." (Exodus 34:5-7)

When we read such verses, we should stop and take careful note! This is God's name that He Himself has spoken!

Do the last couple lines of His name make you tremble a little bit – maybe more than a little bit? … They should! We should all have a healthy amount of fear in light of God's authority over all things, including the final verdict when it's our time to be judged. Most fearful – indeed, terrified – should be those who are guilty of persisting in unbelief – those who are comfortable wallowing in the iniquity of rejecting Jesus as their Savior. Such people are complacently following the misguided footsteps of so many who have come before them, oftentimes their own ancestors. What lies at the end of the path of complacency? People who persist on this path to the bitter end will attempt to stand on their own merits before God, and will find this to be impossible in the face of His wrath.

As you can see, God's name includes the severity of the fully brewed manifestation of His anger. … What makes God angry? As discussed previously, what makes Him angry is sin, unrepentance, and unbelief (Chapter 2 – "A preemptive strike" section).

But as you can also see, God's name includes that He is "slow to anger." … What makes God's smoldering anger cool to ashes? As discussed in the same section referenced in the preceding paragraph, God's anger toward our sin is quenched / satisfied by our repentance and our belief: gifts of the Holy Spirit. Specifically, our belief is in Jesus' redeeming work, which is nothing less than His payment in full for every one of our sins. This has already been accomplished – once and for all – by Jesus' sacrifice on the cross; that is where we see God the Father's anger toward each and every one of our sins finally – at the fullness of time (Galatians 4:4-7) – completely manifested, overflowing in a torrent and ultimately upended, being entirely poured out on Jesus. This is the awesome way by which God the Father's slow but justified anger – perfect, righteous anger –

toward all sin has been fully quenched / fully satisfied. Because of this, Jesus has two other very fitting names that we call Him: our Redeemer and our Savior.

~

In this section, I've reminded you that – from a literal perspective (often mine) – God is on the quiet side, and this has helped us to stop and take notice when He speaks; and not the least of the things that He has spoken is that part of His name is "slow to anger" (Exodus 34:6).

Knowing that this is part of God's name causes believers to stop and take notice every time we remember Jesus' redeeming work; God the Father's righteous anger toward all sins of all people, believers and unbelievers alike, was made manifest – and was fully quenched – in a magnificent way.

Unbelievers, on the other hand, have not yet stopped and taken notice of any of this. If they continue down this wayward path, following each and every one of their unspiritual predecessors, then God's slow anger toward their willful, persistent sins of unrepentance and unbelief will catch up with them when it comes time for them to be judged. Then, they will clearly see the manifestation of His righteous anger toward unrepentance and unbelief, which in their case is still smoldering and even now erupting. Finally, He will have their full attention, and they will have no choice but to stop and take notice.

~

How should we believers apply what we've learned in this section to our personal relationships?

As I've amply described, when someone has a quiet nature, we stop and take notice when they have something to say. Similarly, when someone is slow to anger, we stop and take notice when their righteous anger is made manifest. In contrast, if someone is talkative, or if someone is hasty to escalate their anger, then we tend to tune them out: They're just adding yet another sub-bullet point to their lengthy list of what they think is important; or they're just interrupting our day, belching loud bellyaches about yet another trifling matter that they're ticked off about.

From this, we can all learn a lesson: Our friends and loved ones will stop and take notice when our tou… – no, always gentle – love for them is made manifest by our righteous anger. By previously demonstrating to them that we are slow to anger, they'll know that our anger is not our hasty reaction to a trifling matter – and they'll know that, even in the midst of such righteous anger, we haven't forgotten our promises to them, not the least of which is: We love them, and always want the best for them.

"Love is not easily angered."

"Love … keeps no record of wrongs" (1 Corinthians 13:4-5 NIV)

As I was growing up, one of the things that I slowly but surely became aware of was that our family had various "lists." I will call the agglomeration of them a "list of lists." Allow me to elaborate: There was the "damn list" – on which was anyone who didn't seem to us to be right with God, or to be living what seemed to us to be a particularly sanctified life. There was the "not us list" – on which was anyone who didn't seem to us to be expressing their patriotism with fervor and from our side of the political aisle. There was the "hippie list" – on which was anyone who seemed to us to be too young and too content. I'm sure you're not surprised that we needed a "charcoal list" – a kind of catch-all, on which was anyone who differed from us on any other matter that we considered important. A whole 'nother category was the "quid quo amateur list" – on which was anyone who didn't satisfy our definition of quid quo pro; to wit, *I scratched your back with verve, but you haven't done nearly as much to tickle my fancy.* And last, but not least, there was what we called simply "The List" (other families call this the "shi_ list") – on which was anyone who made it onto more than one of our other lists.

Whether you made it onto only one of our lists, or you made it all the way onto The List, one thing was certain – you were on there to stay. That's the whole point of a list – so we don't forget!

There's another, more personal, list that each of us keeps. We don't need to write down the names and the circumstances because we will not forget. We keep this list in our heart, our deeply wounded heart. It's the list of those who have hurt us severely by sinning against us in a grievous way. Our counterpart in this circumstance may not even have been on any of our other lists. Yes, we are most deeply hurt by those we trust – by those we don't expect to hurt us – by those we love.

There are many ways by which otherwise loving counterparts can hurt one another in a profound and "permanent" manner. Two common – unfortunately… – examples are infidelity and abuse. When we sin against our counterpart, or our counterpart sins against us, in such a damaging way, our lives are changed forever – we will never be the same. This goes for our relationship, as well as for both of us as individuals. As with all sins and hurts, no matter what we do in the present and future, those sins and hurts are part of our history. The infidelity and the pain it caused are permanently part of our history; the abuse and the pain it caused are permanently part of our history. What is our reaction to be?

I'm sure many of you noticed that in the preceding paragraph, several times I referred to such sins and hurts as being permanent. And some of you may even have questioned my wording it that way. … *Good! It's right for you to question such things! I'm glad to see that you're getting what it means to live in love!* … While our sins and hurts are, from one perspective – the perspective of this life, this physical world – a permanent part of our history (We cannot change the past), we should not allow our history to define our present and future.

But how can we do a difficult thing like restore a relationship that has been wounded by an egregious sin of one against the other? How can we trust our counterpart again? How can we pick up the pieces, and forgive such a grievous sin against us? Yes, how can we truly forgive, and not seek a way to hurt them in return – to try to even the score, as it were? After all, they started it! Yes, the easiest responses for us are retaliation and giving up. Our selfish, sinful, human nature makes it impossible for us, on our own, to consider anything other than retaliation and/or severing the relationship permanently. Retaliation is the easiest answer, and is always wrong. Severing the relationship permanently – cutting our counterpart off forever – is another "easy" (relative to reconciliation) answer; but instead of making such a rash decision quickly, initially please only take the first step, which is a timeout period. The purpose of a timeout is for both parties to gather their thoughts, process their feelings, and – *Don't forget this important part!* – to reconvene when they're calmer, hopefully to start the reconciliation process. So, when we're hurt, how do we pursue anything other than the easy answers? How do we pursue reconciliation? And I'm talking about true reconciliation, where we are a driving pair that's focused on the road ahead, not our rearview mirrors. Staring into our rearview mirrors only serves to remind our counterpart of their sin and to hinder us from letting go of our resentment and coming to peace with our hurt. Careful readers already know the answer: We can only do such a difficult thing based on submitting to the Holy Spirit, who alone has the power to help us stop looking inward, and rather look outward – to pursue the best for our counterpart and for our relationship.

When we make a minor mistake, or when someone mildly irritates us, a small adjustment is probably a good idea. In contrast, when we commit a grievous sin against someone, or when someone hurts us very deeply, a large change is absolutely necessary! Which is worse: being deeply hurt by someone we trusted, or living in the regret of deeply hurting someone who trusted us? Both are extremely difficult. I'll address both scenarios in turn. Which shall I address first? … I have no choice but to order them in this way.

- **When our grievous sin deeply hurts someone who trusted us**: How long does it take us to realize that we need to stop such behavior? How long does it take us to stop being selfish and comprehend how our actions are impacting our counterpart? How long does it take us to repent? In the example of abuse, how long does it take us to open our eyes and see the pain in the eyes of the one we are abusing? In the example of infidelity, how long does it take us to confess our sin, and vow never to be unfaithful again? The answer to all these questions is: *If the question pertains to us, then it already has taken us far too long. We must stop immediately! We must confess immediately! We must repent immediately!* Yes, the moment we start an egregious sin against someone, the time to stop is now.

  Why do we stop? Why do we repent? Why do we change our behavior? I'll provide more commentary on this, below, but next please consider the following lyrics.

> *I'm sorry that I hurt you*
> *It's something I must live with every day*
> *And all the pain I put you through*
> *I wish I could take it all away*
> *And be the one who catches all your tears*
> *That's why I need you to hear*

I've found a reason for me
To change who I used to be
A reason to start over new
And the reason is you[2]

Why do we stop? Why do we repent? Why do we change our behavior? Is it to benefit ourselves? While stopping / repenting / changing will benefit us personally, rarely does changing for the sake of ourselves provide sufficient motivation. It's easier to stay the way we are. Yes, it's easier, so we generally prefer the status quo. So, what provides sufficient motivation? Motivation – profound motivation – is provided when we stop looking inward, and rather look outward. Only then do we see clearly how our behavior is impacting our counterpart. Only then do we see clearly why we have to change.

- **When we have been deeply hurt by the grievous sin of someone we trusted**: Just as in the previous bullet point, the main issue again here is our selfish attitude. When we focus on ourselves – *Which is so easy to do when we are hurt, isn't it?* – we focus on our pain and our resentment toward the one who hurt us. In contrast, when we focus on what's best for our counterpart – *Which at such times is so difficult for us, isn't it?* – we focus on helping them become a better person, a better person in all respects: emotionally, psychologically, and spiritually. The emotional and psychological aspects are for this life – and, yes, ideally we're still included in life together with them, based on reconciliation. More importantly, the spiritual aspect is for both this life and the life to come.

  The spiritual element is the only part of this whole discussion that truly is permanent. Our infidelity, our abusive behavior, any other ways that we've wronged someone else, our guilt and regret over such sins of ours, our feelings of being hurt by the sins of others, our feelings of resentment toward others who have hurt us: all such things are, spiritually speaking, *not* permanent. As permanent as they are in this life, where our history sticks to us like cat fur on a cashmere sweater, in the context of eternity they surely are not permanent! In this life, sometimes we have difficulty not dwelling on our history – not looking back to focus on our hurts, the sins that caused them, and the people who committed these sins – as Lot's wife couldn't help but look back toward a den of atrocities (Genesis 19:26). But in the life to come, our hurts and the sins that caused them are blotted out: "Though your sins are like scarlet, they shall be as white as snow; / though they are red like crimson, they shall become like wool" (Isaiah 1:18); "I am he who blots out your transgressions for my own sake, and I will not remember your sins" (Isaiah 43:25); "Behold, I am making all things new" (Revelation 21:5).

In heaven, we'll have neither the time nor the interest to be giving further thought to our hurts, our regrets, our sins, or the sins of anyone else. In heaven, we'll have higher priority things to focus on, and we'll at last drown in the unfathomable depths of God's complete forgiveness.

"Love keeps no record of wrongs."

~

I'd like to close this section with a prayer for reconciliation. If you're in a relationship where one or both of you have been deeply hurt by the other's grievous sin, I've written a prayer on your behalf – as a way to try to encourage you to work together toward reaching true reconciliation. In this life, love is not always easy. When love is challenging – when you're experiencing emotional pain because of an unexpected trial within a close relationship – don't give up, but rather pray. In addition to your own prayers, please read the following prayer I've written for you, know that God loves you – both you and your counterpart – and wants to help you strengthen your relationship, and then close your eyes and ask God what the next steps should be. (This is written assuming that you are a married couple, one of whom has recently hurt the other very deeply. Change the details as needed.)

- *Heavenly Father, this couple that You hold dear is struggling severely.*

  One has hurt the other – very deeply. One has dishonored the other, in a most disrespectful way. One has been extremely selfish, and disregarded the other. One has broken their marriage vows. One has egregiously sinned against You and their spouse.

  And one is feeling a pain they never knew before. One is hurt in a way they never dreamt they would have to experience. One knows that what has happened can't be changed – their life will never be the same. One is wonder-ing if they can ever forgive the other. One is wondering if they can ever trust the other again.

Heavenly Father, I ask You to help these two dear offspring of Yours turn their focus from inward to outward. Help them both remember how much You love them, no matter what.

Help the one who committed the sin to experience true remorse, to be motivated by their regret to pursue meaningful change, not only for their per-sonal development but more importantly for the sake of their spouse and for the relationship. Help the one who committed the sin to clearly demonstrate that they've learned from their mistake, that they know they can't mistreat their spouse in this way, or any other way…, again, that they'll work with their spouse to make meaningful changes, and in these and other ways prove, in time, that they're again trustworthy.

And please help the one who was sinned against. Oh, God, they're hurt-ing! They've been treated unfairly, and are struggling with how to cope with this. Help them get through any feelings of revenge, spite, or wanting to shut out their spouse forever. Give them time to heal. Give them the space to examine their own heart, to identify ways that they may have contributed to strains in the relationship with their spouse. Help them attain an openness that the relationship may be restorable.

And please help the couple work together to build their relationship back up, piece by piece: to communicate more effectively, to resolve conflicts by talking and listening to each other, to learn how to change, to learn how to process their feelings and eventually let go of resentment, to learn how to come to peace with hurts, to learn how to come to peace with regrets, to learn how to give and receive forgiveness even in difficult circumstances, to start to build trust again, to start to show affection again, and in such ways, and in due time, experience mutual healing and renewed love for one another.

And help them remember that even though relationships in this life some-times encounter challenges never anticipated – challenges that become an unalterable part of our past here on this earth – such sins and hurts truly are drowned forever in your ever-flowing forgiveness and grace. We are thankful that we experience such eternal blessings, all because of the sacrifice of Jesus, our Savior. In His name, Amen.

"Love does not delight in evil" (1 Corinthians 13:6 NIV)

In the previous section, I focus on the impact of sins within a close relationship. Are these the only sins that impact us? *Heavens no!* In this world, we are wading through swamplands where evil lurks just below the murky surface. Sometimes we bump up against evil in our own meanderings (for example, we slowly evolve from the maladaptive habit of gazing at handsome / beautiful models in the Sears catalog to the maladjusted addiction of yearning for thespians of hardcore pornography). Other times evil leaps out at us – toothy jaws snapping – from what at first glance seemed to us to be a serene alcove (for example, we attend a concert and suddenly find ourselves diving for cover as bullets fly). I have much to say about evil, and what our reaction to it should be, in the "What if you encounter evil in the world?" section (Chapter 9). For now, let's focus on what is always (1 Thessalonians 5:17) a good idea – prayer. If you ever have trouble thinking of the right words to say as you pray, I suggest going to the psalms. If you don't know what to pray for, just open your Bible near the center and pick one. If you know that you want to pray about the impact of evil on our lives, may I suggest Psalm 5? Below, I provide the first four verses.

> Give ear to my words, O LORD; consider my groaning. / Give attention to the sound of my cry, my King and my God, for to you do I pray. / O LORD, in the morning you hear my voice; in the morning I prepare a sacrifice for you and watch. / For you are not a God who delights in wickedness; evil may not dwell with you. (Psalm 5:1-4)

A common position of skeptics is: *If there is a God, then He's neither perfectly loving nor perfectly powerful because He allows us to be impacted by evil.* But while they're busy doubting God, they forget to take a look in the mirror. All their doubting cannot change the awful truth that it's *us* who chose to play in Satan's sandbox instead of to submit to God's will in all things, and in such a way remain in the sanctuary of the Garden of Eden (Genesis 3). If we throw sand in our playmate's eyes, are our parents being unloving to our playmates? No, *we are* being unloving to our playmates! In the same way, when we carry out evil deeds that hurt others, it isn't God who is unloving or out of control.

Are we, God's creatures, perfectly in line with God's nature?
- The definition of love that is simultaneously most succinct and most expansive is: "God is love" (1 John 4:8, 16)
  - o   It's God's nature to love, but we are often unloving, like a cacophonous throng of sandy-haired toddlers slinging handfuls in every direction
- God and evil do not mix – they are entirely opposed to one another: "You are not a God who delights in wickedness; evil may not dwell with you" (Psalm 5:4)
  - o   It's God's nature to oppose evil, but we return to Satan's sandbox every day

Obviously, none of us on this side of eternity are living perfectly in line with God's nature! Does this come as a surprise to you? It seems to come as a surprise to skeptics. Apparently, their many doubts lead them to conclude that each of us is a marionette, with God pulling the strings that control our every action, and with each of our actions being in total alignment with God's nature. I, for one, am very skeptical of their skepticism and have reached the conclusion that their conclusion is of a dubious nature. I reached this finding based on the following research.
- I tried to find a translation of the Bible that says that we are love. I searched high and low, but I can only find "God is love" (1 John 4:8, 16).
- Likewise, I tried to find a translation of the Bible that says that evil may not dwell with us. But I can only find "Evil may not dwell with you [God]" (Psalm 5:4).
- I don't give up easily! I kept pushing on, and tried to find a translation of the Bible that says that we do not delight in wickedness / evil, but I can only find the following *two* things: "You are not a God who delights in wickedness" (Psalm 5:4), and "Love does not delight in evil" (1 Corinthians 13:6 NIV). I was so proud of myself for finding two things, but then I realized that these really only qualify as one thing because – by definition – those are equivalent statements.

Love does not delight in wickedness; You are not a God who delights in evil.

"Love … rejoices with the truth" (1 Corinthians 13:4, 6)

I discuss in Chapter 1, at the beginning of the "Antonyms of love" section, that certain things are seen more clearly with the opposite as the backdrop. I give three examples: light / darkness, good / evil, and God / Satan. I'd like to elaborate further on another, similar, example: truth / lies, specifically the lies of Satan.

One phenomenon that my wife and I have experienced frequently is our becoming aware that Satan is trying to thwart something that we're doing. Years ago, we'd fret about this and get upset. But over time, we learned to look at it differently. Now, when we see Satan trying to stop us, we know that we're on the right track. We've said to each other, on multiple occasions, that a project we're working on is obviously going to be very impactful and God-pleasing because Satan is trying very hard to throw monkey wrenches into it. We have seen this so many times that it has risen to the status of a bona fide law, and I like to call it the Law of Satan's Backed Up and Overflowing Cesspit of Lies (LOSBUAOCOL).

There are two corollaries of this law that I want to impress upon you (listed below). But before I get to that, be mindful of this: The law itself, these two corollaries, and any other corollaries there might be, only hold true when we're in tight prayer with God. Satan is wily. He'll try to trick us with his lies. He can easily deceive us, with one exception: It's impossible for him to mislead us if we're in close communication with God. When we "pray without ceasing" (1 Thessalonians 5:17), Satan has no chance. Satan is cunning, yes, but God is always working an infinite number of moves ahead: "For he who is in you is greater than he who is in the world" (1 John 4:4).

- The first corollary to LOSBUAOCOL is: When it comes time to make a decision, determine which option Satan wants to stop more, and there's your answer!

- The second corollary to LOSBUAOCOL is: When Satan realizes that he can't thwart our God-pleasing plan, his next move is to try to come between those of us who are involved in carrying out this plan. In other words, Satan doesn't give up easily; so, when he sees that he has no chance to stop what-ever God-pleasing thing we're doing, he'll next try to make our lives miser-able. He especially likes to drive a wedge between loving counterparts. This particular breed of wedgie is what I like to call – oh, no, I shouldn't; there are ladies and gentlemen present. Anyway, the point is: Especially when under a lot of stress, for example because of working hard on something to further God's kingdom, please be on the alert for Satan to try to get you and your counterpart to turn on one another. When he realizes that he can't stop the overall project, he turns his attention fully to trying to cause strife between us. Such strife will still give him satisfaction – very much satisfaction, in fact. If we sense the birth pains of such conflict, let us remind ourselves – and our counterpart – that this is further proof of LOSBUAOCOL; in this case, what's being made more clear is that we're in a loving relationship that God wants to remain strong, so we must make a correction immediately to keep it that way. Satan has a lot of lies at his disposal, as he tries to destroy God-pleasing relationships. He might try to convince you that your counterpart isn't pulling their weight. He might try to convince you that your counterpart is a slave-driver who doesn't appreciate your contributions. He might try to convince you that your counterpart is a dictator who doesn't give any consideration to your ideas. He might try to convince you that your counterpart's sigh means that they're annoyed with you. He might try to convince you that your counterpart has the communication skills of a bag of rocks, except, of course, when they're interrupting you, which they're clearly doing as a small but integral part of a complex power move that you've seen developing for some time now. … See how it can elevate? Elevate right to the bottom of Satan's cesspit.

Every relationship has its challenges, and Satan is very happy to contribute his two cents. This is especially the case when it's a God-pleasing relationship. Please teach your counterparts the law – change the name, if you must – that what is God-pleasing is more easily seen against the backdrop of what is trying to oppose it: Satan's lies. And teach your counterparts to be especially mindful of the second corollary. Pray with each of them – without ceasing – that your relationship will remain strong. In such a way, Satan's lies are surely thwarted.

"Love rejoices with the truth."

"Love bears all things" (1 Corinthians 13:7)

I'd like to start this section with what may seem like a small example of "bearing with one another in love" (Ephesians 4:2). This example seems to be a thorn in my side, or at least it used to be. I hope that this resonates with some of you, and that the rest of you don't find it too annoying. … You are unaware that I've just introduced the topic for you. Yes, I'd like to elaborate on the topic of our being annoying / irritating to others. I'm most assuredly an expert on this topic. Surely, you already know that I have honed skills in the arena of being annoying: verbose elaborations, every scenario scrutinized, awkward elephants addressed, bullet points galore, in every shape and size *(Be thankful that this book was not printed in color!)*, many puzzling word choices, ornate analogies that are not for the prudish or faint of heart, a curious and sometimes heavy-handed obsession with semantics, an unabashed fondness for ellipses… I could go on, but I think that's sufficient evidence to convict me. What are we left with when we boil such attributes down? … *Annoying!* Let me specify just one more attribute that's in my cauldron. How's this for annoying? *I find each and every one of you just as annoying!* Oh, that's right, I don't know all of you, so let me put it another way: *If I knew you, you can rest assured that I'd find you just as annoying!* How can I be so sure? Because you're different from me, and sometimes I don't like that. And this is the same reason why sometimes you're annoyed with me – I'm different from you, and sometimes you don't like that.

In my past, when I was annoyed by someone, I'd have a hard time being loving to them; likewise, when I became aware or sensed that someone was annoyed with me, I'd have a hard time accepting that they still loved me. I think differently now, and here's why: Finding one another annoying from time to time is to be expected because each of us is unique. Our uniqueness is something to celebrate, despite the fact that it occasionally gives rise to annoyance / irritation. Becoming annoyed with someone is analogous to getting angry with them. Both things rise up from our differences. In the midst of anger or annoyance, such differences are usually not appreciated. But when we reach the reconciliation stage, we remember that it really is the differences between us that are at the core of what we cherish about one another. The next time your counterpart does something that annoys you, don't overreact and don't dwell on it. Rather, remind yourself that they simply are different from you … and isn't that wonderful?

~

Let's face it – annoyances are usually relatively mild and short-lived. Life throws many more serious challenges at us. So, let's move on to another, more profound, way that we bear with one another in love – a way that probably resonates with more of you. As most of us have experienced, it's rare to travel very far in a relationship without encountering a challenging situation, and sometimes it may appear to be a roadblock or even a collapsed bridge. For example, one of us may become seriously ill or sustain multiple, severe injuries in a bad accident; other times, we may be faced with a family crisis, even as critical as a suicide attempt. At such times, it's common to feel confused and wonder why we must bear such heavy burdens. Never fear, I'm not going to do either of the following: I certainly am not going to chastise you for having such feelings; these are an entirely natural part of how we process adversities. And I'm not going to try to explain, at least not fully (Romans 11:33-34), why God allows us to experience such difficulties. However, next I describe a perspective that you may not have considered before, and I hope you find it helpful when faced with a true hardship.

You've probably heard it said that we can be blessed by our hardships, for example because they can make us stronger. I have a problem with this statement, and here's why. *(Consider yourself forewarned that another semantics lesson is surely coming!)* My problem is that this statement can easily be misconstrued to mean that we are blessed directly by a hardship itself. No, we are *not* blessed directly by a hardship itself. Hardships are ultimately the result of sin in this fallen world. We are not blessed by sin, or anything that is a direct result of sin*. God did not intend for us to experience hardships. At The Fall (Genesis 3), we were the ones who chose to suffer with adversities instead of submitting to God's will in all things. But God surely continues to bless us, even though we made that awful choice. One way that He blesses us, while we're in the midst of experiencing difficulties, is to influence how we and those around us *react* (both immediately and down the road) to these difficulties. God turns hardships into blessings, and those who love Him are well-equipped to recognize, appreciate, and express thankfulness for such blessings (Romans 8:28).

- For example, let's consider a scenario where we're directly impacted by a natural disaster. Below I describe two ways that we can react to this.

o One reaction is for us to become bitter about the inconveniences and the more profound difficulties the disaster is causing for us and our loved ones; to complain to rescue and relief workers that they're not doing enough to rectify the situation – at least not on our timeline; to become fearful and anxious about what the future holds, especially now that we've seen that calamity can strike at any time; and to become angry with God because He is allowing such things to happen to us

o A better reaction is for us, as empowered by the Holy Spirit, to look at the situation as an opportunity to receive and give help, enabling bonds between people to be strengthened; to thank and honor others who are trying their best to rectify the situation; to appreciate more deeply that we should cherish everyone in our life, especially now that we've seen that calamity can strike at any time; and in such ways to see more clearly "that for those who love God all things work together for good" (Romans 8:28)

With either reaction, the hardship itself was not a blessing. But in the second case, we've experienced rich blessings nevertheless. This life isn't always easy, but when our reactions to the challenges that come our way are guided by the Holy Spirit, ultimately we're strengthened, no matter what sin and Satan try to crush us with.

"Love bears all things."

> *Note: Above, I wrote, "We are not blessed by sin, or anything that is a direct result of sin." When I wrote this, I tried to think of an exception. The closest thing to an exception that I could think of is conception when the act of sex was a sin. I most definitely consider every conception to be a blessing. The Creator has created a new person. The previous sentence is a hint for how I came to the conclusion that conception when the act of sex was a sin is not an exception to what I wrote above. Why did I come to this conclusion? Because I don't consider conception to be a *direct* result of anything that *we* do, whether the sex involved a married couple coming together in a beautiful expression of love, or it involved any number of sinful acts that I will not try to list. In every case, conception of a human being is a direct result of the Creator being about His work; our involvement in the conception is *indirect*.

When we sin and are nevertheless blessed – *And doesn't this happen every day?* – we certainly aren't blessed *because of* our sin; we're blessed *despite* our sin. By the way, what I've just discussed is grace, which means: God blessing us, even though we don't deserve it.

"Love … always trusts" (1 Corinthians 13:4, 7 NIV)

You know by now that I'm generally pretty careful about my choice of words. And I don't think you'll be shocked beyond recovery to learn that I pay close attention to the word choices of others… *one of my most annoying attributes!* Which word in the title of this section caused me to do a bit of a double-take? … *Anyone?* … There are only three words. No, it's not "love" – I'm feeling pretty good about that word. … No, it's not "trusts" – love and trust should go together. … But "always"? *Really?* Love *always* trusts? What if our counterpart has hurt us very deeply? What if they've done this multiple times, there is a pattern developing, and there doesn't seem to be a path toward reconciliation? What if it's best for our physical and/or emotional wellbeing to separate ourselves from this person? … Love *always* trusts?

It comes down to what exactly love is leading us to trust. Is love leading us to trust that others will never sin against us again? No, that's not it – not at all. Then what are we to trust? And how does love lead us there? I can see two perspectives that speak to this.

- No matter how untrustworthy we find others in our life to be, God is always completely trustworthy. While others may regularly break every one of their promises, God never breaks any of His promises. God is perfectly trustworthy. God wants to have an intimate, loving relationship with each of us. Within this relationship, we come to understand that we are a totally dependent creature, and this brings us great comfort. What a relief to know that our God always knows what's best for us; and no matter what we're facing – challenges, disappointments, setbacks – we trust Him to guide our ways.

- When it comes to our interpersonal relationships, I've already mentioned that we cannot trust that our counterparts won't sin against us again. Yes, even the people who love us will sin against us again. And we will sin again, even against the people we love. How can we trust one another in light of this? … Is it hopeless? … No, in light of God's love it isn't hopeless. As enabled by the Holy Spirit's hand, while we still struggle with sin, we nevertheless trust that our loving counterparts will be forgiving of us, and we of them. When we love someone, we always aspire to forgive, no matter what (Chapter 9). And no matter how hurtful the sin is, within a loving relationship there is always a path to reconciliation.

I don't use the word "always" loosely. But in this section I've used it many times. When it comes to any attribute of God, "always" is always an appropriate word to use. God is certainly dependable, to be sure. And when it comes to forgiveness and reconciliation, "always" is an appropriate word to use when we're talking about believers in a loving relationship.

When two believers love one another, one thing this means is that we feel remorse whenever we hurt the other in any way; and this means that we apologize in short order; and this means that our counterpart forgives us; and this means that we're very soon working together to resolve issues related to the sin; and this means that we're not dwelling on the past; and this means that we're hopeful that the future will be different; and this means that we trust that this particular sin will not recur. And if this particular sin *does* recur, we trust that there is again remorse… and the path to follow is familiar…

In the preceding paragraph, it is love – the love that the counterparts have for one another, and more importantly God's love for both of them – that is the guarantee that forgiveness and reconciliation are pursued. We trust that we will forgive and reconcile, no matter what.

But what if one counterpart becomes unwilling to follow this familiar path? … Do we trust now? … When our counterpart chooses not to follow this path, they're choosing to fall out of love with us. Our conditional love relationship is disintegrating; our bond is breaking. When we fall out of love, then we can no longer trust that forgiveness and reconciliation are going to be pursued. This is a shame, and our response in such situations should be to love our counterpart unconditionally, as one-sided as this may be, and ask God to help us restore, if it is His will, a loving, two-sided, bonded relationship with this person.

When we fall out of love with someone, the inference is that we had previously fallen *in* love with them. Look back at the reasons the two of you fell in love in the first place. Remind your counterpart of these reasons, and – *Don't stop there!* – remind them that, no matter what, you still love them unconditionally. Perhaps this – and a little patience – will be enough for you to find that your counterpart is, at the end of the day, trustworthy after all.

"Love always trusts."

"Love … hopes all things" (1 Corinthians 13:7)

For each of us who is a Christian – who trusts in Jesus as our Savior from sin, death, and Satan – we know the joy of the assurance that we are saved. And what a comfort this is! I can't imagine going through life without ever knowing the certainty of God's promise to save all who trust in Him. I can't imagine it because I've been empowered by the Holy Spirit to believe God's promises; thus, I've taken them to heart and I'm a new person (2 Corinthians 5:17). Amongst other things, this blessed perspective enables me to see that if I let go of God's promises, I have nothing left but despair and hopelessness – a relentless wind across a vast expanse of nothingness that the Holy Spirit shelters me from. But many people not only imagine a hollow life – one where they continuously reject God's promises – they live it every day.

How are we to help someone who has mired themselves in such an empty life? There's so much they're rejecting! They're rejecting the fact that they're a sinner. They're rejecting their need for a Savior. They're rejecting Jesus. They're rejecting God's forgiveness – His promise to cover their sins forever in the righteousness of Jesus. They're rejecting God's promise to save all who turn to Jesus (repent), and trust only in Him. They're rejecting God's love. … Is this a long and daunting list? How do we know where to start? … In my view, it's not as daunting as it may first appear. In fact, I don't find it daunting at all. Didn't David slay Goliath (1 Samuel 17)? Weren't about 3,000 souls baptized on the first Pentecost after Jesus' ascension (Acts 2)?

We start by laying aside our puny, brittle weapons, and seek the weapon that only the Holy Spirit can provide. Then, we consider our "enemy." This is not very difficult, because they are like us – actually, they are exactly like us, at least the way we were before we believed. Part of our selfish, sinful, human nature – all of ours – is to don thick armor, as a way to try to get through this life on our own. But, to be sure, we all have a chink in our armor. Then, just as sure, once our armor is breached, we all have a part of ourselves that is most susceptible.

First things first: Where is the chink in our armor? … If you look carefully, you can find it. … *See? There it is…* It's at the seam between perfection and reality. This is the seam that tries to reconcile our desire for perfection with the harsh reality that everything about the secular, temporal world is imperfect. When living in a nonspiritual way:

- We want to have it all, but we see the reality that no matter how many material things we accumulate, we still feel empty inside
- We want others to admire us, to follow our lead, but we see the reality that at our first sign of faltering, their snickering starts and shortly thereafter they scatter like rats fleeing a burning building
- We want others to love us, but we see the reality that our inability to truly love anyone in return causes us to experience the barrenness of loneliness and isolation
- We want to live forever, but we see the reality that people are dying all around us

This seam between perfection and reality tends to loosen easily. We keep sewing it back up with all the care we can muster, all the while fretting about it. The Holy Spirit knows full well that we fret about this. He zeroes in on our seam – takes careful aim – and with awesome strength lances us with the cold-steel fact that *everything* about the secular, temporal world is imperfect – *including us!* The Holy Spirit does not miss. He hits the seam in our armor, square and true, and we are surely impaled – yes, all the way through – with the agonizing truth that it is *not possible* to reconcile our desire for perfection with anything that this world has to offer. As we writhe in misery, we have no choice but to admit that we are imperfect; saying this another way – in God's language – we have no choice but to admit that we are a sinner.

How do we recover from this? There are only two ways that this can be resolved: (i) We persist in independence – which is gruesome death, or (ii) we submit to dependence – a dependence on God, which is life itself. What does our selfish, sinful, human nature choose? Without fail, we choose blinding pain that leads nowhere other than agonizing death. Left to our own devices, we insist on remaining independent. We lay exposed and alone for days and nights, groaning and clutching at the thick pole through our bowels, wanting nothing more than to pull it out, but all our attempts are in vain – the shaft is too heavy and the working end is barbed. We lie in indescribable anguish, with our life slowly draining out of us.

What can be done? Recall that earlier I mentioned that once our armor is breached, we all have a part of ourselves that is most susceptible. Is it our bowels? No, we remain independent, even though our bowels are ripped to shreds. Is it our head, our mind? No, we remain independent, even though our thoughts are tortured with unsatisfactory rationalizations as to how our choice can possibly make sense. If it is neither our bowels nor our mind, then what can it be? *Any thoughts? … Nope, that's not it. Anyone else? … Nope, certainly not that… My goodness… Anyone else? … Yes, you're right! You've been paying attention! It's our heart.* Depending on our circumstances, we may have forgotten about our heart. Even as we lay in agony, we may not remember that we have a heart. … When is the last time we felt like we mattered? When is the last time we felt cared for? When is the last time we felt touched by love? … Even if we have no prior experience with such feelings – rare, but it can happen – our heart is susceptible to being receptive to change that God wants for us. For it is in our heart that we know (Romans 2:14-15) that life is meant to be more than a futile search for perfection in an imperfect world. And it is in our heart that we know that life is meant to be more than lying alone in anguish. The Holy Spirit knows full well that we understand this. For one thing, He Himself taught us! He zeroes in on our heart – takes careful aim – and with awesome gentleness embraces us with His warm touch that assures us that despite mankind's rebellion (Genesis 3), which makes everything about the secular, temporal world imperfect, He still loves all humanity – *including us!* Unless we react to even this with a stubbornness of an incomprehensible magnitude – an inexplicable hardening of our own heart – once the Holy Spirit embraces our heart, we finally give in and are engulfed with overwhelming mercy and grace – yes, fully penetrating – with the blessed truth that He loves and cherishes us, through and through: body, mind, heart, and soul. As we bask in His love, our body, mind, heart, and soul have no choice but to admit that we are totally dependent creatures – that we are totally His.

Earlier, I wrote that helping someone mired in a painful, fruitless, empty life is not a daunting task. But what I've written since then may sound quite daunting! But I stand by my earlier statement. That's right, I don't find it daunting at all to shower such a person in love. Don't you see? It's a domino effect – it's a package deal. Each of those things that our selfish, sinful, human nature rejects – *Remember that "long and daunting list"?* – each of them evaporates in the warmth of love. Yes, even the very first thing on that list – *They're rejecting the fact that they're a sinner* – yes, even that, the first thing that needs to be addressed, is not daunting in the face of love. Oh, it's hard for us. Impossible, in fact! But it's not daunting at all when we ask the Holy Spirit to provide the sturdy weapon and His awesome strength and gentleness. When our counterpart rejects the fact that they're a sinner, the most loving thing we can do for them – *And this is such a wonderful expression of love!* – is with one arm impale them, and with the other arm seek to embrace them. They may reject initially, but after we confront them with the truth of their sinfulness, we must persistently seek to embrace them. Neither of our arms is strong enough for such tasks. So, we must ask the Holy Spirit first to provide the sturdy weapon and His awesome strength to wield it all the way through our counterpart – our counterpart we love; and, in turn, we must ask the Holy Spirit to provide the gentleness to touch their heart. Once this is accomplished, unless they react with incomprehensible stubbornness, all reasons to reject God and to reject all His promises disappear like a morning fog submitting to the warm rays of the sun. When we admit that we are a sinner and stop rejecting God's love, it follows naturally that we stop rejecting His promise to forgive us *(Of course He forgives us. He loves us!)* and His promise to save us if we trust in Jesus *(Of course He saves all who trust in Jesus. He loves us!)*. So, you see, what seems like a daunting list of difficult tasks boils down to one simple task: All we need to do is love.

~

But do all respond to the Holy Spirit's mighty weapon, awesome power, and awesome gentleness in the way I elaborated upon above? No, as I alluded to, some respond, even in the face of all this, with incomprehensible stubbornness – an inexplicable hardening of their heart. What are we to do? Nothing… except pray…; nothing, except be patient…; nothing, except be available to be guided further by the Holy Spirit's hand; nothing, except hope.

Consider the relatively common example of a believer who is married to an unbeliever. The believer has a special task; she or he has been placed in just the right spot, as beautifully orchestrated by our Maestro, to be just the right witness for their spouse. The believer has strongly wielded the Holy Spirit's mighty weapon with one of their arms, and gently embraced with their other arm. Nevertheless, their spouse has – so far…, and as far as any of us can tell… (None of us know what's truly in their heart) – reacted with incomprehensible stubbornness. What is the believing spouse to do? Nothing… except pray…; nothing, except be patient…; nothing, except be available to be guided further by the Holy Spirit's hand; nothing, except hope. "And hope does not put us to shame, because God's love has been poured into our hearts through the Holy Spirit who has been given to us" (Romans 5:5).

If you are a believer and your spouse is not, I've written a prayer on your behalf – as a way to try to encourage you to keep up the important work that you're doing. Yes, you are an effective witness to your spouse. You are an effective witness because your spouse knows that you are a believer, and they cannot help but see this reflected in all your loving ways. For whatever reasons, your spouse has so far (at least apparently) been resistant – incomprehensibly stubborn – but I want you always to remain hopeful that they will turn to Jesus (repent). As you read the following prayer, know that God loves you – both you and your spouse – and is pleased with your desire for your spouse to be saved. After reading this, close your eyes and pray your own prayer, and ask God to help you in your specific situation. (This is written assuming that you are a believing woman, whose husband is an unbeliever. Change the details as needed.)

- *Heavenly Father, please look down in love at this dear woman. See what a faithful witness she is! See how much she loves You, and how she wants everyone in her life to put their trust in You. See how she rejoices in the intimate relationship she has with You. But also see her distress – yes, she's saddened to tears because her husband doesn't have such a relationship. See her concern for his spiritual welfare. See how much she loves him – she wants him to be with You forever. See how much she treasures him – she wants to be with him forever too, along with all believers in heaven. Be gracious to her! Reassure her that she's just the right woman for her husband, and that You are pleased with her resolute witness – her one-of-a-kind, special love for her husband. Strengthen her with patience and hope. Also comfort her with the knowledge that her witness is all that You are asking of her in this matter – it's not her responsibility to change her husband's heart. Remind her that You love her husband, and want him to be with You forever. It's Your job to change hearts. It's her job to persist in love, remain patient and hopeful, and in all things place her trust in You. ... I also pray for her husband. Work in his heart, so he finally sees Your love, which is plainly evident in all creation, including, in a special way for him, the loving kindness of his beautiful wife. In Jesus' name, Amen.*

"Love hopes all things."

"Love ... endures all things" (1 Corinthians 13:7)

This is very similar to the earlier section, "Love bears all things." What's the difference between bearing all things and enduring all things? When I think of endurance, I think of running a long race – persevering over the long haul.

In the earlier section, I describe scenarios that usually are fairly short-lived: ranging from minor annoyances that may last only a day or two, to more serious problems that often resolve within a few months. But sometimes we encounter challenges that are more sustained. In the earlier section, I give a few examples of the kinds of hardships we can face: becoming seriously ill, being injured in a bad accident, and being faced with a family crisis. As many of you know first-hand, sometimes such adversities can be so severe that they permanently change our life: What if the only treatment for our illness causes life-long side effects, and even shortens our life expectancy? What if there is *no* effective treatment? What if the injuries from our accident leave us permanently disabled? What if our family crisis resolved in tragedy?

At times like these, it's natural for us to question what good can come of it. I'm not going to try to explain why God asks us to endure lifelong burdens. But one thing's for sure: God will find a way for good to come of it, in one manner or another. We may not even be aware of the blessings, but that does not stop them from coming. For instance, maybe the positive example we show – contentment, peace, hope, faith, in the midst of our severe challenge – through the power of the Holy Spirit serves to strengthen someone else, emotionally and spiritually. Maybe they don't even tell us the impact our behavior (enabled by the hand of the Holy Spirit) is having on them, for example because the relationship between us is not particularly close. We all know that God wants to use us to edify others; what we may not know is that sometimes what He asks is very painful for us –

sometimes so painful that our life is changed forever. I understand that it's natural to look inward, as we consider the impact such pain has on us. But I'd like you to look outward, and ask the Holy Spirit to use your reaction to your pain to bless others spiritually, so their lives can also be changed forever.

"Love endures all things."

"Love never ends" (1 Corinthians 13:8) / "Love never fails" (1 Corinthians 13:8 NIV)

Careful readers have noticed that while listing these various facets of love, I sometimes use the ESV translation and I sometimes use the NIV translation. For this facet, I'm providing both translations. Guess what that means? … That means I'm going to provide commentary on both! *Oh, yes it does!*

"Love never ends" (1 Corinthians 13:8)

In the "Love … endures all things" section, above, I do not specifically state it, but I do allude to a scenario where a family member commits suicide ("What if our family crisis resolved in tragedy?"). First off, if you've experienced this, I'm so sorry – this is an extremely painful, lifelong hardship. Part of this hardship may include doubts about whether God can forgive someone who commits suicide. You even may have been told that He can't. But what I just wrote shows that such judgmental messages are faulty. To be clear, what I just wrote is: "He can't." That's ridiculous. God certainly can forgive any sin. Yes, suicide is a sin. It's a very large sin. I would even go so far as to call it a heinous atrocity; to be sure: "Thou shalt not kill" (Exodus 20:13 KJV). But can God forgive someone who commits a heinous atrocity? … Jesus has already paid the full price for all sin. So, hell yes – God certainly can forgive a heinous atrocity! … Careful readers have noted that so far in this section I've only gone so far as to write that God "can" forgive. Why didn't I write "does"? What is the contingency for our receiving God's forgiveness? Some judgmental people will say that God's forgiveness is contingent on us confessing our sins, and in the aftermath of a suicide will add: "And how are we supposed to confess the sin of suicide, since we're dead?" We should confess our sins, of course, but does God's forgiveness depend on that? No, God has already forgiven all believers. The only contingency for our receiving God's forgiveness is that we are a believer. Believer of what? Believer in Jesus as our Savior from sin, death, and Satan. If a person who committed suicide believed in their heart – all the way up to the end, despite their feelings of despair – that Jesus is their Savior, then God had already forgiven them for every sin they committed, including their last, awful, heinous sin. God's forgiveness doesn't come in chunks, with each chunk coming as a result of our confession, like a hamster getting a pellet when he pushes a button on his feeder. No, God's forgiveness is a never-ending flow. Our confession comes as a result of our sorrow over the impact our sin is having on our life and the lives of others, our desire to live a more sanctified life (a life that becomes more and more Christlike), and our acknowledgment that it is God who is the ultimate source of all forgiveness.

Before I change topics, there are a few more things I want to add on the topic of suicide.

- Foremost, if you struggle with suicidal thoughts yourself, please – please – do not misconstrue what I've written to be the "green light" for you to turn such thoughts into action. No, take to heart the following perspectives, including that they are both true simultaneously.
  - Don't forget that we all must give an account to God (2 Corinthians 5:10; Hebrews 4:13). He has great plans for you – even if you don't see that now, in your current dark place – and a person who commits suicide will need to give account as to why they gave up on their life and God's plans for it. In addition to God's plans for your own personal growth, consider the people who will be positively impacted by you – *(Don't fool yourself, negatively thinking that this isn't possible…)* – if you allow yourself to be a part of their future. Typically, wiping away the cobwebs and realizing that you can indeed have such an impact will help to lift your spirits, and see that it is worth it, after all.
  - No matter how deep your feelings of despair and hopelessness are, please know that God loves you as much as ever – you are His dear offspring. His love for you does not depend on your feelings. Be passive, and allow His pervasive love for you to penetrate through your dark thoughts, all the way down to your heart and soul. Don't shut Him out. It's my sincere hope that this will be facilitated by your turning right now to p. 333, and praying that prayer and reading the surrounding paragraphs.

- Second, if you are enduring the hardship of the suicide of a family member or a close friend, I have written a prayer on your behalf – as a way to try to comfort you and help you get a little bit closer to closure on your dear one's death. Please read this prayer, know that God loves you and wants to help you move forward with your life, and then close your eyes and ask God how this can best be accomplished. (This is written assuming that you are a mother who has lost an adolescent child. Change the details as needed.)
  - *Heavenly Father, Your cherished one here is struggling because she has experienced a great loss. She is finding it most difficult to accept the finality of what has happened. Her dear child is gone! This is a heavy burden for her to endure. Her life will never be the same. Please have mercy, and shower her with love, so she will be comforted by Your gifts of grace, peace, and a blessed life infused with hope, contentment, and, in due time, even joy again. Any feelings of guilt she has about what she did or didn't do, what she said or didn't say, before her child left – wash them all away! Yes, wash every one of such worries away in the continuous flood of Your forgiveness – a forgiveness that overwhelms any sin we have ever committed. Wash all such worries away in the continuous flood of Your love – a love that overwhelms any regret we can ever feel. And help her remember that, if her child was a believer, they will be reunited, to share a life together again – an everlasting life with You. In Jesus' name, Amen.*
- Last and certainly least, I'd like to take a slight turn here, walk to a street corner many of us are familiar with, and provide a bit of drollery. I'm going to briefly describe a scenario which will surely put an end, once and for all, to the ridiculous notion that God can't forgive someone who commits suicide because they're sinning when they die: Imagine that our friend Baxter – a believer – is standing on a street corner on a very hot summer afternoon. Bax sees a young woman walk by, and she obviously checked the weather forecast before getting dressed on this particular day. Bax doesn't even remember what he had been thinking about as he turns his attention fully to looking at her with lustful intent – committing adultery with her in his heart (Matthew 5:27-28) with intense focus. Bax is so captivated and distracted by her that he doesn't see a bus bearing down on him as he steps off the curb to get a better view. Bax is instantly killed by the bus. Does Bax go to hell because he didn't confess his sins of adultery and disrespect for a woman before he

died? … *Your heads should be wagging from side to side right now… There you go.*

o I hope that you don't find this example to be in bad taste. But God's forgiveness being an unceasing flow that continuously floods all believers is such an important point that I'll go to any length to make it clear.

Sometimes in life, we get distracted by unedifying things, whether that be impure thoughts about a young woman walking down the sidewalk on a hot summer afternoon, or dark thoughts that lead us to despair and hopelessness. And sometimes our distraction becomes so focused that there are dire, irreversible consequences. Let us instead fix our eyes on Jesus (cf. Hebrews 12:2 NIV), so we clear our head and live the life that He intends for us.

~

Mourning the death of a loved one is always hard, regardless of the circumstances, and sometimes the context of their death causes us lifelong hardship. As I describe in the Prologue and elsewhere, my mother's struggle with breast cancer that ended in her surprising (to me) death when I was six years old has caused me some difficulties, I think mainly due to my emotional immaturity at that time. While I've finally gotten close to closure, I don't anticipate reaching full closure in this lifetime. So, yes, my mom's death is indeed a lifelong hardship for me – my life is changed forever. One thing that has helped me along the way – to approach closure – is to remember that the hardships of this life will melt away in light of the love we'll experience in heaven (what I refer to as perfectly requited love – see Chapter 1). Indeed, as St. Paul wrote: "The sufferings of this present time are not worth comparing with the glory that is to be revealed to us" (Romans 8:18). As I have aged, I can look back and see that what started as an inward focus, and one that considered almost exclusively the present, slowly evolved to an outward focus that considered more and more the future. I sometimes used to look at my mother's death as an abrupt end, not only to her life but also to our relationship and furthermore to my feeling comfortable entering into other loving relationships, including one with God. If I had persisted in looking inward, focusing on and being distracted by my hurts, in a very real sense I would have cut myself off from many, if not all, of the blessings of loving relationships.

But fortunately I've learned, based on the Holy Spirit's guidance, that a better view is to look at my mother's death as a reminder that this life is short, which means we should cherish everyone we have a relationship with, and shift our focus away from the pains of this short life to the joys of … *(Do you think I'm only going to mention heaven here? No!)* … *both* this short life *(Yes, there are many joys in this life!)* and our everlasting life in heaven, where we will be re-united with all believers and, more importantly, where we will be with God Himself. "Behold, the dwelling place of God is with man. He will dwell with them, and they will be his people, and God himself will be with them as their God. He will wipe away every tear from their eyes, and death shall be no more, neither shall there be mourning, nor crying, nor pain anymore, for the former things have passed away" (Revelation 21:3-4).

"Love never ends."

"Love never fails" (1 Corinthians 13:8 NIV)

I mentioned at the beginning of the Prologue that I'm generally not expressive with my emotions. That's certainly true, but also certainly true is that I very much like to ponder feelings and emotions internally. This is an illustration of how we can't tell what's in another person's heart based on outward appearances. For example, when watching a movie or when singing praise songs during a worship service, sometimes I'm almost moved to tears. Can anyone around me sense this? Yes, if they can sense that a stone-faced man with no expression and no physical movement of any kind is feeling this way, in which case I applaud their psychic abilities.

I've just given you an example of something that can fail us – our perceptions of others. And I've hinted at something else that can fail us. … *What is it?* … *Yes, that's right!* It's our emotions. Our emotions sometimes fail us because they are dependent on our frames of mind and heart at that particular time. I already told you that some praise songs – (We all have our favorites) – sometimes almost lead me to tears. What important word did I include in the previous sentence? … *Sometimes…* That's right. *Sometimes* I'm almost moved to tears, but *other times* I'm depressed or angry or annoyed or what have you, and nothing is going to make me feel elated at that particular time. If I don't feel elated by a song or a Scripture reading or a sermon that would normally cause me to feel this way, does this mean that something is wrong with my relationship with God? ... No, there's nothing wrong with our relationship: I still believe in my heart that Jesus is my Savior; I still am saved; God still has forgiven me; God still considers me inherently valuable; God still loves me. All such things are not dependent on feelings and emotions.

There's nothing wrong with feeling elated during worship, unless we start to assess our faith on the extent of this feeling. When we do this, all is well when we're in a good mood, but what about when we're deflated? When it comes to our relationship with God, too much focus on our feelings and emotions leads to an oscillation between grabbing for what God has already given us during our up times, and severe doubts or disturbing thought distortions during our down times. To mitigate against such a rollercoaster ride, I recommend that our thoughts be passive during worship. It's fine for our actions to be assertive (singing loudly, dancing, hugging, smiling, laughing, crying, etc.), but let our thoughts be passive. What do I mean by this? Our focus during worship should be on our total dependence on God in all things, not on the consistency of our response back to Him. It often feels good to have a response – and an assertive response can be encouraging and edifying to those around us – but our response will vary from day to day, week to week, and that's OK. What doesn't vary is God's love for us. We are like a baby being cared for by our mother. Sometimes we coo back, and other times we scream and fuss. But our mother loves us just the same.

As C.S. Lewis wrote, "The great thing to remember is that, though our feelings come and go, His [God's] love for us does not."[3]

~

It's a common assumption that love between people, especially romantic love, is based on emotions. Love between people should evoke emotions within us. How can it not? But authentic love between people is not *based on* emotions – it *gives rise to* emotions. This may seem like a chicken-and-egg problem *(Which came first?)*, but let me assure you – love comes first, and emotions follow. Do you doubt this? If so, go back to Chapter 1 and reread my 103-word definition of intimate love between people. The "CliffsNotes® version" is: *To love means we remain true to ourselves, and we use our unique attributes to give gifts – prayers, thoughts, words, and actions – to our counterpart to affirm their inherent value; to be loved means another does this for us; and to be in love means two do this for one another.* If we only do this when we are emotionally elated, then our relationship is going to be a rollercoaster ride – a very bumpy, rickety ride with loops when we least expect it. Authentic love between people means that we do what I just summarized regardless of our feelings. Is it challenging to love when we are feeling down? Yes, it can be, but I can't think of a better way to come back up – in due time – to elated feelings. Yes, love does evoke emotions within us, and for good reason, but authentic love does not arise from emotions – (Any amorous or pseudo-amorous behavior that is based on initial emotions is infatuation, not authentic love) – and is not reliant on sustained emotions. And that's a good thing because emotions do fail us sometimes.

"Love never fails."

Love is greatest (cf. 1 Corinthians 13:13)

Right here is where I was when it happened. I'll never forget that evening. The first person I saw after the explosion was right over there – a young girl with striking eyes. She couldn't have been more than 12 years old. The look of fear on her face haunts me to this day.

That girl reminds me of my best friend. I only see her a few times a year now because she moved to the outskirts when she got married. But when we were young, we saw each other almost every week for several years.

When I was 12 years old, my mother started sending me on errands, usually to get something from the market. The first time I went there by myself, as I was leaving my mother warned me: "Now be a good boy and don't go wandering off. The best market is the one at the edge of our neighborhood, so go to that one. Be careful not to go further, because that is a dangerous place."

One day at the market, I saw off to the side a girl playing on the ground with a baby. The girl was about my age. I stood there looking at her and the baby for a few moments. The girl looked up at me, and smiled. I will always remember that smile, and those sparkling eyes. She looked different from any of the girls in my neighborhood. I asked her if I could play with her. She said something that I didn't understand, but she smiled again and motioned for me to join her. She continued the game that she was playing with her baby brother. I did my best to understand what she was doing, and then I tried to mimic her. She laughed, and smiled at me again. We played like this for maybe ten minutes, and then suddenly I realized that her parents were standing over us. I'm not sure how long they had been watching us. I looked up at them and smiled. They did not smile back, but they did not seem upset either. The mother picked up the baby, and the father reached out his hand for Fatima / Naomi* – that's my friend's name. My friend waved goodbye, and they left.

*Note: In this story, I use several "word- or phrase-pairings," for example: "Jews / Muslims," "Arabic / Hebrew," "Eid al-Fitr / Simchat Torah," and "Fatima / Naomi." The word- or phrase-pairings are to indicate that the narrator of this story may be either a Jew or a Muslim, and his friend is from the other group. To be clear, I mean that the narrator may be a Jew, in which case his friend is a Muslim named Fatima; just as likely, the narrator may be a Muslim, in which case his friend is a Jew named Naomi. I want it to be ambiguous – either group could fit either side of the story. Each word- or phrase-pairing is marked with an asterisk the first time it is used. Within each pairing, I have written the two options simply in alphabetical order. Also, while this story is written with the enmity being between Jews and Muslims, please do not misconstrue this to mean that I consider people who claim to be Christians to be immune from such biases and participation in hate crimes. Unfortunately, our selfish, sinful, human nature makes none of us immune from such antagonistic actions and thoughts. Let us keep praying that the Holy Spirit will steer us clear from our joining in such discord, and empower us to surprise others with kindness, again and again, even in the face of animosity.

After that, when I went to the market, I would always look for her, and I would take an extra-long time shopping, hoping that she would come in while I was there. It was about two months later when I finally saw her again. She was there with her family when I walked in. This time, her mother was holding the baby, and the four of them were together. I stood still for a moment, looking at them, when Fatima / Naomi turned and saw me. Her eyes lit up, and she immediately smiled and waved. I smiled and waved back. She motioned for me to come. So, I did, and her parents saw me as I was walking toward them. This time, they smiled too. Her mother said something to me, but I couldn't understand her. When her father saw my reaction, he said in slow and halting Arabic / Hebrew*, "Hello. We see you again." He reached out his hand toward me, and I reached out to take his. Then they all started saying things that I didn't understand, but I could see that they were happy. They resumed their shopping, and I started mine. Fatima / Naomi followed me around, and helped me pick out the fruits and vegetables. She giggled at some of the other things I put in my basket. After my friend's parents paid for their food, they came back to get her. We both were sad to part, and we waved goodbye.

The next couple times that I went to the market, I stayed over an hour longer than I needed to, hoping to see my friend again. My mother got upset with me, especially the second time, wondering why I was taking so long. I said that I wanted to get the best fruits, and it took me a long time to do that. She looked at me like she didn't believe me.

The next few times, I didn't take as long, because my mother scolded me before I left. So, I tried a different idea – going at different times of day, thinking that their regular time must be different than mine. I was sad every time that I went and didn't see my friend. Finally, about a month and a half after our second meeting, I saw her and her family again. They came in when I was almost done. When I saw them, I pretended that I had much more to get. I basically just followed them around. When we got close to the place off to the side – where Fatima / Naomi and I first met – I motioned that we should play our game with her baby brother. She quickly agreed, and we spent the rest of the time (while her parents finished shopping) doing this. When her parents were done – (They didn't take very long because they never bought much in this market) – they came back to get Fatima / Naomi and her brother. I was sad, but then her father asked me, "Do you want to visit to our home?"

I grinned widely, and stood up quickly to leave with them. As we started to go, her mother looked at me inquisitively. At first, I wondered why she did that, and then Fatima's / Naomi's father said, "Do you pay?"

… I had forgotten! I was embarrassed, and exclaimed loudly, "Oh!"

I turned around and quickly grabbed two more things, and then paid for what was in my basket. They waited for me, and then we walked to their home. We went in the opposite direction from the way to my home. I remembered what my mother had told me, but I felt safe with my friends. Not long into our walk, there was a soldier with a gun; he recognized my friends, but he looked at me funny. Then the streets looked different than any I had seen before. The people looked different too. Some of them looked at me funny, but not for very long. We got to their home, and went inside. It was very different from the inside of my home, but that didn't bother me. I was just happy to be with Fatima / Naomi. We played for about an hour. Her mother made lunch, and motioned for me to join them. I didn't really like it, until we had sweets for dessert. Those I liked! They could see that, and smiled and laughed. After we ate, I said that I should get home because my mother would be wondering where I was. They looked at each other, and Fatima's / Naomi's father said something that seemed to help them understand. He then said to me, "You go to Mother, yes?"

I nodded, got my things, and said "Thank you," as I started toward the door.

Her father said, "Wait – we walk to market."

I looked confused, and he said, "We see our friend with gun."

Fatima / Naomi said something to her father, and then she looked at me. Her father said something in return, and she smiled and came toward me. I was glad that she was going to come along on our short walk back to the market. As the three of us were walking, her father said, "Do we meet next week?"

My eyes lit up, and he said, "Yes, we meet next week. We meet at that time."

When we reached our friend with the gun, we waved goodbye, and then I ran all the way home. When I got there and went inside, my mother yelled at me: "What are you up to, boy?! How long does it take to pick out this?" I didn't mind her yelling. I was so happy inside. I told her, in a faltering way because I was still catching my breath, "Mother, … I met a friend at the market. … I spent some time with them afterward. … I had lunch with them, … and they want to play with me again next week."

"What's wrong with your friends on this street?" she asked.

I just stood there, breathing hard. … I wiped the sweat off my forehead. … Then, she looked at me differently, and asked, "Oh, is it a girl?"

At first, I didn't give any kind of response, but finally I nodded, and couldn't help but smile a little bashfully.

After that, Mother never yelled at me about how long it took me to come home from the market. The first few weeks, I stayed at Fatima's / Naomi's home just a little bit longer than the previous week, but finally it became clear that I could stay all afternoon. Looking back, I'm surprised that my mother never asked what neighborhood my friend lived in. At first, I figured that Mother assumed it was not past the market. A few years later, it occurred to me that maybe she was afraid to ask – and preferred not knowing. When I was 16, I finally told her where my friend lived. Mother looked somewhat disappointed and worried, but she did not have as strong of a reaction as I thought she would. All she said was, "Be careful not to become too attached to her. Remember, there are many nice girls at your school."

~

It was Monday after work when it happened. Many people were outside – walking, shopping, enjoying the beautiful evening. It had rained for several days before this, and the weather had finally cleared. I was walking along a narrow street bustling with people when we heard it. The sound was very loud, and I think the ground shook a bit. I figured that the explosion must have been very near. I looked to see if anyone was hurt, and was relieved that everyone I could see was not. I was surprised when I later learned that the explosion was two full blocks away. I was saddened – but not surprised – when I learned that it was an air strike by armed forces / the work of a suicide bomber*: seventeen killed, close to a hundred injured – all civilians. Many of the casualties were women and children.

Every evening that week, when I went to bed I would lie there thinking about those impacted by the attack: those whose lives were ended so abruptly, those who lost loved one(s), those who were maimed and their families, and all of us who were not impacted directly this time but live in various levels of fear of the next attack. I did not get much sleep that week.

On Friday / Saturday*, I went to worship, as I usually do. Both before and after, outside the mosque / synagogue*, there was much discussion about the attack. Many men were concerned, and their talking just seemed to make them angrier. Worship was a welcome break from the growing restlessness outside.

Monday evening, as I walked home from work, I noticed a small crowd had gathered over in the main square. At first, I didn't think much of it. Such gatherings are common in this square. But as I continued to walk, I started to hear some cheers from the crowd. Usually, such gatherings are fairly quiet. The enthusiasm of the crowd got my attention, and I went over to see what it was about.

Ah, of course, I thought, as I got close enough to hear the speaker. *Of course there is a gathering about last week's attack. And this evening is a good time, as it's the one-week anniversary.* There was a man standing on top of the usual park bench – (There is one most commonly used for this purpose) – so people could hear and see him. When I joined the group, we were about five deep, in a semicircle around him. He was saying that we must respond to the attack. He went on with much energy for several minutes. He didn't seem to have reached any particular conclusion when he suddenly stopped and stepped down off the bench. Another man took his place immediately. A short line had formed; more men wanted a turn on the bench.

Each took five to ten minutes. Some of the men talked about retaliation – our leaders must organize a response quickly, and strike back with numerous suicide attacks / overwhelming force*; this would show the Jews / Muslims* that they could not get away with it – the price to pay would be too high. Others talked about renewing peace negotiations – the two leaderships need to get together to resume talks. Others talked about the inflammatory nature of military checkpoints / the need for more military checkpoints*. Most speakers focused on one of these points, and they would do their best to make their case – the crowd occasionally reacting with claps and sometimes even shouts of agreement or disagreement, often both simultaneously. This went on for well over an hour. By then, it seemed that most of the men who wanted to talk had already said their piece. The time between speakers was starting to get longer and longer.

There was one man near me who appeared quite anxious; he obviously wanted to say something, but he was too reluctant to climb up onto the bench. At one especially long pause, with some in the crowd starting to leave, I told him, "The bench is free. Why don't you go up and say what you want to say?"

At first he shook his head, no. But I said, "Everyone else has said their piece. People are starting to leave. It looks like this might be your last chance."

He stopped shaking his head, and he just stood there frozen, looking at the bench. I didn't say more, but I motioned for him to go. He finally started moving forward, and he slowly climbed up. He turned around, and when he laid his eyes on the crowd – it had grown considerably since I had arrived – he looked very nervous. The crowd grew quiet, waiting for him to start. A few seconds passed. He coughed. A few more seconds passed. Finally, he started speaking. He was kind of mumbling, as he looked down toward the ground in front of him. "I grew up just a few streets from here. One of my first memories is hearing distant gunshots in the night. I asked my parents what it was, and they said, 'The Jews / Muslims are murderous people, and kill us without warning. They cannot be trusted. We pray that they be driven out of our land. We hope this happens in our lifetimes. We pray that if we don't see it, you and your sisters will.' ... Our parents have since died. They did not see it. I'm tired of waiting. ... I'm getting married in a few weeks, and especially after what happened a week ago, I think it's best for us to move out of this region. ... [There was some murmuring from the crowd.] ... We want to have children. I don't want them to have to live like this."

Some people started yelling. First, several were emphatic that none of us should move away – that would be giving the Jews / Muslims exactly what they want. Then there were renewed calls that we must fight back. This seemed to be the opinion of the vast majority, at least of those who had been vocal up until this time. My new friend looked very nervous now.

I had not previously thought of getting up on the bench myself, but suddenly I felt compelled to get up there. I was partially motivated by what my new friend said, but that on its own would not have been enough for me. What made me move forward was I noticed that there were a couple angry men making their way through the crowd. I had already worked my way up closer to the bench when my new friend went up to speak. So, it wasn't far for me to get to it. My new friend looked relieved when he saw me coming up. He quickly traded places with me, and he successfully melted back into the crowd.

The first thing I did when I climbed up onto the bench was to look around. I was surprised to see how big the crowd had become. I knew it had grown, but now I realized it was a couple hundred people, at least. I knew that I needed to start talking, but I hesitated. A couple people yelled out (again) that we need to fight back. I think most people figured that was going to be my message as well. The angry men who wanted to speak were getting close to the bench, so I had no choice but to start talking. At first, I don't think that many people could hear what I was saying. Some shouts were continuing, and I do not have a very loud voice. To my surprise, this seemed to quiet the crowd down. I was too nervous to look at faces in the crowd, especially the angry faces. I started by looking at the ground, but then it occurred to me to look toward where I had been standing. I was relieved to find my new friend who had spoken before me; he had taken my place in the crowd. That made me feel more at ease. I looked at my new friend, and spoke as if only to him.

"I also grew up near here. I also remember hearing gunshots and worse things, at night and sometimes during the day. I also have a girlfriend, and we are starting to talk about marriage. We also want to have children some-day. We also want them to grow up in a safer place. We also have talked about moving away, as the last speaker is thinking about doing when he gets married and starts a family. When we think of our children, we need to think of all the possibilities. We need to think of a better way. … Moving away is one idea, but I saw a better way years ago. … I never knew who to tell about this. … Let me tell you now. … I was a spy. I took a 15-minute walk – not many streets – and visited the enemy. I spied on them. I looked them in the eyes. Yes, I did. When I did that, what did they do? … They surprised me. … They smiled at me. … And when they did that, I couldn't help but smile back at them. It was then that I realized that this is not my enemy. No, this is a cherished friend – a precious friend like I've never had before or since. This is her young brother – who I came to think of as the younger brother I never had. This is her dear mother, who always greeted me with a kiss. This is her affable father, who laughed the biggest laugh I've ever heard, amused me with his stories, and one time even sheltered me with his family when we heard gunshots just down their street. These people are not my enemy. These are people just like me and just like my family, my other friends, my girlfriend, and the children we hope to have some day. … They are not the armed forces / terrorists* who attacked civil-ians last week. They are not the angry men who wander our streets at night. … My Jewish / Muslim* friends are our allies, also wanting a better life for their families. … We should not be retaliating against Jews / Muslims. We – not just the politicians, but all of us peace-loving citizens, both Jews and Muslims – should work together to bring an end to all attacks on civilians, whether caused by armed forces, terrorists, or angry people wandering our streets."

I couldn't think of anything else to say. People were very quiet – quieter than they had been since I had arrived. As I finally looked around at some of their faces, I couldn't really tell what people were thinking. They didn't seem upset, but they didn't appear to be motivated either. I looked down to figure out how best to get back into the crowd. I was about to start toward my new friend, when my eyes met those of a young woman standing just ahead of him. She looked very intense and determined, and it startled me. I had been in a kind of fog ever since my new friend started talking, and the energy in this woman woke me up. I hesitated, and the next thing I knew she started up toward me. I was taken by surprise and tried to get out of her way, but she grabbed my arm and whispered quietly but firmly that she wanted me to stay up there with her. I didn't give any kind of response, and she was satisfied with that.

When she turned around to face the crowd, she was not scared, as my new friend and I had been. She did not hesitate to start talking, as my new friend and I had hesitated. She did not avoid looking people directly in the eyes as she spoke, as my new friend and I had avoided doing. She did not mumble or speak softly, as my new friend and I had done; no, she spoke clearly and loudly. I felt awkward standing next to her; I felt very out of place – like a new recruit standing high up on a platform next to a seasoned war veteran who was confidently addressing a large group of soldiers. But she would not let me leave. She grabbed me tightly around my shoulder, and the first words out of her mouth were, "This man has seen the enemy, as he just eloquently told you."

When she said that, I literally started to shrink back. She grabbed me even tighter and pulled me up even taller, all the while not missing a beat in what she was saying. "This man has looked into their eyes, and he sees a better way. For as long as we can remember, we have fought back and sometimes we have even tried peace negotiations. Sometimes, one or the other approach seems to work: The Jews / Muslims get the message that they need to pay – pay dearly – when they attack us, or other times we all honor a peace treaty for a time. But such things have only worked for a short while. These tactics do not last. And military checkpoints cannot stop all determined individuals / military checkpoints rub salt into the wound*. Inevitably, someone gets impatient and the fighting starts again. Usually, it starts as a relatively small incident, and it grows from there."

She sensed me starting to slouch and draw back a bit, so she reached her hand up to the back of my neck and started to pinch me hard. That got me back in line. "So far today, until this man had the courage to get up here, we've heard nothing new – just the same ideas we already know don't work. And some are even thinking of retreating! …"

For the first time in her speech, she paused for a moment. … For the first time, I saw her smile. She smiled at my new friend briefly, and then she looked up to the crowd again, and said loudly, "I understand why some of us want to leave. The man who spoke earlier, and was brave enough to admit that he wants to leave – what was he saying? He was saying that our ways are not working, and it cannot be tolerated anymore! That's right! We cannot tolerate this anymore! … If you have children, and want to leave for their sake, that's fine with me. But I don't have children, and I don't plan to have any soon. I am staying."

For the first time since I had started talking, the crowd voiced a reaction. It started as verbal affirmations of what my new, fearless friend was saying. That led some to murmur in disagreement, but not very many did this. I think it was the disagreement that motivated her to continue with fervor: "I am staying with you! I know you! We played on the street as children. Don't you remember me? I remember you. We laughed together. We sang songs together. We celebrated Eid al-Fitr / Simchat Torah* together. Remember? And remember our friend here? [She grabbed me tighter, and looked me in the eyes.] He was there with us too. Most of the time, he was there too. But other times, he would wander off… Don't you remember that? … I remembered what he did, and in time I had the courage to wander off and meet our enemy too. I have looked in their eyes, and they have looked into mine. I have smiled, and they have smiled back. They have embraced me, and I have returned the favor. … When I was a child, like my friend here – [She held me closer again] – and our friend who spoke before him, I too wondered about sounds I heard in the night. I too asked my parents about what the sounds meant. They too told me that they were the sounds of hate. … We can all see that we've tried hate, and it doesn't work. … Let's try something different. … When we were children growing up, our parents also taught us about love. They taught us to love those in our family. They taught us to love those in our neighborhood. They taught us to love all Jews / Muslims. … But let us expand beyond what our parents taught us. Let us expand even wider than this. It's not far for us to go: just a few streets further, just a 15-minute walk. [She hugged me tighter, and for the first time it felt comfortable.] Let me teach you some ways that love is far, far more powerful than hate: Hate cannot stop people from fighting, but this is easily done by love. Hate cannot stop people from demanding that others leave their territory, but love sees that this land is for all peaceable people – Jews and Muslims, and, yes, people of other heritages and faiths as well. Hate cannot stop people from remembering atrocities from the past, but love looks forward with hope. Hate leads only to death, but love leads to life that abides. Let us reject the ways of hate, which we have tolerated for far too long. We know in our heart whether we are a Jew or a Muslim or something else. Let this knowledge in our own heart be enough for us. When we look at any other person, let us discard such labels, and simply call them friend."

Which character(s) in this story do you identify with?

I identify most with the narrator and with his new friend who speaks before him at the gathering. I don't identify very much with the bold woman who speaks after them. I'm not as confident as she is, especially when speaking in front of a group. But maybe my "soft-spoken, mumbling" story here, that some may find contrived in spots, will nevertheless inspire a bolder, more confident, more knowledgeable, and more eloquent person to inspire one or more others, and them in turn still others, eventually giving this unfinished story a lovely ending.

Each character in this story influences at least one other character, and in that sense contributes to – maybe just a little bit, but that's OK – the fearless woman's speech. One of the wonderful things about life is that even the little things we do have an impact on others, very often in ways we never know. In this story, a little girl who looked fearful after an explosion reminds the narrator of his dear friend. Fatima / Naomi is engaging and extremely open to forming a long-lasting friendship with someone very different from her. Her baby brother is involved in her first activity with her new friend. Her parents are quite accommodating to her wishes as she befriends a boy from "the other side of the tracks," as it were, and in the process her parents also form bonds with him. The narrator's mother is not so controlling that she forbids her son from seeing Fatima / Naomi and her family on a weekly basis. The victims of the attack remind the narrator that there is a better way. His new friend who speaks before him at the gathering – despite his hesitancy, nervousness, and mumbling – expresses an unpopular point of view (not an easy task, but often very important) that gets the crowd thinking, and this starts a bit of a domino effect with the next two speeches. The narrator is then compelled to say his piece and – despite his mild manners and uneasiness speaking to a group – provides a backdrop for his new, fearless friend to build on his thoughts, to articulate them in a way that more people can appreciate, and hopefully to get some traction.

I say hopefully because I understand that such idealistic viewpoints are often not easily actualized. Real traction – by this, I mean movement toward substantive and lasting change – needs buy-in from diverse people willing to work together. The bold woman's testimony will for some fall on deaf ears; for some others sound good until the next gathering's topic distracts them; and for some others sound good until the next attack, at which time the seductive call of hateful retribution becomes too difficult for them to ignore. Despite such reasons for real traction to seem elusive, we should nevertheless say our piece, be true to what it means to live in love, and play our role as we are able, which for those of us who believe in Jesus as our Savior includes empowerment by the Holy Spirit. And while at times it may seem impossible, ultimately love will surely triumph over hate, for love is greatest.

~   ~   ~

After-hours

Bob unplugged

In the "Love … does not insist on its own way" section, I provide an elaborate analogy to make it clear that we should be looking to our trusted counterparts for their advice, instead of living in isolation and stubbornly insisting on our own way. In my example, my mentors stood up for you and were not shy about advising that I go back to the van to change my beachwear. But sometimes our counterparts are hesitant to bring something like that up. So, we should ask them to give us their honest opinion. To get their honest opinion, we need to be careful with our choice of words. For example, "Does this dress make me look fat?" has only one answer (and I've learned that this one answer does not begin with, "If you have to ask that…"). A much better question is: "Which of these dresses looks better on me?"

- Here's your assignment: In the coming month, I'd like you to ask at least two of your trusted counterparts one personal question about yourself, carefully worded to invite their honest feedback
  - Ask two counterparts the same open-ended question at separate times. If their input is incongruent, ask a third counterpart, as a tie-breaker. After getting sufficient feedback, ask yourself: "Should I go back to the van to change my beachwear?"

To give you a better idea of what I mean, below I give three examples, each of which starts with a closed-ended question that I don't recommend (because your counterpart may choose an easy out, which may negatively enable you), followed by an open-ended question that is more likely to yield meaningful feedback.

- Don't ask, "Am I negative?" Rather ask, "Recently, I've learned that there are benefits of positivity. Do you have any suggestions for how I can better achieve this frame of mind more consistently?"

- Don't ask, "Am I a doormat?" Rather ask, "Lack of assertiveness is something I've struggled with for years. Recently, I've been trying a few things to improve in this area. It's all a little new to me, and I'm starting to feel overwhelmed. Based on what you've seen of my interpersonal interactions over the past few months, can you tell me what's working and what isn't?"
- Don't ask, "Isn't my boyfriend a dreamboat?" Rather ask, "As you know, Bob and I have been going out for a while now. We're starting to get pretty serious. (It is Bob, after all…) Before I get in over my head, I want to check with a couple of confidantes, to see if I have blinders on in any areas. To this end, can you tell me at least three things that you like about Bob, and at least three things that you don't like, or that concern you, about him?"

Step up to the microphone

The very first facet in Paul's definition of love is, "Love is patient" (1 Corinthians 13:4). Some people think that a synonym of patience is doing nothing – simply waiting. However, doing nothing is better characterized as apathy or laziness. I searched high and low, but I didn't find a single verse that says love is apathetic or lazy.

- What are better synonyms for patience?
- Under what circumstances do you find it most challenging to be patient?

In the "Love is … kind" section, I provide many examples of a kind reaction that contrasts with the expected reaction. Think back to your experiences, and remember at least one example where you received a kind reaction that surprised you; likewise remember at least one example where you gave a kind reaction that surprised someone else.

- Can you make a commitment to surprise someone with kindness at least once per month going forward?

In the story in the "Love is greatest" section, the narrator refers to others as "friend" very readily. For example, he didn't meet the man who speaks before him at the gathering until that time, yet he frequently refers to him as "my new friend," and this seems to reflect his feeling at that time, not only in hindsight. Similarly, he refers to the woman who speaks after him at the gathering as "my new, fearless friend."

- Does this seem reasonable?
- How would you define friend?
- How long does it take to start a friendship?

For parents: I'd like you to follow up on the conversation you had with each of your children back in Chapter 4. Remind them of the strengths or gifts you talked about, and this time emphasize that 1 Corinthians 13 teaches us that we should be using such strengths and gifts to serve others in love. Ask them to tell you at least one specific way that they'll do this in the coming month. … Then, follow up again, to ask them how it went.

For intimate couples: I'd like both of you, in turn, to choose at least one "Love is …" phrase discussed in this chapter, and apply it to your partner. In other words, tell them how they exemplify that particular aspect of love. (If you're really imaginative, I just might accept your creation of a new "Love is …" phrase that's not specifically covered in 1 Corinthians 13, although if you say "Love is Hildegard," or whatever your partner's name happens to be – *[I'm so sorry if it's not Hildegard]* – then I am giving you an F.)

Chapter 9 – What If … ?

I hope this book isn't coming across as too simplistic – just do this and do that, and your whole life will be rosy. I hate oversimplifications like that. Life is messy, and sometimes we get awfully grimy. In real life, it's rare that easy answers are enough to get us back on course. In the chapters before this one, at various points it occurred to me that there are important perspectives that I wasn't addressing adequately. Instead of scurrying down rabbit holes within those chapters, I decided to create a separate chapter devoted to exploring such perspectives in more depth. *Welcome to that chapter!* Each section of this chapter is devoted to a question, and each question starts with the words "What if." Perhaps some of these questions have crossed your mind as you've been reading.

Yes, there are a lot of "What if … ?" questions in life – more than I can possibly address here. But I hope that I'm touching on many of the main ones for you.

There are so many important questions. Where do I begin? How do I prioritize?

I've decided that I must begin at the bottom – rock bottom.

What if you hit rock bottom?

In the section after this one, my emphasis is that we are to help each other. To be sure, we are to "Bear one another's burdens" (Galatians 6:2). There, I focus on us helping others. But sometimes we are the ones who need to be helped. If you have a heavy burden in your life, I implore you to reach out to others: family, friends, pastor, other church-worker, social worker, professional counselor. All these people want to help us. Don't worry about reciprocation (returning the favor). When we're bogged down, let's prioritize disentanglement from the mire; after we get the mud washed off, then we'll be in a position to reciprocate – not necessarily to the same people who helped us, and that's fine (Chapter 6 – "360 degrees of reciprocation" section).

Sometimes we feel hesitant to ask others for help. Perhaps we're embarrassed about the particular mud we're stuck in. Or maybe we want to avoid the potential of burdening anyone else. I'll address both perspectives in turn.

- If we're embarrassed, let's keep in mind that there are only so many different types of mud on the farm. Sure, we have our unique concoction of humus stirred into our slurry, but there's no type of mud we're in that The Farmer (God) and His farmhands (us) haven't seen before. If for whatever reason you don't want to talk to a family member, friend, pastor, other church-worker, or social worker, then please reach out to a professional counselor. They certainly provide for us a safe environment. It's their job to help people in our situation. I hope no one finds the following analogy inappropriate: The first time a girl or young woman needs to go to the gynecologist, she may be a little embarrassed, but nevertheless she makes an appointment, goes to the office, waits a while, gets called back to a private room, waits a while longer, the gynecologist does their job, and all is well. … Do you need to make an appointment with a "gynecologist"? Don't be embarrassed. You're seeing someone trained to help you. Part of a professional counselor's training is to keep the details you share with them strictly confidential between the two of you (unless they see evidence that you may harm someone, including yourself), and to interact with you in a nonjudgmental way.

- If you are worried about burdening others, or feel bad about simply taking up some of their time, may I ask you a question? Do you have low self-esteem? Each one of us is inherently just as valuable as anyone else. We're all in this together, and when any one of us stumbles, all the rest of us should turn to help them up. Do you know that special joy you get when you help someone? Don't deny others that experience by not reaching out to them when you need help. Some of my greatest joys in life have come from helping someone in need. If they had not reached out to me, I would have missed out on that. I'm very thankful that they didn't worry about "burdening" me, or feel bad about "taking up my time." I always make a point to thank people for telling me about their burden. Why? I'm thanking them for their expression of love to me. Yes, by reaching out to a family member, friend, pastor, or other church-worker, we're telling them that we love them – that we trust them enough to make ourselves vulnerable to them. I've never met anyone who doesn't appreciate being loved in this special way.

My experience with rock-bottom situations is that we oscillate between episodes of truly hitting bottom and times of coming up from that, at least a little bit. If this is your experience too, please take advantage of the times when you feel better to talk to someone about your lowest feelings. Don't be fooled into thinking that you won't drop down again. Oscillations are common. Without meaningful changes being made, if you have already experienced oscillations, then you should expect to go back down again.

I don't know what's worse: oscillations or staying consistently down. I suppose it depends on the person. Just as we each have our unique preferences related to the joys of life, we each have our unique antipathies that cause us the most pain – our special array of fiends. What may be merely disheartening for one is unbearable for another. Let us keep this in mind as we help others who are in a shadowy place. What may seem merely dim to us may be pitch black to them.

~

If you sometimes feel so much despair and hopelessness that you've considered suicide, I'd like you to talk to God about it right now. Remember, cast "all your anxieties on him, because he cares for you" (1 Peter 5:7). If you can't think of the words to say, may I suggest the following prayer?

- *Heavenly Father, You know that I've been struggling, and it seems to be getting worse. Sometimes it gets so bad that I don't see any hope for me – only blackness – and I feel that it's best to give up. At times like that, I'm convinced that no one cares about me; I conclude that I'm of no value, so most people wouldn't give it a second thought if I was gone forever, and everyone would be better off without me. When I'm feeling OK, I know that You care about me, but when I'm not feeling OK, I sometimes wonder why You have let me drop so low. I remember that You have promised that when I'm burdened with something that's more than I can endure, You will provide a way out (1 Corinthians 10:13). I confess to You that I'm burdened with the temptation to end my periodic feelings of worthlessness once and for all – to escape, in my own rash way. I'm crying out to You now; I know that I can't bear this temptation on my own. I need Your help to find another way – a more loving and God-pleasing way – out of this spiral. God, help me!*

Yes, God wants to help you. One of the ways He does this is through the people in your life. Don't shut people out. As much as you may want to do that when in your dark place, don't shut people out! Is there someone you trust and can be completely open with? If so, please open up to them about what you're struggling with. It's therapeutic to hear ourselves verbalize our disconcerting thoughts – as opposed to holding them inside, allowing them to grind away. You will be amazed by how much simply talking about your situation can help you – even if "all" your counterpart does is listen attentively.

If a family member or friend like that isn't available, then talk to your pastor if you have one, and if that's not an option then talk to a social worker or professional counselor. If there's not time to meet one in person, call a 24-hour lifeline such as the National Suicide Prevention Lifeline at 800-273-TALK (8255), and if you would prefer to chat online, this is an option at www.suicideprevention lifeline.org.

Take it one step at a time, and one of the first steps is to remember that no matter how bleak things look, no matter if we see nothing positive in our future, no matter if we feel that everyone hates us and rejects us, no matter how different from others we feel and judged for that, no matter how mistreated we have been, no matter how heinous a thing we have done to others, no matter what, God still loves us the same as ever; we are still His cherished loved one, with inherent value so great that words cannot express. God will never withhold His love, waiting for us to "get our act together" – that would be conditional love. Whatever should change in your life (and we all have things that should change), wait until you're feeling better (i.e., you remember God's unconditional love for you, and you no longer feel like giving up), and then talk to God about what changes are appropriate for you and ask for His help in doing this.

If you were struggling because of the weight of sin, remember that, if you trust in Jesus as your Savior, God has already forgiven you – Jesus has already paid the price for every sin we'll ever commit, no matter how atrocious. And God will provide a way for you not to persist in this sin (1 Corinthians 10:13).

If you were struggling because you were hurt by someone, especially someone you trusted and made yourself vulnerable to, remember that while people disappoint sometimes, God never disappoints. And just because one person disappointed you or even severely mistreated you, this doesn't mean that you can trust no one. Give it some time, and ask God to help you build healthy relation-ships with loving people.

What if someone else in your life hits rock bottom?

No matter how inspiring a message may be – and I hope that this book is at least in some small ways inspiring – if someone is in a certain mindset, then they may not be particularly dispositioned to be inspired. For example, even if some-one was to read this book cover to cover, if they're truly in a dark place, then all my words aren't going to be enough to flip the light switch on for them. They need more help to get up from where they are. They need, with the Holy Spirit's guidance, someone – ideally, in many cases, someone who already knows them – to learn the specifics and get down in the mud with them. If you're not in a terribly dark place yourself, then I want this book to inspire you to get down in the mud with others who are. There are four main points I want to emphasize about getting down in the mud.

- The first is pretty obvious, and it's that we are to help people in our life who are in need (Luke 10:25-37)
- Second, often it's best if we already have a close relationship with the person we're helping. This is one reason why it's important that we form strong bonds with others – we're establishing a network of people we can help. (Don't use this as an excuse not to help someone in need who's in your life but you don't know very well, for example someone who lives across the hall in your dorm. Again, Luke 10:25-37 is a suitable reference, as the Good Samaritan did not have a prior relationship with the man he helped.)
- Third, to give our best loving, we need to learn the specifics – we need to know what type of mud we're dealing with. Sometimes the specifics can be difficult for our counterpart to talk about. This is another reason why it's often best if we already have a close relationship with them.
- And, fourth, armchair confabulations are usually not enough. To give our best loving, we need to stop philosophizing and give our counterpart tangible help, and that means it's going to get messy.

I mentioned above that people who are in a dark place aren't easily inspired. Let me draw an analogy (and be forewarned that I'm going to attempt to give you a little comic relief here). If I'm in the mood for – you know – but my wife is tired, had a terrible day, is stressed, has a headache, feels nauseous, has allergies, stubbed her toe, accidentally erased the latest episode of *Real Housewives of Bobsville* from the DVR, has to get up early in the morning, has a big meeting at 7 A.M. that she's supposed to lead but she's not prepared, and her team just lost Game 7 of the World Series by blowing a nine-run lead in the ninth inning (you know, the full list and then some), then no matter how inspiring I am (and I can be pretty inspiring…), it just ain't gonna happen… Talk about rock bottom! (I mean for her…)

Let me get back on track here, but I'm going to continue with my analogy. In all seriousness (my comic relief is officially over), in such a scenario, instead of sulking I should be patient, stop focusing on my own desires, and turn my attention to helping my wife feel better. *No, not to get what I wanted in the first place!* I need to show her love in a different way.

She is at a low place, so I need to help her up. And I need to help her up from where she actually is – not from where I wish she was. I had plenty of ideas for how to make her feel good, but I need to set those aside and help her with her specific situation.

With our friends and loved ones, we may have certain ideas for how to make them feel good – *(And maybe you've gotten some new ideas from this book!)* – but we should always keep at least two things in mind: First, what are their preferences? Their preferences may be very different from ours. Does she really want a bobblehead – *the most outlandish one in the catalog!* – as a hood ornament for her car? And, second, is there anything you're aware of that's much higher priority in her life now? For example, if you know that your friend is being abused by her husband, then by this point in this book I hope you realize that an outlandish hood ornament isn't what she needs right now. That's not going to inspire her to make the necessary changes in her life. That's not going to do anything meaningful to address her top priority (secularly speaking).

Did I hear one of you say: "But then I don't get to see a tangible increase in the eccentricity of our parking lot when I look out my office window"? *Well, boo hoo…*

That's right – boo hoo… When we become aware of anyone in our life getting anywhere near a rock-bottom scenario, helping them up from that is Priority One. We need to roll up our sleeves, put on our big-girl or big-boy pants, drop our plans for a parking lot laden with limited edition, oversized BOBbleheads, and get down into the mud with them.

~

An important point is: How do we know if someone in our life is at or near rock bottom? Many times we're unaware. Other times we have an inkling but don't realize the extent of the issue. Even someone we consider a close friend may be holding something back. Maybe they're embarrassed; maybe they don't want to bother us (previous section). So, we must keep our eyes open and ask questions.

- Look for changes in mood or behavior, either oscillations within a relatively short period or a more consistent change from the more distant past
- Listen carefully to what they say and watch their body language. Again, look for changes from your past experience with them.
- Be especially mindful of people who seem *too* consistent. They may be masking other feelings. No one is happy *all* the time…
- If anything causes you to wonder, make a special point to ask them how they're doing. Even if they say they're fine, be sure to tell them that you're always there for them. If you're not convinced that they're really fine, then keep asking them questions in the upcoming days and weeks, and get more specific. For example, "Are you really OK? You haven't seemed as sociable over the last couple weeks. Is there anything you want to talk about?"
- If you're comfortable, be more open with them. This may encourage them to be more open with you too. In other words, add strands to the bond between the two of you.

~

Before I bring this section to a close, I want to list some of the more common ways that we can hit rock bottom. I was a little hesitant to make such a list because I don't want to miss anyone's reason. Yes, there are so many ways we can hit rock bottom, and a comprehensive list would have billions of entries because each encounter with the lowest ebb is unique.

With so many routes to rock bottom, trail markers are few and far between. The fog is thick and the forest overgrown. How do we know when we've reached that distressing destination? … All I can say is that you know it when you get there. You know it because the only feelings that remain are despair and hopelessness.

When someone else in your life has fallen down like this, reach out your hand and grasp theirs firmly. They need to relearn other feelings, and a good place for them to start is with the simple but wondrous feeling that you care about them.

Below is my general list of common ways we can fall down. If you or someone close to you has hit rock bottom in a way not listed here, please forgive me and know that I'm simply making an attempt to help your fellow readers understand how dark it can get for some.

- Love Zero: This is the thought distortion that there is no one – no family member, no friend, not anyone, not even God Himself – who loves us and will ever love us; see the Prologue for more details
- Other severe doubts about God's nature
- Chronic depression, or other mood disorder
- A debilitating phobia, or other anxiety disorder
- Dependent personality disorder (I specifically mention this one because many sufferers are susceptible to being abused), or other personality disorder
- Abuse – emotional, psychological, physical, sexual
- Sexual harassment
- Rape, and its aftermath
- Being cheated on
- Partner involved in an emotional affair
- Abandonment / Chronic neglect
- Caught doing something heinous or embarrassing
- Fired from job / Loss of livelihood / Expelled from school / "Blackballed"
- Homelessness
- Bullied
- Victim of racism
- Victim of a hate crime
- Diagnosed with cancer or other life-threatening or life-altering disease
- Addiction
- Struggling with sin, with no apparent resolution

- Overwhelmed with guilt / shame
- Unresolved grief, for example induced by a suicide or other tragedy, especially if there is a likelihood that the deceased did not have saving faith

These are truly hardships that can sometimes lead to suicidal thoughts (previous section). It's important for us to help people struggling in such ways. But how do we prioritize? When looking for wheels to grease (i.e., people to help), it's very convenient when a wheel is squeaky, but let's not forget that some quiet wheels are near their breaking point as well. Sure, let's clean out our ear wax, but let's also continue to sow what may seem to us to be small gestures, for example, a few encouraging words, or a fun gift that's in line with our friend's preferences. It's a team effort, after all, and a small gesture from us may help develop more traction. Every bit helps, and our (new) friend turning their corner is higher priority than keeping track of who helped them achieve this.

What if you turn to Jesus (repent) after committing countless heinous atrocities?

Jesus said, "Whoever comes to me I will never cast out" (John 6:37). This is a promise you can trust. Jesus – True God – always keeps His promises (Numbers 23:19; Psalm 18:30; Psalm 145:13; 2 Timothy 2:13; Hebrews 10:23).

Even if you've committed every sin discussed in this book – arrogance, bullying, prejudice, terrorism, mass murder (via an act of terrorism), emotional abuse, physical abuse, sexual abuse, infidelity, sexual harassment, rape, lewd thoughts, covetousness, to name a few – and even if you've committed every sin in the unrated version of this book – murder of an individual, torture, bigotry, manipulation, incest, to name a few – if you repent, if you turn to Jesus, He will not cast you out. Even if you rejected Him before, if you now believe that Jesus, God the Son, is your Savior – Your Lord – who has paid the price for all the sins of the world – even your sins – by dying on the cross and being raised from the dead as proof that His sacrifice is acceptable to God the Father, then you will be saved (cf. Romans 10:9). Turn to Jesus! Repent of your sins, ask for His forgiveness, and receive it.

Are you concerned that Jesus won't welcome you because your sins are too great? Sister and brother, we're all in the same boat. Have you heard of St. Paul?

Pretty important guy in the early Church, huh? Do you know that he called himself the worst sinner? Yes, he did heinous things (Acts 8:1-3; Acts 9:1-2; Acts 22:19-20). Brother Paul wrote: "The saying is trustworthy and deserving of full acceptance, that Christ Jesus came into the world to save sinners, of whom I am the foremost" (1 Timothy 1:15). Paul wrote that after He turned to Jesus.

Are you concerned that Jesus won't welcome you because you waited too long? Until the time of God's judgment of you, no wait is too long for Jesus: "With the Lord one day is as a thousand years, and a thousand years as one day. The Lord is not slow to fulfill his promise as some count slowness, but is patient toward you, not wishing that any should perish, but that all should reach repentance" (2 Peter 3:8-9). Even if you happen to know that it's your last day on earth, it's still not too late to turn to Jesus. Remember the repentant criminal who was crucified alongside Jesus? This criminal did something heinous – he was receiving the death penalty for his crime. Did he wait too long to turn to Jesus? Here's what that criminal said to a third man, an unrepentant criminal, also being crucified alongside Jesus: "'Do you not fear God, since you are under the same sentence of condemnation? And we indeed justly, for we are receiving the due reward of our deeds; but this man has done nothing wrong.' And he said, 'Jesus, remember me when you come into your kingdom'" (Luke 23:40-42). And Jesus replied, "Truly, I say to you, today you will be with me in paradise" (Luke 23:43). The repentant criminal heard this after He turned to Jesus.

Are you concerned that if you come into the kingdom of God there will be a permanent record – even a video recording… – of all your sins for all to see? Are you concerned that you'll be forced to wear *The Scarlet Letter* – a large, heavy one that has been chiseled carefully, with every one of your sins meticulously accounted for in the intricate design – for all eternity? Don't fret my friend, but trust in what the LORD says: "Though your sins are like scarlet, they shall be as white as snow; / though they are red like crimson, they shall become like wool" (Isaiah 1:18); "I am he who blots out your transgressions for my own sake, and I will not remember your sins" (Isaiah 43:25).

Are you concerned that when you come into the kingdom of God, you'll be snuck in reluctantly – slipped through the back door, so to speak – with half-hearted acquiescence? No, you'll be warmly welcomed with great rejoicing (Luke 15:1-10)!

~

While the above is valid all the way until the time of God's judgment (Luke 23:43), don't delay to turn to Jesus! None of us know when it's our time to be judged. If you delay, you're continuing to live controlled by willful sin, and God's wrath remains on you (cf. John 3:36).

~

Turn to Jesus! I want to rejoice over you. And I want you to rejoice over me. Don't let me down!

We are in the same boat now – two sinners in need of God's forgiveness – and, if you turn to Jesus, we will be in the same boat for all eternity – two forgiven children of God, with Him forever, with no time or interest to watch videos or wear letters. Our only scarlet adornment will be the blood (sacrifice) of Jesus – our wondrous insignia.

What if you continue to commit heinous atrocities after turning to Jesus (repenting)?

Repentance – turning to Jesus – means that we have a changed heart. When our heart is changed in this way, we begin a journey called sanctification (becoming more and more Christlike). The bus driver on this journey is the Holy Spirit. Even if we're clinging to the roof of this bus by our fingertips, far be it from us to commit an atrocity, heinous or otherwise! Yes, all of us in or on this bus continue to sin because we're imperfect humans living in a sinful world. However, if we've turned to Jesus, then we have a changed heart – a heart that loves our neighbor. We're changed from our former, selfish way of living, and follow God's will as empowered by the Holy Spirit. St. Paul – who called himself the worst sinner (1 Timothy 1:15) – puts it this way: "I have been crucified with Christ. It is no longer I who live, but Christ who lives in me. And the life I now live in the flesh I live by faith in the Son of God, who loved me and gave himself for me" (Galatians 2:20).

Some people who call themselves Christians do commit heinous atrocities. If they ever really were on the sanctification bus, they certainly fell off. If you commit a heinous atrocity after turning to Jesus (repenting), then you have fallen off the bus and need to turn to Jesus (repent) again. My recommendation for you is to read the first paragraph of Chapter 2 and start walking; yes, start the long walk of reminding yourself what it's like to be on your own – all on your own. After a few hours in the blazing sun, no shade or water in sight, how does it feel to be all on your own now? You're never going to make it. Can't you see that? That valley looks even farther away now than when you started. … Think back. … Can't you remember? … You've been in this wilderness before. Maybe it was years ago when you turned to Jesus, but don't you remember? There is a way. Yes, there is one Way (John 14:6). Turn to Jesus again, and you'll make it – not on your own, but you'll make it across this wilderness.

What if someone sins against you?

This one's too easy, right? If they are remorseful about what they did wrong – show an openness to change their behavior – then, yes, this is too easy: *We are to forgive – under all circumstances – no exceptions.*

~

So, let's see here. What's the next "What if … ?" section on the list? … Oh, wait a minute. There is a little more to say about forgiveness.

All stopwatches will be confiscated at the starting gate

For us mortals, forgiveness is a process that takes time, especially when the sin is severe. While it's easy for me to say, especially in light of Luke 17:3-4, that we are to forgive under all circumstances when our counterpart is remorseful and has an openness to change their behavior, that doesn't necessarily mean that we'll be ready to flip a switch at a moment's notice.

How would you define forgiveness? Every time I ask this question, I get a different answer. It is a complex topic. Below is my definition of interpersonal forgiveness, and while you may not agree, at least now you know the framework I'm working within.

- Interpersonal forgiveness includes *all* of the following milestones
  - We commit not to retaliate; that is God's department (Romans 12:19; Appendix Ↄ); *and*
  - We commit to free our counterpart from any "debt" we felt they owed us personally – (I'm not talking about any debts they owe society); *and*
  - We commit not to harbor feelings of resentment; rather, each time these feelings come, we acknowledge them, and then we let them go
- Interpersonal reconciliation (applicable when the two of us had a relationship) goes a step further than forgiveness – namely, both of us commit to playing our role in the restoration of a healthy relationship

Is forgiveness a brief journey? I advise that it not be, especially when the sin has hurt us severely. Some feel pressured to try to speed through the process, and I can relate. … "Let it go, let it go."[1] … You've caught me with my hand in the cookie jar. Yes, I'm feeling that special tug – the one that beckons us to join countless preteen and otherwise youthful damsels singing at the top of their lungs along with Elsa, as she guides us toward a fulfilling ending. We'll have our sing-along in due time, but before we join the chorus, let's not forget to show ourselves some compassion. It's not emotionally healthy to try to cancel debts and let go of resentment before we acknowledge all of our feelings and take the journey called coming to peace with having been hurt. How long does this journey take? Sometimes minutes, sometimes decades (especially if our counterpart is not remorseful) – and take careful note that I measure progress not with a stopwatch but with a pedometer. Whether our path is one step or thousands, we're always making good progress when we're taking our current step.

One important question, and two important answers

After calibrating our pedometer, let's take a closer look at the particular path that lays before us. What if it's an especially arduous passage – what if the one who sinned against us is *not* remorseful – what if they have *no openness* to change their behavior? There are actually two correct answers, but before I get to them, let me tell you about my forgiveness class.

I'm in Remedial Forgiveness 101. I recognize some of you from class. Do you recognize me? Let me jog your memory: Remember when The Teacher moved me to the front row because I kept nodding off in class? He knows that

I'm having a tough time with this course – just barely passing. He really wants me to pass! You know, graduation day is coming soon, and He really wants me to graduate (1 Timothy 2:3-4; Titus 2:11 NIV; 2 Peter 3:8-9). All of us who stay awake in forgiveness class will get our diplomas on graduation day – based on Jesus' righteousness (Romans 1:17; 1 Corinthians 1:30; 2 Corinthians 5:21; Philippians 3:9), certainly not our own – but some of the graduates are gifted students who aren't in our forgiveness class. No, they're taking the honors class in advanced forgiveness. Both classes, remedial and honors, teach the same concepts about forgiveness. But when faced with the following question on the final exam – *How are we to respond if someone sins against us and they are not remorseful – they have no openness to change their behavior?* – I scribble stick-figures with a crayon, while my gifted colleagues compose poetry with an angel's quill.

I've already told you that there are two correct answers to the question I repeated a few lines above this. Even I have figured out the first answer, but for the second answer I need to peek at my gifted colleagues' final exams. … Let's see here. … I'm starting to get a glimpse. … What am I seeing? I'll try to make my scribblings legible for you.

- The first answer is that we strive to, at a minimum, *offer* forgiveness (i.e., it's conditional upon our counterpart's repentance) – under all circumstances – no exceptions
- The second answer is that we aspire to forgive – not just offer forgiveness, but truly forgive – before our counterpart repents

The first answer is relatively easy: We start down our path – for example, extend an olive branch – no matter how arduous the path appears. The second answer is definitely not easy: We commit to our *full* journey, no matter how arduous the path *is*. This requires more discussion, and below I provide commentary relevant to offering forgiveness and truly giving forgiveness from both of the following perspectives: our giving unconditional love and our being in a conditional love relationship.

Offering forgiveness – and truly giving forgiveness – in light of unconditional love

First things first

Let me start right out of the gate here by clarifying that unconditional love does not equate to universal, unconditional forgiveness. (This is analogous to unconditional love not equating to universal salvation, as discussed elsewhere.) Yes, it is possible to love someone unconditionally and withhold forgiveness from them. *Have I just shocked you? Please keep reading.* When someone injures us or disrespects us, and they show no remorse for it – no openness to change – loving them unconditionally includes that we want what's best for them. If they are a fellow believer and they are causing spiritual damage to or are otherwise hurting one or more people, then what's best for our erring believer (and all involved) is that we follow the guidelines spelled out for us in Matthew 18:15-17 (instructions for trying to reconcile with a fellow believer), and let this run its course. If at the end of this portion of the journey, they're still not remorseful – still not willing to change – then they should be excommunicated (removed from fellowship with the church) (Matthew 18:17; John 20:23; the unfortunate but necessary paragraph [Prologue]; the first paragraph of Chapter 2). Does excommunication mean that we no longer love them? No, not at all! We still love them unconditionally. Excommunication is not meant to be the last step of the journey. Desired next steps are a time of separation (a timeout) followed by repentance, forgiveness, and reconciliation. We want them to return to fellowship with us at church. And when such reconciliation occurs, by definition this means that we have also completely forgiven them for all they did wrong in the past (2 Corinthians 2:7-8).

What I've written above is the minimum requirement as taught in Remedial Forgiveness 101. Our gifted colleagues in the honors class will remind us that we aspire to truly forgive while actualizing Matthew 18:15-17, not only when the one who was excommunicated returns to fellowship with us. *Why do we aspire to do this?* I'll get to that shortly.

Nonspecific guidance

That was pretty easy.

OK, but what if the person who sinned against us is not a fellow believer? My view is that we still follow the same general (not specific) guidelines of Matthew 18:15-17.

But before we jump into that, let me remind you that if we're in a potentially dangerous situation – i.e., there's a reasonable chance that our counterpart will harm us – our first priority is to distance ourselves from this person. (The same applies to the fellow-believer scenario, described in the preceding subsection.)

Now that that's settled, let's take *general* guidance from Matthew 18:15 by somehow reaching out to our counterpart ourselves, in a one-on-one fashion, to offer forgiveness – to say that we're willing to forgive if they show remorse for hurting us and are willing to change their behavior. If possible, this conversation should be in person. If that's not a viable option (we're not in close proximity, or being together is reasonably likely to put us in danger), then other ways are via phone, email, or snail mail. If extending an olive branch in such a way doesn't result in traction toward reconciliation or at least a peaceable settlement, then let's take *general* guidance from Matthew 18:16-17 by getting more people, potentially even proper authorities, involved in the conversation(s) – for example a mutual friend, a social worker, a professional counselor, a lawyer, a judge. If the outcome is that the person who hurt us is still not remorseful – still not willing to change – then I advise that we (further) distance ourselves from this person. This is a timeout period that hopefully will end in reconciliation or a peaceable settlement, by which time of course we have forgiven them. Throughout all of this, we still love them unconditionally, always wanting what's best for them; simultaneously, we love ourselves, which includes that we respect ourselves, don't let ourselves be taken advantage of, and we take measures not to be hurt further by this person.

What I've written above is the minimum requirement as taught in Remedial Forgiveness 101. Our gifted colleagues in the honors class will remind us that we aspire to truly forgive during this process, not waiting for the reconciliation / settlement stage. *Why do we aspire to do this?* I'll get to that shortly.

A high calling

I think that was pretty easy too. Are you still with me?

OK, but what if – *(How many of these am I going to have?)* – the sin hurt us very deeply? To make myself clear, I'll answer this from the extreme circumstance that our life has been impacted by a heinous atrocity, such as abuse, rape, torture, murder of a loved one, a terrorist attack, or a similar hate crime. Of course we endeavor to bring the perpetrator(s) to justice, punishing them for what they did wrong, with the punishment being fully commensurate with their offense. Of course we denounce their hurtful behavior. Of course we take it seriously that it may be best to distance ourselves, and all others already impacted or potentially impacted in the future, physically and emotionally from the perpetrator(s). Of course we do what we can to reduce the likelihood of repeat violations by the perpetrator(s) or copycats. If the perpetrator(s) are members of our church and it's unambiguous that they have caused spiritual damage to or have otherwise hurt one or more people, of course we are justified following the steps toward excommunication. Of course we comfort and support all those impacted by the hurtful behavior, including making them aware of the aforementioned actions. But these are not our only responses. All these responses are under the umbrella of unconditional love for the perpetrator(s) – we want what's best for them – and at this time it's best for them to be punished to the full extent of the law. But there's one more response I haven't included yet, even though it should be simultaneous with the other responses. … Do you know what it is? … It's also under the umbrella of unconditional love for the perpetrator(s). We strive to, at a minimum, offer to forgive them. Yes, that's right – no typos. We offer to forgive them. I understand that this is not always easy. Unconditional love in all circumstances is not easy.

And what if the perpetrator(s) of a heinous crime *do* demonstrate true remorse for their misconduct? … No, we don't let them off the hook; they still need to pay their full debt to society. … Take a step back and look at the big picture. … I already gave you the answer in the very first paragraph of this "What if … ?" section. I know that was a long time ago now, so I'll repeat it again. If they're remorseful: *We are to forgive – under all circumstances – no exceptions.*

A higher calling

There is a larger and more difficult step that some gifted individuals are blessed to take. Let me illustrate this beautiful – no, exquisite (Chapter 6) – step with a scenario where the perpetrator(s) of a heinous crime are *not* remorseful. Based on total submission to the Holy Spirit, some are empowered to go beyond *offering* forgiveness to *truly forgiving*, even when very deeply hurt by someone who is not remorseful. I already told you that all of us who trust Jesus as our Savior will get our diplomas on graduation day – based on Jesus' righteousness, not our own – but there are gifted individuals among us who are not only in the honors class in advanced forgiveness, they are acing it with a string of plusses. Such individuals surely have the spiritual gift of healing. I do not. Don't rat me out, but I'm peeking at their final exams again... Looks like they have a few questions that aren't even on mine. I've never been tested like this... What am I seeing? I'm seeing that all of us, not only those of you with the spiritual gift of healing, should aspire to truly forgive – not only offer forgiveness – under all circumstances. Yes, that's right – no typos. We aspire to truly forgive, no matter what. *Why?*

I've been promising to answer this question for a while now, and here I finally address it. Is it to let the sinner think that they didn't do anything wrong? Is it to let the sinner think that there's no benefit to their changing? Is it to let the sinner off the hook from their debt to society? ... Even I know that the answer to all these questions is, "Of course not." ... *OK, then why?* ... There are two reasons.

1) Just as God continuously showers us with an unlimited supply of uncon-ditional love because He wants us to be His forever, we, in turn, strive to shower others in our life with unfettered unconditional love because this points them to God. And sometimes God calls us to kick unfettered up a notch, to the level of our grabbing hold of a fire hose with the spigot fully open, holding on for dear life as we aspire to aim the writhing stream at our unrepentant counterpart. There are circumstances where the exquisite step of giving true forgiveness in the face of no remorse will touch the heart of the sinner mightily. These are the kinds of mechanisms by which people are born again. When someone deeply hurts us, and shows no remorse for it, let us ask God to give us the strength to love in this special way.

2) Whether this powerful stream of forgiveness hits the intended target or not, there's always a benefit to us personally. By truly forgiving, we're coming to

peace with our anger, breaking free from resentment's internal stranglehold. Harboring resentment toward our counterpart allows them to have some degree of control over our life. God wants us to forgive and experience the serenity of living entirely under His control, which includes relying on Him to be final judge. Pray that God's judgment of this sinner be the same as His judgment of us; in other words, pray that this sinner trust in Jesus as his or her Savior. We're all in the same boat. We're all in desperate need of God's mercy (not punishing us, even though we deserve it – Jeremiah 3:12; Joel 2:13).

When we're blessed to give surprising, exquisite forgiveness in such a circumstance, I view this as analogous to being a martyr. We accept the blazing pain that sometimes flares up in this broken world – taking long, deep breaths of oxygen so the fire burns hot and to completion. When the flames subside, we sweep away the ashes of our resentment and pray that another benefit may be a change in the sinner's heart. Sometimes God calls us to be martyrs.

A different point of view

Are you still with me? Let me illustrate a main message of my last several paragraphs from a different perspective. Imagine for a moment that you are a perpetrator of a heinous crime; you are being punished and in other ways shunned by society; you are feeling a lot of hate from a lot of people; you are getting the message loud and clear that you are an awful person; the world is very dark for you right now; and you react according to your selfish, sinful, human nature – unconditional hate for all. If, in the midst of this, you become aware that someone – especially someone directly impacted by the crime – considers you a person who did an awful thing, not an awful person (please note the distinction), and they are offering you forgiveness – possibly even actually forgiving you! – because they have the love of God in them, you have just received a powerful message. You have just received a message that, if you take it to heart, will change your eternal destiny. Yes, if you take this message to heart, you will hear Jesus say to you what He said to the criminal being crucified to one side of Him: "You will be with me in paradise" (Luke 23:43).

An important point in my preceding paragraph is that to have maximum impact, our offering forgiveness – or our giving forgiveness – should be in conjunction with God's love. In other words, it's a beautiful thing to say: "I'm willing to forgive you, if you acknowledge that what you did is wrong," or "I forgive you;" but it's an exquisite thing to be more specific and say: "I'm willing to forgive you, if you acknowledge that what you did is wrong – because 'If we confess our sins, he [God] is faithful and just to forgive us our sins' (1 John 1:9)," or "I forgive you because I believe in God – and 'God is love' (1 John 4:8, 16)."

~

While unconditional love under such challenging circumstances is not easy, it is important. And for us to do a difficult thing like truly forgive, not only offer forgiveness, under all circumstances, we look to Jesus as our model. What was His response to cries of "Crucify, crucify him!" (Luke 23:21) and the brutalities that ensued in the wake of that? Was His response anger, resentment, hate, and retaliation? No, His response was unconditional love.

"Forgive and …" How does that go again? I forget.

Every time I sing the chorus of "Let It Go" – (Yes, *that* often!) – I'm reminded of the familiar advice of others to forgive and forget, and of my advice to forgive and remember. … What am I suggesting that we remember? … Even after we've reached what appears to be the end of an arduous path of forgiveness, it's OK to have occasional feelings of anger and resentment related to how our counterpart hurt us. This is normal. And when this happens, let's simply acknowledge our feelings and then remember the decision we made to forgive our counterpart. Our decision to forgive is a recurring commitment. While God can – *and does!* – say, "I will not remember your sins" (Isaiah 43:25), it's not emotionally healthy for us mortals to disregard our feelings, for example when we encounter a trauma trigger. It's also not emotionally healthy for us to be *dwelling* on bitter feelings. This is why we acknowledge our feelings and remember our recurring commitment. We remember that we have chosen to forget / to let it go.

Offering forgiveness – and truly giving forgiveness – in light of conditional love

Forward-pedaling on a path to reconciliation

What should we do if the one who sinned against us is in a conditional love relationship with us, for example they're our friend? Depending on the severity of their sin, the friendship may be profoundly damaged, possibly even severed, at least for a time. Regardless of how significant the negative impact is to our conditional love relationship, we should always love them unconditionally as described above. Again, I'm not saying this is easy.

A new emphasis relevant to a conditional love relationship damaged by sin is that no matter how much the bond has been frayed – yes, even if it has been completely severed – we should always be open to the possibility that there's a path by which there will eventually be reconciliation.

A conditional love relationship by definition has conditions associated with it. A path to reconciliation of conditional love has one standard condition. Sometimes we'll identify more conditions to be met, but there's always one that absolutely must be met for the relationship to be a healthy one. This is that our counterpart must have some measure of remorse for what they did wrong and an openness to change. Does this seem like I'm backpedaling? Didn't I just say that we should aspire to forgive even in the absence of any remorse? Yes, I did, and thank you for reading so carefully. But let me clarify that the prior discussion is in light of our giving unconditional love; now we're talking about reconciliation in a conditional love relationship.

In a healthy conditional love relationship, a condition that must be met for the bond to remain strong is for the one who wronged the other to have some measure of remorse and an openness to change. In contrast to forgiveness given via unconditional love – where only one is required to love, where only one is required to express forgiveness to have it land properly – forgiveness (and reconciliation) in a healthy conditional love relationship does take two. Allow me to make an analogy. In a healthy sexual relationship, every time we have sex, the two of us join together in an expression of love, and we both participate enthusiastically. The analogy is that in a healthy conditional love relationship that has been weakened by the sin of one against the other, forgiveness (and reconciliation) come when the two of us join together in an expression of love. Yes, such forgiveness is a coupling, and it comes in one of the following forms: (i) One offers forgiveness, and the other accepts (including meeting the one standard condition of remorse and an openness to change), or (ii) one apologizes (thus meeting the one standard condition), and the other forgives. Either way, the result is the same – the two have joined together in a beautiful expression of love.

What I've written so far in this subsection implies, for simplicity, that one of the pair is the "sinner" and the other has not contributed to that particular strain in the relationship. But usually things are not so clear cut. In real life, it's rare for a strain to be all one counterpart's fault. So, does my analogy fall flat? No, you can still apply my analogy to your relationship with full confidence, as long as you assure me that neither one of you dominates over the other when it comes to initiating encounters. If one never or rarely initiates, that's not satisfying, and my assignment for you both is to read "Dr. Bob's sex advice" (Chapter 9) and apply what you learn to your forgiveness encounters.

When complications set in

When you offer forgiveness with this one standard condition and any other conditions that may be appropriate based on the circumstances, your counterpart may not accept your forgiveness right away. Be patient. Also, to be fair, keep in mind the possibility that you've sinned against your counterpart by setting unreasonable conditions; perhaps in the heat of anger you asked for too much. If you later realize that this is the case, then you should tell your counterpart that you're sorry for that and want to talk more with them so better conditions can be established. But be careful – only change the conditions if you're really convinced that's appropriate – don't be manipulated. This is getting complicated – *(Conditional love can get complicated!)* – so let me illustrate with an example. In this example, I try to address concepts from throughout this "What if … ?" section, including the unconditional love portion. Remember that conditional love relationships should include some measure of mutual unconditional love. The backdrop to this example is an extramarital affair, and I apologize if my treatment of such a deplorable experience comes across as flippant in any of what I've written.

- Imagine that you've discovered that your husband is having a sexual affair. As you should, you immediately kick him out of the home or leave yourself (to stay at a friend's home, for example). After some time to cool off, if he has not contacted you, I recommend contacting him to say that despite him hurting you very deeply, you're willing to go to counseling if he'll come with you and if he'll immediately stop the affair. You add that, because you're a Christian, you can imagine a scenario where you'll forgive him and the two of you will be able to restore a healthy relationship (reconcile), but this is only if he fully participates with you throughout the counseling, he stops cheating, and you both cooperate to make other improvements in your marriage. You further add that while looking at credit card statements, you noticed that he bought the other woman some items (meals, gifts, etc.). You demand that she pay you back at twice the value. To be clear, what she received cost $750, so she owes you $1,500. He agrees to the first three conditions (he'll come with you to counseling, he'll stop the affair, and he'll work with you to try to achieve other improvements in your marriage), but he wants to talk about the $750 at the first counseling session. There, you agree that you were acting hastily in anger about the $1,500, and now see that in the big picture being paid back anything is not that important. So, you apologize for demanding money, and let it drop. He tries to weasel out of coming to future counseling sessions, but you stick to your guns and say that you won't budge on that condition.

o   Preferred ending: After extensive couples therapy, the two of you reconcile and begin to live together again, and you both continue to cooperate to strengthen your marriage

o   Alternate ending: It becomes apparent that your husband has been lying to you about who he was/is having an affair with. He did stop seeing the one woman you first found out about, but he has continued being with several others, even to this time.

"With God all things are possible" (Matthew 19:26), but from what I'm seeing right now the outlook doesn't look good, and it's probably appropriate to divorce this man. Too many important conditions (fidelity [Matthew 5:31-32] and honesty) are not being met, and this is during a separation and counseling.

Even if you divorce such a man, you should show him unconditional love, and from that perspective you strive to offer forgiveness and you aspire to truly forgive. I know this is not easy. But don't forget that offering or giving forgiveness doesn't infer restoration of a conditional love relationship, even if your counterpart accepts your (offer of) forgiveness.

And forgiveness never condones the hurtful behavior itself. Your counterpart is in no way let off the hook. Ask God to give you the strength to offer or truly give forgiveness in this way.

To bring this alternate ending full circle, here's a suggestion for what the woman in my example could say to offer forgiveness to her soon-to-be ex-husband.

- *You've hurt me deeply, and I'll never be the same. I'm saddened beyond words that you haven't loved me the way that a husband should love a wife. You've disrespected and dishonored our marriage, and I don't see any indication that you'll change. I need to move on with my life, and I'm going to do this with people who are loving to me. So, I'm leaving you. I'm a Christian, so I take it seriously that I want the best for everyone in my life, even those who disappoint me. In our current situation, the best for both of us is to part ways and start separate lives. So, I must say that despite my disappointment, I do hope the best for you in your new life and – this is hard for me to say but I believe it's the right thing to say because I confess my sins to God and know that I'm forgiven – if you sincerely apologize to me for disrespecting and emotionally hurting me by cheating on me with multiple women, for chronically lying to me about it, for not being willing to stop, and for not trying to cooperate with me in these and other ways to restore our marriage, then I will forgive you. If you're not ready to do this now, you can let me know later. If you ever reach out to receive my forgiveness, I want to be clear that my forgiveness would in no way condone your behavior, and I'd be forgiving you as one human being to another – you're not a friend anymore. I believe that "with God all things are possible" (Matthew 19:26) and, yes, I would indeed consider it a miracle if there's any path by which you and I would ever be friends again, based on all that has been tried already. What you did is wrong and it has caused you to lose me, but I don't want the past to hinder the future for either of us. By offering to forgive you, I'm taking an important step in my journey toward coming to peace with my anger, and toward freeing myself from resentment. By so doing, I'm empowering myself to start a new life without hindrances related to our failed relationship.*

Expanding our repertoire

I'd like to end this "What if … ?" section with an (I think) interesting side note. While most of my friends give me plenty of opportunities to forgive them… two of my friends are – *How do I put this?* – considerably considerate. So, I've never had anything meaningful to forgive them for. In the past, it occurred to me multiple times that I would like to show them love by expressing forgiveness to them for something significant. In case you think I had *completely* lost it, let me explain that these friends don't, as far as I can tell, have saving faith. So, I was wanting to include expression of forgiveness in my repertoire of witnessing tools. My quiver was getting heavy – I wanted to shoot more arrows – and what else shows love quite like forgiveness?

Be that as it may, let's work with the cards we're dealt, and then stand pat; we all have plenty of opportunities to forgive. I have come to realize that another way to shoot an arrow in exquisite fashion is to thank a considerably considerate friend for being that way.

What if you are struggling to forgive yourself?

Before we get ahead of ourselves, let's remember that if someone else has been hurt by our sin, then we shouldn't be thinking very long about whether we can forgive ourselves until we ask them for their forgiveness. We need to put them first – seek their forgiveness before we seek our own. After that, even if they don't have the spiritual maturity to forgive us, then let us proceed as follows.

If we're struggling with guilt, whether that be for a sin which has hurt someone else or for a sin within our own heart (for example, lustful thoughts), this infers that we feel remorse for our sin and that we have an openness to change our behavior. If you're reading these "What if … ?" sections in sequence, then you already know from the previous one what we do when someone feels remorse and has an openness to change. It's so important that I actually wrote it twice in the previous section. I know that both occurrences were a long time ago now, so I'll repeat it yet again: *We are to forgive – under all circumstances – no exceptions.*

In case I'm not being clear, no exceptions means no exceptions. Close your eyes, confess your sin to God, ask Him to help you change, know that He forgives you, and – *Don't stop yet!* – apply this no exceptions policy to yourself.

Some people are harder on themselves than they are on others. Are you like that? Do you have an easier time applying what I've now written three times to others than to yourself? One thing I find helpful when I'm having a hard time forgiving myself for a sin I've committed against another is to imagine that someone else committed that sin against me, and further that they've come to me to ask for forgiveness, and I can tell that they're sincere. Similarly, when I'm having a hard time forgiving myself for a private sin within my own heart, I imagine that I've somehow become aware of that type of sin within the heart of someone I love, and further that they're truly remorseful about that and want to change. Thinking this way helps me put my sins in proper perspective. It helps me forgive myself. Similar to the point that I've made several times in this book – that we are just as lovable as anyone else – we also are just as forgivable as anyone else, provided that we're remorseful and have an openness to change our behavior.

Jesus has already paid the full price for all sins of all people. If we're a believer, not only are we forgiven by God, but also we're reconciled with God, i.e., we have a restored relationship with Him. Do we know better than God? Are we going to be so bold as to disagree with Him by withholding forgiveness from ourselves when He has already given us this prerequisite to reconciliation? Such disagreement is disappointing to God. Not only are we just as forgivable as anyone else, provided that we're remorseful and have an openness to change our behavior, but also we are just as reconcilable as anyone else – and this is fully consummated when we trust in Jesus as our Savior. Please don't disappoint God, especially on the topics of forgiveness and reconciliation.

What if you are struggling with an addiction?

Please read and apply the previous section. Furthermore, your addiction may cause you to doubt whether you can adhere to one of the phrases that I keep using. Specifically, you may doubt that you have an openness to change your behavior. If you're addicted, by definition it's difficult to change your behavior. But if in your heart you want to change, even if you're not able to do this on your own, your desire to change certainly qualifies as openness. So, if you're addicted, please forgive yourself, and move on with your life by finding the necessary help to end your destructive behavior. Don't be embarrassed. People want to help you! The danger comes when you don't have a desire to get out from under your addiction, in which case it does become willful, persistent sin.

Living in the shadow of a persistent, habitual sin is not God-pleasing (1 John 3:4-10) and we're not showing proper love to ourselves. The loving thing to do for ourselves is to admit that we need help escaping from the grip of addiction. If we have a close friend we can talk to about it, that will help. We can also talk to our pastor. In most situations like this, we'll need some form of professional assistance. This can start simply by talking to a counselor, and they can help us identify what's most appropriate in our situation.

If you're struggling with an addiction, won't you pray about it right now? Below, I've written a prayer-testimony of someone who has recently discovered that they're addicted. Please give it a read. Maybe you can identify with certain elements of this. Then, tell your own story to God, and ask for His guidance on your journey to conquer your addiction.

- *God, You know that I like to think of myself as being very organized and in control of the situation. I can juggle a lot of balls, and it's rare for any to drop. At work, I'm known as The Goalie – Nothing gets by me! – and I'm very proud of that reputation. Yes, it's stressful to juggle so much, but I thought I could handle it, especially since I knew that I could go home at the end of the day and relax – really let go! Sometimes my friends and I get a little crazy. But I work hard and deserve it, right? Although, there are times when I go too far and do things that I'm not proud of. You know I'm sorry about that; I've been confessing that sin every week for over a year now. Up until a couple months ago, I had always considered it just a casual sin – no big deal. I could decide not to do it… right? That's what I had thought. But I was starting to notice that I was doing it more and more often. It was becoming rare for me to make it two days without doing it again. You know that I started to get more remorseful – even to the point of accepting that I should stop, not simply reduce the frequency. You know how proud I was just a couple days ago – I had made it three whole days without doing it. It was on my mind frequently – at least a couple times an hour – but I was resisting! But then came yesterday morning. I think I had a dream that triggered it. The first thing I clearly remember is lying in bed and feeling an incredibly strong desire to do it again. My eagerness to do it had rarely been that strong before. I literally couldn't think of anything else. A part of me wanted to resist, but that voice that had gotten me through three and a half days now was becoming weaker, until it finally was overpowered by another part of me that doggedly wanted to submit to my habitual sin again. So, I did. That made me feel much better... but also much, much worse... It felt dreadful because that's when it hit me that I have a problem. It finally dawned on me that this is really out of control. You know how fervently I prayed about this as I scrambled to get dressed and drive to work. It was after 9:00 A.M. by the time I got in the car, and seeing the time reminded me of the important 8:00 A.M. meeting... Oh, God, what was I going to tell my boss? ... Should I call in sick? ... My heart sank as the truth set in: It's getting harder and harder to manage my... my... addiction... That's the first time I've applied that word to myself. Yes, it looks like I really do have an addiction. So, this is what it feels like – to not be able to resist. I've always thought of myself as being strong, so much in control of my life. But this is clearly more than I can handle. I'm embarrassed about this, but I must talk to someone. The person I trust the most – I've known him since we were kids – is just 40 miles away. I want to call him tonight, and ask if he can set aside a few hours this weekend to meet with me. Over the years, we've both shared some pretty personal things. So, I know he won't judge me or overreact. Lord, thank You for giving me such a friend! And, Lord, thank You so much for forgiving me for this sin again and again... and again... And thank You for making the severity of my sin so prominent yesterday morning – it makes me finally realize that I have to stop. You keep on forgiving me, but You also want what's best for me – and living with an addiction certainly is not. Lord, be with me as I take the first step toward recovery, with the help of my good friend.*

What if you are struggling with the sin of your own abusive behavior?

Before you think that this section cannot apply to you, please take a moment to consider the people in your life. Is there anyone you've started to treat unfairly? Is there anyone you're hurting by what you say or do? It's common for an abuser to shift blame to others and to rationalize that what they're doing is not that bad – to minimize it. Abuse almost always starts small, and then builds slowly as the abuser keeps pushing the envelope, seeing how much they can get away with. And the slow buildup allows desensitization to play a role. What would have seemed unimaginable a year ago has become routine.

Abuse is an antithesis (opposite) of love, but an abuser commonly victimizes someone he loves, or at least loved previously. Why is that? A large component is vulnerability, which is an ingredient of a conditional love relationship. Vulnerability allows us to become close to another, so is usually a beautiful part of a relationship. However, with certain people and in certain circumstances, one feels entitled to take advantage of the other's vulnerability.

Are you taking advantage of anyone's vulnerability?

The sin of abusive behavior has a way of sneaking up on us. The hurtful episodes don't need to be very frequent for the overall behavior to be considered chronic abuse. Think about it – the worst cases of abuse started with a single hurtful episode, and built from there. If you hurt someone in a single hurtful episode, is that truly a "one-off," or could it be the start of a new pattern? Has there been more than one hurtful episode? Are they becoming more frequent?

Maybe this section applies to you after all. If it does, or you're not really sure, please take it to God right now.

If you've sinned in this way, look to God for forgiveness and healing. He wants to help you become more loving. Pour out your story to God, and be open to His guidance to put the pieces back together.

As a model for this, although I sincerely hope that your situation has not progressed as far as this, below I've provided the thoughts of a man who has physically abused his wife for years, and is finally (much later than it should have been) confronted with the reality that he has no choice but to stop. Please read this prayer-testimony, think about those elements that relate to your story, and then open up (make yourself vulnerable) to God. He will never take advantage. Seek His forgiveness – and find it (cf. Matthew 7:7-11). Ask for His guidance toward recovery. Ask that He put into your heart compassion for the one you've been hurting.

- *God, I never thought she'd do it. I never thought she'd actually leave me. I thought it could go on forever. I mean, it started so simply. No big deal, right? And the steps were small. It was like building a house of cards – each card put on so carefully. Why did she go and knock it over now?*

  It took me a while to even realize that she was gone. I got home from Bible study, and I didn't think much about her not being there. I figured that she was just at the grocery store or something. I was tired from a stressful day at work, and Bible study had run a bit long – lots of important prayer requests this week. And I stayed after with one of the new guys; his wife has recently been diagnosed with ovarian cancer. I don't know him well, and I've never met his wife, but I felt so sad when he was describing the situation that my eyes started to well up with tears. I couldn't really think of the right words to say, but he seemed to be comforted simply by knowing that I was there for him. I often don't know what to say, but I've been told by several people that I'm a good listener.

  To decompress from the long day, I played a video game and – You know how those things are – the next thing I knew almost an hour had passed. I started to become concerned that my wife still wasn't home. Eventually, I went into the kitchen to grab a snack, and that's when I saw it. There was a note on the kitchen table. At first, I figured it was just letting me know where she had gone for the evening. But there was an awful lot of writing... ... What's this? ... What?! ... I felt numb from what I was reading. It was like I was tangled in a dream: "... don't understand you ... can't take it any longer ... don't know what to do ... have to leave." But where did she go? She didn't say where!

  My heart was racing, and I had to sit down. How could she do this to me? How could she abandon me?

  Once the initial shock started to wear off, I really wanted to find out where she was, and it occurred to me to start calling our friends until I found someone who knew. ... Oh, but what was I going to say? Why did I not know where she was?

  That was three days ago...

  Last night I got a call from Pastor. He told me that my wife had contacted him earlier in the day, and that he needed to talk to me too. At first I was relieved, but then a feeling of dread started to slowly envelop me. I wished it was anyone but Pastor. How much did he know? … I didn't say anything, and just waited to see what card he would play next. … After an awkward silence, he said that she had contacted him to tell him that she had left the house, and he repeated that he needed to talk to me too. I didn't address his request to talk to me – I just asked where she was. He said he had promised her that he wouldn't tell me, but that she was safe. … I felt a sinking feeling. Why else would he add that she was safe? He must know something… But what, exactly? … The silence was getting uncomfortable, so I just said that I need to know where she is. "I'm her husband, after all."

He didn't say anything. I started to get agitated. "Why won't you tell me?"

He still didn't say anything. There was silence for what seemed like an eternity. Finally, he said that she was scared to be with me, that she wasn't sure what to do, and that he really needed to talk to me. There was silence again. I was about to say something when he said that he learned that things had gotten pretty bad – with anger and fighting – and he wanted to help me address my anger issues. There was silence again. I was trying to figure out how much she had told him, but he wasn't saying anything specific. I suddenly blurted out, "Well, sometimes she makes me mad. And now she's twisting things around to make it seem like it's all my fault. Like what she's doing now – talking to you, and saying that I have anger issues!"

Then he said in a quiet voice that he did want to hear my side of it, but there is also one very important thing that needs to be addressed. … Silence again… I was resolved to say nothing. I could wait longer than him. Finally, he said that he had asked my wife if she wants to press charges. … When he said that, I really started to panic. But I did not give up hope. Maybe he only knew a small portion, so I played dumb and said, "What do you mean?"

He said that she had described enough about what has been going on that he advised her that she could press charges. … There was silence again. … I could literally feel my heart sinking lower and lower as I thought about what he might know. I was speechless. … He finally said that her response was that it all sounded so confusing, and that she would need help to do that. The last thing he said was that he would pray for me, pray for my wife, and call me again at 8 o'clock in the morning so we could talk about this more.

Press charges... Would she really do that? ... Press charges... Would she have a case? It depends on how much she would tell... and show... She's careful about covering up her bruises, and I've always assumed that she would be too embarrassed to talk to anyone about it. But now I know that she's said something to Pastor. Who else did she tell? What did she tell them? What did she show them?

People have seemed kind of aloof lately, although I've never been very social anyway. But there was that barbeque at the neighborhood park a couple weekends ago. That seemed especially awkward. I was running a little late, and my wife went ahead of me. When I got there, I was looking for her but didn't see her at first. But then I heard her laugh, and I looked and there she was – laughing and smiling with a friend. ... Then she turned and saw me – immediately her countenance fell. Just like that, her laugh and smile were gone. I wondered if anyone else noticed the change in her, and that it happened just as she saw me. The person she was talking to seemed pretty oblivious to it – that was good... I looked around, and everyone seemed busy. Oh, but then I saw all the way across the lawn another one of her friends – one of her best friends in fact – and she was looking right at me. She didn't look happy at all, but maybe that's just her resting face. I raised my hand a little and tried to smile. She just turned away. ... What does she know?

Oh, God, I must admit that I'm starting to get really scared. If my wife has been talking to people, and now has support to press charges, then I'm in very, very serious trouble.

It all started so simply – just some yelling. I've never liked to get confrontational, so I just try to avoid fighting altogether. When growing up, everyone in our family was that way. We almost never voiced disagreement, and I don't remember any yelling. When any one of us got mad, we would just give the silent treatment. But my wife is much more expressive than I am. That was another thing – in addition to her laugh and smile – that drew me to her. She makes it so much easier for me to be social; I rely on her to break the ice. And she can even tell when someone is making me uncomfortable; she always finds a way to divert the conversation. I really appreciate that. And when we're alone, she's very affirming of her love for me and often quite passionate when we make love. But over the past few years this has been tapering off, and more of her anger is showing through. Not long after we met, I quickly learned that she is also expressive in anger. But I always just considered it a minor drawback related to so many things I appreciate about her.

Every time she yells, I get flustered. Early in our marriage, I didn't know what to say – how to respond to her yelling – and a few times I even ended up breaking down in tears. That always made her stop. She would see that she upset me, so she'd stop. Then, we'd begin to talk in a calmer manner about whatever we were arguing about, and eventually we'd make up. But then there was that one fight where out of the blue she criticized me for falling behind in updating the prayer chain with the new prayer requests that were coming in. Why did I volunteer to do it, if I couldn't keep up? Something about that made me snap, and I suddenly found myself spewing obscenities at her, and calling her awful names. Even in the middle of it, I was shocked by the dreadful things I was yelling at her. But I couldn't seem to stop myself from doing it. When I finally realized that she had stopped yelling, I stopped too. I apologized quickly for what I had said, but she needed more time to process what had just happened. Even hours later, she still seemed different. The next morning, we went our separate ways (to our workplaces), and things seemed to go back to normal, more or less.

But it didn't take long for it to become apparent that there was a change in us. For whatever reasons, I now found myself feeling more comfortable yelling at her. It was as if I had discovered that I could do it, with seemingly no real consequences. But the deplorable things I would call her… Oh, it just got worse and worse. … Looking back, I think what I was trying to do was to make her stop by showing her that I would always win any fight she wanted to start. But within a few weeks, she would get angry again. What was I supposed to do? I felt like she didn't respect me.

And then there was that one time when – in the thick of another fight – I couldn't believe her nerve when she actually said that if anyone in the congregation knew what one of their Elders had just called his wife, they would be appalled and disgusted. I yelled back that it was her fault because she was always the one to start our fights. The look of anger on her face – she was seething! … Why did she hate me so much? … I couldn't take the rejection implied by this, and in my rage I surprised myself by shoving her. She had made me so mad, that I actually shoved her. That made her stop.

As usual, when I cooled down, I apologized for what I said, and this time I needed to add that I was sorry for pushing her. I was proud of myself for feeling sorry – I mean, deep down I want to be gentle and loving – and I just wished we would never fight again.

But just a few weeks later, she started another fight. All I said was that I didn't like what she had made for dinner – that she seemed to be getting lackadaisical. She started a fight over a simple thing like that. And this time, she didn't stop even when I pushed her. Instead, she said, "How would you like it if I told the whole prayer chain what you just did?" I couldn't believe she was being so disrespectful. So, I pushed her harder. Finally, she stopped. Later that night, I felt bad about pushing her. I told her I was sorry, and that I don't like to fight.

But, sure enough, just like clockwork barely a month had passed and she pushed my buttons again. Why can't she learn? Why does she blame me for everything? Nothing I say ever seems to be enough to make her stop.

I remember the first time I pushed her so hard that she fell down. I'll never forget the look on her face. ... I also remember the first time I really hit her – I mean with my fist. That even shocked me a bit – but only the first time... It's amazing what a person can allow themselves to become accustomed to.

I can't get that look on her face out of my mind. She had just been yelling and so animated about it, but when I shoved her down her countenance changed immediately. She looked up at me, but her eyes seemed ... empty ... no expression. I had never seen her look like that before. After that, our fights became a little different. She's not as animated. She basically just looks scared. And inevitably I end it with a hard shove or a hit. But it has never again been like that one time, because now she doesn't even look at me.

Then there was that time about a month ago. Boy, did she make me mad! I think that's the maddest she has ever made me! She had the audacity to tell me – me! – that I need to change. She was mumbling something about forgiving me if I change. I couldn't really follow most of it, except there was something about talking to a counselor and she kept saying things like, "If I stop," "If I change," and "If I admit that what I'm doing is wrong." How dare she! Why was she blaming me? I was showing restraint, but enough is enough! I had to stop her. I warned her. I told her that if she didn't stop, I would put a stop to it myself. So, I had no choice but to end it right there. In the past, I had always held back. I mean, I don't consider myself to be brutal. There's a limit. So, I would hold back and not hit too hard. But this time, she made me so mad that I pushed such inhibitions aside, and I really let her have it. That's right, I hit her as hard as I could. Only once – that was enough to make her drop to her knees. That made her stop. As usual, she wouldn't look at me. But this time, something was different. All the other times, when I made her stop, she shut up. But this time, after maybe a minute of silence, she started to cry.

... Looking back – I've never thought about this before – I'm realizing that over all this time she never tried to really hurt me. I mean, she's almost as big as me and she works out – she could have gotten a few shoves in, if she had wanted to. But she never went there. And sure, she yelled at me a lot – sometimes very loudly! – but she never said anything really nasty to me. I slung plenty of dirty labels at her, but she never went there. I mean, even that time I left her crying on the floor, as I stormed out I screamed that she is a __ing __ , but she just sat there.

...

Oh, God, who have I become?

...

If she presses charges... If she presses charges, then I'm in a heap of trouble... For one thing, she still has that huge dark bruise on her left breast. I was so careful to hit her there, so no one else would see. But if she has the nerve to press charges, then maybe she would show someone even that... And if she will show that, then is there anything she won't reveal? Oh..., she's got a case all right...

...

Oh, God, look at the time... I've gotten no sleep, and it's only half an hour now before Pastor's calling back... What am I going to say? I have never been so scared in my life...

~

If you are struggling with the sin of your own abusive behavior, I implore you to get the help you need to stop before it slips any further. It must be stopped – and this must be far before it slides anywhere near as far down as it did in this story. And it's not just about you stopping; don't forget the one you were abusing! They need a lot of love in the wake of being the victim of abuse. Turn your abusive behavior on its head, and give them love instead. Work together to reconcile and start a new life.

To help you better understand the point of view of the one you've been abusing, and to help you both begin to make positive changes together, I'd like you to read the next section, and then sit down with your counterpart and tell them that you're ready for change.

What if you are being abused?

Please read the previous section. Does that story sound at all familiar? Are you being treated unfairly by anyone in your life? That story is about physical abuse, along with some emotional abuse, which is hurtful and manipulative language and other nonphysical behavior with the (possibly subconscious) intent to control another and make them feel threatened or bad about themselves (inferior, ashamed). Another type of abuse is sexual abuse, which I describe in Chapter 7 ("Sexual abuse in an adult relationship" subsection).

If you are being abused, I'm so sorry, and you need to get out of the situation, at least for a timeout period. Creating a safety plan, identifying a safe haven, and initiating a timeout may seem difficult, but you need to do it. While it's good to open up to a close friend about this kind of predicament, unless they're experienced in such matters you should talk to a social worker or professional counselor for help with establishing a safety plan tailored for your circumstances. If your situation is such that it's difficult to meet with a social worker or counselor in person, then contact a 24-hour hotline such as the three listed below. But, as always, call 911 if you are in immediate danger.

- National Domestic Violence Hotline: 800-799-SAFE (7233), and if you would prefer to chat online, this is an option at www.thehotline.org
- Safe Horizon Hotline: 800-621-HOPE (4673), and see www.safehorizon.org for more information about their services
- National Sexual Assault Hotline: 800-656-HOPE (4673), and if you would prefer to chat online, this is an option at www.rainn.org

~

If you are the victim of abuse, I have written a prayer on your behalf – as a way to support you. Please read it, know that God loves you and wants what's best for you, and then close your eyes and ask God what your next steps should be. (This is written assuming that you are a wife being abused by your husband. Change the details as needed.)

- *Heavenly Father, please look down with grace on Your dear child here. She is hurting very badly. Someone she loves [or, loved] – indeed, the person she promised to love the most: her husband – is not treating her with respect and love. He is trampling on her vulnerability. Yes, Lord, she is the victim of his abuse. When I think of the kinds of things she has had to endure, I am saddened to the point of tears. This is not what you intended marriage to be. Please bless her! Provide a path by which she will feel loved again. May her friends and family support her, encourage her, love her. Help her never to forget that she is a beautiful woman – yes, she is to be cherished! You cherish her. Never let her forget it. Please comfort her with Your love – cause it to penetrate deep into her heart. Let her reflect Your love with a forgiving attitude, yes, even toward her husband – and an openness that there may be a way that the marriage can be restored. Strengthen her, so she has the courage to stand up for herself, not allowing her husband to take advantage anymore. Open her eyes so she can see what needs to change, and please provide the resources for such change to be accomplished. Please transform the heart of her husband, both for his sake as an individual and because this is a prerequisite for their marriage to have any chance of being restored. If their marriage cannot be repaired, please help this dear woman move on with her life gracefully. She needs to be loved. I ask that You display Your love by surrounding her with loving people. In Jesus' name, Amen.*

~

I'm not ready to end this section yet. I want you to read the following prayer-testimony of the wife in the sad story of the previous section. Also, please don't miss my commentary after her prayer-testimony, where I include a few words about things that should have been handled differently. This situation got very violent and dangerous. Action must be taken sooner, so it never reaches this point.

- *God, the last few days have been very scary for me. If my husband finds out where I am, who knows what he's going to do? I'm still a little shocked that I really left him.*

   I know, especially now, that I should have left long ago, but I didn't know where to go. And I didn't want to talk to anyone about it because I was embarrassed that something like this was happening to me. My friends have been asking me how I'm doing – am I really OK – more and more over the last year or so. I know my mood has been different, and I guess it was more obvious than I thought. I always just said that I'm fine.

   That is, until a few months ago. It was a little while after he had started actually hitting me – with his fist – when I finally told my best friend a little bit. I said that we were fighting more and more, and that he was starting to get physical. My friend started crying. She hugged me – really tight. It didn't take long until I started crying too. At first, just a little, but as I started to think back over the last few years, I cried harder and harder. My friend held me the entire time. It must have been several minutes. Then she did something that touched me in a special way. She looked me in the eyes and said, "I love you." (We have been close friends for years, but we hadn't used that word before with each other.) I didn't say anything back. My tears said enough.

   ...

   I didn't even tell her that day about the hitting, but she already knew enough. She prayed with me. She asked God to help us learn what to do next.

   She had never been in a situation like this before, but the next day she told me that she found out that across town there is a shelter for victims of abuse. She said that I was of course welcome to stay with her, but we both agreed that could be dangerous because my husband might find me there.

   She encouraged me to leave right away – she even said that she would drive me there – but I just couldn't do it. I said I wanted to try to talk to my husband about going to counseling before just leaving. She was skeptical, telling me that I should have talked to him about that a couple years ago at least (I know she's right), and that I should be talking to the police, not him. But I knew what I wanted to do – it seemed right to me. I was looking for a good opportunity to talk to him, but it never seemed to come.

As the weeks dragged on, my friend kept asking me if I had talked to him, and she was starting to get a little upset with me. By then, she knew it had escalated to hitting – I had finally showed her some of my bruises – and she was concerned for my safety. She was agitated that I wasn't moving this along faster. She wanted to call the police, but I asked for more time.

Finally, about a month ago, I thought a good time had come. And I remembered that my friend was getting anxious, so I actually mustered up the courage to talk to my husband about counseling to help with our situation. We had just had a nice weekend. The weather was beautiful. We went for a long bike ride on Saturday, church on Sunday morning, and a nice long stroll on the beach on Sunday afternoon. We even held hands a little bit and reminisced about when we first started dating. That evening, we made love and it reminded me how tender he can be. Afterwards, he was so peaceful – I hadn't seen him look like that in a long time. So, I told him how much I enjoyed the weekend, and how I wish more of our time together was like this. I told him that I don't like to fight so much, that I should work on talking things through more calmly, and that he scared me when he got angry. I told him that I thought we needed professional help, especially since he was starting to get more physical when we fought. I told him I love him but he shouldn't hurt me like that. I told him I would forgive him for it, if he would stop. ... He had been just kind of lying there, not looking so peaceful anymore, but still just lying there – maybe a little zoned out, actually. But when I said "if you stop," that got his attention, and he propped up on his elbows. ... I continued, and said I would forgive him if he would change. That was the word – "change." He suddenly flew into a rage. He yelled at me to stop blaming him for everything. Maybe I should have not said any more, but I didn't appreciate him implying that it was my fault that he can't control his temper. I didn't yell because I didn't want to come across as overly emotional, but I said calmly that I would forgive him if he would admit that what he is doing is wrong. That word hit a trigger. Never before had I told him that anything he has done is wrong. He lost it. He screamed that I am a disrespectful b_____ , and that I had to shut the _____ up or he would make me wish I had never started this. He continued to yell obscenities, and not long into that he took a swing at me like I've never seen before. In that split second when I first saw it coming, I couldn't believe he was really going to hit me that hard. Surely, he was going to hold back, at least a little bit, before he actually hit me. But no, he didn't hold back. I've never felt so much force. I think he knocked the wind out of me. I slumped to my knees ... clutched my chest ... struggled to catch my breath ... and ... ... cried.

...

I was at the end of my rope.

...

I didn't know what to tell my friend. I couldn't tell her what happened because she'd make me leave. I was too scared to leave.

My friend kept asking me when I was going to have that talk with my husband. After the third time that I responded that I still hadn't found the right time, she got upset with me. She told me that I'm enabling his behavior if I don't confront him, and then leave immediately if necessary. This made me mad, and I yelled, "You don't understand what I'm going through! You don't know anything about things like this! Why do you keep telling me what to do, like you know better?! And I don't appreciate the way you're starting to make it sound like it's my fault!"

"Of course it's not your fault that he's hurting you! But you can't go on like this. If you don't talk to him tonight, then I'm doing it tomorrow. You have 24 hours."

I sat there a little stunned at the ultimatum that she had just thrown down. I said "But... but..." I didn't know how to finish this, so I just started crying. It only took her a few seconds to sit next to me and give me another long hug. Again, I started crying harder and harder. That's when I told her about what happened that weekend. She got very angry. I've never seen her like that. She asked me where my husband was. At first, I was scared because I thought she was going to go where he was. I just kind of sat there, and she asked if he was at work for the rest of the day. I nodded, and she immediately took me by the hand, drove me to my house (just a couple houses away), and told me that I had 30 minutes to get everything I wanted to take. I was in a kind of robotic haze, following her orders. I kept walking slowly between the bedroom and the bathroom. I couldn't seem to focus. She was standing downstairs, looking out the open front door. I leaned over the banister to ask her how many changes of clothes I should take, and she just snapped back: "A lot!"

We were just about to leave, when it occurred to her that I should prob-ably leave a note for "that snake." I couldn't think of what to say, so she helped me write it.

She drove me to the shelter she had found previously. She stayed with me all the rest of that day. She said a prayer for me, and included that she was glad that I was safe and finally taking action, and then she asked God to help us with next steps.

My friend has come back to be with me every day I've been here. I'm so thankful for that. When I think of how mad my husband must be, I do get scared. But I always feel better when my friend is with me.

Yesterday, I finally called Pastor. It was hard to know where to start. I was kind of stumbling along about fights with my husband, when Pastor asked me where I was. I hesitated. He asked me if I was still at the house. I still didn't say anything. It wasn't until he said that I should leave, that I started crying and told him where I was, and I quickly added that he couldn't tell my husband. All he said was, "I won't tell him, and I'll be there in 15 minutes."

I said "OK," but he had already hung up.

Pastor and my friend were with me all afternoon. He prayed with me and told me that he would help me. He and my friend encouraged me to press charges against my husband. At first, that sounded so dire to me, and I told them that I don't know anything about how to do it. But as I finally really opened up to them, as well as to the caseworker who had been assigned to me when I checked in at the shelter, and told them all the details of how bad things had gotten – (It got easier and easier for me, the more I told) – it became clear to all of us that we should get the police involved. Pastor, my friend, and the caseworker all started to ask about evidence, and that's when I showed them most of my bruises, and then I showed my friend the biggest one that was on my breast. When she saw that, she broke down and sobbed. After a few minutes, she said faintly but clearly: "I will help you do whatever it takes to bring him to justice; and I will help you reclaim your life and dignity."

I stroked her hand … looked at her … and said quietly … "I love you."

~

Yes, the husband must be brought to justice. He also needs other elements of unconditional love (see the "What if someone sins against you?" section, earlier in this chapter). In situations like this, we should be praying fervently that his wife's reclamation of her life and dignity can include reconciliation with him – restoration of a healthy conditional love relationship. As perilous as their current situation is, with professional help they may, in time and with practice, be able to manage future interpersonal conflicts in a God-pleasing way, including the husband learning how to respond to his anger in a nondestructive manner. When focusing on the awful things he did and said, it might not seem realistic that such changes are possible, but never forget, "All things are possible with God" (Mark 10:27). If you relate to the husband's story, don't despair; take it to God and get ready to be changed.

If you relate to the wife's story, don't delay doing what she and her friend finally did – retreat to safety and take it to God: "*She said a prayer for me, and included that she was glad that I was safe and finally taking action, and then she asked God to help us with next steps.*" God helps with next steps by providing us with good friends like this, and with pastors and professionals trained to deal with such circumstances. Your situation will not improve by continuing to hide; identify the right people, tell your story to them, keep praying, and get ready for change.

Before we move on from this story, let's circle the wagons and acknowledge that the wife and her friend did make at least a couple mistakes. For example, the situation would have played out better if the wife didn't wait so long to try to talk to her husband about counseling. Her years of hesitancy followed by doing it in person was a little misguided. If before leaving him she wanted to talk to him one-on-one – something I always recommend – then since she had waited until the violence had escalated to the point it did in this story, a better idea would be to contact him in another way, for example a phone call from a safe place. This way, she would not be physically hurt during her attempt to reach out to him. (But no matter what mistakes she made, she shouldn't be blamed for that vicious attack, or any of the prior attacks. She is certainly a victim. I'm simply providing a recommendation for a better way to handle the situation.) Also, the police should have been called in much earlier. Because the wife was hesitant to do that, her friend should have insisted when she finally found out there was chronic violence, even before she eventually learned the horrible extent of it.

You can see that both mistakes are related to the wife's reluctance to talk about the situation. If you are the victim of abuse, you must talk to people about it! Start with whomever you feel most comfortable – a friend, family member, pastor, other church-worker, social worker, professional counselor, 24-hour hotline such as the three listed above – and together build from there.

And if you learn of someone being abused, you must take action immediately. The level of violence would need to be much less than in this story for alternate avenues to be explored other than leaving the home and contacting the police.

What if your friend is being abused?

Taking action immediately when we learn of someone being abused can be difficult, but we do it regardless. How do we do it? We overcome our fears related to bringing up an uncomfortable topic, not knowing what our (new) friend's reaction will be, and not knowing what their abusing counterpart's reaction will be.

- What's more uncomfortable?
  - Initiating a loving conversation with a friend, demonstrating that we care about their wellbeing and want to help
  - Or waiting until irreparable damage has occurred, and living with the regret that we didn't do more when we had the chance
- What reaction is better for our friend?
  - They withdraw from us because they're embarrassed and angry that we called the cops
  - Or they never take action on what should be their top priority (secularly speaking) because we enable them to avoid the topic
- What reaction is better for their abusing counterpart?
  - They threaten us because they discovered that we got involved, so we (further) distance ourselves and, if necessary, establish a restraining order
  - Or they are polite to us and are enabled to continue to slide undeterred down the slippery slope of abusive behavior because we don't want to feel uncomfortable

Note that the above fears are based on the short term: we're worried about initiating an uncomfortable conversation or putting a strain on a relationship. But when someone we know is being abused, let's change our focus to the long-term benefits for our (new) friend and for all of the relationships they choose to cultivate.

What if you have experienced trauma?

The dear woman in the section before the previous one experienced the trauma of escalating physical violence. The precious child in the "One black stepping stone" section of Chapter 5 experienced the trauma of escalating sexual harassment that led to rape. I had the traumatic experience of losing a loved one unexpectedly. These are just a few of the many ways by which we can experience trauma. Maybe you have witnessed firsthand a vicious attack, a terrible accident, the catastrophic effects of a natural disaster, deplorable dysfunction in your childhood home. Maybe *you* were the one attacked, injured, or otherwise a target during distressing circumstances or a shocking single event. Whatever the trauma – even after it has become part of our distant past – it can manifest itself as a deep imprint on the way we view the world. What is to be done?

I don't have much to say on this topic. For this, you need to do the talking. I don't care if your trauma occurred 50 days ago or 50 years ago, or at various times in between, if you have found yourself consciously or subconsciously fixated on the imprint then you are stuck at an anxious, hypervigilant impasse until you do the talking.

- Who do you need to talk to? Is this the time to isolate yourself and replay the event(s) over and over in your mind, mumbling to yourself as you try to make sense of it? Is this the time to pretend to "be strong," and play the lone wolf? No, this is the time to be strong and reach out to a close friend and/or support group and/or professional counselor.
  - And if your trauma is proving to be tenacious, ask your therapist if they think supplementing your treatment with Bilateral Stimulation – which is not what its two-letter acronym implies (Appendix S) – will be helpful in your case

- What do you need to talk about? Is this the time for "Just the facts, ma'am"[2]? No, this is the time to stop walling ourselves behind our favorite defense mechanisms and let our true emotions out, even the painful, unpleasant ones.

The time has come for our empathetic counselor / support group / friend to provide a sanctuary where it's safe for us to let it *all* out. The time has come for us to receive compassion, including from ourselves. We have found a secure place, and the time has come for our emotions – *(Oh, yes, they're down there; don't doubt that for a second)* – directly and indirectly related to the trauma to finally see the light of day.

> *All the times that I've cried / Keeping all the things I knew inside*
> *It's hard / But it's harder to ignore it*[3]

What if your counterpart is afraid?

The most recent time I was with someone who was afraid, I convinced myself that I had just discovered a sixth love language. I picked up the basic vocabulary with remarkable ease, and it wasn't long before I was well on my way to crafting my own dialect, infused with several imaginative expletives. I like to call this facile language: Stern lecturing on the high likelihood of survival through the night, sprinkled liberally with statistics that support the practicalities of this point of view. This is not quite as succinct as the names of the first five love languages, but when you're planting your flag deep into the wet sand of newfound territory, brevity is not a high priority.

If you've ever stepped over the brink of discovery, you know that a hurdle to be cleared is acceptance by your peers. To wit, to claim a discovery, it's helpful to have others agree that the claim is valid. … When it comes to my assertion of discovering a sixth love language, suffice it to say that my fearful counterpart did not validate my claim.

Why are there still only five love languages? Because I learned that fearful counterparts are not comforted by lectures, as practical as they might be. Concurrently, I learned that empathy should not stop when we simply pick up on our counterpart's emotional state. Empathy should take another step, and provide our counterpart with a good measure of understanding and/or compassion and/or –

especially relevant when our counterpart is afraid – comfort. And all of this can be provided by the love languages that have already been surveyed and drawn on our maps.

Comfort can come in the form of words, although keep in mind that comforting words are typically neither stern nor saturated with statistics. And if our fearful counterpart is physically present with us, comfort is well-provided by physical touch. A hug goes a long way, and a good cooldown after a fear-mitigating hug is staying right next to our counterpart, ideally for an extended period of time. So, when someone in our life becomes afraid for any reason, let's infuse them with the following antidote for their fear: quality time that includes soothing words of affirmation and prayer, and ideally our physical presence alongside them.

~

Fear is highly contagious, but sometimes our immunity to such a contagion is so strong that we get frustrated and turn into stern lecturers to those who have become infected. For example, just because we didn't opt for the movie with *Chucky* in the title when we split up at the movie theater doesn't mean that our response to our counterpart's ensuing fear of being attacked in the night should be a cold-hearted explanation of how unlikely this is, all the while sitting across the room with our arms crossed.

Fear is a complex emotion. Sometimes it's very helpful, as it guides us toward changes that are best for our physical and emotional wellbeing. But sometimes fear goes overboard and lures us to take illogical excursions. When this happens, level-headed, logical guidance from our friends and loved ones can help us get back on the right track.

So, what's the take-home message? … Here's how I'm going to phrase it: If your counterpart is afraid, do your best to balance a jug of water on your head as you help them identify any changes that may be beneficial and, just as importantly, throughout all of this be understanding, compassionate, and comforting, even if you know beyond a shadow of a doubt that the nearest Charles – whether this be a man unlike you or me; a clown; a marionette; a ventriloquist's dummy; or a creepy, orange-haired doll in urgent need of a haircut – is blocks away.

What if you are afraid?

Several times in this book, I say that there are circumstances where we should distance ourselves from someone for our physical and emotional wellbeing. But sometimes this is easier said than done. For example, what if we're noticing an increase in vandalism in our neighborhood? What if the word on the street is that break-ins are on the rise? What if we occasionally hear gunshots in the night? What if it's even worse, and there has been a long string of serial rapes or killings nearby? What if there are no suspects? What if we slip into unfair, stereotypical thinking, as we start to notice more and more people in our neighborhood who are unlike you or me?

While my last example is *not* a fair, rational reason to be fearful, there are plenty of well-founded reasons to be afraid and, as mentioned in the previous section, sometimes fear is constructive as it helps us identify prudent changes to make. For instance, maybe we should do more to increase our privacy and home security. Maybe we should think twice before going out alone, especially after dark. Maybe we should call the police and ask for their advice about what can be done in our specific circumstance.

Such mitigations should help assuage our fears, at least a little bit. But there are a couple more things to be done, and these are what provide us with real relief.

- We should seek level-headed guidance and tenderhearted comfort from our counterparts who are not known for their lectures, stern or otherwise (previous section)
- We should pour out our fears to God, allowing Him to convert them to peaceful contentment. We may not understand why events are playing out the way they are. We may not understand why some people are different from us. We may not understand why some people even seek to harm us. We may think it's unfair when we change our lifestyle because of such dangers. But we can rest assured that – come what may – we are in God's hands. Even if a so-called worst-case scenario actually does come to pass, we are comforted in knowing that we are His forever – no matter what.

What if you encounter evil in the world?

What is evil? Have we discussed it yet? Not specifically, but we visited its suburbs a few times, including in the previous section and especially in Chapter 1 where I describe antonyms (opposites) of love: neglect, indifference, selfishness, revulsion, manipulation, abuse, cruelty, malevolence, vindictiveness, and hate. A person carries out an evil deed when they put such sins into willful action with the intent to harm one or more people.

As with any sin, we sinners have no one else to blame but ourselves for choosing to carry out an evil deed. We certainly cannot blame God, and we can't even place very much onus on "the evil one" (Matthew 13:19 and elsewhere), a.k.a., Satan, the devil. Did the cheerleaders win the football game? … *Have I lost you? Let me explain immediately.* … Satan is surely cheering us on whenever we choose to sin in any way – and he's a big fan of evil deeds – but we are always making *our own* choice whenever we submit to his desire and to our own selfish, sinful, human nature. Whenever I hear anyone say, "The devil made me do it," my response is, "Hooey!" Sure, sometimes Satan disrupts the game himself – for example, runs across the field, inattentive to his pink miniskirt swirling in the breeze – but is that distraction to blame for your horse collar tackle of the other team's first-string quarterback, done in such a vicious fashion that the injury prevents him from returning to the game?

A common question is: *Why does omnipotent God allow evil deeds to be carried out? Sometimes the impact on us is truly terrible. Sometimes we're hurt very badly – sometimes permanently (with respect to this life). The damage is palpable: physical, emotional, psychological, or all of the above. Sometimes there's even death. Why does omnipotent God allow such things to happen?*

In light of Romans 11:33-34, I certainly am not going to claim that I can fully answer this question. But a part of the answer is that *we* chose the path that led to this. Don't you remember? … Think back. Think way back to the Garden of Eden. At The Fall, *we* chose to follow the lies of Satan (Genesis 3:1, 4-5) instead of following God's will (Genesis 3:3). *We* chose the way of sin instead of the way of obedience. *Our* awful choice is what led to our banishment from the Garden of Eden, "to work the ground" (Genesis 3:23) – the "cursed … ground" (Genesis 3:17). Ah, yes, now you remember! You've been trying to block that memory out, trying to blame the curse on everyone else, especially two people with the initials A and E. But not thinking about it doesn't make it go away. Deep down, you remember that we're all in the same boat. Deep down, you remember that we all have the same selfish, sinful, human nature, and when left to our own devices, we all submit to this nature – every time.

Another part of the answer is that while God absolutely does not plot evil, He does allow some measure to be carried out by us because this is one way – not the only way… – for us to see God's love clearly. What do I mean? The dichotomy that is established when evil is carried out – the dichotomy of evil and good – provides a clear distinction between Satan's ways and God's ways. When the atmosphere becomes murky with the fumes from Satan's putrefying excrement, that's exactly when we can expect to see brilliant hues on the horizon – yes, a spectacular tapestry (Chapter 1 – "Antonyms of love" section). When we're impacted by evil, we're being asked to bear tremendous hardship. For those of us who love God, bearing – with His sustaining power – such burdens is a clear way that we serve Him. We are part of His response to evil, for He responds with awesome contradictions, bringing blessings – brilliant, spectacular blessings – to people who heretofore were nearsighted, not able to see the distinction between Satan's ways and God's ways.

What if you are directly impacted by an evil deed?

If we're directly impacted by evil, we're being hurt not only by the perpetrator(s) of the evil deed but also by none other than Satan himself. One or more sinful humans willfully committed the act – to be sure – but, as I alluded to above, Satan is surely on the sidelines twirling his pom-poms and attempting cartwheels, and occasionally he even ventures onto the field. Why is Satan intent on cheering the perpetrator(s) along? Why is Satan intent on hurting us? With Satan, there's always only one reason for why he does anything. He doesn't have diversified goals; in fact, he has only one goal. Sure, he has a whole bag of tricks that he drags behind him as he lurches along: sometimes he lulls us into indifference, sometimes he causes us to doubt God's promises, sometimes he lures us into thinking that we know better than God, sometimes he tempts us to commit evil deeds ourselves, and sometimes – most relevant to this subsection – he causes us to question why God allowed someone else's evil deed to impact us. Despite his plethora of weapons, Satan is of one mind – he has one purpose – and that is to turn us away from God. When it comes to a situation where we've been impacted by evil, Satan wants us to turn away from God based on our erroneous conclusion that God doesn't care about us. Satan influences some of us to wonder: *If om-nipotent God cares about me, then why did He allow me to be impacted by evil?* This is very similar to the question posed in the third paragraph of this overall section, except the question in the current paragraph is more personal. Just before this subsection, I did start to get personal – I did give a reason why God some-times asks us to bear the burden of being impacted by evil. And what a glorious reason that is! Nevertheless, in light of Romans 11:33-34, I'm not going to claim that I've fully answered the question, neither with my partial answer above nor with the following partial answer: When we are impacted by evil, we have a clear demonstration that we (each of us, as individuals) are wholly dependent on God to save us from the consequences of sin, whether the sin be someone else's evil deed that hurts us in this life, or, more impactful in the big picture, a thought within our own heart that causes us to deserve eternal punishment in hell (Appendix G). In both scenarios, and everywhere in between, without God it is hopeless. We are wholly dependent on Him for deliverance.

Evil in the world presents us with a fence that is far too splintery for any of us to sit on (Romans 2:7-8). When we don't submit to the power of God to deliver us from the consequences of sin, we instead submit to the whims of "the ruler of this world" (John 12:31; 14:30; 16:11). Did you know that this is one of Satan's nicknames? Well, now you do. As dire as this name may sound, and as dire as submitting to his whims actually is, don't ever forget that God is stronger than Satan (1 John 4:4) – indeed, God places a limit on Satan's power and influence (Job 1:12). Jesus Himself told us two things that bring us comfort whenever we're hurt by Satan: "The ruler of this world is judged" (John 16:11), and "My [Jesus'] kingdom is not of this world" (John 18:36). So, if we're directly im-pacted by an evil deed, our response should not be to question God – to doubt that He cares for us. No, our response should be to wholly rely on our stronger God – our strongest God – our caring God (1 Peter 5:7). Only He provides us with the strength required to get through the ordeal itself, the shock of the imme-diate aftermath, the grief that we may have to bear, and whatever other terrible consequences there might be. And not only does He get us through all of this, but also He turns evil on its head by blessing us with the assurance that He will cause good to come from it. No matter how impossible this may seem to us in the wake of our being directly impacted by an evil deed, it's certain: "We know that for those who love God all things work together for good, for those who are called according to his purpose" (Romans 8:28). If God allows you to be impacted by evil, I understand that this is a great hardship, but in due time please be comforted in knowing that, if you love Him, you and/or others will experience firsthand His blessings as He turns the hardship into gracious wonders – for He is our omnipotent God.

What if you are never directly impacted by an evil deed?

If we're never directly impacted by an atrocity, does any of this "What if … ?" section apply to us? Yes, it all still applies to each of us! The title of this overall section is, "What if you encounter evil in the world?" As usual for the sections in this chapter, this includes an "if." However, I would argue that this particular "if" is ridiculous. Why? Because – unfortunately – we can easily see evidence of horrendous evil on any given day: simply check the news. However, when we're not directly impacted – but only see and/or hear news of a shooting, a terrorist attack, a murder, a rape, a hate crime, or similar atrocity – what's our usual reaction? For far too many of us, we're moderately disturbed for some time, but then our life returns to "normal" in fairly short order. But that's just the problem, isn't it? Why should our lives return to normal?! Have we become so desensitized that we can accept bumbling along from one tragedy to the next, giving each one hardly any more thought than we do a disappointing result on the sports page? Is the fact that we weren't directly impacted a good reason to do nothing? … *I'm waiting for your answer to this! Wake up!* … Let me ask it another way: Is the fact that we don't know the victim(s) good justification for us to pass "by on the other side" (Luke 10:31, 32)? … *Why do I only hear mumbling?* … Let us learn a lesson from our fearless friend in the story at the end of the previous chapter. Remember what she said? *And she didn't mumble when she said it!* … "It cannot be tolerated anymore! That's right! We cannot tolerate this anymore!" She was speaking in response to the targeting of a large group of civilians by Israeli armed forces or one Palestinian terrorist. Either way, it is terrorism. Either way, it is evil. Either way, it cannot be tolerated. And it's obvious that evil doesn't always target a group – sometimes it focuses in on an individual victim. Either way, it is evil and cannot be tolerated. And let us not forget that evil doesn't always result in death or physical injury – sometimes it gashes horrific wounds of lifelong emotional / psychological trauma. Either way, it is evil and cannot be tolerated.

What should our response be? Should it be: *God allows us to be impacted by evil from time to time, so who are we to do anything about it? Who are we to say that it cannot be tolerated? …* If that's your attitude, then I'm very disappointed.

- Have you so soon forgotten: "We know that for those who love God all things work together for good, for those who are called according to his purpose" (Romans 8:28)?
  - Don't you want to be a part of thwarting Satan's schemes? Don't you want to play a role in God's plan to bring blessings out of ruins?
- Have you so soon forgotten: Our God is "not a God who delights in wickedness" (Psalm 5:4)?
  - We should not tolerate anything that does not delight our God

Here's a better response: *God, You allow us to be impacted by evil from time to time – for reasons that we don't fully understand (Romans 11:33-34) – and we trust that You will make good come of it, for those who love You. In prayer, we come to You, asking what our role should be in such transformations. In faith and hope, we look forward to Your bounteous blessings and the healing they bring. In compassion, some of Your blessings are distributed through us as we help those impacted by evil – perhaps showing them God's love in a way they've never experienced before. In boldness, we work diligently toward inhibiting future evil acts, never tolerating what does not delight You. We understand that if in Your infinite wisdom You want to allow a particular incident to happen, then You will allow it, but far be it from us to conclude that we should stand idly by and in such a way enable it ourselves. We do our best to thwart evil schemes, as empowered by the Holy Spirit, and when they nevertheless occur we respond in love. We proclaim Your message: "Do not be overcome by evil, but overcome evil with good" (Romans 12:21).*

How is evil overcome with good? Please allow me to elaborate on ways that come to mind: Besides the obvious steps of punishing the perpetrator(s) of the evil deed to the full extent of the law, and in other ways loving them unconditionally; caring for the victims and their loved ones, and in other ways loving them unconditionally; and getting the undivided attention of the applicable leadership, making our voices heard, so change becomes the only option; let us also overcome evil through the power of prayer. If you do not already pray on a daily basis, you need to start doing so. Every day, I'd like you to supplement your prayers by spending at *least* five minutes praying about a specific occurrence of evil that you're aware of – whether that be within a stone's throw – (Don't submit to the temptation that this convenience provides) – or on the other side of the globe. When doing so, pray for *all* of the following who are still alive: the victim(s), their loved ones, rescue and relief workers, eyewitnesses, others who are struggling to process what has happened and why it happened, the perpetrator(s), and their loved ones. No, I was not trying to be sneaky by slipping the perpetrator(s) in toward the end of my list – although I did notice that a few of you were starting to doze off right about then. Yes, we do need to pray for the perpetrator(s). They are in desperate need of prayer! I want you to pray on their behalf. If you have a hard time doing this, may I suggest the following?

- *Heavenly Father, I'm very angry about what happened – and rightly so! Look at the irreversible (with respect to this life) damage that has occurred. Look at the lasting impact this will have on people's lives. But even in the face of all this, please help me to channel my anger such that it helps to bring about positive change – helps to identify a better way. In my anger, I'm sorely tempted to judge the perpetrator(s) myself, and to want more than justified punishment – to want revenge. Please help me not to give in to this temptation, but always to remember the alternate path that You want me to take: "Repay no one evil for evil … never avenge yourselves, but leave it to the wrath of God, for it is written, 'Vengeance is mine, I will repay, says the Lord'" (Romans 12:17, 19). Help me to be patient, and remember that You will judge rightly (Psalm 9:7-8). You are patient, and I do remember the reason for this: "With the Lord one day is as a thousand years, and a thousand years as one day. The Lord is not slow to fulfill his promise as some count slowness, but is patient toward you, not wishing that any should perish, but that all should reach repentance" (2 Peter 3:8-9). God, I do pray that the perpetrator(s) will be led to repent of their awful crime. … When I think of this tragedy, it makes my heart break. Why do such things happen? What led them to commit this awful crime? What led them to do this evil thing? I don't know the whole backstory, but I know who's behind this – who's partially responsible. Please release the perpetrator(s) from the grip of Satan. Please help the perpetrator(s) learn somehow – maybe by their punishment, maybe by finally looking deep inside themselves and finding remorse for how much pain they've caused, maybe by a surprising response of someone impacted by their evil deed – that what they did is wrong, that they need to change, and most importantly that they need to turn to Jesus (repent) and start a new life. Jesus, help me remember that You Yourself said: "Whoever comes to me I will never cast out" (John 6:37). Jesus, I pray that those who did this awful thing will turn to You, and instead of casting them out You will instead graft them back into Your olive tree (Romans 11:23). Again, Lord, I know that You will make good come of even this. Is there something I can do to help? Is there something You want me to do in addition to praying?*

"Do not be anxious about anything, but in everything by prayer and supplication with thanksgiving let your requests be made known to God. And the peace of God, which surpasses all understanding, will guard your hearts and your minds in Christ Jesus" (Philippians 4:6-7).

What if someone hates you?

When someone hates us, they're breaking the Fifth Commandment (Exodus 20:13; 1 John 3:15). So, we proceed as described in the "What if someone sins against you?" section, earlier in this chapter, all the while remembering what Jesus teaches in the Sermon on the Mount.

> You have heard that it was said, "You shall love your neighbor and hate your enemy." But I say to you, Love your enemies and pray for those who persecute you, so that you may be sons of your Father who is in heaven. For he makes his sun rise on the evil and on the good, and sends rain on the just and on the unjust. For if you love those who love you, what reward do you have? Do not even the tax collectors do the same? (Matthew 5:43-46)

Anyone who has the audacity to hate us is surely persecuting us, and Jesus says that we should pray for them. What should we pray? Should we pray that they be struck by a lightning bolt? ... No (Appendix K), we should pray that God will change their heart to be more open to receiving God's love, and in turn be more loving to others. We should also pray for patience. When I struggle with patience, it helps me to remember Psalm 37:7a – "Be still before the LORD and wait patiently for him." Why should we be patient when there are people who hate us, and we don't see evidence that their hearts are changing? We should be patient with each person in our life because God is patient with each of us, even when our hearts are slow to change (2 Peter 3:8-9).

What else should we pray about when someone hates us? … We should thank God for His love for us; we should thank Him for every loving person in our life; and I suggest adding the request to be blessed by experiencing tangible love to offset the audacious hate we've endured. Pray with confidence! Remember that Jesus said, "Therefore I tell you, whatever you ask in prayer, believe that you have received it, and it will be yours" (Mark 11:24).

And there's at least one more thing to pray about if we're being hated by a family member or someone we had considered a friend. We should pray for reconciliation, and simultaneously we should ask God what specifically we should do, with the Holy Spirit's guidance, to foster reconciliation. If it's our child, we should be especially patient and hopeful.

Importantly, if we're being hated by someone who's demonstrating the potential to do us physical and/or emotional harm, then we should pray for protection, and distance ourselves from them. Of course, we should not retaliate (Matthew 5:38-42; Appendix Ɔ) or otherwise treat them in an unloving way.

What if someone disappoints you?

Ah, this is a tough one for me! We all have those things that are especially challenging for us. I never want this book to come across as easy answers, or that I, being the author, can do all of this effortlessly. So, here I'll take the opportunity to admit to you that an area I especially struggle with is forgiving someone who disappoints me. While I generally find it relatively easy to forgive someone who wrongs me in a way that comes out of left field for me, the stars align on my anger whenever either of the following two differences from that general statement apply.

- The first is if it does *not* come out of left field for me. Consider a scenario where my counterpart and I share a background that relates specifically to their sin / offense. We've talked about the situation before. They know that I have strong feelings about it, and they said that they understand and will proceed in a certain fashion. When they don't proceed in this way, but rather willfully sin / offend, I'm sorely disappointed. This is a trigger for me. Why? Because I highly value reliability (Chapter 4) and not to follow through on something we talked about is a severe (at least I consider it severe) breach in reliability.

- o Do such experiences cause you to feel angry too? If so, I'm glad that you can relate – *(Please indulge me, as I finish this sentence with some comic relief. I need some…)* – although I assure you that in such situations you handle anger better than I do, with your anger being like one tiny ice crystal on the tippy top of my gigantic iceberg. *(I feel a little better… Thank you…)*

- My iceberg of anger turns into a whole *iceberg field* of anger if a second change is made to the general statement I wrote above, and am repeating here for clarity: *I generally find it relatively easy to forgive someone who wrongs me in a way that comes out of left field.* Changing one word of this infuriates me. Any guesses as to what this one word is? … It's a small word. … It's "me." That's right: If someone disappoints me by wronging *me*, then my iceberg of anger melts relatively quickly (long before the next ice age). If, on the other hand, someone disappoints me by wronging *a friend or loved one of mine*, then the stars *and planets* have aligned! *Two* triggers of mine have been pulled simultaneously! A full-blown ice age has begun!

  - o That is, I unleash a full-blown ice age of anger unless I stop acting self-ishly, and instead submit to the Holy Spirit. Below, I give a little commentary about how to love unconditionally in such a situation, but here I want to pause for a moment to remind you that none of us, myself included, can follow the advice in this book without submitting to the Holy Spirit. Several times when writing this book, I did a double-take and thought to myself: *How can I write this, when even I can't do this?* Every time I thought this, I was comforted by the Holy Spirit leading me to remind myself: *Yes, that's absolutely right, I – on my own – am utterly incapable of truly loving anyone by any means, even by the simplest advice in this book; the only way I can truly love is by submission to the Holy Spirit's guidance.*

~

I'm going to let you in on a little secret: I didn't write this book in sequence. *(Pick your jaw up off the floor!)* In some cases, I chose to write a particular section while I was experiencing highs or lows associated (often only loosely) with that section's topic. Not surprisingly, this made it easier for me to express certain things. A good example (and one where there was a tight association) is that I was very much feeling unconditionally loved when I wrote about what that feels like (Chapter 6 – "Basking in unconditional love given to us by another person" section). Certainly, I never could have written that without ever having experienced unconditional love. Just as certainly, I never could have included in that description certain subtle feelings, if I hadn't written that section while I was actually in the midst of those feelings. (To remind myself of those subtleties, I can't rely on my memory – I need to go back and reread that section myself.)

As I'm writing this paragraph, I'm not feeling that way. No, right now I'm angry. Right now, I happen to be roughly half way through writing this book. Just last night, I was even more angry than I am right now. As I tossed and turned in bed, I was anxiously fretting about something a friend had done – (In a nutshell: belittled someone and took a portion of the credit the other deserved, with some irreversible consequences) – and I literally didn't know what to do about my anger. One thought that entered my mind was the consideration that I should not continue to write this book. It seemed hypocritical for me to write a plethora of ostensible easy answers, and yet myself harbor resentment toward a friend.

What did I do about it? I prayed for God's guidance, and I waited.

~

What was God's answer? I feel that it came in three parts. The second and third points I list below certainly came from God. I feel that the first point did as well. But *(comic relief…)* if you're hating this book – if you wish it had never been finished – then I'm sure you disagree with me!

- Early the next morning, I felt compelled to start writing this "What if … ?" section. Here's another little secret: When I started to write this section, I did not know how to end it.

- I didn't need to wait very much longer to hear clearly an important part of God's answer to my prayer. Actually, the act of writing what I was feeling helped me see this point.* What was it? … Some of you already know. *You're catching on!* … I was sinning. Yes, it was sinful for me to harbor such disdain for my friend. Part of my sin was that I was hoarding my anger – letting it fester inside of me – instead of telling my friend how I felt. So, I did. There was nothing that could be done about what had happened, but instead of following my unfortunate tendency to avoid conflict (Chapter 4), I told them why what they did made me angry, including the parts about how we had talked about it before, and that it had a detrimental impact on someone else.

  *Note: Journaling (writing down our thoughts / feelings / emotions, usually in an informal manner) – and even creating audio messages for ourselves to listen to later ("audio-journaling") – are effective ways to process what is discouraging or upsetting us. For this reason, journaling is often an important part of a regimen to heal from depression or anxiety.

- But before I talked to my friend, I heard yet another, just as important, part of God's answer to my prayer. What was it? … Careful readers already know. … I should forgive my friend. Call off the ice age and forgive. *Why?* The answer is clear: Don't I disappoint God? Don't He and I share a background that relates specifically to my sins? Haven't He and I talked about the situations before? Don't I know that He has strong feelings – no, passionate demands – about these things? Haven't I said that I understand, and that I'll try to proceed in the right ways? Haven't I then immediately not proceeded in those ways, but rather willfully sinned again? As if that's not enough, haven't I sinned not only against Him but also against people He cares about? Haven't I done enough to pull God's triggers to unleash an ice age of wrath against me? Yes, I've done more than enough for Him to unleash countless ice ages, all of epic proportions and with no thaw in between them (cf. Matthew 18:21-35). But how does God respond? Am I cast out into subzero temperatures, lashed by a biting wind thick with sleet, blinded such that I can only listen as my frail boat – the makeshift contraption I built with my own feeble hands – is crushed by the relentless, encroaching ice? No, He disciplines (Hebrews 12:5-11; Revelation 3:19) me by reminding me of His demands, and then He immediately rights my boat – the seaworthy craft He prepared for me at the beginning of time (cf. Ephesians 1:4-5) – repairs the sails I damaged in my folly, places me back at the helm, provides an ample breeze behind me, and guides me to places I do not know yet eagerly pursue; by night, I am guided by stars that are not aligned but rather in their proper places; by day, I am guided by pleasant landmarks, as I bask in the warmth of the sun against my skin, and marvel at the beauty of the light shimmering off the surface of the sea.

~

I cannot forgive with that kind of effect – only God's forgiveness is that impactful. Indeed, it is infinitely more impactful than I tried to describe.

But I did forgive my friend. I did not unleash an ice age of any proportion on them. I did not crush their boat.

~

Anger is a natural emotion that we all experience, and it's not maladaptive when handled correctly. I'm not sure how great of an example I just gave, but it's an example where anger led me, with the Holy Spirit's guidance toward a proper application of my anger, to a conclusion I may not have otherwise reached. At least I did not tee off, which would have been a misuse of my anger. Neither did I bury it inside, avoiding conflict, which also would have been a misuse of my anger.

There were two things I did that were key: I prayed to God and I told my friend what I was upset about. Oh, that's right, there was a third thing that was key: I waited patiently for God's answer to my prayer before I talked to my friend; I took a timeout instead of marching on a beeline to a tee box, intent on unleashing my fury. Yes, a few nights ago I was seriously tempted to do this. I was even rehearsing my tee shot!

During my timeout, God drowned me in His forgiveness and steered me away from that rocky shoreline. I was guided toward calmer waters, and I forgave my friend. It's amazing how quickly an iceberg of anger melts in the warmth of forgiveness.

It's times like these you learn to live again
It's times like these you give and give again[4]

~

Anger can be a useful emotion, but it should be what I like to call a distant cousin emotion. What do I mean? Anger is an emotion that pays us a visit periodically – shouldn't be very often – and after a night or two we kick it off the couch. Our brief visitor has taught us something new – possibly even something profound that gets our journey of life back on the right course – but, for heaven's sake, give me my couch back!

~

It has been one week since I wrote what has come so far in this "What if … ?" section. *How am I doing?* you ask. Thanks for asking. I'm generally doing OK, but I did have one relapse. It's behind me now, but two nights ago, as I was driving home from work, I fell off the wagon. A part of me got to thinking… A part of me got to thinking again about what my friend did… Yes, anger paid me another visit. *(Back so soon!)* A part of me grabbed the helm and started to turn my boat a different direction. That part of me was successful at getting my full attention. I got to thinking about how calm I had been when I told my friend how what they did made me feel; I had used a putter, but now I wished I had used a driver. I remembered how they didn't seem very sorry – kind of defensive actually… I started to feel that I had let them off the hook… I started to feel that they should know how angry I had been! Or, more accurately, how angry I still am! I started to feel, "Eye for eye, and tooth for tooth" (Matthew 5:38), conveniently disregarding the rest of that chapter.

While telling my wife about these new feelings, I said, "I think I asked too much of myself" – referring to forgiving my friend without them being more demonstratively remorseful.

She said, "But you know that we are called to forgive in the same way that God forgives us. It's reasonable that you wanted to let your friend know that they disappointed you, but you've done that sufficiently already. You need to move on, for your own sake and for the sake of your friendship."

It's times like these you learn to love again
It's times like these time and time again[4]

I already told you (in the "What if someone sins against you?" section) that I'm struggling to pass Remedial Forgiveness 101. I'd surely fail this class without the Holy Spirit helping me. And one way He's helping me pass the course is He has provided for me a tutor who's a student in the honors class in advanced forgiveness. My wife is not only in the honors class, but she's acing it!

You can see that my tutor reminded me of the importance of balance in such a scenario. Some degree of chastisement for what my friend did is reasonable. *Why?* Because we want our counterpart to learn how to act differently in the future, not only with us but also with others in their life. But we also want our counterpart to learn about forgiveness. And what better way for them to learn about it than to receive it? Such balance is important so we don't burn bridges, and we keep the door open for reconciliation. Whether our friendship continues is largely up to our counterpart. If, in a case like I've described, they take our moderate chastisement to heart, don't get overly defensive in a long-term fashion, and they accept our forgiveness, then we can move on together. If, on the other hand, they feel bitter about the chastisement and don't understand what they're being forgiven for, then perhaps we're entering another chapter of our lives where we're not as close as we used to be. Sometimes we need to turn the page to the next chapter.

~

This book definitely is not filled with answers that are easy for any of us – on our own. Even the students with a full schedule of honors classes are continuously at the feet of the Holy Spirit, soaking it all in. Surely, there's no way any of us could do anything like what I describe above on our own.

On a dimly lit corner of our sinful nature is an alluring temptress, enticing us toward the vindictive satisfaction of slamming our heart's door in the face of anyone who disappoints us by wronging us or especially a friend or loved one of ours. In our past, we've spent countless nights with her – our eager harlot, who enthusiastically accommodates our lustful desire. Only the Holy Spirit's influence gives us the strength to roll up our window and drive home, denying our beguiling seductress our passionate affections. It is His strength that keeps our heart's door of forgiveness open.

For us – on our own – forgiving someone who disappoints us (rolling up our window and driving home) is impossible; but we do it – no, He does it through us – when we submit to the Holy Spirit. And He forgives through us with indescribable ease; it is, after all, His nature.

~

It has been six months since I wrote what has come so far in this "What if … ?" section. *How am I doing?* you ask. Thanks for asking. The Holy Spirit hasn't let me fall off the wagon. That distant cousin is not coming back. I've had some visits from a few other distant cousins, but my distant cousin from the part of town I've described above is so far over the horizon now that they have slipped off the edge of the earth (cf. Psalm 103:12).

> *I'm a new day rising*
> *I'm a brand new sky to hang the stars upon tonight*[4]

What if someone makes you get angry?

The title of this section is incorrect. No one *makes* us "get angry." Anger is a feeling, and our feelings are our own. And we are responsible for how we express our feelings. We may choose to respond to what someone says, doesn't say, does, or doesn't do by expressing anger, but they don't make us get angry.

Each of us – no one else – is responsible for our own actions at *all* times. When we feel angry about what someone says, doesn't say, does, or doesn't do, we shouldn't tee off and we shouldn't bury our anger inside ourselves, avoiding conflict. We should choose a middle ground. A moderate amount of conflict can be healthy and fruitful. Sometimes expressing anger to our counterpart is the appropriate choice to make; yes, expressing a moderate amount of anger can be healthy and fruitful. Moderate anger and conflict can help us learn better approaches going forward.

The preceding section addresses this from the perspective of interactions with a friend or loved one.

If, on the other hand, we become angry with someone who's not a friend or loved one – especially if they have not demonstrated that they are loving and trustworthy, and most especially if they are demonstrating the potential to do us physical and/or emotional harm – then we should be very cautious of entering into conflict. Conflict is healthy and fruitful when it involves loving counterparts; we may not seem particularly loving to one another in the midst of the conflict, but things don't get out of hand and our loving attitudes become clear again when we reach the resolution phase. Conflict has much less chance of being healthy and fruitful when either counterpart doesn't have a loving attitude toward the other. In such cases, I strongly advise a timeout period until both parties completely cool off, and in the meantime distance yourself from the individual, for your physical and emotional wellbeing. In your prayers, ask God how you should interact with your counterpart when you both have cooled off, and then patiently wait for His answer.

What if you have an argument?

For those of you who are disappointed that this book is not a conventional "how to" book, allow me to make it up to you now. I was tempted to title this section, "How to have an argument," but something about the wording of this doesn't seem to fit the theme of this particular chapter.

As amply discussed in the preceding two sections, sometimes we get angry, and sometimes this is appropriate. When we have justified anger, we should not let it fester inside but rather communicate our feelings to relevant counterpart(s). In the off-chance that they don't agree with our point of view immediately, it's reasonably likely that an argument will ensue in short order.

Arguments can also arise when other(s) have justified anger, and we are a relevant counterpart. In the off-chance that we agree with their point of view immediately, then we will find no reason to argue.

Arguments can also arise when anger is the furthest thing from both / all of our minds, and on our pleasant journey together we happen to stumble upon something that – as unimportant as it might be – causes us to agree that we should take a detour such that we can mutually explore our newfound disagreement in a more thorough manner.

How many of you like detours? … I'm not seeing any hands go up, and that's not surprising. But sometimes detours are exactly what we need. Whether there's something ahead that's as dire as a bridge out or as benign as a few trees that are due for a little trimming, sometimes we need to take a detour to reach our destination safely. Likewise, while few, if any, of us enjoy having an argument, consider that this can be an efficient way for both / all viewpoints to be presented, for all involved to learn a thing or two, and for a path forward to be established: with all of this occurring within indomitable, loving relationships.

So, how do we proceed on such an efficient detour? There are two phases.

The dispute phase
- We shouldn't only think about what we want to say, but we should also listen to our counterpart(s) and do our best to empathize – which during a dispute manifests itself as seeing their point(s) of view, even if we don't agree
- We shouldn't go overboard by doing any of the following
  o Being disrespectful
  o Dredging up irrelevant things from the past
  o Pushing buttons – poking sore spots
  o And otherwise being hurtful, emotionally or physically
- It's usually best and appropriate not to view the situation as black and white, with one point of view being completely right and the other(s) being completely wrong
  o An exception is if it's clear that a fellow believer has caused spiritual damage to or has otherwise hurt one or more people; if the situation is truly unambiguous, then this is a black-and-white issue that we are justified dealing with in accordance with Matthew 18:15-17
  o If, on the other hand, there's no decision that must be made, or action that must be taken, then it may be best to simply "agree to disagree," as they say, and not dwell on such differences
  o If a decision or action is needed and it's a gray-area issue, sometimes the best thing to do is reach a compromise, whether this compromise is fully manifested at this particular juncture – ("Let's choose pale gray") – or further down the road – ("We'll go with black this time, and white next time")

- If a decision / action is needed eventually, but it can wait a while, then after sufficient time for all points of view to be presented, let's take a timeout and agree to meet again later. It's amazing how different a situation can look when we take the time to cool our boilers.

The resolution phase
- When a decision / action is established, or when the dispute is otherwise "over," typically there are some lingering bad feelings between the participants. We should address these without undue delay.
  - For example, when there's a decision / action, and it's more or less in alignment with our preference – let's say that we wanted white, and the decision / action is very pale gray – then at all times we should be gracious to our counterpart(s) who wanted black. To this end, it may be appropriate to acknowledge that their point of view has merit and we can see that sometimes darker gray or even black would be best.
  - Sometimes bad feelings between the participants can be thoroughly addressed immediately as the dispute phase winds down. More commonly, however – especially if the dispute became heated – it's best to revisit the situation after there has been a sufficient cooling-off period. Whether this timeout is just a few minutes or hours or even days, at the end of it we should initiate what I like to refer to as an aftermath discussion.
    - The aftermath discussion is not a time to revisit the dispute or rub salt into any wounds. Rather, it's often appropriate for both / all parties to apologize for going too far in one way or another. As always, whenever someone apologizes to us, we should express our forgiveness.
    - While we should have been empathizing all along, this can be hard to do when we're in the heat of anger. So, the aftermath discussion is a great opportunity for us to be more demonstrative with our empathy toward our counterpart(s), with whom we may still disagree. This is good practice, as we seek to form habits that will guide our behavior the next time we find ourselves in a dispute phase.
  - If we were disputing with a close friend, it's especially important to have a meaningful aftermath discussion. Sometimes we can do this with essentially no time gap between the two phases – transitioning almost immediately from disputing to resolving – and a benefit of this is it allows

us to reconnect without time for wounds to fester. However, let's not push for premature closure if either of us is not ready. Sometimes we do need a period to internally process what just happened before we're ready to discuss resolution with our friend. During such a timeout, we should pray about how best to proceed. Once we're ready, let's not wait for our counterpart to be the one to initiate the aftermath discussion. Rather, let's reach out to them to say we want to talk about what happened, and we're wondering if they're also ready. Even if they thought they weren't ready, chances are that when they see us reaching out to them, they'll be ready immediately or in a relatively short time.

We don't need to be anxious about what we'll say to our friend during our aftermath discussion. It's straightforward.

- With rare exception (for example, if you happen to have lapsed into a brief state of perfection during the dispute phase), the first thing we say is that we're sorry for our role in what went wrong during the dispute

- If our counterpart apologizes for their role, we should express our forgiveness

- The next thing to talk about is what we'll do differently in the future, with respect to both not repeating the same dispute again, and not repeating the same mistakes in any other dispute that may arise between us

- The resolution phase between friends is not over until we reaffirm our love for one another. Again, let's be the initiator, affirming it first. As we do this, let's drive to the hoop, which in my vernacular means give a hug and use the L-word.

o If the close friend we were disputing with is our spouse, the aftermath discussion is critical. Everything in the preceding set of bullet points applies, with a special emphasis on reaffirming our love for one another.

- Disagreements are bound to come, especially in the closest interpersonal relationship of all – a marriage – and it's important that by the time the dust settles we both are reminded that we still love each other. Such mutual affirmation, especially in the wake of a difficult interaction, is liberating.

- Thus, it should come as no surprise that after a married couple has a meaningful aftermath discussion, they often find that they share mutual eagerness to embark on the welcome and prolonged detour that I like to call launching for the hoop from beyond the free throw line, which in my vernacular means make-up sex
- Is there anyone we're forgetting? There is if we have children and they're aware of our former dispute. It's important for them to know that we have resolved our conflict, and that we still love one another. They are watching closer than we think, and resolution after a dispute is an important lesson for them to learn. And while they aren't going to see the full highlight reel, let's make sure that they see us hug and use the L-word.

~

I'll close this section with a word of advice for those of you who are dating and considering becoming engaged. If at all possible, don't commit until you have a dispute with your boyfriend / girlfriend over a significant issue. It's important for both of you to see how the two of you interact during such a challenge. I'm not saying that you or your counterpart should be looking for perfection in this (or any other) area – and it goes without saying that you will not be launching for any hoops (Chapter 7 – "Should we have sex before marriage?" section) – but it's valuable to see tangible evidence that your special friend is well-suited to enter into an indomitable, loving relationship with you.

What if you feel ineffective giving unconditional love to someone?

What do I mean by "feel ineffective"? Do I mean the empty feeling we get when our love is not reciprocated? No, that's not what I'm talking about here. *(You have to wait until the next section for that!)* We can't make any specific person love us, and we shouldn't try. So, I'm *not* going to give advice here or elsewhere about how to have your love reciprocated by any particular individual in your life.

Disappointment related to unreciprocated love is only applicable when we desire to have a conditional love relationship. When we give unconditional love

– the focus of this section – let's always remember that we give such love without any thought to it being reciprocated. Yes, it's possible for unconditional love to be completely one-sided (Chapter 1).

Can one-sided unconditional love be ineffective? It depends on your definition of "effective." My definition of effective is that the other person is loved. Based on this definition, it's impossible for our unconditional love for another to be ineffective. They are loved, and that's that.

But if we sense or become aware that our expression of unconditional love makes our counterpart uncomfortable, or worse they don't appreciate our love, or still worse they don't believe that they are truly loved, then I understand that we can feel ineffective. Encouraging you not to be overwhelmed by this feeling – encouraging you not to give up – is what this section is about.

~

I just gave you my definition of effective one-sided unconditional love. How can I be so bold as to say that effectiveness is achieved merely by our loving? Don't we need to see a result, and better yet a result that makes us feel warm and fuzzy inside?

Let me draw an analogy to prayer. What makes prayer effective? My definition of effective prayer is that a believer prays. That's it. If we believe that Jesus is our Savior, then we pray for something – or better yet someone – and we know that it's effective. How do we know? We know because God hears our prayers (Psalm 66:17-20; 1 Peter 3:12; 1 John 5:14-15) and always answers in the very best way (Psalm 34:17; Matthew 6:6). Sometimes when we pray, we ask for something specific – we think we know what's best. Is our prayer effective only when God provides what we asked for, and on our timeline? Of course not! Only God knows what's best in the big picture, and He always answers our prayers with this in mind. Here's an interesting question, I think: Since God already knows what's best, then why do we pray? Here's my interesting answer: We pray because God wants us to communicate with Him to strengthen our connection, to thank Him for everything *(Yes, I said everything)*, to voice our specific requests to Him, to acknowledge our complete dependence on Him, to express our faith, to demonstrate our care for others by bringing them to God's throne, and to offer ourselves for tangible involvement in the answers to our prayers, if He so chooses to use us in this special way. When our prayers aren't answered in the way we were hoping, do we stop praying? You already know the answer to this.

When we give one-sided unconditional love to someone, it's like a prayer. We're praying – figuratively and it should also be literally – that our counterpart experiences the joy of receiving unconditional love. And what a joy this is! If we feel that such a prayer isn't being answered in the way we were hoping, do we stop loving? You already know the answer to this.

Here's another interesting question: Is it possible that our figurative and hopefully also literal prayer – that our counterpart experiences the joy of receiving unconditional love from us – will be answered with a resounding "*No*"? … I was a little tricky when asking this question. Careful readers have already noticed that this question has a couple extra words when compared to how I phrased this in the preceding paragraph. What words did I add? … *You're right!* I added "from us." Yes, it *is* possible that our one-sided unconditional love for our counterpart will *not* result in them experiencing the joy of receiving unconditional love *from us*. Before you slunk off depressed, let me also say that I'm not aware of any circumstance where our figurative and hopefully also literal prayer will not result in our counterpart experiencing some measure of more love in their life. They may not appreciate or even know that we're praying a special type of prayer for them, but eventually they will know more love. Are you doubtful? I challenge you to try to prove me wrong!

~

OK, so what should we do if we pray this special prayer – give one-sided unconditional love – but our counterpart doesn't seem to be positively impacted? I hope that I've already convinced you that we shouldn't give up. If I haven't yet convinced you, consider a case where the other person is our child. At times like these, of course we don't give up. We make an adjustment to try to love them with more impact. While I'm sorely tempted to write several bullet points with various intriguing scenarios, it's probably better for me to simply say that we should learn their preferences for how they would like to be loved.

What if our counterpart isn't in our family? My view is that we should never give up on anyone. We ask the Holy Spirit to help us love each person in our life as best we can, making adjustments as appropriate, of course remaining true to our personality and not slipping into the chasm of being overly accommodating to them (Chapter 7), which is not being loving to ourselves. As with so many things in life, here too we strive to keep a proper balance.

Keep in mind that someone who doesn't seem to appreciate our love may still be receiving some benefit from our loving them. Don't get discouraged. And don't obsess over it. There are plenty of people (indeed, everyone in our life) for us to bless with love, and each person will receive our love differently.

If we feel ineffective with a particular counterpart, we should ask God if there are others who are better suited than us to give impactful love to this person. By now you know that I'm not suggesting that we stop trying ourselves. What I am saying is that it's always a good idea to ask God to supply other people to join us in loving our counterpart. Yes, this is true even if our counterpart is our child. In such a situation, good co-lovers with us include other family members, teachers and classmates, youth group leaders and the youth themselves. Sometimes the most loving thing we can do for another is to give them some space to grow apart from us, at least for a time, all the while ensuring that they're receiving loving support from trustworthy people.

We all continue to change over the course of our lives. While our unconditional love for another specific individual may feel ineffective at times, that doesn't mean we stop loving them. With the Holy Spirit's guidance, we adapt to the changing landscape and we "pray without ceasing" (1 Thessalonians 5:17) that our counterpart experiences the joy of being loved unconditionally, if not by us then by others in their life, with the ultimate goal always being that they encounter more facets of God's love through such people. Praying and loving in this way is indeed most wonderfully effective, by any definition.

What if your love for someone is not reciprocated?

OK, *now* we get to talk about scenarios where we feel that singular pang that comes when our love is not reciprocated. Such scenarios are in the realm of (longed for) conditional love relationships. But don't forget that any healthy conditional love relationship should include some measure of unconditional love (Chapter 1). Yes, I just gave you a hint about how to respond when our love is not reciprocated. You already know the core of the answer, don't you? ... *You are getting this!*

Let me start by reminding you that we can't make any specific person love us, and we shouldn't try. None of my advice has anything to do with trying to have our love reciprocated by any specific individual. If you ever think I venture into that quicksand, repeat the following four words over and over until you forget what the words mean: *He's talking about fishing; he's talking about fishing; he's talking about fishing...* We've been traveling together long enough now that you've noticed my fondness for analogies. And here's another! This time, the subject under consideration is cultivating friendships. … When we get up before the sun and put our waders on, we are excited to go fishing, but do we know what specific, individual aquatic beast we're going to catch? Unless we're Captain Ahab in *Moby Dick*, obviously we do not. But does that deter us from fishing? When we drop our line into the lake, using the most attractive worm we have handy, we wait patiently for any top, middle, or bottom dweller to find this worm utterly irresistible. When we drop our net in the sea, using the silkiest net in our collection, we wait patiently for any school of natatorial creatures to take a field trip in our direction. What do we do when it's long past breakfast time and we haven't gotten a tug on our line or net? Do we give up? *No!* We try a different worm and we cast our net on the other side; sometimes such adjustments can make all the difference (cf. John 21:6). So, you see that while we don't try to catch any specific, individual denizen of the deep or shallow, it's often a good idea to make adjustments throughout the day.

In a similar way, while we can't make any specific individual love us, by adapting but all the while staying true to our personality, we won't catch every occupant of our pond but our net will be sufficiently full.

~

OK, where were we? Oh, yes, you feel that your love for someone is not being reciprocated. The first thing I'd like to ask you is: Is your love for this person truly not reciprocated, or does it only seem that way? Some people have difficulty expressing their love for others. If there's someone whom you would like to befriend, but they don't seem very interested, one possibility is that they have difficulty showing love to anyone. Now, we can't go around assuming that everyone who doesn't seem interested in being our friend is simply having a hard time expressing their love for us. I hate to break this to you, but some people *really are not* interested in being our friend! And the loving thing to do in those situations is not to push it, but instead give them the space they want. More on this in the following paragraphs. But here I'd like to say a few words about how to distinguish between those who aren't very interested in being our friend and those who aren't very able to express love. Yes, there really are people who so far in their lives have had great difficulty loving others, or at least conveying it. Maybe they have been abused (even to this day). Maybe they haven't received much love from others throughout their life. Maybe they struggle with post-traumatic stress disorder of abandonment. Whatever has happened in their past to cause them difficulty, it usually boils down to a general distrust of others and/or a feeling of low self-worth. To help you assess the situation, ask yourself the following questions:

- Do they not have a wide circle of diverse friends?
- Are they quiet / shy / antisocial?
- Are they not assertive or proactive?
- Are they extremely private about their personal life, even when asked about it?
- Are they not expressive with their feelings and emotions?

If the answer to most of these questions is "yes," then you may have found someone who simply has a hard time expressing love in general. Now – be honest – if you consider someone you've never met before and for whom the answer to most of my questions is "yes," would you have a strong desire to become their friend? Many of us would say, "Not particularly…" But I want to challenge you to think differently. Such a person – whom I'm going to label as having a flower personality – deep down inside is just as interesting and has just as much to offer as anyone else. I have several friends who fit this general description, and I love them dearly. Is my love reciprocated? Yes, it is, even though it's not always very obvious. In such situations, we simply need to be more sensitive to the signs, and be patient. There are few greater joys in life than the long, slow journey of getting close to someone who doesn't get close to others easily. Especially toward the beginning of such a journey, we may feel like our love isn't being reciprocated. We may be tempted to hold back our love, selfishly thinking that our continuing to show love is "not worth it." Boy, that sounds a lot like conditional love to me! While a friendship is indeed a type of conditional love, it should also include some measure of unconditional love, and sometimes we need to *begin* with this type of love in order to get a friendship started. I don't need to remind you that unconditional love includes loving even when it's not reciprocated. We shouldn't get stuck in feelings of bitterness or resentment, but rather continue loving in a respectful way that doesn't cause our counterpart to feel uncomfortable or burdened. At this stage – which may be the furthest we get in our journey of loving this person – we should be satisfied with the knowledge that we are loving them (previous section). If we're fortunate and patient, we may eventually know that they're experiencing love in an impactful way. If we're even more fortunate and impeccably patient, we may actually reach the point where we know that they genuinely appreciate our love for them. Sincere appreciation is an expression of love. If they do become our friend, they'll find even more ways to express their love later on down the road. Trust me.

OK, so what about people who make it clear that they currently are not interested in being our friend? My answer might surprise you! I advise that we proceed exactly as above and see how it goes! What do I mean? What I describe in the preceding paragraph is a journey that begins with our unconditional love for another person and hopefully reaches the stage of friendship. And I just reminded you that friendship is a type of conditional love. The specific condition being met in the preceding paragraph is that our love is reciprocated in the form of appreciation, which in turn causes us to feel loved. But when we started the journey, we didn't know that our love would ever be reciprocated. In my example, odds were good because we were loving a flower personality – that is, someone who is waiting for another to initiate. What I'm saying now is that even if our apparently disinterested counterpart doesn't have a flower personality, while the odds may be lower we should still try. Yes, we should love them anyway, in an unconditional fashion. How do we express our love in such a scenario? Well, for one thing, we should love in a way that doesn't cause the other to feel uncomfortable, always giving them adequate space. And for another thing, we should pray for them. We should always give love by praying. Prayer is always effective, even when all else seems to fail. What should we pray for? In my view, it's usually best not to emphasize *our* wants in the situation – for example, our desire to be loved by our counterpart. (Refraining from such an emphasis is in line with the concept that we can't make any specific person love us, and we shouldn't try.) It's always appropriate to pray that *they* feel loved – by God, by themselves, and by others in their life. If they feel loved, their love for others (although not necessarily us (Chapter 6)) will eventually blossom. Trust me.

~

In all of this, I implore you not to slip into shadowy thoughts, fretting over whether your potential friend loves you or not. To love us, or to love us not, is of course our counterpart's choice to make; we need to respect that, and we should never let an apparent lack of love from anyone negatively impact our regard for ourselves. Sometimes this is not easy – believe me, I know.

- When I have such doubts about someone relatively new in my life, I find it helpful to say to myself: *I'm not really sure if this person loves me or not. I respect their choice, whatever it is. I also understand that it's usually not so black and white. My counterpart's rose petals may be a stunning shade of gray. I'll keep praying for them, asking God to bless them. And I thank God that He loves me just the way He made me, and that He has provided me with family and friends who also love me this way. I know that I'm inherently valuable, regardless of what some may think.*
- When I have such doubts about someone I've had a friendship with, I find it helpful to pray: *God, I'm not really sure if my (former) friend loves me anymore, and that makes me sad. Please help me identify appropriate ways to try to reconnect with them – all the while remaining true to my authentic self – and to respect their wishes, even if they choose not to be as close to me as they used to be. Come what may, help me to never stop loving them unconditionally. Thank You for loving the authentic me, and thank You for providing me with family and friends who also keep loving me this way. Amen.*

Be true to your authentic self, love yourself that way, thank God for making you no other way, and thank Him for all the loving relationships you do have. Your garden is sufficiently full, even in the extreme case that He's the only rose blooming there. When we're unsure about any other rosebush, the last thing we want to do is pluck rose petals one after another. Roses – including the marvelous gray ones – are healthier and prettier with their petals left on.

~

I'll wind this section down with a few words about circumstances where the form of love that is not reciprocated is sexual attraction within a friendship. In contrast to the next two sections, here I'm referring to a scenario where neither counterpart is married.

It's not uncommon for a platonic friendship to evolve such that one counterpart finds themselves sexually attracted to the other, but this feeling is not reciprocated. The moment this becomes evident, the two of you are at a fork in the road and you need to decide which way to go: maintain the friendship or go your separate ways. The very first thing to do is have a timeout – time for both of you to think and pray about which way is appropriate in your specific circumstance. This timeout may not need to be very long, but don't end it until both of you know in your own heart which way you want to go.

- *Either* of you can resolve that the friendship will not be maintained, at least for the time being. If this is the decision that either of you makes, then the two of you are to start a longer timeout period. Such a breakup may never end, but on the other hand it's possible that the passage of time and the maturing of both parties will allow for the friendship to be reestablished.

- *Both* of you need to agree, if there will be an attempt to maintain the friendship. And, if so, both of you need to honor the new conditions. A friendship is by definition a type of conditional love, and in this case conditions that are appropriate are those related to maintaining a platonic relationship. Appropriate conditions for any platonic relationship include:
    - Physical affection is OK, provided that it's limited to simple hugs, touching shoulders, and similar common signs of affection between friends
    - No lascivious comments or behavior, even in jest
    - Both of you will always respect your counterpart's other friends, especially your counterpart's sexual partner
    - No periodic inquiry as to whether a sexual attraction has developed in the one who had no such feelings before the timeout; that one is to decide on their own terms if, when, and how they want to let their counterpart know of any such new feelings

I already warned you that conditional love relationships can get complicated. And feelings of sexual attraction give rise to elaborate complexities that range all the way from a couple scaling with great exertion the thin-aired heights of passion arising from mutual desire, to an individual slipping over the edge of the familiar precipice that I refer to as the pang of unrequited yearning.

What if your friend wants to have a sexual or emotional affair with you?

Short answer: *Run for the hills!*

Longer answer: Unrequited yearning is a natural part of life before marriage. When we get married, we should lose all familiarity with that precipice. In marriage, we have a climbing partner to whom we're attached with a dynamic climbing rope, and there's only room for two on the narrow ledge we're ascending. Yes, I'm talking about sex, but I'm also talking about emotional closeness, which is another essential part of a healthy marriage.

At the end of the previous section, I discuss a scenario where there is unrequited yearning of a sexual nature, and both counterparts are unmarried. This section is similar, except at least one counterpart is married and I'm including a second type of yearning that may be felt, and that is a desire for deep emotional closeness. When we go too far and at least one of us is married, our vocabulary needs to include the word "affair." I think we all know what a sexual affair is. An emotional affair is a situation where there's no physical intimacy (at least not yet…) but there's a high degree of emotional intimacy, so much so that it's similar to, if not surpassing, the emotional intimacy we have with our spouse. An emotional affair is often a precursor to a sexual affair. So, for several reasons, an emotional affair is already way beyond many lines we shouldn't cross. While it's healthy to share thoughts and feelings with each of our friends, we shouldn't be sharing things that would cause alarm if our spouse becomes aware of the specifics.

Regardless of which one of you is married, the one who is yearning for the other is not respecting the sanctity of marriage and, if the yearning includes sexual desire, is committing adultery in their heart (Matthew 5:27-28). Even if there isn't outright seduction being attempted, *neither* of you has any chance of getting a pass from me on this. The matter is settled: Once even a "simple yearning" for any type of affair comes to light, the coveting one must drop to their knees, weeping repentant tears, and the coveted one must run for the hills – I mean those gentle, rolling foothills down there, way below the clouds – leaving their counterpart far, far behind.

Yes, if anyone wants to have a sexual or emotional affair with you, the matter is settled. If this is someone you considered a friend, you need to stop the friendship immediately and with no ambiguity about it. Friendship requires trust – and how can you trust someone who doesn't respect marriage? The friendship is severed – yes, just like that – and you need to make that clear to your former friend. They disrespected and emotionally hurt you and the spouse(s), and the most loving thing you can do is distance yourself from your former friend for your emotional wellbeing and to show them that their behavior cannot be tolerated. If the friendship can ever be restored, it's only after a *very long* timeout period and there will have to be tangible evidence of real change in their life.

In the scenario that I just described, my advice to sever the friendship immediately may sound a bit harsh. But, no, it is *not* too harsh! *Not at all!* We loved – yes, and we still do love – our former friend. And when we love someone, sometimes we need to be firm with them. We always want the best for those we love. Because we love ourselves and our former friend, sometimes the best for both of us is to tell them in an unwavering manner that their behavior is wrong and cannot be tolerated. We still love them unconditionally, and in such cases this means that we offer to help them change; we strive to – at a minimum – offer forgiveness, and we aspire to truly forgive ("What if someone sins against you?" section, earlier in this chapter), neither of which means that the friendship is restored immediately; and we pray for them. But, importantly under the circumstances, all of this does *not* mean that we tolerate their behavior. That would be enabling, which is not at all loving.

What if you are married but sexually attracted to someone else in your life?

The first thing you need to do is initiate a timeout from this person, pray about the situation, ask God for forgiveness, and know that you are forgiven.

The next thing you need to do is ensure that your timeout will be prolonged, for your emotional wellbeing and for the sake of your marriage. If you can't completely stop all contact with this person (for example, you work together), then do everything you can to avoid physical and emotional closeness.

You must focus on someone else. Here's a clever idea: Pay more attention to your spouse!

All of this should be relatively straightforward if the person you're attracted to is not actively seeking you out. First, let me tell you what *not* to do. Absolutely do *not* tell them that you are attracted to them! I cannot emphasize this enough! If perchance they feel the same way about you (which could become more likely simply because of you sharing your feelings), then you've suddenly found yourself on the edge of the cliff of a sexual affair. *Back away!* If you need to talk to someone about your attraction, then talk to a close friend, a counselor, or a pastor. It's also a good idea to talk to your spouse about it. While obviously this is a difficult conversation for both of you, it's much easier than telling them that you had an affair. If your spouse has a good measure of unconditional love for you, their love won't be swayed by such falterings*. And when you see such love from your spouse, you'll find that others aren't so attractive after all.

> *Note: Some will say that it's OK for us to be sexually attracted to people other than our spouse, and that such thoughts are not "falterings," as I refer to them. If the other people aren't in our life, for example they are celebrities or someone we happen to see walking around, then I just might be able to agree with this to some extent – provided that we don't dwell on the feeling. But if the other people are in our life – even people we have no relationship with, but nevertheless see regularly – then I have to say that I cannot compromise on this! We all sin, and it's not uncommon for us to have such thoughts from time to time, but what I am saying is that we must not allow ourselves to dwell on these feelings, as this is an early step toward ensnarement in sexual fantasies, or worse an actual affair.
>
> If you struggle with intrusive thoughts, please see Appendix G – "Thought-action fusion."

If, on the other hand, the person you're attracted to *is* actively seeking you out, then you have a larger problem on your hands. Back away from the cliff as far as you can and muster up the fortitude to talk to someone (close friend, counselor, pastor, spouse) about the situation and that you're starting to feel uncomfortable. In short order, you have to cut off your connection to your seducer. Probably the best way is to tell them that you're happily married and consider it inappropriate to have a relationship of any kind with them. Avoid the temptation to compromise and "just be friends," as this is far afield from where you need to go. Any such relationship is not going to be a healthy friendship, and it would only stir your attraction which – let's face it – is not just going to fade away. Don't worry about hurting their feelings. They are hurting you and your spouse, and you need to be firm in your rejection of their indiscretion. You are on the brink of an affair unless one of you can draw a clear line. *Be the one!* In such a situation, the most loving thing you can do is avoid an affair at all costs, because an affair is as unloving as it gets…

What if your friend is of the opposite sex and is married?

Is it possible to have a healthy friendship with such a person? My last few pages may make it seem like this is impossible. Oh, no, it's not impossible – far from it! If we guard ourselves from the pitfalls that can occur, as I've amply described in the last few sections, we can enjoy beautiful and fulfilling friendships with members of the opposite sex – yes, even if they're married. *(Shocking, I know!)*

The first step is respect – respect for them, their spouse, and their marriage. A healthy friendship means we want the best for our friend. And the best includes a healthy marriage. If for whatever reason (for example, envy) we want anything less for our friend than a healthy marriage, then we find ourselves on a slippery slope and of course we're not being a good friend.

The next step is clarity in our intentions. In a shallow relationship, this isn't really relevant because there's unlikely to be a misunderstanding. But I'm talking about a true friendship where there is a degree of emotional intimacy, and in such cases our intentions could be misinterpreted. There are simple things that can be said that are in line with you wanting only a platonic relationship: "I'm happy that we're friends." "I love you like a brother / sister." "I'm glad that you and your wife / husband are finally able to take that trip you've been saving for!" "How is your wife / husband doing? You mentioned that they were stressed out last week." If such statements are proving to be too subtle, it's best to be more clear, for example, "I like spending time with you, and I appreciate our friendship. We're starting to get to know each other pretty well, so I want to be sure I'm not giving you the wrong impression. Please let me know if I ever make you uncomfortable, or if I start getting too personal." If nothing else, a discussion that starts like this should help both of you remember that while such a relationship can become close, there are boundaries. To demonstrate to your friend that you understand these boundaries, ideally they'll know that you also have other friends who are of the opposite sex and married, and that they all have found you trustworthy. And if you're married yourself, talk about your spouse often and always in a loving way (even if there's a need to report a problem in your marriage), and suggest that both spouses be included when planning activities.

It goes without saying that you should *not* start down the path of playful flirtations (no matter how innocent they might seem) or sharing of many private thoughts. Anything shared between the two of you should be OK for your spouses to find out about. If either of you wants to keep anything shared from their spouse, you may be teetering at the starting gate of an emotional affair – an icy, two-person bobsled run that can end in the ruins of a sexual affair.

Rather, treat your friend in a respectful, honorable, and loving way, thanking God for a unique relationship with a valuable person you are fortunate to know.

What if your partner is unfaithful to you?

Please be sure to read the "What if someone sins against you?" section, earlier in this chapter. Unfaithfulness is an especially difficult case because it's such a blatant breach of trust. The one you are currently most vulnerable to – your current sexual partner – has turned against you and hurt you very deeply by being physically intimate with another. This is hard to take! Only after a long time of communication about underlying causes is there a chance for reconciliation. It's very possible that the relationship needs to end. It should end, unless your partner makes it abundantly clear that they have become trustworthy and that they have learned the special importance of being faithful sexually.

While of course this applies most especially to a marriage, cheating on your boyfriend / girlfriend is obviously deeply hurtful to them. While God intends sexual intimacy to be reserved only for male-female marriage relationships (Genesis 2:24; 1 Corinthians 7:2; Exodus 22:16; Matthew 5:27-28; Hebrews

13:4), if you are nevertheless in a sexual relationship before marriage, you should treat your partner in a loving way. It's difficult to be more unloving than to cheat on our sexual partner. If you are in a sexual relationship before marriage and your partner cheats on you, then you should break up immediately unless both of you commit to professional counseling. This is serious. You shouldn't be sexually intimate with someone you're not considering marrying. And you shouldn't consider marrying someone who has cheated on you, unless they're sincerely sorry and willing to change immediately, in which case you should only consider working on restoring the relationship with them if this includes professional counseling. I cannot emphasize this enough. If you casually marry someone who has cheated on you, there is a high likelihood of similar troubles down the road.

~

In light of the seriousness of sexual unfaithfulness, I'd like to take a step back and encourage all of us whose sexual partner is faithful to make a point of telling them how much we appreciate their faithfulness. A faithful partner is a great blessing! Let's verbally thank them for this specifically. We shouldn't be silent on the subject, waiting until we have something to be angry about.

~

Before we leave this section, I'd like you to read the following story of a man whose wife drifted into an emotional affair and finally cheated on him. In contrast to the promiscuous husband in the "What if someone sins against you?" section, here we have a woman being sexually unfaithful one time. Does that make it OK? *No, it is not OK...* When we are tempted, let us remember not to fall into the trap of "just this once." For one thing, that's a slippery slope – "just once" turns into "just twice," and what's going to stop us? And for another thing, one time is of course deeply hurtful to our partner; it is a life-changing injury.

An important message in this story is that the narrator's wife drifted into an emotional affair because she was helping a friend and things got out of hand. This is a good reminder that while we are of course to help our friends – and this book has many ideas for how to do this – we need to refrain from becoming so enthusiastic in helping that we become *too* close. By too close, I mean approaching the level of closeness we have with our spouse.

   Finally, I feel compelled to say that this is not based on a true story. My wife is faithful. And so am I. While the narrator in this story is from one perspective not an adulterer, from the perspective of Matthew 5:27-28 he is *very much* so. Let us beware from allowing our mind to meander down such paths anywhere near as far as this – it's an icy descent, my friends.

   I'm not very outgoing. Nevertheless, I've never had trouble attracting the ladies. Even back in high school, they just kept coming from every direction. I happened to be captain of the football team, but that wasn't the half of it. Apparently, there's something about my eyes. Every girl – no exceptions – I've ever gone out with has commented on my eyes. And most of them added that I have a great smile. When I hear things like that, I get a little embarrassed. My usual response is to laugh, and I found that they seem to like that too…

   In high school, I did go on a lot of dates and it did end up being with quite a few different girls. Four years is a long time, after all… Most of them were courteous girls, but there were a few who wanted to do more than kiss and similar simple forms of physical affection. I always told them the same thing: "I don't want to be intimate with anyone I'm not considering marrying, and I'm too young to be thinking about marriage."

   I thank my mom for teaching me this.

   The girls I had to tell this to always looked at me like I was crazy, and things inevitably fizzled with them in short order.

   I didn't meet my eventual wife until our freshman year in college. There was definitely something different about her, and I had never felt this way about anyone else. She didn't need me to tell her my view on intimacy, but eventually I felt it was best to explain myself. We had gone out about five times, and I didn't want her to think that I wasn't attracted to her. When I told her, she didn't look at me like I was crazy. Actually, if anything, she seemed relieved.

When we finally felt ready to be intimate with each other, it was the first time for both of us. On several occasions, she has thanked me for waiting. She knew that I had plenty of chances, and it meant a lot to her that I waited for her. I thanked her for waiting too.

After college, I got a job in a physical therapy office. There's not much to tell about that, except there was a woman who worked there who – I'm not gonna lie – is beautiful. I don't use that word very often, but this woman is beautiful. I also consider my wife to be beautiful and I have never cheated on her, but when I was not with my wife I often had lewd thoughts about my coworker and committed adultery with her in my heart. And that was fueled by the fact that she obviously was attracted to me – a lot. And she wasn't shy about it. She was always so happy to see me, and as we got to know each other better she would make those same comments I had heard so many times – the eyes, the smile, the laugh – and she added more that I hadn't heard quite as often – the hair, the cheekbones, the Roman nose, and, when she really wanted to turn up the heat, effusive compliments about various specific attributes of my physique. Most of this didn't get to me very much, but what really tempted me was the way she would look at me. She has this look that I don't know how to describe other than a combination of playfulness and eagerness.

She was relentless. She knew I was married, but that didn't stop her from making suggestions that became less and less subtle. I was afraid that she could sense some of my feelings for her, and I tried to be careful never to give evidence that might cause her to suspect the extent of the truth. I remember how relieved I was when out of the blue she announced that she had eloped the past weekend. She was married! I figured that would end her advances on me. But how wrong I was. I think she got a kick out of tempting me even more after she was married. She knew that I was acquainted with her husband – Bob and I had been on the football team together in college – and she would drop little comments about their… marital relations… I found myself with a new feeling – burning envy. I have never been so jealous of a man in my life. She seemed to know this, and she kept giving me that same look and dropping hints that she was feeling limited with only one man. If I had been single, I just might have submitted to my desire. But I remembered my wife, and my promise to her. However, I am embarrassed to admit that when I was not with my wife, my thoughts turned to my coworker even more often than before – again and again committing adultery with her in my heart.

It was truly a blessing when I got a new job just over a year ago. It was a huge relief to get away from that treacherous woman!

My wife got a new job at about that same time. She really likes it there. She says everyone's so friendly, and they have lots of team-building opportunities: workshops, seminars, special camaraderie events, parties, picnics – you name it. I'm not sure if they actually get any work done, but I guess that's not my problem.

After about nine months there, she mentioned that they just had another fascinating seminar, and a group of them were so inspired by what they had learned that they were going on a weekend camping trip together in a few weeks. The highlight was going to be introductory level rock-climbing – something about honing their trusting skills. She asked if I wanted to come along. I tried to act not completely disinterested, and said, "Oh, uh, that sounds interesting honey, but, uh, thanks but no thanks. I've got a big meeting that following Monday morning, and I'm sure I'll need to spend some time over that weekend preparing."

She didn't seem disappointed that I declined.

That weekend came and went, without much fanfare. But in the days that followed, I noticed her spending a lot more time than usual texting on her cell phone, usually with a big smile on her face, and occasionally she would emit an exclamation of glee.

One evening, she was sitting on the couch texting, and I called down the stairs to her, "Hey, honey… I'm going to bed now… but actually… wouldn't you know it… I'm really not that tired."

I'm sure every couple has their unique ways of letting each other know when they're in the mood. I'm generally not a very direct person, and that type of playful talk is one of my ways. She didn't seem to have heard me, so I said, "It feels like there's something wrong with the mattress… seems kind of uneven… Why don't you come up and let me know what you think?"

Still nothing. I was running out of material, and getting a little annoyed, actually. And when she giggled again and resumed typing madly on her phone, I shouted down, "Hey! So, you don't have time for me but you have time to prattle with your friends about tonight's episode of *Real House-wives of Bobsville*?!"

I thought that would get her attention. It wasn't until another ten seconds of typing that she finally looked up at me, and said, "Oh, I'm sorry honey. I'm really tired. Can I take a rain check?"

"OK, I understand. … But that means you're coming up to sleep soon, right?"

After some more typing, she said without looking up, "Yeah, I'll be up soon."

I went to bed and was lying there wondering about her new hobby – what my reaction should be. … And she didn't come up. … And she didn't come up. … Finally, about an hour had passed, and I was really getting irritated. I walked down the stairs – a little surprised at myself for controlling my anger – but became even more agitated when I saw that she was still text-messaging. She was so focused on this that she didn't even notice me coming down. It wasn't until I was standing in front of her that she suddenly looked up – startled. She could tell that I was mad, and she preempted me by saying, "Oh, I'm sorry honey, it's just that I've got this friend at work who's going through a divorce. This is really hard on him, so I'm helping him process things."

In line with my nature, I avoided getting confrontational by making a quip: "Well, why don't you help him process the concept of getting a good night's sleep."

She gave me a little smile, and said, "Yeah, you're right honey. I'll let him know that we should call it a night."

I went back upstairs, thinking to myself – *This guy's getting a divorce, so my wife's too tired to come up and check the mattress…*

Then, the following Friday night something unusual happened. I had gone to bed early because I had an exhausting week. I woke up after midnight, and was surprised that my wife wasn't in bed. The house was dark, except there was some flickering light coming from downstairs. Was that the TV? I didn't hear much sound – just a little. I walked along the upstairs hallway and discovered that, yes, it was the TV. I thought my wife didn't know that our cable package included this type of programming. For a few moments, I watched too from the top of the stairs. I had seen this movie before, and it was getting to an especially enticing part: An exotic and voluptuous woman began to receive copious intimate attention, and she became more and more unabashedly vocal about how much she was relishing this. My wife was so focused that she didn't see me, even when I started to walk slowly down the stairs. I had never seen her watch anything like this before, and I must admit that I was more than a little turned on by her level of interest. When I got to the bottom of the stairs, she finally realized that I was there – and boy was she embarrassed! She kind of gathered herself together and sat on a corner of the couch with a blanket, looking very sheepish. Again in my nature, I tried to defuse the situation with some humor: "So, how many guys does she have? … Oh, my, well I can do better than the both of them put together!" I reached out to her, smiled, took her by the hand, turned off the TV, and we went upstairs.

The next morning, when I woke up I was surprised that she was out of bed. When I went downstairs, she was already on her cell phone, typing and giggling. I asked her, "What's so funny?"

"Oh, he says the funniest things."

I got a little irritated. "Him again? Can't you give that a rest? It's 8 o'clock Saturday morning, and you're already back at it. He's going to start thinking that you have a thing for him!"

That made her look up. She immediately got defensive and said, "Oh, come on, I'm just telling him some of my childhood experiences – like I told him my favorite memory. What's wrong with that?"

"I don't even know what your favorite memory is."

"Oh, you know, the time I walked up that hill with my mom."

"I have no idea what you're talking about. You've never told me that story, let alone tell me that's your favorite memory. I don't ever remember even talking about favorite memories."

At first, she seemed a little bashful. But after a few seconds the look on her face changed. We just looked at each other for a moment, and then she took a turn I wasn't expecting. She said – actually, she started yelling – "Maybe I would tell you things like that if you took the slightest interest! Whenever I tell you about my childhood, you just start whining about your hardnosed dad, and how tough you had it. Well, maybe it's time you stopped sniveling about him neglecting you, not loving you, not forgiving you, not listening to you, and whatever damn else you accuse him of, and act like a man! Real men talk to their wives about both of their childhoods, and both dads, and both moms, and both sets of dreams and aspirations and disappointments and failures. You never want to talk to me about things like that! You never want to talk about anything that has the slightest thing to do with feelings or emotions. You won't even say 'I love you'! When's the last time you told me that you love me?"

I was about to say something, but she cut me off. "Mumbling 'Love you too' doesn't cut it, buddy!"

She stormed out of the room, and that was my cue to go outside to walk around the block a few times. I do that sometimes when things get heated. It helps me calm down and put things in perspective. Looking back on that day, I wish I had tried to reconcile with my wife when I came back inside. I was feeling better, but I guess I kind of forgot about her feelings and how upset she was. I never have liked confrontations. When I came inside, my wife was sitting on the couch, and she looked up at me. I couldn't really tell if she was still mad or not. I just mumbled something like, "I'm sorry that I don't express myself more and talk to you about things." That seemed to make her feel a little bit better. She was still looking at me, but I just went into the kitchen and asked her if she wanted me to make us something for breakfast.

Later that day, she apologized to me for yelling and saying certain things. She told me that she knows I love her, and she added with a wry smile, "I love you too." We both chuckled at that, and we hugged.

But in the coming days the texting and giggling continued. One time – I didn't even have to ask who it was – I said, "Doesn't he have any other friends?"

"Oh, honey, you know that he's going through a tough time. A lot of his friends are friends with his wife too, so it's kind of awkward right now for all of them. Isn't it great that I don't know his wife?"

I didn't say anything to that, but thought to myself – *Yeah, just great...*

Then she added, "Oh, and guess what? Perfect timing! At work, you know how we've been having those all-day, team-building workshops once a quarter? The next one is next week – *How time flies!* – and guess what the topic is? ... Oh, you'll never guess. This is perfect for my friend! It's ... I just can't believe it. Listen to this! ... 'Making yourself vulnerable to strengthen bonds.' ... Oh, I'm really looking forward to it! This is just what he needs!"

Again, I didn't say anything, but I thought to myself – *I've met enough divorced men to know what kind of bonds they want to form... I think what this guy needs is a cold shower...*

Then, a couple weeks later, came a day that I will never forget. I came home from work early because I wasn't feeling well. When I came in the front door, I thought that I heard something upstairs. Was it the shower? No, it wasn't the shower. Was it the TV? No, it wasn't the TV. I softly shut the front door, and listened more carefully. But by then it seemed to have stopped. I quietly walked up the stairs; I could hear my wife say something, but I couldn't make out what it was. Then, as I walked along the upstairs hallway, there was utter silence. I thought it was unusual that our bedroom door was closed. When I reached it, I stared at the doorknob for a moment, and a feeling of dread enveloped me. Finally, I turned the knob, slowly opened the door, and ... there they were... They weren't doing anything anymore, but there they were in bed – *our bed!* My wife had pulled the sheets up, but I could see her face looking at me. I have never seen that look before. She looked scared. I felt numb, and I hardly remember walking down the stairs. I think my wife called out weakly to me, but I'm not really sure. I walked out the front door, got back in my car, and drove off. I didn't know where I was going. All I wanted to do was drive away.

Not long into this, my cell phone started ringing, but there was no way I was going to answer it. Every time a call finally timed out, after a few seconds the ringing would start again. I finally caught a red light, and shut my ringer off.

Eventually, I decided I should check into a hotel, so I pulled into the next one I happened to see. While waiting to check in, I habitually looked at my cell phone. There were 16 new text messages – no, now 17. My wife kept writing about how terrible she felt about what happened, how sorry she was, that she had never done anything like that before and never will again, that she really wanted to talk to me, and she wanted to know where I was. … I ignored them all.

That first night, I ate nothing and slept little. I kept ruminating: *How many times had she been with him? When was the first time? Have there been other men? Sure, she texted me that she had never done anything like that before – but was she lying?*

I called in sick to work every morning for the rest of the week. After a couple days, I finally ate a few things from the vending machine. Then it occurred to me to buy a few shirts, simple toiletries – things like that.

When Saturday morning came, I decided to take a walk on the beach. I thought that might help me clear my mind, and even get me to start thinking about what happens next. I wasn't making much progress, and then I saw some women playing beach volleyball. That did grab my attention. I decided to walk in that direction, and I was doing my best to look at them just enough to get the gist of it without obviously leering. I was so intent on maintaining this balance that I didn't even see her until she was five feet in front of me. It was the woman from the physical therapy office. She was smiling and telling me how happy she was to see me again. I was just kind of standing there. Maybe I managed to say something but all I remember is – *wow*… I had never seen her with so little on. *Wow*… I was a little stunned. And I was afraid that she knew what I was thinking because she gave me that look again. It had been over a year since I had seen her, but I didn't forget that look. And now I've seen something else that I will not easily forget! I was just kind of looking dumbfounded, and – yes, she definitely knew what I was thinking – she went to another level and gave me a hug (she had never done that before), lifted one of her feet back, and exclaimed, "Oh, it's so nice to see you!"

When her foot dropped back down into the sand, I figured our hug was drawing to a close. But she had other plans. She drew me a little closer and whispered, "I've missed you." … Time stood still for a moment. I became powerless in her spell. I allowed my thoughts to carry me away, so I could savor this brief respite. She was wearing only a bikini. When our hug began, I had felt awkward about that. Now, I found it incredibly alluring. Her skin felt like satin, and this contrasted wonderfully with some grains of sand that were caught in the small of her back… She looked up at me, and smiled. But this was a look I had never seen before from her – she simply looked contented. She closed her eyes. Her thick, wavy hair was wet, and smelled strongly of seawater… I closed my eyes too, and heard only the waves… … This ethereal diversion took maybe 10 to 15 seconds – like a dream, so much was experienced in such a short time. She woke me from my blissful trance – abruptly ending our embrace as she asked in a matter-of-fact way, "So, you're not still married, are you?"

I just bumbled, "Uh, yeah…"

"I dumped Bob."

I confess that my mind started to go somewhere when she said that… But then she continued, "I decided that I liked one of his friends better, so I got a divorce and married him instead! We just got back from our honeymoon. I've always wondered what Jamaica is like. We were there three weeks, and I still don't know!" She laughed, and gave me that familiar look again.

"Oh, um, I guess congratulations. Um…, so I guess it'll be hard to go back to work next week?"

"Oh, no, I haven't worked since the divorce. My new husband's a pilot. So, we either just hang out at his place – oh, I guess I can finally start calling it our place now – or I fly off with him to who knows where. But this time I didn't go with him. I knew I'd be tired out from the honeymoon, so I told him that on his first stint afterwards he'll have to be all alone for five whole nights. Well, this way he can recharge… So, poor little me is all by her lonesome while he's meandering all over the globe. My days are pretty packed, though. Let's see… Oh, yes, especially today… Here's what's on the schedule for today: go to the beach, go home and take a shower, lie by the pool, 'forget' to take a towel when answering the door when the groceries are delivered, watch the delivery boy do the same balancing act you were just doing with those volleyball players… I saw that…, lie by the pool and fantasize about the delivery boy, and – I can't keep putting this off – unpack from the trip. But that shouldn't take long. How long does it take to unpack one small, ultralight duffle bag? (She gave me that familiar look again… She was loving this…) Oh, and you'll like this. We've got an awesome hot tub that overlooks the city – great view, especially at night. Why don't you come over and check it out? You and I have so much to catch up on! I've missed you so much! Pretty please?"

The whole time she was talking I was just kind of in a haze. When I realized she had stopped, I stammered, "Uh… well… it was nice seeing you again, but I really have to go," and I just started walking away.

"Aww, you do? What a bummer! At least give me a call. My phone number hasn't changed!"

I didn't say anything. I just looked back one last time and nodded, and then I turned away and walked off in a fog.

I went back to my room and committed adultery with her in my heart, my vivid memories assisted by the smell of seawater lingering in my nostrils, and the tingling from the sand between my curling toes. … When I was finished, my memories returned to the last time I was home: a faint noise followed by silence, a closed door, bed sheets, the look on my wife's face.

...

It's not surprising that when the pain becomes unbearable, we are most open to change. When the tide is the lowest, it becomes easier to make progress along the shoreline of life.

...

I spent the rest of that day pouring my heart out to God. I had not talked to God since my awful discovery. Now, I could think of nothing else but praying. As I prayed – well, I don't know if you would really consider it praying – I had never prayed like that before – it didn't take long for me to realize that I had to contact my wife. If nothing else, I knew I should at least tell her that I'm OK and that we need to figure out what happens next. When thinking about how best to contact her and exactly what I was going to say, it also occurred to me that at some point I was going to need to decide whether I forgive her. I already knew that she said she was sorry, and she certainly seemed sincere about that. I even remembered that we are to forgive people who tell us they're sorry. ... But how could I possibly forgive her for that?!

Even though I was nowhere near ready to forgive her, I knew that I needed to contact her. I still could not face seeing her or even talking to her. So, I texted her. I wrote that I'm OK and that I might be ready to talk to her soon. I also asked her if she wanted to go to marriage counseling. She immediately texted me back to say that she was relieved to hear from me, was so sorry about what she had done, had immediately cut off all contact with him, had never done anything like that before, will never make such a mistake again, and wanted to talk to me and go to marriage counseling. I wrote, "OK, and maybe I'll be ready to talk tomorrow."

The next morning, the first thing I thought of when I woke up was that I had to call my wife. It suddenly struck me how long it had been since we had talked, and I felt bad about that. I didn't want to call her out of the blue. So, I texted her that I was ready to talk, and asked her to call me when she was ready. Immediately, she called me. It was all happening so fast. I looked at my phone as it was ringing. I had been rehearsing, but suddenly I didn't know what to say. I hesitated, and the only thing that made me answer was that I didn't want it to timeout. All I said was "Hi," and my wife just started crying. She couldn't say anything. Finally, I said that I think the best thing for us is to go to couples therapy. I said that I remembered Pastor had mentioned there is a counseling group that is Christian, and that I would prefer to go to a place like that. I added that I was not ready to come home yet, and that I was going to continue staying here. She asked me where that was, and it dawned on me that I hadn't even told her where I was. Again in my nature, I tried to lighten the mood a little bit by making a slight chuckle as I said, "Oh, yeah, I guess I should tell you that! I forgot you didn't know."

She didn't really laugh, but she did sniff her nose as she said she was ready to write it down.

After that, I didn't know what to say. The silence was becoming a little uncomfortable. I was about to say that I'd make an appointment, when she asked in a quiet voice if I could ever forgive her. All I said was: "I'm not sure."

She was quiet again – I think she was crying a bit – and she finally said quietly and with faltering speech, "I'm sorry for what I did, I promise never to do anything like that again, and I hope you can find it in your heart to forgive me."

I didn't know what to say to that, so I just said that we should go to counseling and talk about it there. I said I would call to make an appointment, and let her know when to meet me and where to go. I said I'd text her the details. She said "OK," and then we both said "Goodbye."

Our first session was a bit awkward. Before it even started, I was running a little late and when I walked into the lobby – there she was. When I saw her face, my mind immediately went back to the last time I had seen her… She still looked a little scared… She got up and started walking toward me like she wanted to hug me. I mumbled "Hi," and walked quickly over to the front desk to tell them that I was there. I tried to make it look like I was concerned about getting checked in – but I could tell that my wife was sad by how I averted her. I just wasn't ready to hug her. I couldn't do it.

I was worried about how long we were going to have to sit in the lobby, waiting to go in. What was I going to say to her? I sat down a couple chairs away, looked around, and said something about the place being kind of hard to find, the traffic being worse than I thought it would be – dumb stuff like that. I didn't have much left, and mercifully our therapist came out to ask us to come inside.

I thought we were going to go straight to the punchline, but our therapist had different plans. She opened in prayer, and asked God to bless our marriage. She said that by the end of the session she, of course, wanted to hear our main reasons for coming in for couples therapy, but she wanted to get some background information first. She had all kinds of questions about our childhood, our parents, how we met, our faith life, etc. When I was telling about my dad, I couldn't help but start explaining that I often felt unloved by him. As I was getting into that, I looked at my wife, expecting to see a little glower of disapproval, but she didn't look that way at all. She was listening attentively, and even added a few things that she remembered from our past conversations. Things were actually going along pretty smoothly, but when the therapist asked about our sex life, she picked up on a change in our demeanor. We both clammed up and got kind of stiff. She immediately took notice and diverted the conversation a little bit. She said to me, "I notice that you sat in the chair, not on the couch next to your wife. Do you have difficulty with affection and closeness?"

I stammered, "I'm not the best at talking about feelings and emotions, as my wife knows all too well, but I usually don't have difficulty showing affection. But something happened…" I stopped, because I didn't know how to finish this.

Without hesitation, my wife said, "I need to tell what happened. I need to tell the real reason why we came in today. … It's very hard for me to talk about. So, I wrote it out, and I'll try to read it."

She read: "I probably can't get through this without crying, so please bear with me."

Our therapist interjected, "That's fine. Take all the time you need."

My wife continued, "I'm ashamed about what I've done. So, it's difficult for me to talk about it, but I have to. It started when an acquaintance at work started divorce proceedings several months ago. I felt bad for him, so I started talking to him more than before. We seemed to get along pretty well, so we became friends. In my enthusiasm to help my new friend, I started opening up and telling him personal things about myself. I wanted him to be comfortable opening up to me. He was very upset about his failing marriage, and he needed someone to talk to. I can see now that I went too far. I was trying to be a good friend, but we made ourselves too vulnerable to one another. He didn't try to come on to me, but we had become so emotionally close that, in hindsight, I guess it seemed – [She paused, and then her voice broke a little] – natural to go further… I made a big mistake by inviting him home for lunch one day. There was a picnic at work that we decided to skip. I cooked him a nice meal, and we were talking about the books we had read when we were in school, and which ones were our favorites, and why. Sometimes we were laughing, and one time I cried. I saw his eyes tear up a bit too. I liked the way it felt to talk so openly with someone. I think he liked it too. We were sitting on the couch together. … Our hands touched – I think accidentally. I don't want to say any more about that, except the next thing I knew we had gone upstairs. My husband came home from work early and found us. … … He has been staying in a hotel ever since, and we agreed that we had to come here."

She was still reading, but she turned to me now and said, "I'm so ashamed about what I've done. I'm so sorry that I hurt you. I hope that over time I can regain your trust. And I hope that you can find it in your heart to forgive me."

She had made it to this point without crying, but now she broke down in tears.

I didn't know what to say. Our therapist thanked my wife for sharing that difficult account, and told us that she was happy we were willing to come in to talk about it. She promised that she would do her best to help us. She then laid her hands on both of us – which was difficult for her because we were so far apart – and prayed for us, as individuals and as a couple.

It was hard for me to do this, but as we were getting ready to leave I did hug my wife. And I told her that I would be praying.

The next few sessions went well. At each one, I made a point to hug my wife in the lobby and then again at the end of our session.

At the session before today's, our therapist started to get into the concept of forgiveness, and how hard it can be to forgive when we are hurt deeply. I shared a little bit more about my dad. My wife cried when I described how I had never heard him say that he was sorry for anything, and what's more the only time I heard him talk about forgiveness was when he was ridiculing someone else for giving it. It felt good to let that out. Some of that I had told my wife before, but not to such depth. Then I moved on to a topic that I thought I would never discuss with anyone. I was recalling memories of my dad, and I suddenly found myself telling about his box of porn magazines. I discovered it one day when I was looking for a pair of pruning shears near his workbench in the garage. I was amazed at the extent of this cache. I immediately committed to memory the positions of this special box and the few things that had been lying on top of it. Over time, I also memorized the order that the magazines were stacked within the box, taking note of changes that would occur periodically. I formed the habit of hiding one of the magazines in my backpack, taking it into my bedroom, and then carefully putting the magazine back in its place when I was finished. I did this several times per week until I moved away for college. I told my wife and our therapist all of this and about the time my dad came into the garage while I was deciding which magazine to put into my backpack that day. I described how ashamed I felt when he caught me, especially when he called me perverted, and told me that I'm a disgusting boy for looking at magazines like that. During the session, I snickered a bit at my dad's apparent hypocrisy. I added that it didn't take me long to find where my dad moved the box – the back of the coat closet by the front door. Then, against my nature, I became a little serious, turned toward my wife, and said, "I had my little secret, but my dad found out. Ever since,

I've tried very hard not to let anyone know or even suspect the truth – that I still often think about being with other women that way. For a long time, I've felt a deep-rooted guilt about this, and I'm tired of hiding. I'm guessing that I've been escaping into fantasy as a way to try to cope with my fear of emotional closeness. I'm hoping it will help me to tell you and to let you know that I'm sorry." My wife had been quiet for a long time, and she still didn't say anything when I was done talking. She was looking down toward the ground, and just seemed sad. I started to wonder why I had revealed so much, and furthermore how she could feel justified judging me. But then she surprised me by slowly moving to the front of the couch cushion, leaning forward, and reaching out her hand to hold mine. We sat like that for what must have been at least a minute. We were almost out of time in the session, so our therapist broke the silence with a closing prayer.

That was a good session, but today's was the best. Last night I was anxious because I had been thinking a lot about the decision I needed to make. I was starting to feel that I'd like to do it. But another part of me was still wondering if I really should. Wouldn't that be like letting her get away with it? I mean, she hurt me deeply – I don't think I'll ever be the same – and it was hard to imagine being intimate with her again without remembering what she had done. I had difficulty sleeping, and that part of me that didn't want to take this step was making some very good arguments. I wanted to shut down the debates so I could get some sleep. So, I prayed about it for a while, and I guess in the middle of that – *Sorry, God…* – I finally dozed off. When I woke up the next morning, the first thing I thought was that I want to do it. It suddenly struck me how long it had been since my wife had told me she's sorry, and I felt bad about the delay.

At the beginning of the session, as usual our therapist asked us where we'd like to start. My wife began to say something, but I cut her off and said, "I want to go first."

My wife quietly said, "OK," and looked down toward the ground.

I also looked down and said, "I have decided that I" … I hesitated a bit, and got a little choked up. "I have decided that" … I looked at my wife and noticed that she seemed a little nervous. "I have decided that I will …

… forgive you if you promise that you won't ever again get as close to someone else as you are to me."

I wasn't half way through that when my wife looked at me and smiled, her eyes glittering. When I finished, she started crying, but she was still smiling at me.

Consistent with my nature, I immediately tried to attenuate the emotions by adding something that I thought might be a little humorous: "I would have added 'and if you're sorry for what you did,' but I already know that you are."

That made my wife cry even harder. For a moment, she dropped her face into her hands and was shaking a little bit, but then she looked up at me again. Suddenly I realized that I was still in my usual chair, and my wife was still alone on the couch. So, I went to sit beside her; I wrapped my arms around her, kissed her on the forehead, and said, "I … I love you."

It's not easy to forgive someone who has betrayed our trust by hurting us deeply, but when the time comes that there is a mutual longing to repair the frayed bond, the natural thing to do is fall back in love.

What if your friend is not a Christian?

If you have such a friend, give thanks to God for handing you – yes, on a silver platter – an opportunity to witness! Who is a better witness than a friend? You have a golden opportunity because you've earned your friend's trust and respect; your friend listens to you, and values your input. God wants you to tell your friend about Jesus' love for them.

Your job, with the guidance of the Holy Spirit, is simply to tell them this message – ideally multiple times and in various ways – and continue to be a good friend to them regardless of their response, or apparent lack thereof. It's not your responsibility to change your friend into a believer. That's the Holy Spirit's job. You are to plant a seed (1 Corinthians 3:5-9). Don't beat yourself up if your friend doesn't seem open to your message. Be patient. And even if they seem unresponsive, that doesn't mean there's no change in their heart. My ice plant looks bland for many months, but blossoms gloriously in the summer.

If your friend is of another faith, look for commonalities between their faith and Christianity. This usually makes it easier to initiate a conversation about religion. For example, several religions lend themselves to easy agreement that God created the world, including each of us. And I'd take another step and add to the conversation that God has a loving nature – that God loves us. Your friend may have a somewhat different view about this, but that's OK. Discussing God's love is always a good idea. And when such a discussion is with a non-Christian friend, this is a good opportunity for you to explain – possibly across multiple conversations (depicted in the following list with cascading bullet points) – that the clearest demonstration of God's love for us is:

- God the Father sending God the Son – Jesus, True God and True Man – into the world
  - to live the perfect life that we cannot,
    - die on a cross, as a perfect sacrifice to pay the price for all the sins of each individual across the world,
      - rise from the dead, validating that God the Father's wrath (because of our sins) has been fully quenched,
        - and ascend to heaven, where He is preparing a place for those who believe that Jesus is their Savior

I've had the honor of doing this, and I'll give an example. I've been blessed with a fairly close friendship with a person of another religion. Over the course of some years, I've been very open about my faith, at the same time inquiring much about theirs, all the while being very respectful. The two of us have talked about such things in one-on-one conversations probably 30-40 times. In due time, I gave them a New Testament in their native language. At another suitable time, within a week of a terrorist attack that was reported widely in the news, I gave them a handwritten card to express that I care about them and how unfair it is for people to judge others because of their home country and culture, and because of what a few men of this culture did. While I have been earnestly praying that the Holy Spirit will find a peaceful dwelling in their heart, I don't know if my friend has saving faith or not – and in a very real sense that is not for me to know. I will find out in heaven.

By the way, in order to protect them, in the preceding paragraph I'm purposely very vague about the timing of all this and any specifics about my friend. Yes, I just gave you a hint about what the other religion is. I'm telling you this as a reminder that we need to be sensitive to such things when we witness to others.

What if your friend or loved one has died?

During this earthly life, one of the special things about any loving relationship is that it's transient. There's a beginning – often a birth or the beginning of a friendship – and there's an end – in many cases, especially in strong relationships, when one dies. The joy we feel at the beginning is countered by the deep sadness we feel at the end. Yes, love is a voyage that requires a continuum of emotions, not only joy and happiness. While emotionally stable people don't actively seek out experiences that yield only disappointments and setbacks, neither do we shrink from establishing relationships due to various fears of what we may encounter along the way – not the least of which is the chance of the relationship ending because of the other dying. For example, we enter into marriage with celebration, aware but not caring that there's a high likelihood that the relationship will end with the death of one. I hope you're not finding this or what follows too melancholy, but if you'll indulge me I'll continue a little further down this path. You may not find my following suggestion easy, but I'd like you to try anyway. The next time you're in a group that's mourning the loss of a friend or loved one – really displaying an outpouring of grief – can you find a way to be soothed by this? Before you throw this book to the floor, let me explain where I'm coming from. I do sometimes feel this way because the outpouring is such a clear demonstration of the depth of love we have for our friend or loved one, plus it provides a natural way for us to turn and comfort one another. This strengthens existing relationships and may even form entirely new friendships; a strand we can add to our bond is the commonality that the deceased was close to us. So, while life teaches us that love between two people (a relationship) on this earth is inherently transient, life also teaches us that love does continue on and on.

The mourning process is important; we need to let our grief pour out. After sufficient time of this – different for each person and circumstance – accept the healing that mourning provides, and move on with life and love.

~

If our friend or loved one is relatively young when they die, one facet of our grief (i.e., sadness due to loss) is that they weren't able to experience more in their life. For example, I sometimes am sad that my mom didn't get to see any of her children graduate from college or get married – all four of us did both. I sometimes am sad that my mom didn't get to hold a grandchild – there are several, and now even some *great* grandchildren! I sometimes am sad that my mom didn't get to spend more time with my dad – he lived over 40 more years. My mom enjoyed writing poetry, and one of her last ones (see the "Backstage pass" subsection, not far below) is about dying in a peaceful manner, written while knowing that she would very soon be with the Lord; I sometimes am sad that she didn't get to write more poems, including ones with themes about the joys of living. Feeling such sadness is a natural part of the mourning process, and that's good. At other times, with increasing frequency as the mourning process winds down, it's also good to consider and be thankful for the things that our friend or loved one *did* experience. For example, my mom was blessed in so many ways. She was born and raised in a loving, Christian family. She was intelligent and well educated, continuing past college and attaining a Master's degree in chemistry – and consider that we're talking about the late 1940s here, when chemistry was largely considered "male territory." She capitalized on this by marrying one of her lab partners. Their marriage was blessed by many years together and four children. She was loving and optimistic in life, and calm and peaceful all the way through her health struggles. She was the first to teach me about unconditional love, patience, contentment, and faith that God knows what's best for us – pretty lofty thoughts for a six year old to try to grasp, and it's still sinking in all these years later. Yes, she was richly blessed, and gave so much to others who are fortunate to have been a part of her life.

~

When your friend or loved one passes away, it's natural to feel sadness of course, but after a time of this shift your thoughts to the specific ways that they were blessed and actively participated in these blessings – for example, I hope they were open to God's love such that they enjoyed a relationship with Jesus.

Take breaks from your own heartache to turn your compassion inside out, looking for ways to comfort and support the surviving loved ones, especially a parent, spouse, or children. Their life has just been turned upside down, and they are in great need of receiving love. There are so many ways that we can love them. Most importantly, if they don't yet have a relationship with Jesus, this is a perfect time for them to get started.

Yes, after a death of a friend or loved one, it's common for people to be more receptive to spiritual matters than usual. At such times, we're reminded of our mortality and it makes us think about what follows this life. For us believers, we're comforted in knowing that death means it's God's will that our earthly voyage is over, and we've reached our destination of being with Him forever in heaven. For unbelievers, such comfort is lacking, and it's common for them to be yearning for satisfying answers to their questions. Pray that the Holy Spirit will stoke the fire of faith in their hearts, and even bless you with the joy of helping with this.

Finally, if you are yourself one of the surviving loved ones, be thankful for the special relationship you had with your dear one, be thankful for the love that you shared, and be thankful for the time you had together, regardless of how short that time might have been. That time could have been even shorter, unless the circumstance was a miscarriage, stillbirth, or death of the mother during childbirth. Importantly, don't seclude yourself but rather open yourself up to receive love from others who want to comfort you, and especially be open to receiving God's love – yes, know that He cares for you.

What if your friend or loved one is near death?

This is a special time because while the end of your present journey together is fast approaching – your one-of-a-kind snowflake is about to melt – be thankful for the opportunity to travel a little bit further with them.

Talk to them about the blessings of their life, and how you and others have been positively influenced by them. Show them love by telling them that they are special and appreciated. Be sincere – don't embellish too much and certainly don't make things up. Be specific – even if it seems small, remember that love is often seen most clearly through the simple things in life. Be personal – say how it impacted you and other specific people.

If they're anxious about death, calm their fears by reminding them *(or telling them for the first time!)* that Jesus loves them and, if they believe in Him as their Savior, they'll soon be with Him forever.

Don't be surprised if you don't get much back; this is your turn to give. If they're able to talk, this is the time to use all your good listening skills! At some point, they may not be able to reciprocate your love. Be content that you're able to show them love. Giving love to a person in their last moments of this life is an amazing gift to give someone. I can't think of a better gift to give.

What if you are near death?

Obviously, not all of us are given much warning that we are about to die. For this reason, important messages that I want you to get from this book are:

- We should live life fully aware that we may not have much time left on this earth, and
- In light of this, we should not delay submitting to the Holy Spirit's gift of faith

If God chooses to give us warning that we will be dying soon but not quite yet, let us use this time wisely! How do we prioritize? … Not surprisingly, I'm going to ask you to think of others. However, let's take this one step at a time. For example, I understand that it may be extremely difficult for us to think of others when we become aware that we don't have much time left, especially if the reason why came as a shock to us. Nevertheless, after we have had some time to process the new situation we find ourselves in, let's take a deep breath and take one last dive from the highest diving platform we can find.

When we hit the water, how do we prioritize?

- First things first: If you've wandered from the faith, or you've never believed at all, then before you think of other people in your life you need to think about your relationship with God. You need to think about what happens after death, specifically what will happen to you after you die. Such thoughts can be scary… but they don't have to be! We can get scared because when we look back on our life, we're going to remember many regrets – many things we'd do differently if we only had the chance. But no matter how embarrassing the contents of our dirty laundry basket are, there's always one place we can go and not feel ashamed, even when the basket is overturned and all is laid bare. God already knows everything in our basket – we're not going to surprise Him. Yes, each of us must give an account (2 Corinthians 5:10; Hebrews 4:13) to God, but we do not need to feel ashamed or fearful when we do this. If you can't think of the words to say to Him when you must give an account, may I suggest the following as an introduction? All of this can be said without shame or fear.

- ○ *God, where do I begin? "I know that nothing good dwells in me, that is, in my flesh" (Romans 7:18). I learned – a little late, but not too late – that I need a Savior to stand before You. I learned – a little late, but not too late – that Jesus died for my sins, and is my Savior. I learned – a little late, but not too late – that Jesus rose from the dead on Easter morning, and is my living Lord. I learned – a little late, but not too late – that my life is in Your hands: "God, be merciful to me, a sinner!" (Luke 18:13).*
  - ▪ Remember that Jesus promises, "Whoever comes to me I will never cast out" (John 6:37). If we trust in Him, He will never cause us to feel ashamed or afraid. "There is no fear in love, but perfect love casts out fear" (1 John 4:18).
- After you're comforted in knowing what you're going to say when you must give an account, now it's time to tell others why you're so confident in the face of death. This is a great opportunity to witness. People will take notice, if you face death in an unfearing way. Let your fearlessness show clearly and – *Don't stop there!* – tell them why you're facing death with confidence.
- As implied by the previous bullet point, please don't isolate yourself. You may be tempted to do so, if you focus too much on yourself. I know I'm asking a lot of you at a very difficult time, but please hang in there and get through this final push. It's important! Besides witnessing as described above, please tell your friends and loved ones how they've positively im-pacted your life. Be specific, as you encourage them to continue in like man-ner with others. Continue to be specific as you tell them why you love them. Why hold back? What are you waiting for? What are you afraid of (1 John 4:18)? Remember, we are to face death fearlessly (Hebrews 2:14-15).

Backstage pass

If we have a young child who doesn't really understand the concept of death, we should try to explain it to them as best we can. It's better to have this difficult conversation than to have them be surprised when a loved one dies. Below is an example of what a mother who knows she's going to die within a few months could tell her young son.

"Son, there's something I want to talk to you about. It's about another part of life that we haven't talked about before. You know that people are of different ages, and that you are younger than most people. But there are some people younger than you, like you know that my sister just had another baby, and the baby is younger than you. And you know that lots of people are older than you – like Grandma. Do you know that Grandma is my mother? Yes, I had a mother and father, just like you. I lived with them, when I was your age. Yes, years ago, I was your age. Did you know that? In life, we grow older. Now, I'm a lot older than you, right? And Grandma is a lot older than me, right? You never met my father – your grandpa. Did you know that you had a grandpa? Here's a picture of him with Grandma. Do you recognize her? This is way back when they got married. I wasn't even born yet. Grandpa lived a long time – a very long time. He lived 88 years. 88 years is a long time, right? You were born only five years ago, a lot less time than 88 years. When Grandpa got all the way up to 88 years, he died. Do you know what it means to die?"

"No."

"When Grandpa got all the way up to 88 years, he got very sick, and after a while he stopped living. To stop living means to die. But if we be-lieve in God – if we trust Jesus – when we die, we stop living the life we know here, and we go to heaven to live with Him there. Grandpa believed in God – he trusted Jesus. Grandpa went to church and Sunday School, just like we go to church and Sunday School. Grandpa believed in God – he trusted Jesus – so when Grandpa died he went to heaven."

"If I get sick, will I die?"

"When you get sick, we take you to the doctor, and they do everything they can to make you better again. Remember when you got an ear infec-tion? I took you to the doctor, and they helped you get better. But there

are a few things that a doctor can't help with. Usually, we don't get that kind of sickness until we're older, but once in a while younger people get sick like that too. That's why when we pray to God, we ask that He keep all of us healthy. ... You know that I've been sick for a while. Your dad and I and a lot of other people have been praying to God that I get healthy again. ... But I have the kind of sickness that a doctor can't help with."

"Why didn't Jesus and the doctor keep you healthy this time?"

"I don't know. We've been asking God to make me healthy again, but He knows what's best for us. We keep asking, but we accept His decision. ... The doctors have tried everything they can do. ... ... They think I probably will die soon..."

...

"Is dying like going to sleep?"

...

"Not really. ... When we go to sleep at night, we're getting the rest we need to feel strong the next day."

"Is dying like going on a trip?"

"Not really. When we go on a trip, we go together to see something new, but then we come back home. Remember when we went out to the desert last spring? We saw lots of new things, but then we came back here. When I die, it means I go to heaven, and I won't come back to this home..."

...

"Do you want to go?"

...

"No, I don't want to go. ... I love you very much. ... I want to stay here with you, your brother, your two sisters, and your dad. I love you all very much. ... I've been asking to stay, but I accept God's decision. ... I'll be with Him in heaven. I'll see Jesus and Grandpa, and lots of other people, and I'll see you there too when it's time for you to come."

"How long will that be?"

"None of us know how long we will live. I've been asking God to keep you healthy and safe – for you to live a long time. God wants us to pray to Him about all kinds of things, but in everything we accept His decision. ... Here are some more things that I don't want you ever to forget: God

loves you and me; God knows what's best; this life is short compared to
our life in heaven – where we will live forever; and … I love you."
    "I love you too."

~

And what if such a conversation did not occur? Perhaps the son would later
write:

"A Restful Place"

If I say "I love you," will you then hear?
Or 'tis too late to pierce the clouded sky?
Is it too dark and far for us to find
A restful place for me within your heart?

I lie and listen, growing weary now.
I wait for your sweet lullaby, but no,
Only the wind – quiet rustling of leaves.
Tomorrow morning – perhaps – I hear you.

If I reach out to you, will you then feel?
Or 'tis too late for there to be such warmth?
Do we expect too much – such comforts? Though
Almost forgotten, they do haunt me still.

I lie exposed, even shivering now.
I wait for your soft warm caress, but no,
Only the wind – so cold against my skin.
Tomorrow morning – perhaps – I feel you.

If I look for you, might we catch a glimpse?
Or 'tis too late for such joys to behold?
If I shut my eyes – shut ev'ryone out,
The darkness call my sole friend – 'tis enough?

I lie but keep watch – daylight much delayed.
I wait for your kind glowing smile, but no.
The night grows long – soon death's dawn for me too;
Tomorrow morning – indeed – I see you.

When you say "I love you," will I then hear?
Not only hear, nay also feel and see?
Then I be like you – you again like me;
The veil between us then finally gone.

No more need I wait – lying all alone;
A restful place in our hearts being found.
And ev'ry morn we both will smile and say,
"Now truly you know how much I love you."

~

And perhaps the son would later write a poem with his mother. Let me explain: The following stanzas that are aligned with the left-hand margin are the poem "Comfort," written in 1969 by my mother, Edith, not long before her death. Interspersed are stanzas, entitled "Comforted," written in 2017 by yours truly – these are aligned with the right-hand margin. Another way to distinguish is that "Comfort" can stand on its own, while my stanzas don't make much sense without my mom's stanzas; also, "Comforted" is spiritually immature at some points within the first half.

  "Comfort"   *"Comforted"*

            Such darkened sadness I ne'er known before;
              Distraught to see my darling suffer so.

Pity me not, / I'm in my Master's arms;
He holds me fast and will not let me go.

> *Pry Him away with all my strength and guile;*
> *To no avail. … Perchance reprieve arrange?*

Envy my lot! / I'm in my Lord's embrace.
With such a lover, who would sigh for change?

> *No lover of mine such pains would allow.*
> *My plan is better. Why won't He take heed?*

Welcome the thought / That Christ thus cares for me.
His good and gracious will is done indeed.

> *Why does His plan have such a bitter end?*
> *Do you accept this lot? Will you not fight?*

Alter naught / My portion no hair's-breadth.
Remove no featherweight of burden light.

> *Sweet Jesus heals, yes, you taught me so well.*
> *But what about this time? Shall we protest?*

Cancel no jot, / No tittle He prescribes.
The Great Physician knows what cure is best.

> *An acrid lesson to learn – I will try;*
> *Give me a moment. … Let my heart be free.*

Weep now for naught, / Since no iota, speck,
Of what the world calls trouble, troubles me.

> *From whence comes wisdom such as this? Pray tell!*
> *Hasten to teach, so I too may employ.*

What hath God wrought? / This little season's pain
He blesses, turns into ecstatic joy!

My plan myopic – God's plan so sublime;
His care expansive – past this journey brief.

Perfect the plot / My Heav'nly Bridegroom plans
Whereby He proves His love. He kisses me!

Much more than a glimpse now – hence I perceive;
His love is tranquil, tender, most profound.

Pervasive joy as I ne'er known before,
To know my darling this elated be.

~

Losing a loved one is always hard, but if they believed in God – if they trusted Jesus – we are comforted in knowing that they are with Him in heaven.

What if your friend is diagnosed with cancer or other life-threatening or life-altering disease?

I find this to be an especially challenging situation, and I think that's because of emotional difficulties from my experience with my mom (Prologue). Right up front here I want to say that while I consider myself to have the spiritual gift of mercy (Chapter 4), this in no way means that I'm perfect in dealing with scenarios that a mercy-giver normally excels in. In the cancer patient scenario, I've swung for the fences and missed the ball, mainly in two ways: (i) going overboard / smothering, and (ii) expressing too much confidence in the outcome. *(Only two strikes! I'm happy to announce that I did not strike out!)* The biggest thing I've learned from my mistakes is that the best support is provided by all the supporters working as a team (even when we don't all know each other – which is usually the case). Each one of us in the entire network plays their role. No one should be swinging for the fences to win the game all on their own. If each of us settles down and hits a single, that will end up scoring a lot more runs than any home run can provide.

Below are several suggestions for how to "hit a single" – how to love someone in our life who has been diagnosed with a terrible disease like cancer.

Some of my suggestions are generally applicable to any health issue, but other examples are specific to cancer. Let such specifics be a reminder that any disease will have its own list of unique challenges. Please be mindful of these. When you want to love someone afflicted with an illness, your first step is not to rush unannounced to their home with a bowl of leftover chicken noodle soup and flowers from your garden. No, your first step should be to learn more about the disease ("know your enemy") and what the patient will be experiencing throughout their treatment.

- **Handwritten cards**: A good way to express our sentiments is via cards. Unless we're a family member or close friend, in-person visits are usually not a good idea. Typically, the patient's schedule is very busy with doctor appointments. In between, they're often fatigued. They also don't need the added stress of keeping their home presentable for visitors. And once their treatment starts, they often are advised by their doctors to minimize contact with people (because of the patient's weakened immune system). An issue with phone calls is that they may come at a bad time. Text messages and emails are better, and of course such methods of communication can be used to set up a time for a phone call or videoconference, if they're up to it. However, cards are always nice because the patient can read them whenever they'd like, and they have something tangible they can keep. Please go "old school" here and handwrite at least several sentences inside your card!
  - **What to write**: It's pretty obvious that the reason we're giving them a card is because of their health issue so, yes, please do write something about that. Sentiments like "Get well soon" don't really make sense in a cancer scenario.

    Cancer patients usually get a lot of warrior imagery and messages about being strong. That can get old pretty quick. I like to give a slightly different message: While they'll be strong often, no one should be expected to be strong all the time, and during such challenging times they can rely on the support of their loved ones and friends.

    It's often nice to add some words about topics unrelated to their health issue, to help them think about other things – for example, what's going on back at the office. However, be sensitive not to go on and on about your latest exciting escapade – such as your recent trip to Fiji – as this may serve little purpose beyond reminding the patient that they aren't able to personally enjoy such freedom at this time. It depends on the relationship and the situation, but my tendency is to lean toward waiting to share much, if anything, about such adventures until the patient is through their roughest patches.

It's always a good idea to write that you're praying for them, and I often will include specifically what I'm praying about. Don't just pray for physical healing. I like to include that they maintain a positive disposition throughout the journey. I always include prayers for their family members.

If something they're doing is inspiring to you – for example, their attitude – tell them that, but keep it simple and low-key. Slathering it on too thick often backfires by causing them to later feel like they're letting people down, if they can't maintain their prior trait. And don't make things up. If someone is severely depressed, a sentiment that says their upbeat attitude is inspiring will ring hollow. Such lack of sincerity is easy to see, and is disheartening. Rule #1 is – *be sincere*.

Even if they're not exhibiting a positive disposition, in your message stay positive and optimistic (in reference to your own outlook about the situation), but do this without going overboard (see next bullet point).

Under most circumstances, the following elements are good to include: I'm happy to help in any way I can; I'm praying for you; God hears our prayers; He is in control; He knows what's best for us; I'm comforted knowing that you are in God's hands; I'm hopeful / optimistic about your outcome; and no matter what happens, know that I love you.

o **What not to write**: Don't make the mistake of saying that they're going to beat it, or of expressing unwarranted confidence. We don't know the outcome. It may be God's will that they not beat it. Rather, write something more along the lines of my previous paragraph. It's very tempting to express unwarranted confidence, but it's devastating when we're wrong. And we might think that the patient wants to hear that everything's going to be fine. But, generally, cancer patients don't want that kind of sugarcoating. Optimism is good (as in the preceding bullet point) but I advise not going further than that.

If you're anxious or worried, pray to God to soothe your fears. Take to heart – "The Lord is at hand … in everything by prayer and supplication with thanksgiving let your requests be made known to God" (Philippians 4:5-6). Some anxiety / worry is natural, but let's not become mired in such feelings. And let's not pass our anxiety on to the patient. Even worse than the mistake of the preceding paragraph is in any way expressing anxiety or worry to the patient.

o **How much to write**: Some of us – we know who we are… – have a tendency to want to say a lot in these types of situations, and this can be overwhelming to someone who's not particularly fond of receiving emotional sentiments. So, as they say, "know your audience," and remember that quantity and quality do not always go hand in hand.

- **Gifts**: As mentioned above, cards are always good, and many times that really is enough. If you want to give a gift as well, I could go on at some length with ideas, but I'll summarize as follows.

o **What to give**: Give something comforting (except see the next bullet point), not too large in size, and most importantly something that you think will really resonate with them. Is there something that symbolizes your friendship? Is there something you remember them telling you that they like or that inspires them?

A framed photograph of the two of you, or of a larger group of friends / family, on a simple stand so it can be easily kept nearby, is a way to help recall pleasant memories.

They probably will have a lot of downtime, so books and movies may be a good idea.

A donation (for example, to an organization associated with their disease) in their honor is a way to give something that they probably will appreciate – and it has the advantage of not taking up any space! One common time to give a donation is when they finish their treatment, but see the bullet point further below about the timing of gifts.

I generally don't like to give gift cards as a present to anyone. However, a time that it seems right is when a patient comes off treatment. They're finally able to start getting out to enjoy life again. So, gift cards to restaurants, movie theaters, and similar are often appreciated.

○ **What not to give**: In many cases, cancer patients aren't allowed to be near flowers and other plants (again, because of their weakened immune system). So, if you really want to give flowers, ask if the patient is allowed to receive them. If they're not, give something else in the meantime and wait to give flowers until they're off treatment and given the green light.

  Similarly, in many cases, cancer patients have diet restrictions and maximum allowable times between when food is cooked and when they need to eat it (again, their immune system). So, if you want to give food, please ask ahead about what's OK.

  While it can be nice to give a cancer patient a blanket, it's a relatively common gift, so I advise not to give this unless you know they need or want another one.

○ **How much to give / Do not smother**: Unless you know that the patient has a small network of family and friends, or has a tendency to feel lonely / neglected, be mindful of not going overboard. Give generously, but allow others in their network to be just as generous. It's not a competition, and we don't want the patient to feel uncomfortable with the degree of attention from us.

  If despite my warning, you still find yourself giving a lot, at least make it clear to them that you don't expect any kind of reciprocation. We certainly don't want to add a burden.

○ **When to give**: Consider focusing on the middle of their treatment period. The most attention naturally falls toward the beginning of them learning of their health issue, and again at the end of treatment. If you're worried about them feeling lonely or neglected, the middle of treatment is probably the most likely time for this, even if they have a relatively large network. I've given in the middle of treatment, as a way to celebrate having made good progress and "light at the end of the tunnel."

• **Tangible help**: As you've probably gathered by now, during treatment it may not be very easy to help in a tangible way. In case you missed it, this is because it's common for cancer patients to need to limit their exposure to other people. But even during treatment, it never hurts to ask. An important point is that when we ask how we can help, it's best to be specific. This makes it more likely that they'll accept. For example, perhaps we can help them drive to and from doctor appointments. Even if they're able to drive on their own, they still may appreciate the company.

Especially if we're a close friend, it's a good idea to ask if we can help with errands or housecleaning, and things of this nature. If for some reason this isn't feasible, an alternative is to give gift cards for grocery stores (especially ones that offer delivery service), maid service, and the like, if we know which vendors they'll use.

- **Is there anyone we're forgetting?** There is, if we forget the immediate family of the patient. The family is under a lot of stress and needs support too. When offering to help, again it's best to be specific. For example, even if cooking for the patient isn't a viable way to help (see above), perhaps we can bring a meal for the rest of the family. I also think cards, gift cards, and other gifts for the family are nice to add to the mix.

~

Before I close this section, I want to say a few words about how I was helped by a cancer patient. One way that I swung for the fences came in the form of my repeatedly giving them lengthy written sentiments rife with emotion. It was an interesting situation because my recipient is someone who – *How do I put this?* – is not particularly fond of elaborate expressions saturated with sentimentalities (a relatively common trait, I have learned). I'm leaving out some details to protect the innocent, but suffice it to say that once the fog started to dissipate toward the end of their difficult journey of treatment and recovery, it finally dawned on me why I felt so deeply comforted writing such things: I had been writing to my friend sentiments like I wanted to tell my mom, but I never was able to. It was doubly soothing to me because it felt like I was expressing these things to two people: both my friend and my mom. This helped me approach closure on my mom's death – to get nearer than I ever thought I could in this lifetime. While basking, I thanked my friend for their impressive patience with my compositions – for letting me be me, even in this way that is not particularly aligned with their preferences. Yes, I felt unconditionally loved.

What if you are worried that something or someone can separate you from the love of God?

Paul writes in Romans 8:38-39, "I am sure that neither death nor life, nor angels nor rulers, nor things present nor things to come, nor powers, nor height nor depth, nor anything else in all creation, will be able to separate us from the love of God in Christ Jesus our Lord."

The only thing that can separate you from the love of God is you, and that is if you reject Him at the time of God's judgment. And it's so easy not to reject Him! "If you confess with your mouth that Jesus is Lord and believe in your heart that God raised him from the dead, you will be saved" (Romans 10:9). And this isn't based on your own intelligence or effort – it's a gift from God: "For by grace you have been saved through faith. And this is not your own doing; it is the gift of God, not a result of works, so that no one may boast" (Ephesians 2:8-9).

Do not reject this gift!

What if you are starting to wonder if this book will ever end?

I'm sure you've figured out by now that I could go on forever with more and more "What if … ?" scenarios. Yes, a few more do come to mind (and some of these are captured as appendices). But if I keep going on forever, then I'll never finish this book! And neither will you! By this point, I'm confident that you can manage to apply what you've learned to your own unique situations. If you get stuck, remember that "Love … never gives up" (1 Corinthians 13:7 GW). If you get discouraged, remember that "Love never fails" (1 Corinthians 13:8 NIV).

~   ~   ~

After-hours

Bob unplugged

In the Prologue, I provide a list of memories about my mom, and I lie to you. After that list, it still says that those are all my meaningful memories of her. I rationalize that this is merely a white lie because that was true at the time I wrote that list. About a year later, I had another memory of her. It's a little disturbing, and apparently for this reason I had buried it deep down inside. This more recent memory is of us kids being our bratty selves at the lunch table, our mom taking notice but not saying a word; rather, she stood up, walked quietly but determinedly to retrieve "the belt," wrapped said belt around her neck such that it dangled over her shoulders like a pastor's stole, and she sat back down to resume eating. She didn't say a word, but the message was loud and clear that if it gets bad enough, physical violence is the answer.

When I remembered this, I was deeply distressed for several hours because I was confronted with the reality that my mom made a mistake – a big mistake… I'm not exaggerating. If anything, so far I've been understating it. The truth is that she made a monumental mistake by modeling the avoidance of verbal expression of feelings and – as if that's not bad enough – otherwise communicating an appalling message.

As it was sinking in that my mom was not the perfect person I had often imagined her to be, I slowly realized that I was learning a valuable lesson. In my tendency toward black-and-white thinking, I had previously considered myself abandoned (Prologue) by a faultless being. … Stop for a moment and think of the implications of reaching such a conclusion. … But my recalled image, while initially distressing, helped me see the situation differently – in a marvelous shade of gray: A regular person gave me her best loving while she was alive, and then she died; it's as simple as that. Sometimes the obvious is so close that we can't see it clearly.

Do I think less of my mom, now that I know with certainty that she wasn't flawless? … Loving despite flaws – let me see – I think there's a phrase that fits.

Yes, the phrase that fits has been used 172 times already in this book, and there are 14 occurrences yet to come. Loving despite flaws is the very essence of unconditional love.

We must be flawed (or otherwise in need) in order to be loved unconditionally, but are we *defined* by our flaws? For example, is my mom defined by the belt? ... No, my mom is not defined by the belt. She was a regular person who made mistakes and was worth loving while she was alive, and is now abiding in God's love because she trusted in Jesus as her Savior.

What if you've made a mistake? ... No, let me phrase it this way: Please close your eyes and think about your mistakes – I mean the big ones, the monumental ones, the ones that have caused – and maybe are still causing – real pain for you and others.

- Do these mistakes define you?
- Are you worth loving?

These are two very important questions, and I'm going to give you a hint about the answers: There is one "yes" and one "no." The order of the answers that you feel applies to you depends on your point of view. If you are struggling with shame, such that you feel the disheartening order of the "yes" and "no" applies to you, please show yourself some compassion and allow yourself to accept the correct point of view.

Step up to the microphone

What defines you?

In the "What if someone disappoints you?" section, I describe having difficulty forgiving a friend. When I get to the part where I realize why I should forgive them, I reference Matthew 18:21-35. This passage is the parable of The Unforgiving Servant. Please read it, and consider the following questions.

- Are you currently withholding forgiveness from anyone?
  - o If yes, do you feel this is justified?

- In the "What if someone sins against you?" section, I say that "unconditional love does not equate to universal, unconditional forgiveness," inferring that there are scenarios where withholding forgiveness is justified. Do you agree or disagree?
- Are there cases – as difficult as they might be – where you're not even extending an olive branch?
  - In the "What if someone sins against you?" section, I advise: "We strive to, at a minimum, offer forgiveness (i.e., it's conditional upon our counterpart's repentance) – under all circumstances – no exceptions." Do you agree or disagree?
- What's your definition of forgiveness?

In the "How to have an argument" section (a.k.a., the "What if you have an argument?" section), I describe the two phases that need to be completed before the matter is settled, and I highlight the importance of empathy in both phases.

Recall a recent argument, and do your best to answer the following questions objectively.
- How could you have been more empathetic during the dispute phase?
- How could you have been more empathetic during the resolution phase?

In the "What if your partner is unfaithful to you?" section, the narrator opens up to his wife and admits that he often fantasizes about being with other women. The story ends before his wife says anything about this. If you were to write an extension to the story, what would you have her say to him on this topic?

For parents: The next time a believer – who is close to your whole family – dies, demonstrate clearly to your children the hope that we have in the Lord. While grieving is a natural part of the healing process, don't be overcome with grief such that it could be interpreted as despair. Rather, articulate to your children that all who believe in Jesus as their Savior have eternal life. Then, when the time is right, gather together as a small group to reminisce about your departed friend or loved one, asking each person to share a memory that is meaningful to them.

Support one another as you give thanks for the time you've had so far with your departed friend or loved one, and emphasize that all who trust in Jesus as their Savior will be reunited in heaven.

For intimate couples (1 of 2): I'd like both of you, in turn, to look your partner in the eyes and promise them that you'll never (again) abuse them, and if abusive behavior is or ever becomes something you struggle with, then you'll go with them to couples therapy – (You're on this journey together). When making your promise, you have to use their name and the L-word.

For intimate couples (2 of 2): At a time separate from addressing the above prompt (so both topics receive full attention), I'd like both of you, in turn, to look your partner in the eyes and promise them that you'll never (again) be unfaithful to them, and if licentious behavior is or ever becomes something you struggle with, then you'll go with them to couples therapy – (You're on this journey together). When making your promise, you have to use their name and the L-word.

Chapter 10 – Just Because

It can be hard to explain why we love someone. Have you ever tried? Some brave souls do at their wedding ceremony, and that can be very heartwarming. And maybe you've written some reasons to share only with your loved one, for example in a Valentine's Day card or anniversary card. Often, such descriptions focus on attributes related to conditional love – things we appreciate, admire, consider strengths. More thorough descriptions sometimes get into less tangible qualities – things that just make us smile, even though it may be hard to put our finger on exactly why. If you think I'm building up to a point where I'm going to snip the horse-hair holding the sword of Damocles, to surely smite you for trying to explain your love, I must disappoint you. Indeed, one of the main points of this book is that we should frequently and effectively communicate – demonstrate and express with words – our love for others, including specifically why we love them. Yes, I urge you to find fresh ways to confess your love for the people in your life, with your confessions infused with elaborate specifics. Demonstrate by serving them in new ways, and frequently affirm with new words, either by writing in a card or better yet verbalizing it, whether that be in private – just between the two of you – or in public. I'll even supply the megaphone, but before you use it don't forget to consider the preferences of your loved one…

I wasn't brave enough to make a speech at our wedding. And while I've made many attempts to express my love in cards, I don't think I should quit my day job to work at Hallmark®. It can be hard to convey our love in words. But that doesn't deter us from trying!

Even harder is trying to describe why we love others unconditionally. I tried to describe the feeling of *receiving* unconditional love in Chapter 6, but I didn't try to describe the feeling of *giving* unconditional love, let alone the reasons for why we give it.

That is, until now!

Why do we love? Let's start to address this from the simpler perspective of conditional love. At least one of the reasons we enter into conditional love relationships is that we receive love back. Again, the sword of Damocles is not about to fall. I wrote an entire chapter about why it's good – no, why we *need* – to receive love from others. … *You don't remember that?! Chapter 5 people!* …

One of the things that makes conditional love so beautiful is that – when it's a healthy relationship – it provides a sanctuary from neglect, indifference, selfishness, revulsion, manipulation, abuse, cruelty, malevolence, vindictiveness, and hate; yes, conditional love provides a safe haven from the opposites of love (Chapter 1). In the midst of these common elements of our sinful world, conditional love provides a comfortable place where we go to find care, kindness, connection, contentment, trust, acceptance – to find peace. Part of God's response to our rebellion against Him (Genesis 3) is to provide a way for us to experience love between people within a world rife with sin. When God saw that we chose to struggle with sin instead of submit to His will in all things, He didn't want us to be overwhelmed by sin. His wonderful design is that with the dichotomies inherent to a sin-filled world (Chapter 7), there are ways that these dichotomies can be tuned – there are conditions that can be met – such that we can still experience love between sinful people. What an amazing example of how God continues to care for us, even in the face of our disobedience! What a beautiful way He provides for us not to be swept away by the swift currents of evil and unconditional hate.

But we don't love only to receive love back. Another reason we love is that we want our counterpart to feel loved – we want their needs to be met – and indeed this is enough for us when it comes to unconditional love. Recall that by definition (Chapter 1), unconditional love isn't given for any form of reciprocation. Consider God's unconditional love for us. Before the time of God's judgment, God loves us even though some of us don't love Him back. Imagine having billions of people not love you back, despite your unconditional love for them. I find it very difficult when one person is unresponsive. God has billions of people being unresponsive! But does that stop Him from loving?

And why do we keep loving, no matter what?

I'm not so much going to try to explain in excruciating detail why we love unconditionally, and what it feels like, as I'm going to illustrate it in two ways. Parents get this first illustration the fastest. Close your eyes and think back to the birth of your child, or if you've never had a child try to imagine what that would be like. The infant is brought into this world with some measure – typically a very large measure, at least for the mother – of anxiety and physical pain. When the infant is delivered, she looks – *How do I put this?* – not like a "Gerber® baby," but instead: red, wrinkly, etc. But what's our reaction? Do we explode in anger at her because she caused us anxiety and pain? Do we turn away in disgust because she's not particularly pleasant-looking at the moment? Of course not. We have a special feeling that's hard to describe. There's a name for it I think… Right on the tip of my tongue… Oh, yes, it's called unconditional love.

Why do we love our newborn infant? That's a stupid question, isn't it? Of course we do, and why am I asking?! OK, let me ask a slightly different question: Why do we "of course" love our newborn? I can think of three reasons.

- We "created" her. Nothing compares to creating something new. And a baby isn't just "something." A baby is a unique human being. There's no one else like her. She's truly one of a kind! She's inherently valuable. It's completely natural that we treasure her. Of course we love her.

- The following is written assuming that the parents have a loving relationship with one another: Specifically how we created her is an embodiment – both figuratively and literally – of our intimate love. Every time we have sex, we demonstrate our love for one another by literally becoming one. In those few times when sex results in conception, we've literally become one in another special way that results in a third person, akin to both of us. It's completely natural that we are spontaneously bonded to this embodiment of our love. Of course we love her.

- The following is written assuming that the caregiver(s) are emotionally stable: We see that she has a need – she is not fully developed – and we are equipped to help her. It's completely natural that we provide care for our dependent. Of course we love her.

Do we unconditionally love only our babies? *(How many rhetorical questions is this short chapter going to have?)* Of course not! The above is only an illustration. And it's only my first! Coming soon (next paragraph!) is the second, and it's similar to the first in the sense that both involve an analogy to relationships within families. People who have younger siblings get the second illustration the fastest. Before we dive deeper, for now simply imagine that you're a child and you discover that your parents are having a baby – of course you love your younger sibling *(Right? …)*. In the same way, because God unconditionally loves us, His offspring, then we should in turn unconditionally love one another. Why? Because all God's offspring are our siblings, and it's natural that we want all our siblings to feel cared for, including by us *(Right? ...)*. "If God so loved us, we also ought to love one another" (1 John 4:11).

Are you with me? ... OK, now close your eyes and imagine that you are Adam or Eve – *(I'm giving you a choice!)* – in the Garden of Eden. You just ate fruit from the tree of the knowledge of good and evil, and God's paying you a visit. What does He say? Does He say, *I hate you*? No, He says, *I love you*. For those of you who aren't remembering Him saying that in the Garden of Eden, let me point you to Genesis 3:15. Here's what God says to the serpent (Satan): "I will put enmity between you and the woman, and between your offspring and her offspring; / he shall bruise your head, and you shall bruise his heel." God is speaking to Satan, but He is telling us that He loves us. How? This verse is a foreshadowing of Jesus conquering sin, death, and Satan, and this has now already been accomplished. How has Jesus done this? Jesus came into this world as an infant, and lived the perfect life that we cannot; He was crucified on the cross to pay the price for all the sins – yes, even yours, even mine – of each individual – yes, even you, even me – across the world; and He rose from the dead to go to heaven to prepare a place for... I'm going to let you finish this by completing the following multiple choice: (a) only those who have proven themselves deserving of – have met the conditions to receive – God's love, or (b) anyone who believes that Jesus is their Savior from sin, death, and Satan. If you haven't dozed off too many times while reading this book, certainly you know that the answer is "b." Yes, this is how God tells us how much He loves us. It cannot be any clearer than this, and this is enough for us to know (and enough to motivate us to love all His offspring). But if anyone would be so bold as to ask *why* God loves us, I would answer, *Of course He does, and a better question is: Why does He of course love us?* I can think of three reasons.

- He created us. ... *God the Father's preemptive strike on our heart is that He created us!* ... Nothing compares to creating something new. And we're not just "something." Each of us is a unique human being, created in God's image and likeness (Genesis 1:26-27; Genesis 5:1-2; James 3:9). There's no one else like us. Each of us is truly one of a kind! Each of us is inherently valuable. It's completely natural that God treasures us. Of course He loves us.
- His creation of each of us is an embodiment – both figuratively and literally – of His love for mankind. The Designer is intensely intimate with each of us, as He lovingly shapes and forms our every characteristic, all the way

down to every detail of our physical, emotional, psychological, and spiritual self. With such closeness and care, He is providing additional tangible evidence that He has not given up on humanity – He is giving us one more opportunity (and another, and another…) – there is more to be accomplished. Part of His attentive design is that we be loved with tender affection, and typically we first experience this through our parents. Indeed, with rare exception, not long after delivery we're in the arms of our loving mother, and literally our mere existence has given rise to indescribable love in her heart. We've simply arrived on the scene and the manifestation of humanity's love has increased, by design. Jesus experienced firsthand this type of love – with His mother. Jesus and Mary shared intimate love. We, like Jesus, are designed to love and to be loved, whether we are a fetus, an adult, or at any stage of development in between. Jesus – True God, True Man, our brother, and our friend – is unified with us, by design. It's completely natural that Jesus is spontaneously bonded to us, because we are embodiments of His love. Of course He loves us.

- God sees that we have a need – we are by nature sinful, and consequently hopeless without a Savior – and He is equipped to help us. It's completely natural that He provide care for His dependent offspring. Of course He loves us.

~

Why God loves us, and why we love the people in our lives, can seem like complex questions. But we get more than a glimpse of the answer when we stop over-analyzing the details, zoom out, and set our sights on the grandeur of the most exquisite love of all – God's love for us. This peak towers above all that are in the mountain range of human relationships – dwarfing beyond compare even the lofty (humanly speaking) peaks of mother-infant relationship, soul mate relationship, and forgiving someone who hurts us deeply and is not remorseful. When we stop resisting and submit to God's love – allowing the Holy Spirit to secure it deep into our heart – then we see and feel that literally our mere existence has given rise to a new expression of the indescribable love already dwelling in God's heart.

~   ~   ~

After-hours

Bob unplugged

Are some people harder to love than others?

I think it's fair to say that most of us find it more challenging to love some people than we do others. Please think about those specific individuals whom you find it very difficult to love. ... Choose one – I suggest the one you find most challenging of all – and now I'd like you to perform the following mind-experiment: Imagine that this person is impacted by senseless violence. How do you feel about them now? Further imagine that you happen to be with this person when there is an emergency and you have an opportunity to help them. What would your reaction be? I hope your answer to both of these questions is: *I set aside our differences; I keep an open mind; I appreciate that they are an inherently valuable human being; I want the best for them; and I do what I can to help them.* Please pray about this, and ask God to help you identify opportunities to love in this way, without waiting for senseless violence or any other kind of emergency.

Step up to the microphone

The title of this book includes the words "Love 360," but this phrase is not used in the text. What does Love 360 mean to you?

What was and is your reaction to my focus in almost all of this book on intimate love (Chapter 1), as opposed to love for groups and humanity in general? Did your reaction change as you read this book? Did I convince you that we are most positively impacted by intimate love? Why or why not?

For parents: Ask your children with younger sibling(s) to describe their feelings when they learned that they were going to have a sister or brother, when their sibling was born, and when their sibling first came home. Do they remember holding their sister or brother for the very first time? What did that feel like?

- Extra credit: I don't want this to be contrived, but if your child spontaneously says that they felt *love* (i.e., they use this word) for their newborn sibling, then please take that opportunity to ask them if they can describe why they felt that way, since all their sibling had done is arrive on the scene. Tell them that you know it's a funny question, but you're just curious as to what reasons they might give, because this is something you've been thinking about.

For intimate couples: I'd like both of you, in turn, to tell your partner why you love them. You both have three choices for how to do this: write them a card, verbalize it with them in private (doesn't need to be an eloquent speech), or take your partner and a megaphone to a busy street corner and have at it.

Epilogue – Closing Prayer

We're almost to the end of our journey, but before we part ways I'd like you to go to a quiet place where you can focus in prayer. This probably will take at least an hour, so you may want to divide it across multiple sessions. Many times in this book, I've attempted to write prayers for this or that specific circumstance. While perhaps some of those came close to hitting the mark for you, here I can't write the prayer for you. Instead, I'd like you to think about the following points, and use your own words and relationships to fill in the details. When you're ready to start, please clear your mind of all distractions and focus on the following expressions of love.

- Thank God for how awesome He is!
- Thank God for how loving He is!
- Thank God that He made you the way He did. Thank Him not only for your strengths but also for those things that you sometimes see as limitations or even wish were different. Yes, thank Him for every bit.
- Thank God for each individual person He has placed in your life, not just in the present but also throughout your whole past
    - For each person, think of at least one specific thing that makes them special / unique – and thank God for that
    - For each person, try to think of at least one specific reason why (Chapter 10) you love them – and thank God for that
        - Such thinking (looking for a specific reason) typically moves toward conditional love, and that's fine! But if this is the case, also think of one specific way that you love them unconditionally. For example: (conditional love) *I love my friend because she greets me with a smile and tells me how happy she is to see me*; (unconditional love) *I've also been frequently moved to show her compassion because her husband died just over a year ago now, and she's still grieving.*
        - If you can't think of anything for a particular person, then pray that God will place some measure of unconditional love for them in your heart. For example: *God, help me be kind to them even though they're mean to me*; or: *God, teach me how to offer forgiveness to them for*

the hurtful thing that they did to me; or: *God, motivate me to assist with one of their needs.*

- o For each person, think of at least one specific way that you can verbalize or demonstrate your love for them in the next month or, if you don't see them that often, the next time you see them
  - ▪ If you can't think of anything for a particular person, then pray for them and include in this a request that they will become aware that you love them
- o For each person (unless circumstances are such that it's no longer possible to have a relationship with them), consider whether there's anything about the relationship that should be changed – and, if yes, pray for opportunities to address that
- *(Here's what I like to call a preemptive-strike prayer!)* Thank God for those people He will be placing into your life in the future!
- Ask God for more opportunities to show love to others, and – if you are so bold *(Yes, do it!)* – go further and ask God to bless you through your experience of being loved by others
- Thank God that He loves you more than words can express!
  - o Thank God that He loves you throughout your whole life on earth: from conception to death or Judgment Day, whichever comes first!
  - o Thank God that – if you believe that Jesus is your Savior … *It's still not too late to turn to Jesus!* – He loves you throughout all eternity: from the beginning of time to our endless experience of the joys of perfectly requited love in heaven

Appendices

Appendix A: What if you are thoroughly and persistently rejecting Jesus as your Savior?

Until the time of God's judgment, God loves you anyway, and wants you to stop rejecting Him. "God our Savior … desires all people to be saved and to come to the knowledge of the truth" (1 Timothy 2:3-4). If, however, you continue to reject God, He is just and will judge accordingly: "Because of your hard and impenitent heart you are storing up wrath for yourself on the day of wrath when God's righteous judgment will be revealed" (Romans 2:5). This is not conditional love, as amply explained in Appendices H and J. In a nutshell, it is God's nature to love ("God is love" – 1 John 4:8, 16) – His love is eternal; if we're not saved, it's not because God changed His nature, it's because we have rejected Him all the way until the time of God's judgment.

An analogy is – (I've never seen such a thing, but allow me to conjecture) – a new-born rejecting their mother, with the infant pushing her away. Does the mother stop loving her child? … And since any emotionally stable mother would remain steadfast in her love for such a child, remaining hopeful that the child will eventually stop resisting her love, how much more will God persistently love us!

If you think this analogy is unrealistic, I agree with you. What newborn would ever reject their loving mother? Likewise, I don't understand why any person would reject our loving God.

~

I am going to change my tone for a moment. I am concerned that what I have written so far in this appendix is not clear enough. Let me be clear. If you are rejecting Jesus as your Savior – in other words, if you are rejecting God's love – then you should be very scared; yes, you should be terrified (Hebrews 10:26-31)! Our loving God wants to have an intimate relationship with you, but you are rejecting. Our merciful God wants to forgive you, but you are rejecting. Our just God wants to cover your sins forever in the righteousness of Jesus – our Redeemer – but you are rejecting. If you persist, then you will be left with a wrathful God (John 3:36), and He will surely punish you (Revelation 19:15). Do you not know that we must all give an account to God (2 Corinthians 5:10; Hebrews 4:13)? In the story about the man who was physically abusing his wife for years ("What if you are struggling with the sin of your own abusive behavior?" section of Chapter 9), his story ends – his house of cards falls – with his thought that I have paraphrased here. You need to note carefully that I have changed a few words for you – not very many. You tell me the words I changed. You think about that. *"… It's only half an hour now before God's demanding that I give an account… What am I going to say?*

I have never been so scared in my life…" I end his story there, but there's more in store for him. The next part is punishment – justice. Oh, yes, he is going to be punished for his crimes. There is no doubt about that! And if you persist in not believing that Jesus is your Savior, you should be very scared – yes, terrified – because the end of your story is clear: You will (attempt to) stand on your own merits before our just God, and – there is no doubt about it – you will receive justice; you will be sorely punished.

~

For those of you who are rejecting Jesus as your Savior – who are rejecting God's love – the previous paragraph is the most loving thing that I can say to you. (This is the truth. I'm not being sarcastic.) I've written an entire chapter on the topic of God's unconditional love for us – indeed, I've written an entire book within which I hope God's love is evident in every chapter – but the full story is that "We should fear and love God."[1] Those of you who are rejecting Jesus as your Savior need more than my book; you need the full story, and it starts with acknowledging your sinfulness – your need for a Savior. Without a Savior, we are dust (cf. Genesis 3:19; Psalm 103:14; Ecclesiastes 3:20; 1 Corinthians 15:48).

Appendix B: The time of God's judgment

"With the Lord one day is as a thousand years, and a thousand years as one day. The Lord is not slow to fulfill his promise as some count slowness, but is patient toward you, not wishing that any should perish, but that all should reach repentance" (2 Peter 3:8-9). Despite God's impeccable patience, time does eventually run out for each of us as individuals. When does time run out with respect to God's judgment of us? I've looked at this from every angle, and I've come to the conclusion that there are three possible answers, listed below, and – for the sake of brevity – throughout this book I use the more general phrase "the time of God's judgment" to cover all scenarios.

- When considering all of human history: For the vast majority of us, our time runs out when we die
- When considering all people alive and yet to be conceived: For the vast majority of us, our time runs out when we die or on Judgment Day, whichever comes first. (See Appendix J for more about Judgment Day.)
- Who's left? I've come to the conclusion that there is a vast minority, specifically, that there is an unknown (to us) relatively small number of people who are judged before they die. A scripturally supported example is Pharaoh, who was kept on earth for a purpose; his heart was hardened (Exodus 7-14) but he still had a role to play (Romans 9:17-18). It seems that another possible example is Judas, because Jesus says of him, before Judas dies: "It would have been better for that man if he had not

been born" (Matthew 26:24). I venture to say that additional possible examples are Adolf Hitler and others of similar ilk. However, we should always remember that we are not to judge (Psalm 75; Matthew 7:1-5; John 5:22; Romans 2:1-3; 1 Corinthians 4:5). Are we all-knowing? From our perspective, we should *always* operate as if it's never too late for *anyone* until they die or until Judgment Day – no matter what. A clear, scripturally supported example of someone of similar ilk who was saved is Saul (Acts 8:1-3; Acts 9:1-2; Acts 22:19-20).

o   (For my commentary on predestination, see Appendix H-4)

Appendix Ɔ: Turning the other cheek (Matthew 5:39)

Jesus says, "Do not resist the one who is evil" (Matthew 5:39a). By this, Jesus means that we are not to retaliate. In the preceding verse, Jesus quotes Exodus 21:24, Leviticus 24:20, *and* Deuteronomy 19:21 – *(Three birds with one stone!)* – reminding us that we are not to go overboard when someone is to be punished for their crime: "An eye for an eye and a tooth for a tooth" (Matthew 5:38). The punishment is commensurate with the offense – one eye for one eye. The punishment does not go overboard – *two* eyes for one eye, for example.

But Jesus goes further by saying, in essence, *NO eye for one eye* (cf. Matthew 5:39-42). Why does He go this far? Shouldn't the person who did an evil deed be punished? Yes, they should pay their debt to society, and if they do not repent they most certainly will be punished. But who is to mete out justice? Sometimes justice is served via our government's judicial system. But is Jesus preaching The Sermon on the Mount (Matthew 5-7) to the Supreme Court or even *12 Angry Men*[2]? No, Jesus is preaching to us as individuals. He's reminding us that we are not to retaliate. And after any justice is served via an earthly government's judicial system, if the person who did an evil deed has not repented – turned to Jesus – then what happens next? Let's step back to a safe distance and allow God's wrath to settle the score with them: "Vengeance is mine, I will repay, says the Lord" (Romans 12:19).

Trying to step back to a safe distance is often advisable, but what are we to do when we are nevertheless treated unfairly? Jesus is very clear on this matter: (i) We are to forgive "seventy-seven times" (Matthew 18:22), i.e., as many times as it takes, *and* (ii) "If anyone slaps you on the right cheek, turn to him the other also" (Matthew 5:39b). The second point is saying that we are to give the one who mistreated us a second chance. Are we to give them seventy-seven chances? There are times when God calls us to serve His kingdom by giving our mistreating counterpart *more* than a second chance; but without a clear calling from God to suffer in such a way, if you are chronically being treated unfairly, my advice is to step (further) back to a safe distance, forgive your counterpart, and take meaningful action to protect yourself.

Let's stop ignoring the *Elephas maximus* in the room. We all know that some have used Matthew 5:39 as a rationale that abusive behavior should be tolerated. Let me be crystal clear: "Husbands, love your wives" (Ephesians 5:25), "Women [are] to love their husbands" (Titus 2:4), and "You yourselves have been taught by God to love one another" (1 Thessalonians 4:9). So, *no one* has *any* rationale for abusive behavior, which is most certainly an antonym of love (Chapter 1), and *none of us* should tolerate abuse.

- If you are in the early stages of being mistreated: Forgive your counterpart, and give them a second chance by talking to them about, for example, how the mistreatment makes you feel, and ideas for how to make your relationship healthier
- If you are the victim of chronic abuse: Forgive your counterpart (again, even if it's the seventy-eighth time), and since you've already given your counterpart ample chances, it's due time to protect yourself by initiating a timeout period, and to work toward the restoration of your dignity and, if possible, the reconstruction of a healthy relationship
  - If the relationship is a marriage, ample chances should be given for the two of you to remember the promises you made to one another on your wedding day. If, despite such attempts to reconcile, your spouse refuses to stop their abusive behavior, then from my vantage point this is justification for divorce.

Appendix D: What if you are considering divorce?

Be sure to read the "What if someone sins against you?" and "What if you are struggling to forgive yourself?" sections of Chapter 9. In addition, an important point is that even in light of significant marriage difficulties, God very much wants us to do all we can to reconcile with our spouse and to honor the commitment we made when we got married. Don't be so quick to use the excuse *"People change"* as justification to give up on the relationship. Of course people change. We all know that. When we make a commitment to become married, part of the commitment is that the two of us will work with each other through such changes.

I understand that there are some circumstances where reconciliation isn't achievable. Any conditional love relationship requires cooperation from both parties, and this is certainly true in marriage. If one or both parties are no longer willing to cooperate, then that certainly calls for a timeout period, and a timeout may become permanent and even legally binding via divorce. Clear grounds for divorce are sexual unfaithfulness (Matthew 5:31-32) and, I would add, abusive behavior without resolution (Appendix Ɔ). A divorce is a sad event, but when all reasonable attempts to reconcile have been exhausted, then divorce may very well be the most loving thing that can be done – a mechanism to free both parties to get on with their lives.

It goes without saying that any children of the divorced couple are in especially great need of love throughout the time leading up to and shortly after a divorce. In addition, the effective modeling of loving behavior by both parents will benefit the children's future relationships. To this end, the two being divorced should be very mindful of continuing to apply to each other the concepts of unconditional love, including that we strive to – at a minimum – offer forgiveness, and that we aspire to truly forgive. This isn't easy, but it's important; the children are watching, and you can teach them a great lesson by continuing to live in a loving way, even in the face of serious difficulties.

Appendix E: What if your parents have told you that you were a mistake?

Even if they didn't use the M-word (which is painful for me to write out completely, but I've done so in the title of this appendix), and even if they didn't express themselves in an intentionally hurtful way, we can misconstrue such messages (that we were not planned / that we were a surprise) to mean that we are the M-word in a broad sense – not only with respect to our parents' family planning. So, parents, please be sensitive to this if you have a child whom you didn't plan. My opinion is that there are very few circumstances where this information will benefit your child. Some things in life are meant to be private. Just as we close our bedroom door when we're intimate with our spouse (and others are present in the home), I advise that we not reveal to our children anything related to our family planning, especially if it pertains directly to them.

As I hinted at in the Prologue, my dad told me multiple times that I wasn't planned, and my recollection is that on some occasions he did use the M-word. He never said these things in an intentionally hurtful way, for example in the heat of anger. Rather, he told me in a matter-of-fact way; I think he honestly thought it was an interesting tidbit of information. When I was younger, there were times when I felt like the M-word in a broad sense. I really can't say definitively that my dad's tidbit of information and questionable word choices exacerbated such feelings in me, but I certainly can say that such things didn't help. So, my recommendation is that you simply not have this be a topic of conversation; choose more edifying subject matter, which should be very easy to do.

If your parents have told you that you were the M-word, I recommend thinking as I do now on the subject: I have concluded that it would be humdrum to the ultimate degree to have been conceived based on the amount of money in my parents' bank account, the number of seats in their cars, the number of bedrooms in their home, the amount of hand-me-down clothes that my siblings had not rendered completely unusable, the phase of the moon (time within a ~ monthly cycle), and such utilitarian considerations related to family planning; I'm delighted to think of my conception as having been the result of spontaneous passion.

Please don't misconstrue my (possibly biased) conclusion to mean that I frown upon the use of contraceptives. Quite the contrary! Appropriate (those that are effective only before conception) contraceptives enable married couples to have God-pleasing sex frequently – at almost all phases of the moon – which is so important for a healthy marriage. And if we ever feel the time is right for us to try to become pregnant, we then embark on another uniquely beautiful experience – making love with our spouse with the intent to conceive. However, as lofty as this peak is, I consider it to be overshadowed by the exquisite experience of a married couple submitting to one another in unplanned passion. And when we mutually submit in this way, occasionally there are ramifications… We may consider it a mistake, but God sees it differently. He has never made a mistake, and conception is no exception. Married couples: Please use appropriate contraceptives with my blessing *(Aren't you relieved?)* – I advise one pallet per lunation *(Look it up!)* – and if you stumble upon an unplanned pregnancy, I recommend thinking as I do now on the subject: When we aren't planning on a child but He is, it's a simple matter for Him to stoke our desire for one another at just the right time and with just the right amount of lack of planning. Yes, God wants married couples to enjoy sex, and on occasion He is very intent on this. "Therefore what God has joined together, let no one separate" (Mark 10:9 NIV).

I'll close this appendix with the following suggestion. If you feel compelled to talk to your child about their conception not being planned (and I advise that you initiate such a conversation only if they already know), then why not word it in such a way as this? *While it's true that your mom and I were surprised when she became pregnant with you, we thank God that He had better plans for us; we are thankful for you, our unplanned (from our perspective), but not unwanted, son.*

Appendix F: What if you need to make an important decision?

One thing I've noticed on life's journey is that it comes with many branch points. This is not an express train. No, there are many stops along our meandering route, and sometimes we even decide to get off our train and transfer to another. How do we know when it's time to make a transfer? And even when we know it's time, sometimes we find that we've stepped into Grand Central Station… So many trains to choose from! How do we decide which one to get on next?

I touch on this topic back in the "Love … rejoices with the truth" section (Chapter 8). There, I focus on two key ways by which we keep a sharp eye on the schedule board. The more obvious point is that we might miss our train if our attention is diverted and we drift away from remaining in tight prayer with God; we cannot doze off in the waiting room of Grand Central Station! The less obvious point is that we should be looking for signs that point to the way Satan wants us to go. When an unfamiliar conductor beckons us to climb aboard his shiny, luxury observation car, we tip our hat so he does the same – and we take a quick look for horns… This is how we know which trains not to get on.

What do horns look like? The ones I'm familiar with require me to compromise in inappropriate ways, for example, cause me to feel disrespected by the conductor of the train, or otherwise go against my values. In such cases, the decision is easy: This choice is eliminated from consideration altogether.

After we've culled out such chaff, we often find that we still have multiple viable choices left to triangulate (a.k.a., consider). This is not nappy time – we need to keep praying. When we're praying for guidance on a decision, what should we be praying about? Besides praying that all conductors on the platform will tip their hats, other things to pray for include:

- Peace of heart, soul, and mind, knowing that in so many instances there is not one right choice, with all others being wrong. God is not a puppeteer, with every one of our movements choreographed; no, much of our dance is freestyle. He allows for us to make our own choices, and – for those who love God – He works them together for good (cf. Romans 8:28). In light of this, there is nothing to fret about.
- Peace of heart, soul, and mind, knowing that in those instances where God *is* calling us to one "right choice," when we maintain an ever-open door of communication with Him (cf. 1 Thessalonians 5:17), then He will make it amply clear which one boxcar He wants us to jump onto. In light of this, there is nothing to fret about.

While we're busy not fretting, we nevertheless may find ourselves approaching a railroad switch, and we need to let the increasingly anxious switchman know which way we want to go. We may think, *OK, I'm comfortable that God is allowing me to freestyle this, but I still need to pick a song on the jukebox*. In such cases, I suggest the following love triangle. (You heard me.)

- The first point to consider is: What is the most loving thing that I can do for myself? For example, which choice will give me the most personal satisfaction, fulfillment, joy? Which choice is the best fit to my personal, long-term goals?
- The second point to consider is: What is the most loving thing that I can do for my family and close friends? For example, do any of the choices have an unacceptable impact on our stress level, or on the amount of quality time that we'll have together? Which choice best lends itself to maintaining proper balance in our lives?
- The third point to consider is: What is the most loving thing that I can do for all others? For example, which choice is the most likely to have a positive impact on society in general? Which choice best serves God's kingdom? Which choice makes the best use of my spiritual gift(s)?

Love triangles can be tricky. In the above type, we must not let any one factor out-weigh the other. It should not be any run-of-the-mill Isosceles triangle that you might happen to come across, and it certainly should not be a right triangle! No, it should be nothing other than a bona fide equilateral triangle. … *Have I lost you?* … I'm so sorry. Love triangles do get me ruffled. The punchline is that when we're busy not fretting about which song to pick on the jukebox, all three points should be given equal weight.

- Selfish people are tempted to give too much weight to the first point. They need to be reminded that – last time I checked – the world does not revolve around them.
- "Social bubble" people, enamored with the status quo – (whom I lovingly refer to as genuine extroverts, or endearing wannabes, who also happen to be in the prodromal stage of emotional lethargy, an infectious disease with a high severity index) – are tempted to give too much weight to the second point. They need to be reminded that we do not live in communal silos, only with our family and with our current social circle, regardless of how large this circle happens to be.
- People with low self-esteem are tempted to give too much weight to the third point. They need to be reminded not to discount their inherent value; they need to be reminded that they are just as lovable as anyone else – it's *Joy*, not *Jo$_y$*, when the topic is love (preamble to Chapter 4).

So, there you have it. When you're having trouble picking a song, just get out your handy dandy protractor, crunch some numbers, and see which choice brings your love triangle closest to the center of the dance floor.

~

I'd like to close this appendix with a reminder to allow, if at all possible, plenty of time for a proposed decision to settle in your mind before making it final – to "sleep on it," as they say. Most decisions don't need to be made immediately, even when some people try to convince you otherwise. A simple example is that a car you're considering buying will likely still be available the next morning, despite what the salesperson says.

Before you literally sleep on any decision, I advise that you write down your personal thoughts and feelings – not letting your mind shout down your heart – on the pros and cons of each song on the jukebox, triangulate as above, discuss with trusted advisors and/or any others directly involved in making the decision, and then go to bed and pray as described above. When you wake up, look again at the pros and cons you wrote down, consider any adjustments that are appropriate in the light of the new day, and ask yourself if you feel comfortable making a decision at this point. If you need more time, that's (usually) OK, and it's often helpful to talk about the situation with one or more good listeners. Love triangles are easier to understand when they're verbalized.

Finally, while it's important to listen to what your heart is telling you, try not to base a decision largely on emotions. When you write down the pros and cons, do your best to be objective, logical, and realistic; and don't forget to consider potential long-term consequences. This is a lot to consider, and you probably will need more than one night to sleep on it if it's an emotional topic, or if you're in a heightened emotional state.

Appendix G: Thought-action fusion

Thought-action fusion (TAF) is the concept that thoughts carry the same weight as the associated actions. From the perspective of psychology, this is a maladaptive belief that is commonly held by sufferers of obsessive compulsive disorder (OCD). From the perspective of theology, TAF is a belief that may be either maladaptive* or adaptive**.

- *If carried too far, TAF leads to religious OCD, a.k.a., scrupulosity
- **If carried the right distance, TAF reminds us that we *all* are sinners in desperate need of a Savior. We all are desperate because God demands perfection – "You therefore must be perfect, as your heavenly Father is perfect" (Matthew 5:48).
  - o Can you convince God or me that you're perfect because you've never literally committed adultery? I, for one, remain skeptical, and here's why: "You have heard that it was said, 'You shall not commit adultery.' But I [Jesus] say to you that everyone who looks at a woman [or man] with lustful intent has already committed adultery with her [or him] in his [or her] heart" (Matthew 5:27-28). "Do not be deceived: neither the sexually immoral … nor adulterers … will inherit the kingdom of God" (1 Corinthians 6:9-10).
  - o Can you convince God or me that you're perfect because you've never literally committed murder? I, for one, remain skeptical, and here's why: "You have heard that it was said to those of old, 'You shall not murder; and whoever murders will be liable to judgment.' But I [Jesus] say to you that everyone who is angry [without justifiable cause] with his brother will be liable to judgment; whoever insults his brother will be liable to the council; and whoever says, 'You fool!' will be liable to the hell of fire" (Matthew 5:21-22). "Everyone who hates his brother is a murderer, and you know that no murderer has eternal life abiding in him" (1 John 3:15).

So, *do* thoughts that are associated with clearly sinful actions carry the same weight as the actions themselves? No*, except from the perspective of our self-reliant merit before God**.

- *It's natural to have, from time to time, unwanted thoughts and strong, uncomfortable feelings. There's no need to feel ashamed. And we should only become concerned if we dwell on such thoughts and feelings, especially if this begins to have a negative impact on our emotional well-being or one of our relationships.

  Not dwelling on unwanted thoughts and feelings is difficult for many of us, and is especially challenging for those with OCD. Intrusive thoughts are common and often can be managed simply by acknowledging them (as opposed to trying not to think about them) and allowing them to pass by naturally (as opposed to trying to push them away immediately), and both steps can be facilitated by prayer and guided meditation. If you need help managing intrusive thoughts, I suggest finding a therapist experienced in exposure response prevention (ERP) therapy, as this is an effective treatment. Note to those struggling with scrupulosity: In my opinion, allowing yourself to experience otherwise unwanted thoughts and strong, uncomfortable feelings during ERP therapy is not sinful because you are doing it for the long-term benefit of your emotional and spiritual health.

- **Some would go so far as to refer to a brief sexual thought about someone other than our spouse, or a brief hateful thought about anyone, as a "featherweight sin." Well, I don't know the weight of your thoughts, but I do know that if our thoughts tick either of these boxes (while not in ERP therapy) then we are certainly disrespecting one or more of God's offspring, and this on its own suffices to render us completely undeserving of inheriting the kingdom of God; the scale that measures our self-reliant merit before God has become maximally tilted against us.

  If this comes as a surprise to you, then you are learning right now that each of us has a sinful nature and is entirely dependent on the righteousness of Jesus – the only One who meets His demand for perfection; it is through Him only that we are saved (John 14:6). Jesus has already carried the full load of all sins of all people – running the gamut from the most featherweight of actions to the most hefty of thoughts. So, when we trust in Jesus as our Savior, He delights in welcoming us into His kingdom – all burdens lifted.

Appendix H: What if someone tells you that God's love is conditional before His judgment of you?

They are wrong. People who like to say that God's love is conditional before we are judged by Him are often quite passionate about this. I think it has something to do with their desire to feel special – better than the rest of us (self-righteous). Naysayers who try to teach us that God's love is conditional before God's judgment of us are false prophets led by the spirit of the antichrist (Matthew 24:8-12; 1 John 4:1-6) and are to be avoided because they erode our spiritual health.

Appendix H-2: Let's dive into the murky waters, shall we?

Below are the most common arguments of the naysayers.

- They assert that even before God's judgment of us, we have to believe / have faith / accept / not reject in order for God to love us. They are wrong because we – of course based on the indwelling of the Holy Spirit – have to do such things in order to be *saved*, but we know that God saves even those who come to faith at the last moment (Matthew 20:1-16). Until the time of God's judgment, God loves us no matter what. The only thing that can cause us to fall away from God's love is our rejection of Him at the time of His judgment.

- They say that there are Scripture passages that prove their point. (See the list below.) They are wrong because they are picking and choosing verses out of context, twisting the meaning to fit their self-righteous fantasies. For example:
  - John 15:9-11 – "As the Father has loved me [Jesus], so have I loved you. Abide in my love. If you keep my commandments, you will abide in my love, just as I have kept my Father's commandments and abide in his love. These things I have spoken to you, that my joy may be in you, and that your joy may be full."

    Naysayers especially like to thump their Bible on "If you keep my commandments, you will abide in my love." But while God wants us to be perfect (Matthew 5:48), He forgives, and our righteousness is Jesus' righteousness (Romans 1:17; 1 Corinthians 1:30; 2 Corinthians 5:21; Philippians 3:9) unless we reject Him.

    But the naysayers don't give up, and say that the last four words of my previous sentence prove that for Him to love us we need to not reject Him. They don't seem to understand that Jesus is talking about abiding (remaining) in His love for all eternity, *at and after* the time of God's judgment. I have already explained that God loves us no matter what up until the time of His judgment.
    - And what naysayers *don't* want you to see is a few verses earlier – specifically, John 14:23-24. Read these two verses carefully, and for clarity I've provided the verse numbers and italicized the words that I'm asking you to focus on here. Jesus says: "[23]… *If anyone loves me, he will keep my word, and my Father will love him*, and we will come to him and make our home with him. [24]*Whoever does not love me does not keep my words*. And the word that you hear is not mine but the Father's who sent me."

      Verse 23 says something similar to what I discuss in the preceding bullet point. (In v. 23, it could almost sound like the Father only loves us when we love Jesus, even before God judges us.)

      Here's something new: In v. 24, note that it certainly does *not* say that the Father does not love us when we do not love Jesus. This is a significant omission in v. 24, and it's not a coincidence.
  - 2 Timothy 2:12 – Speaking of Jesus, Paul writes: "If we deny him, he also will deny us."

    Again, this is talking about our rejection of Him at the time of God's judgment.
  - Malachi 3:7 – "Return to me, and I will return to you, says the LORD of hosts."

    It's hard to sound more conditional than this! That's right – I already told you (Prologue and Chapter 2) that salvation is dependent on belief; and I'm telling you now that God promises to bless those who give generously in their offerings to Him (Malachi 3:10).

- Luke 2:14 – "Glory to God in the highest heaven, and on earth peace to those on whom his favor rests" (NIV).

  ... Shh! ... Is that the sound of reindeer on the roof? ... No, that's the sound of a grumpy naysayer, trying to ruin our Christmas Eve by thudding his Bible rhythmically as he recites, "those on whom His favor rests." But just a couple words before that it says, "peace to those." This peace means reconciliation with God the Father – salvation. Such reconciliation is reserved for believers (see the fortunate and necessary paragraph (Prologue)).

- Romans 7:18a – Paul writes: "I know that nothing good dwells in me."

  Naysayers will stop right here (not reading further in this verse) and twist this to try to convince us that there's nothing inherent about us for God to love... Think about that for a moment... Think about what they're saying! ... They'll admit that we have a changed heart when we come to faith, leaving the dire situation we find ourselves in when we insist on independence: "The heart is deceitful above all things, and desperately sick" (Jeremiah 17:9), to attain the joys of dependence on God: "I [God] will give you a new heart, and a new spirit I will put within you" (Ezekiel 36:26). But naysayers forget that there *is* something inherent about us for God to love, even before we come to faith. ... *What is it?* ... Yes, there really is something: Humans are God's creatures, and not just any creatures; He has always created and still creates each human in His image and likeness (Genesis 1:26-27; Genesis 5:1-2; James 3:9); He creates each of us with an "inmost being" (Psalm 103:1 NIV; Psalm 139:13 NIV); yes, we are "fearfully and wonderfully made" (Psalm 139:14). For such reasons, it's certain that each human is inherently valuable, even to the everlasting God (Matthew 13:44-46; Luke 15). How can I be so confident? Because it is the everlasting God's nature to love – "God is love" (1 John 4:8, 16) – and He cannot go against His nature. God's nature to love – yes, to love even sinners – was manifested throughout Jesus' earthly ministry, where it was unambiguously clear to all who were observing that "This man [Jesus] receives sinners" (Luke 15:2). God's nature to love was made most abundantly and awesomely clear on Good Friday, when Jesus died on the cross to save His "fearfully and wonderfully made" creatures. And never forget that Jesus did this before we could do anything that might look like we "deserve" His love. "Christ died for the ungodly ... God shows his love for us in that while we were still sinners, Christ died for us" (Romans 5:6, 8).

  As I alluded to above, the naysayers like to stop reading when it no longer supports their point. They don't even need to go into the next verse to see that what Paul actually writes is: "I know that nothing good dwells in me, *that is, in my flesh*" (Romans 7:18, emphasis mine). Of course God doesn't love my sinful flesh. God doesn't love me because of what I've become, by my own effort and drifting; no, He loves me because I'm inherently valuable to Him, just the way

He made me, at conception – nay, even before that (Psalm 139:16; Jeremiah 1:5a). I am much more than sinful flesh! Sinful flesh is not part of my "inner being" (Romans 7:22; Ephesians 3:16); sinful flesh has nothing to do with what "in his own image" (Genesis 1:27) means.

Appendix H-3: Whom God "hates" and when

- ○ Romans 9:13 – God says: "Jacob I loved, but Esau I hated."

   OK, now the naysayers are really grasping at straws. Where do I begin? First of all, the reference to Jacob and Esau here is referring to nations, not individuals. Jacob refers to the Israelites, and Esau refers to the Edomites. Before you think that sounds even worse, let me remind you that "loved" here simply means chosen, and "hated" here simply means not chosen. Are the Edomites the chosen people? Sometime between our earliest days in Sunday School and right now, we have learned that they are not. Does God only love the Israelites? We know that the answer to this is "No."

- ○ Revelation 2:6 – Jesus says: "You hate the works of the Nicolaitans, which I also hate."

   Apparently, naysayers like to speed read. It looks like they've missed a few words here. They think this verse means that Jesus hates the Nicolaitans. Oh, wait – it doesn't say that, does it? No, it certainly does not say that! It says He hates *the works of* the Nicolaitans. We already know that God hates sin.

- ○ Psalm 5:5-6 – "The boastful shall not stand before your eyes; you hate all evildoers. / You destroy those who speak lies; the LORD abhors the bloodthirsty and deceitful man."

   I grow weary of such picking and choosing. … *How long must I endure this? "How long will you torment me and break me in pieces with words?" (Job 19:2).* … Ten slow, deep cleansing breaths… … OK, now I'm ready. … The verse before this states something all the rest of us know by now: "You are not a God who delights in wickedness; evil may not dwell with you" (Psalm 5:4). And just a few verses after this, it's made abundantly clear that those being referred to in vv. 5-6 "have rebelled against you [God]" (Psalm 5:10). One of my first memories – way, way back – is being taught, in no uncertain terms, that those who rebel against God – those who thoroughly and persistently reject Jesus as their Savior – cannot stand before God; yes, they will be abhorred – a.k.a., not chosen – when it's their time to be judged.

- ○ *More?* Yes, there's more… Here's one of their favorites: Proverbs 6:16-19 – "There are six things that the LORD hates, seven that are an abomination to him: / haughty eyes, a lying tongue, and hands that shed innocent blood, / a heart that devises wicked plans, feet that make haste to run to evil, / a false witness who breathes out lies, and one who sows discord among brothers."

This is strong language, and naysayers take such passages as the green light to hate some others. So, we can see that in addition to picking and choosing Bible passages, naysayers have taken their narrow-minded thinking a step further and are now even picking and choosing people to love or to hate. But the rest of us know that this list of things God hates is an abbreviated list – nowhere near complete. We understand that God hates *all* sin and will condemn to hell ("hate" at and after their judgment) *all* people who persist in rebellion against Him in any way – who have chosen to live a life, all the way to the bitter end, directed not by Him but by their unique, personal list of sinful desires that are aligned with their own preferences. Here are more things that God hates: the sin of a judgmental attitude (Matthew 7:1-5; Romans 2:1-3), and a man or woman who at the time of their judgment has nothing to show except a life directed not by Him but by their own singular brand of hate, rejecting a life of mercy and forgiveness. When it's our turn to give an account to the only rightful Judge, I do not suggest that one of our discussion points be that we have chosen hate, and thus have rejected a life of mercy and forgiveness...

Appendix H-4: Predestination & universal salvation

- And I've saved the best for last! What naysayers really foam at the mouth about is predestination, specifically their misinterpretation that this means that some (not all) people are predestined *not* to be saved. (Actually, they prefer to say "predestined to go to hell.") No, predestination means that some (not all) people are predestined to be saved. More on this distinction in the next paragraph, but first let's discuss "not all." It seems to contradict 1 Timothy 2:3-4 which states: "God our Savior ... desires all people to be saved and to come to the knowledge of the truth." You might think that I'm now going to go on at some length trying to disprove predestination or even to go a step further and try to prove universal salvation. No, I'm not going to do either because predestination is truth and universal salvation is false. But how can predestination and God's desire for all people to be saved (which is not the same thing as universal salvation) both be true? This is an example of a mystery that we cannot understand, but both are true regardless. Do we know the mind of God? No (Romans 11:33-34), as Job is reminded at some length in Job chapters 38 and 39.

  Now I'm going to address how the truth that some people are predestined to be saved does *not* mean that some people are predestined to go to hell. First, please read Jesus' words in Matthew 25:31-46 carefully. I've provided a portion of that passage below, and within this I've italicized and bolded the words I'm going to address further.

    When the Son of Man comes in his glory, and all the angels with him, then he will sit on his glorious throne. Before him will be gathered all the nations, and he will separate people one from another as a shepherd separates the sheep from the goats. And he will place the sheep on his right, but the goats on the left. Then the King will say to those on his right, "Come, you who are blessed by my Father, inherit the kingdom *prepared for you* from the foundation of the world. ..."

Then he will say to those on his left, "Depart from me, you cursed, into the eternal fire *prepared for the devil and his angels*. ..." And these will go away into eternal punishment, but the righteous into eternal life. (Matthew 25:31-34, 41, 46)

Note that in the first paragraph it says "prepared for you" (v. 34). This is in line with some people being predestined to be saved.

Note that in the second paragraph it says "prepared for the devil and his angels" (v. 41). This is *not* in line with some people being predestined to go to hell. (If they were predestined to go to hell, then why wasn't hell prepared *for them*?)

Are you with me? The main takeaway here is that no one should ever – ever, ever – think that they or anyone else might be predestined to go to hell. That is rubbish! Please see Appendix J, not far below, for more on this topic. In a nutshell, until the time of God's judgment, it's not too late for you or anyone to stop rejecting Jesus as Savior.

OK, so what the heck does all this have to do with the naysayers' view of God's love? Quite simply, they say that God never – never, ever – loves people who are predestined to go to hell. I hope that by now I've convinced you that this is a warped and nonsensical point of view, wrong on multiple levels.

Am I saying that no one will go to hell? No, I am not saying that. Surely, those who reject Jesus as their Savior at the time of God's judgment will go to hell (v. 41). Am I saying that there are no people alive whom God already knows will go to hell? No, I am not saying that either! I am open to the possibility that there is a vast minority of people – none of whom would tolerate reading a book like the one you're reading right now, most certainly not this deep into the appendices – who have become forever lost but are kept on earth for some purpose; for example, Pharaoh's heart was hardened (Exodus 7-14) but he still had a role to play (Romans 9:17-18). I am open to the possibility that there may be some people for whom the time of God's judgment has come while they are still alive. If such people indeed exist, shouldn't we try to figure out who they are, so we can hate them? No, we can't know for sure if someone is in this category. For one thing, we're not to judge (Psalm 75; Matthew 7:1-5; John 5:22; Romans 2:1-3; 1 Corinthians 4:5). For another thing, I am open to the possibility that there really is no one in this category. Am I backpedaling? No, I'm simply acknowledging that God has the power to graft anyone back into His olive tree (Romans 11:23).

~

Don't be lured by the siren song of the naysayers. Their message that God does not love us unconditionally might sometimes resonate with our human way of thinking – that love must be earned – so be careful when they come after you! Satan wants you to be swayed by them, so don't be surprised by the frequency and vitriol of their attacks (Matthew 24:11-13). But it really is remarkably easy to refute their message – all we need to do is look to *all* Scripture, not just their favorite verses that they like to take out of context and twist to stroke their self-righteous fetishes. I can pick and choose verses too! And mine are not out of context! For example, how about Galatians 5:12? (Yes, I'm checking on whether you're really looking up all my Scripture references.)

I'll now settle down and end this appendix with the following: Let's pray for the naysayers, show them love, and who knows? Maybe they'll be swayed by us!

Appendix I: What if you are worried that you are not predestined to be saved?

Your concern is a symptom of your desire to have a relationship with God, and this means that the Spirit is working in you. If knowing this isn't enough, and you're still anxious about whether you're predestined to be saved, trust me when I tell you that God loves you no matter what your past looks like, and absolutely wants you to be saved (1 Timothy 2:3-4; Titus 2:11 NIV; 2 Peter 3:8-9); then – *Don't stop there!* – read the following prayer, believe it (take it to heart), find a church that believes the same thing, and regularly worship God there. Yes, when you confess this belief (Romans 10:9), nothing will be able to separate you from God's love (Romans 8:38-39).

- *Heavenly Father, I believe that Your Son Jesus is not only the Savior of the whole world – yes, He is Lord of all – but is also my personal Savior – yes, He is my Lord. I do believe that Jesus died to pay the price for all my sins, was raised from the dead, lives and reigns with You, and is preparing a place for me to live for all eternity in the presence of Your everlasting love (Psalm 100:5; Isaiah 54:10; Jeremiah 31:3; Lamentations 3:22-23; Romans 8:38-39). Please grant me peace, especially during those times when I hear confusing messages that can cause me to doubt these truths. Throughout the rest of my life, help me to stand steadfast in Your amazing love. Amen.*

Appendix J: What if someone tells you that since God is love, all people are saved?

They are wrong. People who like to say that all people are saved are avoiding clear passages such as John 3:36 – "Whoever believes in the Son has eternal life, but whoever rejects the Son will not see life, for God's wrath remains on them" (NIV), and Mark 16:16 – "Whoever believes and is baptized will be saved, but whoever does not believe will be condemned." People who try to teach us that God's unconditional love means that He cannot condemn people to hell are false prophets led by the spirit of the antichrist (Matthew 24:8-11; 1 John 4:1-6) and are to be avoided because they erode our spiritual health.

Yes, "God is love" (1 John 4:8, 16), but there comes a time when people who persistently reject God will no longer have access to this love. This time is commonly referred to as Judgment Day, and the Bible uses many phrases for this. The ESV translation refers to "the day of judgment" (Matthew 10:15, 11:22, 11:24, 12:36; 2 Peter 2:9, 3:7; 1 John 4:17), "the great day" (Zephaniah 1:14; Jude 1:6; Revelation 6:17; Revelation 16:14), "the day of wrath" (Proverbs 11:4; Romans 2:5), "the day of the LORD" (Ezekiel 30:3; Joel 1:15; Obadiah 1:15; Zephaniah 1:7; and many others), "the day of the Lord" (1 Corinthians 5:5; 1 Thessalonians 5:2; 2 Thessalonians 2:2; 2 Peter 3:10), "the great and awesome day of the LORD" (Joel 2:31; Malachi 4:5), "the great and magnificent day" (Acts 2:20), "the last day" (John 6:39, 40, 44, 54, 11:24, 12:48), "that day" (2 Thessalonians 1:10), and, my personal favorite, simply "the day" (Ezekiel 30:3; Joel 1:15).

In light of all this, it's hard to argue that there's not one Judgment Day – one final time when all who have ever lived will be either raised (if they've already died (1 Corinthians 15:20-23, 42-50)) or transformed (if they've not died (1 Corinthians 15:51-53)), and those who believe in Jesus as their Savior will have eternal life in heaven (Matthew 25:34) and those who don't believe in Jesus as their Savior will have eternal damnation in hell (Matthew 25:41).

Yes, there is a time when this will be revealed to all. Nevertheless, I want to emphasize that time does eventually run out for each of us as individuals, and for most people throughout history this time is before Judgment Day. So, in this book I use the phrase "the time of God's judgment," referring to when, for each of us as individuals, our time is up – God's judgment of us is set (Appendix B). For each of us, there will come a time of God's judgment, and consider this – not only is it not the same time for all of us, but also none of us know when it is! All we do know is that it's whichever of the following that comes first for us: (i) Judgment Day, (ii) our death, or (iii) a time in our life when we are forever lost but kept on earth for some purpose (as I think Pharaoh was; Appendices B and H-4).

Scripture makes it evident that God loves us all the way until the time of God's judgment. Until that time – *(And remember, we don't know when that is!)* – we are still loved by God, and no matter what we have done, no matter what we have said, no matter what we have thought, and no matter how bad we might feel about any of this and more, He is ready and willing for us to bask in His love and start a new life.

~

It's amply clear from Scripture that not everyone is saved. But you have nothing to fear about the time of God's judgment if you remain in His love, which simply means that you don't reject Jesus as your Savior.

God is both merciful and just. When it's your time to be judged, which will you experience firsthand: mercy or justice? ... Remember, Jesus has already paid the price that justice demands. On the cross, Jesus experienced justice. Based on His payment, we will experience everlasting mercy, if we trust in His redeeming work. Yes, if we remain in His love, we will experience firsthand that "Mercy triumphs over judgment" (James 2:13); God will accept us because Jesus' righteousness is our righteousness (Romans 1:17; 1 Corinthians 1:30; 2 Corinthians 5:21; Philippians 3:9). In this way, we are assured that we will live forever with Him in heaven, where we will fully experience perfectly requited love (Chapter 1).

Appendix K: Imprecatory prayers

In the Top 25 of my least favorite questions is: "Should we pray imprecatory prayers?" If you must ask, then my answer is yes and n... – no, let me rephrase that – yes and I don't recommend improvising. Allow me to explain myself.

Imprecatory prayers – which are prayers for God to punish evildoers – are part of Scripture (e.g., Psalm 69), so, yes, I encourage you to read those parts too. These particular prayers have been written by inspired writers, and as such they happen to know that the people they are asking God to judge harshly or otherwise punish are outside of God's kingdom. God will certainly punish severely all those who reject Jesus as their Savior at the time of His judgment, rendering themselves outside of God's kingdom. So, yes, it's reasonable to pray that God punish such people; actually, this is part of the sentiment when we pray, "Thy kingdom come, Thy will be done in earth, as it is in heaven" (Matthew 6:10 KJV), and I hope you pray this frequently.

Some people may find it cathartic to create their own imprecatory prayers from time to time, but to them I say, *Tread very carefully*. Do we know who is outside of God's kingdom? Many times in this book, I say that we are not to judge. With this in mind, below is my advice on how to create your own imprecatory prayer, and I recommend not going down this path unless you are experiencing something truly heinous, and you are feeling angry or scared or both.

- In all our prayers, it's always a good idea to include expressions of our feelings. If you are creating an imprecatory prayer, predominant feeling(s) for you are probably anger or fear or both. If we're fearful, of course we should take it to God. Likewise, if we're angry, of course we should take it to God. However, at all times (in and outside of conscious prayer), be careful that your anger does not slip into hate. Anger is a feeling. Hate is a choice; and in light of 1 John 3:15, I do not recommend making that choice.

- I can imagine scenarios where it may help some of you process your feelings by asking God to pour out His wrath onto another person or group of people. I can accept this, under one condition: Such a request must be preceded by asking God to provide this person / these people ample opportunities to repent – turn to Jesus. The call to repentance comes before judgment (Matthew 4:17; Luke 13:3, 5).

The closest I plan on getting to creating an imprecatory prayer myself is already provided in the "What if you encounter evil in the world?" section (Chapter 9). Toward the end of that section, there is a prayer for the perpetrator(s) of an evil deed. If you'd like to add more wrath, may I suggest the following alternate ending to that prayer? *Heavenly Father, if at the time of Your judgment of the perpetrator(s) they do not believe in Jesus as their Savior, then judge them justly.* That may not sound very wrathful, but – truth be told – God judging unbelievers justly is as wrathful as it gets (Hebrews 10:26-31; Revelation 19:15).

Appendix M: Dr. Bob's tips on how to take MBTI tests in an unbiased manner

Myers-Briggs Type Indicator (MBTI) tests are in abundance on the internet, for example, at the following web addresses: www.16personalities.com, www.truity.com, and www.mbtionline.com.

To increase the likelihood that you'll obtain an accurate result for yourself, try your best to be unbiased / impartial. Generally, the most accurate result is obtained when the MBTI test is administered by a trained professional, because they can help evaluate whether you're answering impartially.

If you take the MBTI test on your own, please note the following advice on how to be unbiased.

- Consider each question thoughtfully before answering. This is not a race; if you rush through, expecting me to give you more recess time, I'm going to disappoint you. Although, some of you – (You know who you are…) – need to refrain from wringing your hands and overthinking it. Your answers should reflect what you truly do feel in your heart, not what you think you should feel or what you wish you felt. It typically doesn't take very long to know what your heart's telling you.

- Don't give an answer that you think someone would want to see. Be honest. No one else needs to see your answers. Pretend that you're giving your answers to a professional counselor.
- Don't think about how you might have answered a question in the past. Think about the present time.
- When you've completed the questions, I think it's a good idea to go through the entire list of questions a second time quickly, just to do a final check to see if your heart's telling you that you were inconsistent in any portions, in which case maybe a few answers should be changed or made more or less extreme. (Those things that you feel especially strongly about should be indicated by giving the most extreme answer. Typically, the questions are yes / no questions, with seven or five answers to choose from, e.g., YES, yes, uncertain, no, NO.)

Appendix Q: Periodic check-ins

Check-ins are one-on-one candid discussions in a safe environment where all topics are fair game. It's beneficial for married couples to maintain frequent check-ins, with good timing being anywhere between a few minutes every day to at least half an hour once per week. If you're not already having periodic check-ins with your spouse, I highly recommend starting now. When forming your new habit, please reach agreement on the location(s), ground rules, and format. Below are a few suggestions that are written assuming you'll establish *both* a weekly thorough check-in *and* a daily quickie.

- Location(s)
  - Anywhere you both feel comfortable speaking freely, are able to focus on one another, and are not likely to be interrupted by others
- Ground rules
  - Kindness, empathy, active listening, and paraphrasing to confirm understanding
  - No judgment, criticism, blaming, or defensiveness
  - No interrupting; take turns giving your counterpart the gift of being heard
  - No hijacking (i.e., no changing the focus to your preference before your counterpart has been able to express themselves fully and receive an empathic response)
  - Don't give advice unless your counterpart asks for it or agrees to your offer to provide it; a good friend is a listener, not a slow- or quick-fix sleuth
  - Defer logistical matters until a later time. (When I remind my wife of this, I like to say in a lighthearted way, "I haven't heard a feeling word in a while.")
  - Commit to meeting regularly, to the extent reasonably possible. Put it on your calendars, and don't form the habit of frequently delaying or canceling.
  - Honor a time limit that's based on your ability to focus and remain enthusiastic for your next check-in. It's generally advisable not to go over 60 minutes.
  - Each gets roughly equal time to express themselves; take turns

- o   If either starts to feel a little uncomfortable or frustrated, de-escalate by saying something like, "I'd like a minute to think about this"
- o   If either feels more than a little uncomfortable or frustrated, or an argument forms, initiate a longer timeout, at least on that particular topic. This timeout may be just a few minutes or all the way until your next weekly check-in, but generally the sooner the better to minimize time of reduced closeness. If you are in couples therapy, your next session may be a good time to revisit the topic.
- Format for weekly
  1) Each describe prominent emotion(s) you've experienced over the past week, and rate the highest intensity of each on a scale of 1 to 10. It's fine if you don't understand why you've had these feelings.
  2) Each give one to a few highlights related to interactions with others outside of your relationship, e.g., other family members, friends, coworkers
  3) Each elaborate on things you appreciate, especially related to your relationship. What has helped the two of you stay connected?
  4) Together discuss points of misunderstanding, conflict, tension, or that are uncomfortable to talk about, especially related to your relationship. How can you better understand one another?
  5) Closing affirmation
- Format for daily
  - o   Not long before going to bed, each of you, in turn, consider your day and choose one item related to any of points 1-4, above. If either choses point 4, definitely add point 5, and I'm hopeful that any way this evolves can never be mistaken for a quickie.

Check-ins shouldn't turn into gripe sessions. Any topic related to point 4, above, is usually best initiated as soon as the issue arises or very shortly afterwards, with the subsequent check-in providing an opportunity to follow up – to have another aftermath discussion. This is generally preferable to launching a new point 4 topic from out of the blue during a check-in, but do what you need to do; it's better to initiate a new point 4 topic during a check-in than never to bring it up at all. Also, it is fair game to bring up a topic from long before the previous check-in, provided that your motivation to unpack the dusty item is to enhance the relationship. It can be tempting to spend a lot of time on point 4, but remember that typically it shouldn't occupy more than a quarter, or at most a third, of your overall check-in time. You may choose to make an exception to this occasionally, and I can accept this if you keep in mind the next paragraph.

Check-ins shouldn't turn into arguments. A check-in is a safe environment with no room for judgment, criticism, blaming, or defensiveness. But there's plenty of room for all emotions, not the least of which is anger. In my opinion, the most important elements of an effective check-in are being heard and authenticity. And sometimes authenticity requires the expression of anger. When you and/or your counterpart expresses anger in a loving way during a check-in, then you can rest assured that the two of you are on the right track: authenticity is alive and well, and mutual understanding is being given a great opportunity to increase by leaps and bounds.

Appendix S: Bilateral stimulation

A common and effective treatment for post-traumatic stress disorder is eye movement desensitization and reprocessing (EMDR). EMDR is the first form of bilateral stimulation to be developed for use in psychotherapy. Other forms of bilateral stimulation are becoming more common, such as the alternating actuation of vibrators held in the palms of one's hands. It may sound like witchcraft, but there is something about the alternating stimulation from one side of your body to the other, just a second or so per side, repeated many times, that really does help many patients unpack and repack traumatic events and the associated emotions.

Your mileage may vary, but my experience has been that it's most efficient to start with conventional cognitive behavioral therapy (CBT) and later supplement with bilateral stimulation. I like to think of it as excavating a tunnel – first drilling holes and planting dynamite sticks at just the right spots with CBT, and later lighting fuses with bilateral stimulation. Such imagery may cause some of you to feel squeamish because I'm relating this to changes within our brains… But never fear – it's just an analogy, and this one's not related to sex.

Appendix X: FAQ #1: *Bob, why do you have so many analogies related to sex?*

Short answer: Because I want to.

Longer answer: This book is about love – a very broad topic that generally is difficult to describe. When we can't quite wrap our head around a concept, using analogies can help because the subject matter is put in terms to which we can more easily relate.

All loving relationships have some degree of emotional intimacy, but it can be difficult to put our finger on adequate words to describe this. Many loving relationships have an extensive degree of physical intimacy (i.e., shared sexual experiences), to which most adults can relate very well. While many of us aren't particularly interested in trying to put our finger on *any* words to describe our sexual experiences, in our mind's eye we see this ethereal concurrence very clearly. We may be speechless, but we can relate nevertheless.

Also, the privacy related to sex lends itself to illustrating the privacy there typically is (at least to some degree) in all of our one-on-one loving relationships – I mean, even the platonic ones. For example, it may be a little hard for me to convince you that it's generally not a good idea to post on your Facebook page what your friend told you in a one-on-one conversation the night before, but you'll get the message when I compare this to your partner posting on their Facebook page details of your sex life.

Appendix Y: Polly

(I read ~ the following at the reception after the memorial service for my sister, Polly, on November 9th, 2019.)

~

Hi, my name's Bob, and I'm Polly's youngest brother.

I'd like to say a few words, but before I get to that, I want to start passing around this picture [second picture on the back cover] of Polly and me from a few years back.

I'm going to start by quoting an Alfred Hitchcock film. In *The Birds*, Melanie Daniels asks Mitch Brenner, "[Do] you know what a mother's love is?"[3]

My answer to Melanie's question is, "Yes, I know, doubly well."

Polly and I were loved by our mother, but then our mom died of breast cancer when we were young. Often, when I've looked back on that loss, I've focused on how hard it was for me. But sometimes, especially recently, I remember how hard this was for Polly too. She was only 18 years old when our mom died. Polly was the oldest of four siblings, all of whom were sad and confused at that time. Polly rose to the occasion by caring for us when our mom was ill and after she passed away.

An image I have from that time period is me sitting alone in my room, sad and lonely. I'm sitting on the floor, looking up through the window, at a tree and the sky. My door is shut, and I'm wondering when someone will find me. ... Polly was the first to find me in my little game of hide-and-seek.

One of my favorite memories involves Polly finding me one evening when I was having a hard time falling asleep. She sat down next to me in my bed, and she read me a book that I liked. Especially meaningful to me is that I dozed off briefly, then woke back up, and was happy to find that Polly was still reading. She hadn't left me.

~

As I began to venture outside of my room more often, from time to time I would get into a bit of a pickle. ... One particularly elaborate quandary has come to be known simply as the blue dye incident. It started as a simple matter. I mean, how much trouble can two boys get into with a white tee-shirt, rubber bands, blue dye, and a pot of boiling water? A kitchen floor isn't that hard to clean, right? My friend, Doug, and I were making good progress on our own until we started traipsing into the dining room which, coincidentally enough, had a thick, lightly hued carpet… Suffice it to say that the task became larger than Doug and I could face, and Polly was called in as reinforcement. We – mainly she… – almost got it all cleaned up by the time our dad got home from work, emphasis on the almost… But Polly pulled a rabbit out of her hat. She found a small throw rug, and put it to good use by placing it in a particularly strategic location of the dining room floor. Sure enough, our dad asked what that was about. Thankfully, he was satisfied with Polly's answer that she was experimenting with new looks. He was none the wiser!

Then there was the time when my friends – Doug, Neil, and Dave – and I decided that our latest adventure on the roof of the shed in my back yard just wasn't complete without lunch. It didn't take Polly long to appreciate the full magnitude of what we were requesting, and it was her suggestion that grilled cheese sandwiches are most suitable for a rooftop meal. It was then and there that my friends and I agreed that their moms would never go to such extremes.

These are the kinds of memories I have of Polly.

~

When I learned a couple months ago that Polly's health was declining, I considered whether I would come out to see her, or if I would prefer to have my last memories of her be as a beautiful woman with an infectious smile, bubbly laugh, and a singular sense of humor. While it would have been fine for me to choose not to come out to see Polly one more time, five weeks ago I decided to go ahead and do it. I figured she would look different, and when I came into her hospice room, I was shocked at what I found… a beautiful woman with an infectious smile, bubbly laugh, and a singular sense of humor.

One of my favorite memories from that visit is when Polly was taking a nap. I stayed in her room with her, sitting by her bed – just the two of us. I used that quiet time to remember another dimly lit room where Polly and I spent time together. During her nap, Polly stirred a few times, looking up briefly to see who was in the room with her – once asking, "Do you want a pillow?" – and then she would lay her head back down.

I'll never forget that room: that's where Polly napped; that's where we told stories; that's where I scratched an itch or two of hers; that's where we looked at picture albums from years gone by; that's where we said goodbye.

Yes, I know what a mother's love is, and I love you too, Polly.

Endnotes

The author claims fair use, based on the fund-raising nature of this book; all net proceeds from the sale of this book are given to the National Suicide Prevention Lifeline, the National Domestic Violence Hotline, and potentially additional nonprofit organizations having similar goals.

Prologue

[1] Mohr, "Silent Night, Holy Night," tr. Young, *Lutheran Service Book* (St. Louis: Concordia Publishing House, 2006), 363, 1

[2] Luther, "From Heaven Above to Earth I Come," tr. Winkworth, *Lutheran Service Book* (St. Louis: Concordia Publishing House, 2006), 358, 13

[3] Havergal, "Take My Life and Let It Be," *Lutheran Service Book* (St. Louis: Concordia Publishing House, 2006), 783

[4] Houston, Joel and Myrin, Jonas. "Broken Vessels (Amazing Grace)." Hillsong Music Publishing, 2014.

[5] Oswald Chambers, "February 7," *My Utmost for His Highest: Selections for the Year* (New York: Dodd, Mead & Company, 1935)

Chapter 1

[1] Mozi, *Book 4 – Universal Love II*, tr. W.P. Mei, (Donald Sturgeon, Chinese Text Project: a dynamic digital library of premodern Chinese, *Digital Scholarship in the Humanities* 2019); retrieved 26 August 2020 from https://ctext.org/mozi/universal-love-ii

[2] Plato, *Phaedrus*, tr. Benjamin Jowett, (Urbana, IL: Project Gutenberg, 2008); retrieved 26 August 2020 from http://www.gutenberg.org/ebooks/1636

[3] https://en.wikiquote.org/wiki/Aristotle (Diogenes Laërtius, *The Lives and Opinions of Eminent Philosophers*); retrieved 26 August 2020

[4] https://en.wikiquote.org/wiki/Augustine_of_Hippo (H. Browne and J. H. Meyers, *The Nicene and Post Nicene Fathers* (1995)); retrieved 26 August 2020

[5] Rumi, *The Masnavi I Ma'navi*, tr. E.H. Whinfield, (London: Global Grey, 2018), 5 (The Prince and the Handmaid); retrieved 26 August 2020 from https://www.globalgreyebooks.com/masnavi-i-manavi-ebook.html

[6] http://www.va/archive/ccc_css/archive/catechism/p3s1c1a5.htm (*Summa Theologiae* I-II, 26 4, *corp. art.*); retrieved 26 August 2020

[7] William Shakespeare, *Romeo and Juliet*, (London: Global Grey, 2019), 15 (Act 1, Scene 1); retrieved 26 August 2020 from https://www.globalgreyebooks.com/romeo-and-juliet-ebook.html

8 William Shakespeare, *Twelfth Night*, (London: Global Grey, 2018), 81 (Act 3, Scene 1); retrieved 26 August 2020 from https://www.globalgreyebooks.com/twelfth-night-ebook.html

9 Johann Wolfgang Goethe, *Erotica Romana*, (Urbana, IL: Project Gutenberg, 2009), XV; retrieved 26 August 2020 from http://www.gutenberg.org/ebooks/7889

10 Honoré de Balzac, *The Physiology of Marriage*, tr. Katharine Prescott Wormeley, (Urbana, IL: Project Gutenberg, 2010), LX; retrieved 26 August 2020 from http://www.gutenberg.org/ebooks/16205

11 Victor Hugo, *Les Misérables*, (London: Global Grey, 2019), 1170; retrieved 26 August 2020 from https://www.globalgreyebooks.com/les-miserables-ebook.html

12 Helen Keller, *The Story of My Life*, (Urbana, IL: Project Gutenberg, 2000), Letters (1887-1901) (June 8, 1891); retrieved 31 August 2020 from http://www.gutenberg.org/ebooks/2397

13 M.K. Gandhi, *Speeches and Writings of M.K. Gandhi*, 3rd edition (Madras: G.A. Natesan & Co., 1922), Gujarat Political Conference

14 Sigmund Freud, *Civilization and Its Discontents*, tr. James Strachey, (New York: W.W. Norton & Company, Inc., 1961), II

15 Bertrand Russell, *The Conquest of Happiness*, (New York: Liveright, 1930), Chapter 12

16 Anaïs Nin and Henry Miller, *A Literate Passion: Letters of Anaïs Nin and Henry Miller, 1932-1953*, (San Diego: Harcourt Brace & Company, 1987), 307 (March, 1937)

17 C.S. Lewis, *God in the Dock*, (Grand Rapids, MI: William B. Eerdmans Publishing Company, 1970), I (4) Q1

18 Jiddu Krishnamurti, *The Collected Works of J. Krishnamurti – Volume V 1948-1949: Choiceless Awareness*, (Ojai, CA: Krishnamurti Publications, 2012), Fourteenth Talk in The Oak Grove (August 27, 1949)

19 https://en.wikiquote.org/wiki/Martin_Luther_King,_Jr. (Loving Your Enemies (Christmas 1957)); retrieved 26 August 2020

20 Kurt Vonnegut, *The Sirens of Titan*, (New York: Dell Publishing, 1959), Epilogue

21 Robert A. Heinlein, *Stranger in a Strange Land*, (New York: G.P. Putnam's Sons, 1961), XXXIII (Note: The 1991 version does not include the quoted material)

22 Lennon, John Winston and McCartney, Paul James. "All You Need Is Love." Sony/ATV Music Publishing LLC, 1967.

23 Mother Teresa – Nobel Lecture. NobelPrize.org. Nobel Media AB 2020; retrieved 26 August 2020 from https://www.nobelprize.org/prizes/peace/1979/teresa/lecture/

24 Katharine Hepburn, *Me: Stories of My Life*, (New York: Alfred A. Knopf, 1991), VI

25 Haruki Murakami, *Kafka on the Shore*, tr. Philip Gabriel, (New York: Alfred A. Knopf, 2005), Chapter 31

26 Antonie van Leeuwenhoek was the first to observe protozoa, and he sometimes referred to these single-celled organisms as "wee beasties" (https://onlinelibrary.wiley.com/doi/abs/10.1002/9781119205791.ch18; retrieved 31 August 2020)

27 Lisa Yount, *Antoni van Leeuwenhoek: First to See Microscopic Life*, (Springfield, NJ: Enslow Publishers, Inc., 1996), Chapter 3

28 Saint Augustine, *The Confessions of Saint Augustine*, tr. E.B. Pusey, (London: Global Grey, 2018), 36 (Book 3); retrieved 26 August 2020 from https://www.globalgrey ebooks.com/confessions-of-saint-augustine-ebook.html

29 *Luther's Catechism: The Small Catechism of Dr. Martin Luther and an Exposition for Children and Adults Written in Contemporary English (Revised) by Martin Luther*, David P. Kuske (Milwaukee: Northwestern Publishing House, 1998), 1

Chapter 2

1 Bathurst, "Oh, for a Faith That Will Not Shrink," *The Lutheran Hymnal* (St. Louis: Concordia Publishing House, 1941), 396, 6

2 Robinson, "Come, Thou Fount of Every Blessing," *Lutheran Service Book* (St. Louis: Concordia Publishing House, 2006), 686, 3

3 Warner, "Jesus Loves Me," *Lutheran Service Book* (St. Louis: Concordia Publishing House, 2006), 588, 2

4 Ibid., 1

5 Townend, Stuart and Getty, Keith. "In Christ Alone." Thankyou Music, 2001.

6 Baloche, Paul and Rossback, Michael. "The Same Love." Columbia, 2012.

7 Alderson, "Lord of Glory, You Have Bought Us," *Lutheran Service Book* (St. Louis: Concordia Publishing House, 2006), 851, 1

Chapter 3

1 Alderson, "Lord of Glory, You Have Bought Us," *Lutheran Service Book* (St. Louis: Concordia Publishing House, 2006), 851, 4

Chapter 4

1 McComb, "Chief of Sinners Though I Be," *Lutheran Service Book* (St. Louis: Concordia Publishing House, 2006), 611, 1

2 Ibid., 2

3 C.G. Jung, *Psychological Types*, tr. Gerhard Adler and R.F.C. Hull, (Princeton, NJ: Princeton University Press, 1971)

4 Isabel Briggs Myers with Peter B. Myers, *Gifts Differing: Understanding Personality Type*, (Mountain View, CA: Davies-Black Publishing, 1980)

5 von Hayn, "I Am Jesus' Little Lamb" tr. *The Lutheran Hymnal, Lutheran Service Book* (St. Louis: Concordia Publishing House, 2006), 740, 1-3

6 Jerald M. Jellison, *Managing the Dynamics of Change: The Fastest Path to Creating an Engaged and Productive Workforce*, (New York: McGraw-Hill, 2006)

Chapter 5

[1] Fred Rogers – Commencement address. Dartmouth.edu. Retrieved 26 August 2020 from https://news.dartmouth.edu/news/2018/03/revisiting-fred-rogers-2002-commencement-address

Chapter 6

[1] Cravalho, Auli'i and House, Rachel. "I Am Moana (Song of the Ancestors)." Walt Disney Records, 2016.

Chapter 7

[1] Gary Chapman, *The 5 Love Languages: The Secret to Love That Lasts*, (Chicago: Northfield Publishing, 2015)

[2] C.S. Lewis, *The Four Loves*, (New York: Harcourt, Brace & Company, 1960), Charity

Chapter 8

[1] Rumi, *The Masnavi I Ma'navi*, tr. E.H. Whinfield, (London: Global Grey, 2018), 134 (The Elephant in a Dark Room); retrieved 26 August 2020 from https://www.globalgreyebooks.com/masnavi-i-manavi-ebook.html

[2] Robb, Douglas; Estrin, Daniel; Hesse, Chris; and Lappalainen, Markku. "The Reason." Warner/Chappell Music, Inc., 2003.

[3] C.S. Lewis, *Mere Christianity*, (New York: HarperCollins Publishers LLC, 1952), Charity

Chapter 9

[1] Anderson-Lopez, Kristen and Lopez, Robert. "Let It Go." Wonderland Music Company, 2013.

[2] Stan Freberg, "St. George and the Dragonet," 1953 (based on https://www.snopes.com/fact-check/just-the-facts/, retrieved 26 August 2020)

[3] Stevens, Cat. "Father and Son." A&M Records, 1970.

[4] Mendel, Nate; Grohl, Dave; Hawkins, Taylor; and Shiflett, Chris. "Times Like These." Kobalt Music Publishing Ltd., Warner/Chappell Music, Inc, Universal Music Publishing, 2003.

Appendices

[1] *Luther's Catechism: The Small Catechism of Dr. Martin Luther and an Exposition for Children and Adults Written in Contemporary English (Revised) by Martin Luther*, David P. Kuske (Milwaukee: Northwestern Publishing House, 1998), 1

[2] *12 Angry Men*. Dir. Sidney Lumet. Perf. Henry Fonda, Lee J. Cobb, and Martin Balsam. Orion-Nova Productions, 1957.

[3] *The Birds*. Dir. Alfred Hitchcock. Perf. Rod Taylor, Tippi Hedren, Jessica Tandy, Suzanne Pleshette, and Veronica Cartwright. Alfred J. Hitchcock Productions, 1963.

Index

.

www.ingramcontent.com/pod-product-compliance
Lightning Source LLC
Chambersburg PA
CBHW080810280326
41926CB00091B/4130